The First Epistle
of Paul the Apostle
to the Corinthians

The First Epistle of Paul the Apostle to the Corinthians

by

Oliver B. Greene

The Gospel Hour, Inc., Oliver B. Greene, Director
P.O. Box 2024, Greenville, South Carolina

The First Epistle
of Paul the Apostle
to the Corinthians

First printing, March 1965
Second printing, February 1966

CONTENTS

Introduction	9
Chapter I	18
Chapter II	91
Chapter III	118
Chapter IV	154
Chapter V	180
Chapter VI	200
Chapter VII	233
Chapter VIII	273
Chapter IX	290
Chapter X	317
Chapter XI	347
Chapter XII	384
Chapter XIII	418
Chapter XIV	437
Chapter XV	478
Chapter XVI	529

CONTENTS

Introduction
Chapter I
Chapter II
Chapter III
Chapter IV
Chapter V
Chapter VI
Chapter VII
Chapter VIII
Chapter IX
Chapter X
Chapter XI
Chapter XII
Chapter XIII
Chapter XIV
Chapter XV
Chapter XVI

The First Epistle
of Paul the Apostle
to the Corinthians

INTRODUCTION

Corinth was one of the outstanding Grecian cities. It was the capital of the Province of Achaia. In the city of Corinth lived the Roman proconsul.

"And when Gallio was the deputy of Achaia, the Jews made insurrection with one accord against Paul, and brought him to the judgment seat" (Acts 18:12).

Corinth was a large city, perfectly situated for commercial purposes, and through commerce carried on with the rest of the world she became a very wealthy city. Thousands of traders from all known nations visited there. Greek civilization flourished there . . . the fine arts were cultivated and well known. Athletic games and schools of philosophy flourished.

However, in this rich metropolis gross sin was prevalent. The entire city was steeped in immoralities of various kinds. It was a city known for drunkenness, gluttony—and above all, for its religiously licensed prostitution. The Greek worship of Aphrodite was of the most degraded nature possible. Moral corruption was so great in the city of Corinth that one living in low moral practices was referred to as one who "lived as a Corinthian."

One outstanding scholar has said, "The geographical position of Corinth was its weal and its woe." The city was so situated that it brought men of wealth from every part of the known world to trade there; but with their riches they also brought their immorality and lust. Thus the city of Corinth was a cesspool of sin.

9

The Apostle Paul first preached the Gospel in the city of Athens and then traveled on to Corinth: "After these things Paul departed from Athens, and came to Corinth" (Acts 18:1). There is no doubt that the Lord used Paul to establish the Corinthian church. The account in Acts 18 verifies this fact.

Paul preached and labored in that city for a year and six months. Jews and Gentiles were saved through the preaching of the grace of God by Paul, the prince of apostles. Some of the outstanding Jews in the city were converted . . . for instance, Crispus, the chief ruler of the synagogue was brought to Christ through the ministry of Paul. However, the majority of those who heard him and believed were Gentiles, and a large number of his converts belonged to the very poor class of people: "For ye see your calling, brethren, how that not many wise men after the flesh, not many mighty, not many noble, are called" (I Cor. 1:26).

There were two exceptions: Erastus (chamberlain of the city) and Gaius (a very wealthy man) were converted through the preaching of Paul, and were baptized. When Paul entered the city of Corinth, preaching the message God had given him, he immediately recognized the fact that he was in a wealthy, wicked city—a city that boasted culture, much learning, and which was filled with pride. But this did not change his mind about the Gospel:

"And I, brethren, when I came to you, came not with excellency of speech or of wisdom, declaring unto you the testimony of God. For I determined not to know any thing among you, save Jesus Christ, and Him crucified" (I Cor. 2:1,2).

The Holy Spirit dealt with Paul in a very special way while he was preaching in Corinth: "And when Silas

10

and Timotheus were come from Macedonia, Paul was pressed in the spirit, and testified to the Jews that Jesus was Christ'' (Acts 18:5). With much fear and trembling, Paul delivered the message God laid upon his heart: "And I was with you in weakness, and in fear, and in much trembling" (I Cor. 2:3).

The apostle knew that he had invaded Satan's playground and that he was not fighting against flesh and blood, but against the very devil himself and the emissaries of hell. God stood by His servant Paul, even though his preaching was not with enticing words of man's wisdom. Paul preached in the demonstration of the Holy Ghost and power, and many were born again: "And my speech and my preaching was not with enticing words of man's wisdom, but in demonstration of the Spirit and of power" (I Cor. 2:4).

Paul left Corinth because of his determination to keep the feast at Jerusalem (Acts 18:21). On his return from Jerusalem he spent three years at Ephesus (Acts 20:31); but the latter part of his stay was disquieted by reports of disorders at Corinth. A very deplorable state of spiritual practices existed in the church there, and many evil things had sprung up among the Corinthians. Because of this condition, a letter had been prepared and sent to the Apostle Paul reporting the state of the church in Corinth: "For it hath been declared unto me of you, my brethren, by them which are of the house of Chloe, that there are contentions among you" (I Cor. 1:11). Here the house of Chloe is mentioned as informing Paul concerning the contentious spirit which was prevalent in the church at Corinth.

No doubt from the same source—and probably from other sources—Paul had heard of even worse things which were making headway in the assembly, even among some of the believers. Gross immorality was being tolerated in the assembly. Lawsuits between believers were being submitted to courts over which pagan judges presided. They had degraded the blessed memorial feast, the Lord's Supper. Some had been getting drunk, some had been acting as gluttons.

There were other matters that were very unchristian in the assembly, such as disorder in public worship, abuse of certain gifts—and it seems that some of the women had attempted to take over leadership in the church and monopolize time in the services.

The epistle itself answers the question concerning the place and the time of the writing. Chapter 16 verse 8 tells us that Paul was in Ephesus and intended remaining there until Pentecost: "But I will tarry at Ephesus until Pentecost."

In the book of Acts we learn that Paul left Ephesus about the time of Pentecost, in the year 57 A. D. It is certain that this first epistle to the Corinthians was written by the Apostle Paul in the first part of that year, probably around Easter.

"Purge out therefore the old leaven, that ye may be a new lump, as ye are unleavened. For even Christ our passover is sacrificed for us: Therefore let us keep the feast, not with old leaven, neither with the leaven of malice and wickedness; but with the unleavened bread of sincerity and truth" (I Cor. 5:7,8).

From Acts 19:22 we learn that the apostle, while still in the city of Ephesus, had sent Timotheus and Erastus to Macedonia: "So he sent into Macedonia two of them that ministered unto him, Timotheus and Erastus; but he himself stayed in Asia for a season." Paul had commissioned Timothy to go to Corinth:

"Now if Timotheus come, see that he may be with you without fear: for he worketh the work of the Lord, as I also do" (I Cor. 16:10).

No doubt Paul sent Timothy to Corinth to lay the groundwork and prepare the way for his visit to the city:

"For this cause have I sent unto you Timotheus, who is my beloved son, and faithful in the Lord, who shall bring you into remembrance of my ways which be in Christ, as I teach every where in every church. Now some are puffed up, as though I would not come to you. But I will come to you shortly, if the Lord will, and will know, not the speech of them which are puffed up, but the power" (I Cor. 4:17—19).

The first letter to the believers at Corinth was taken to the city and presented to the church by Stephanas, Fortunatus, and Achaicus: "I am glad of the coming of Stephanas and Fortunatus and Achaicus: for that which was lacking on your part they have supplied" (I Cor. 16:17).

This first epistle to the Corinthians gives us more than any other, an inner view of the Church, the assembly of the living God. It deals with the practical daily conduct of the believer. It also deals with the public walk of the assembly. It maintains that Paul wrote by the authority of the Holy Ghost. It denounces party spirit—or cliques—in the church. This inspired letter exposes worldly wisdom and how foolish it is to profess to be wise apart from the fear of the Lord. The message of I Corinthians insists upon the power of the Holy Ghost in the individual believer, and also in the church and all of its activities. The message of I Corinthians urges godly order in the church at all times in all services, and it also urges godly order in the use of the gifts bestowed upon believers by the Holy Ghost. I Corinthians commands

13

holy discipline in the church. The letter calls for personal purity and holiness. It counsels the saints concerning social and family difficulties. It gives instruction to the believer concerning his relation to unbelievers—both publicly and privately, both men and women.

I Corinthians leaves no grounds for speculation concerning the future state of the unbeliever. It clearly teaches the faith once delivered unto the saints concerning the resurrection of the righteous. It instructs us concerning our future state with our Lord, and warns that anyone who accepts or supports error concerning the future state of believers is denying the faith and is in jeopardy concerning the faith and spiritual living in the church and with those who are unbelievers.

If we do not believe in the bodily resurrection, Paul declares that our faith is vain, our preaching is vain, we are still in our sins, and all who have died have perished. The bodily resurrection of the Son of God was the greatest bombshell ever to explode in the face of an unbelieving world. Paul left no stone unturned to instruct the believers in Corinth concerning the Bible truth as having to do with the resurrection, each in his own order.

In the closing chapter of the epistle, Paul gives instruction concerning the collection for poor saints. He was not afraid to talk about money matters. It is true that the love of money is the root of all evil; but it is just as true that God loves a cheerful giver, and if we sow sparingly, we reap sparingly. Paul did not hesitate to give clear, concise instructions concerning the collection for the poor saints, and collections for the work of the ministry.

As we study this great epistle and examine the verses therein, we will see manifest in detail the holy wisdom, the burning zeal, and the deep love of the Apostle Paul as he, through the Holy Ghost, yielded himself—heart, mind, soul, and strength—in the name of the Lord Jesus to the glory of God the Father, to be used in the ministry to which the Holy Ghost had appointed him.

As Paul penned down the words recorded in these sixteen chapters of I Corinthians, to anyone but Paul it might have seemed that the eighteen months he labored in that great wicked city had been spent in vain; but Paul did not feel that way about it. He loved the Corinthians with a deep love. He longed for them God's best. He was willing to spend and be spent to serve them, to help them, to encourage them. He said, "I have much people in this city," and he commended them for their faith and their love to God before he sounded out the solemn warning and the stern rebuke that the Holy Ghost impressed upon him to write to his children in the church in the wicked city of Corinth.

There were *two outstanding reasons* for the epistle: First, various defects and delinquencies had come about in *doctrine*. Second, various defects and delinquencies had come about in their *daily practice of life*. These defects and delinquencies in doctrine and practices had made tremendous inroads upon the welfare of the church in the city of Corinth, reports of which had reached the Apostle Paul. Many perplexing circumstances and conditions had arisen, and because of these circumstances and perplexing conditions in the church, a letter had been written and sent to their beloved apostle, seeking his counsel and advice.

These facts are clearly seen in the first fourteen chapters of the epistle. The last two chapters deal with doctrine and practical Christian living in the church and in the individual believers. The subject of disorders in the local assembly is primarily dealt with in chapters

1:10 through 6, and in chapter 7 we have a series of replies to the subjects inquired about. It would have been very natural to expect that under ordinary conditions and circumstances Paul would in the very beginning after his introductory remarks have acknowledged the letter and answered the questions immediately. However, he did not. The evils, the ungodliness, the sinful practices among the saints in the notoriously wicked city of Corinth called for immediate discussion and treatment. The answers to their questions could be postponed to a later place in this important epistle.

So far as Paul being led by the Holy Ghost was concerned, disorders must be dealt with first. Then the difficulties could be dealt with later.

However, even though the disorders among them must be dealt with, and dealt with only as God would have them dealt with, after the introduction in the first three verses Paul does not immediately go into the exhortation and commands that must of necessity follow. Everything in which Paul could find pleasure and cause for praise to the believers in Corinth, preceded the rebuke. Were they not his own children in the Lord? Had he not preached the Gospel that had won these Gentile pagans and religious Jews to Christianity? Was not their deliverance from the gross sin and immorality from which they had been saved brought about through his testimony? Had he not come to them in weakness, in fear, and in much trembling? Had he not undergone great hardships to preach the grace of God to them? He loved them with a deep love that sought out every point of praise that could be found before he used the Gospel pruning knife to attempt, by the grace of God through the Holy Ghost, to cut off the branches that were hindering the growth of the true vine.

Paul said, "I thank my God always on your behalf,

for the grace of God which is given you by Jesus Christ; that in every thing ye are enriched by Him, in all utterance, and in all knowledge; even as the testimony of Christ was confirmed in you: So that ye come behind in no gift; waiting for the coming of our Lord Jesus Christ" (I Cor. 1:4–7).

Paul assures the believers that the Lord would "confirm" them "unto the end," so that they who were truly born again "might be unreprovable in the day of our Lord Jesus Christ." Then he reminds them of the faithfulness of God, who cannot and will not deny Himself: "God is faithful, by whom ye were called unto the fellowship of His Son Jesus Christ our Lord" (I Cor. 1:9).

The state of things in the assembly at Corinth was indeed sad, grievous, and heartbreaking. Paul knew the conditions that existed there, and the praise and thanksgiving is not a compromise concerning the evils that existed in the lives of the believers. Paul did not condone their evil, but he believed that love is the more excellent way. Therefore he assured them that he loved them in spite of their failures—and even moreso, *the God who called them loved them* in spite of their weaknesses and grievous shortcomings.

Then he lays down one by one the commands and the exhortations dictated by the Holy Ghost who had appointed him an apostle to the Gentiles.

CHAPTER ONE

1. Paul, called to be an apostle of Jesus Christ through the will of God, and Sosthenes our brother,

2. Unto the church of God which is at Corinth, to them that are sanctified in Christ Jesus, called to be saints, with all that in every place call upon the name of Jesus Christ our Lord, both their's and our's:

3. Grace be unto you, and peace, from God our Father, and from the Lord Jesus Christ.

4. I thank my God always on your behalf, for the grace of God which is given you by Jesus Christ;

5. That in every thing ye are enriched by him, in all utterance, and in all knowledge;

6. Even as the testimony of Christ was confirmed in you:

7. So that ye come behind in no gift; waiting for the coming of our Lord Jesus Christ:

8. Who shall also confirm you unto the end, that ye may be blameless in the day of our Lord Jesus Christ.

9. God is faithful, by whom ye were called unto the fellowship of his Son Jesus Christ our Lord.

10. Now I beseech you, brethren, by the name of our Lord Jesus Christ, that ye all speak the same thing, and that there be no divisions among you; but that ye be perfectly joined together in the same mind and in the same judgment.

11. For it hath been declared unto me of you, my brethren, by them which are of the house of Chloe, that there are contentions among you.

12. Now this I say, that every one of you saith, I am of Paul; and I of Apollos; and I of Cephas; and I of Christ.

13. Is Christ divided? was Paul crucified for you? or were ye baptized in the name of Paul?

14. I thank God that I baptized none of you, but Crispus and Gaius;

15. Lest any should say that I had baptized in mine own name.

16. And I baptized also the household of Stephanas: besides,

I know not whether I baptized any other.

17. For Christ sent me not to baptize, but to preach the gospel: not with wisdom of words, lest the cross of Christ should be made of none effect.

18. For the preaching of the cross is to them that perish foolishness; but unto us which are saved it is the power of God.

19. For it is written, I will destroy the wisdom of the wise, and will bring to nothing the understanding of the prudent.

20. Where is the wise? where is the scribe? where is the disputer of this world? hath not God made foolish the wisdom of this world?

21. For after that in the wisdom of God the world by wisdom knew not God, it pleased God by the foolishness of preaching to save them that believe.

22. For the Jews require a sign, and the Greeks seek after wisdom:

23. But we preach Christ crucified, unto the Jews a stumblingblock, and unto the Greeks foolishness;

24. But unto them which are called, both Jews and Greeks, Christ the power of God, and the wisdom of God.

25. Because the foolishness of God is wiser than men; and the weakness of God is stronger than men.

26. For ye see your calling, brethren, how that not many wise men after the flesh, not many mighty, not many noble, are called:

27. But God hath chosen the foolish things of the world to confound the wise; and God hath chosen the weak things of the world to confound the things which are mighty;

28. And base things of the world, and things which are despised, hath God chosen, yea, and things which are not, to bring to nought things that are:

29. That no flesh should glory in his presence.

30. But of him are ye in Christ Jesus, who of God is made unto us wisdom, and righteousness, and sanctification, and redemption:

31. That, according as it is written, He that glorieth, let him glory in the Lord.

The Believer's Position in the Grace of God

Verses 1 and 2: "Paul, called to be an apostle of Jesus Christ through the will of God, and Sosthenes our brother, unto the church of God which is at Corinth, to

them that are sanctified in Christ Jesus, called to be
saints, with all that in every place call upon the name
of Jesus Christ our Lord, both their's and our's.''

In the very outset of this epistle Paul asserts his
divine commission. This was necessary because a party
had arisen which was inclined to dispute it. In the second chapter of Galatians we read of the ''false brethren
unawares brought in'' whose doctrine Paul was compelled
to withstand and to assert the divine origin of his own;
and in the second epistle to the Corinthians we find many
allusions to those who rejected his authority, as in II Corinthians 3:1; 5:12; 10:2,7,10. It is worthy of notice that
in the two epistles to the Thessalonians, written before
the controversy began, no such clause is found.

In Corinth, Paul was well known to the saints. He
was used of the Holy Ghost to establish a church there,
and had borne witness to his apostleship with the labors
of his own hands. He preached the Gospel, caring for
the spiritual needs of the people there, and then labored
with his hands, making tents, to provide for his own physical needs, thus bearing witness that he had not come to
them for material gain.

In the opening words of verse 1, the literal Greek
reads, ''Paul, an apostle by calling.'' He assured the
believers at Corinth that he had not taken up the ministry
as a vocation. He was not appointed by the apostles in
Jerusalem, but was an apostle by divine calling, by the
appointment of God the Father through the grace of our
Lord Jesus Christ.

He also reminds the believers at Corinth that they
themselves were saints by calling—not through any merit
or ability of their own, but by the calling of grace which
is in Christ Jesus, our Saviour. It was grace which saved
them and made them saints. It was grace that chose

Paul—not as a saint only, but as an apostle.

We have here the principle of Christian ministry, as well as the principle of the salvation of the soul. It is by God's will that we are saved. God saves us for Christ's sake; it is not His will that any perish.

Paul adds, ". . . A called apostle of Jesus Christ by God's will." Paul wanted to impress upon their hearts the fact that he was not an apostle by his own ability and merit, nor through the choice of men, but through God's sovereign goodness and grace. It is God—God's love and His grace—that makes us saints and calls us into His service as ministers, pastors, missionaries, and even laymen. It is God—not a group of church leaders—who sets ministers and leaders in the church according to His will:

"And God hath set some in the church, first apostles, secondarily prophets, thirdly teachers, after that miracles, then gifts of healings, helps, governments, diversities of tongues" (I Cor. 12:28).

No doubt Sosthenes, mentioned here as "our brother," is the same Sosthenes mentioned in Acts 18:17: "Then all the Greeks took Sosthenes, the chief ruler of the synagogue, and beat him before the judgment seat. And Gallio cared for none of those things."

Sosthenes, like Paul, was once "a persecutor and an injurious person." The experience through which he had passed when he was an enemy of Christ was instrumental in bringing him to the Saviour. When he was chief ruler of the synagogue he was the enemy of Christ, but now through the grace of God he had become "a brother beloved."

The message is addressed *"unto the church of God which is at Corinth."* The Greek word *ekklesia* used here and translated "church" signifies "called out."

That is, persons called out *from* the world, *unto* the Lord. The descriptive phrase "the church of God" is used in the New Testament on many occasions to designate a company of born again believers acting together in a local capacity, serving God together in a local assembly, meeting in a designated place to study the Word, pray, fellowship, and observe the Lord's Supper.

The statement "the church of God" signifies that such a company of believers is God's possession, purchased and paid for by His own blood: "Take heed therefore unto yourselves, and to all the flock, over the which the Holy Ghost hath made you overseers, to feed *the church of God, which He hath purchased with His own blood*" (Acts 20:28). Paul uses the phrase in both First and Second Corinthians when speaking of the local church there. He also uses it concerning the church at Jerusalem which he persecuted before he was converted: "For I am the least of the apostles, that am not meet to be called an apostle, because I persecuted *the church of God*" (I Cor. 15:9). He uses it again in Galatians 1:13: "For ye have heard of my conversation in time past in the Jews' religion, how that beyond measure I persecuted *the church of God*, and wasted it!"

In Acts 8:1 and 3 we read, "And Saul was consenting unto (Stephen's) death. And at that time there was a great persecution against the church which was at Jerusalem; and they were all scattered abroad throughout the regions of Judaea and Samaria, except the apostles. . . As for Saul, he made havock of the church, entering into every house, and haling men and women committed them to prison."

Paul uses this same term in Acts 20:28, obviously referring to the local assembly at Ephesus. In this verse the elders of the church in Ephesus are commanded to *"feed* (or tend) *the church of God*, which He hath purchased with His own blood." The company of believers is spoken of as *"the flock"* over which the Holy Ghost had made the apostles overseers, and the term "the flock" seems to limit the meaning to the local church in that particular city.

In I Timothy 3:5 the statement is again used with reference to the church at Ephesus where Paul had left Timothy in charge, and in verse 15 Paul uses the term, *"the church of the living God."*

It is extremely important for the student of the Word of God to carefully distinguish this local use of the term "CHURCH" from its application to *the entire Church—* the body of Christ—*which is never used in any local or earthly significance.* There are absolutely no scriptural grounds for the term *"the* Church on earth." The Scripture clearly teaches us that *our citizenship is in heaven,* and "we sit together in heavenly places in Christ Jesus." In chapter 5 of his letter to the Ephesians, Paul plainly points out that Christ is the head of *the Church* and we are members of His body—bone of His bone and flesh of His flesh.

*The Church of the living God—*of which Jesus is the head and the foundation and of which we are members baptized into that body by the Holy Ghost—is a heavenly organism. We are members of this organism through the miracle of the spiritual birth that takes place when we believe on the Lord Jesus Christ and are baptized into His body (I Cor. 12:12,13). We will study this more fully when we arrive at chapter 12.

To deviate from scriptural phraseology is to bring about unscriptural organizations, unscriptural human traditions, sectarianism, and man-made programs wearing the attire of a church but not possessing the heart and soul of *the Church of the living God*.

We read of the churches of Galatia, of Asia, of Macedonia, and of Judaea—but not *THE Church* of Galatia . . . nor was it *THE Galatian Church*. The Word of God recognizes no such statements. There is much gross error abroad in the land today concerning *the Church of the living God*. There are many groups who claim to be the true Church. They preach that *they* will make up the bride, and all who do not belong to their little group will be "friends of the bridegroom." They do not consign others to hell, but they give all others a secondary place in God's economy concerning the future state of believers.

There are many preachers who teach that unless you are baptized by one of their group, you do not belong to the bride of Christ (or to the Church of the living God). They demand that their members believe that their local assembly is THE Church; but such teaching is due to gross ignorance of God's Word. If the devil cannot cause a minister to become a liberal or a modernist, he will try to run him down a blind alley. Satan cares not how long nor how loud one preaches, so long as he mixes error with the preaching and fails to lift up the Lord Jesus Christ as head of the Church, the Saviour of the body, the One who gave His blood to purchase *the Church of the living God*.

It will be a happy day in the lives of some ministers and teachers when they fully learn that God saves sinners for Christ's sake (Eph. 4:32). God is highly pleased with the Son of His love, and whatsoever we do to the glory of any person or persons save the Son of God is sin.

Notice in what character the Corinthian believers are addressed as Paul writes, under the inspiration of the Holy Ghost: ". . . To the church of God which is at Corinth" — (meaning the called out ones—members of the

24

body of Christ). It is only through the power of the Holy Spirit of God sent down from heaven that men become members of the *assembly of God* — the New Testament Church.

As we study, we will see that the state of the Corinthians was frightfully bad, and certainly the testimony of many of them brought shame and reproach upon the local assembly. But we must also remember that in commanding them to deal with the most despicable case of all, Paul does so on the Bible grounds of the spirit being saved in the day of the Lord Jesus. This one who had committed so grave a sin was to be turned over to Satan for the destruction of the flesh *only*.

". . . To them that are sanctified in Christ Jesus, called to be saints, with all that in every place call upon the name of Jesus Christ our Lord, both their's and our's." The fact is clearly stated here that all the believers were sanctified. The term "sanctified" signifies *"set apart to God"* and is applicable to all believers. It does not mean merely a process going on day by day, but it has to do with a sanctification that is complete. Positionally, the believers were sanctified; the inner man was stamped with separation unto God in Christ Jesus. In being set apart to God, in contrast to their former unregenerate condition, Christ was made unto them sanctification. And because they were separated unto God in Christ Jesus they were "saints *by* calling." The phrase "called to be saints" does not simply assign the name to them, but signifies "saints by calling"—just as in the first verse Paul describes himself as an apostle by calling.

Through this divine truth, Paul was making an appeal to the heart and conscience to consider their spiritual standing and live accordingly. All born again believers are sanctified the moment they are saved. They are sanctified from the beginning of the work of grace in their souls: "But of Him are ye in Christ Jesus, who of God is made unto us wisdom, and righteousness, and sanctification, and redemption" (I Cor. 1:30).

Of this the Holy Spirit is the agent: "Elect according to the foreknowledge of God the Father, through *sanctification of the Spirit*, unto obedience and sprinkling of the blood of Jesus Christ: Grace unto you, and peace, be multiplied" (I Pet. 1:2).

"That I should be the minister of Jesus Christ to the Gentiles, ministering the Gospel of God, that the offering up of the Gentiles might be acceptable, being *sanctified by the Holy Ghost*" (Rom. 15:16).

"But we are bound to give thanks alway to God for you, brethren beloved of the Lord, because God hath from the beginning chosen you to salvation through *sanctification of the Spirit* and belief of the truth" (II Thess. 2:13).

The Word of God also clearly and definitely teaches a *progressive* sanctification . . . we are to desire the sincere milk of the Word that we may *grow* thereby; we are to study, and through the study of the Word grow in faith and knowledge — but *positionally* we are sanctified the very moment we trust Jesus as our personal Saviour. We are sanctified because of God's will: "By the which will we are sanctified through the offering of the body of Jesus Christ once for all" (Heb. 10:10).

Paul is saying to the believers in Corinth that they are set apart to God. Sanctification here is not an attainment on the part of a believer through righteous living, but is definitely a divine relationship into which God's grace calls the believer on the grounds of the sacrifice of Christ Jesus on the cross: "By the which will we are sanctified *through the offering of the body of Jesus Christ* once for all. . . Wherefore Jesus also, that He might sanctify the people with His own blood, suffered without the gate" (Heb. 10:10; 13:12).

The phrase *"in Christ Jesus"* points out the positional relationship of the believer as dependent upon union with Christ Jesus in resurrection. In Bible language, every true believer is *crucified with Christ, buried* with Christ, *raised* in Christ Jesus *to walk in newness of life*. According to Paul's teaching in Colossians 3:3, we are dead, and our lives are hid with Christ in God. *"In Christ Jesus"* expresses the intimate spiritual union by and through which believers share Christ's life and character. Believers are different because they possess divine nature.

Christianity is not to be compared with any other religion on earth. Christianity is *Christ in you* and *you in Christ*, hidden *with Christ* in God. Thus the Bible language describes the condition and the position of a true, born again Christian, even NOW.

Since we are "in Christ Jesus," we are "called saints." We are not going to *become* saints at some future time or place, but every born again, blood-washed child of God is a saint NOW. The literal Greek reads, "called saints." All believers are saints because they have been called of God, born of God, and possess the divine nature.

Since believers are saints, since believers are sanctified, they are responsible for leading a life in keeping with the Bible fact that they are separated to God. Every believer should live a life of true holiness and true righteousness, the life into which he has been called, the life which he possesses in Christ Jesus. It is the divine purpose of Almighty God in saving the sinner, to separate the sinner from evil. We are taken out of the world of evil and placed over into the realm of righteousness. We are taken from the family of the devil and placed into the family of God: "Beloved, NOW are we the sons of God . . ." (I John 3:2).

However, the separation from evil (which God desires for every believer) and the separation which is the divine purpose for believers, is to be learned from God's Word—God speaking to us through His Word. The separation and life of true holiness which God desires for His children is to be apprehended practically by sincere, earnest, and undeviating obedience to the will of God; and this obedience can be realized only by the power of the Holy Spirit: "For God hath not called us unto uncleanness, but unto holiness" (I Thess. 4:7).

"Sanctify them through thy truth: thy Word is truth. As thou hast sent me into the world, even so have I also sent them into the world. And for their sakes I sanctify myself, that they also might be sanctified through the truth" (John 17:17–19).

"Follow peace with all men, and holiness, without which no man shall see the Lord" (Heb. 12:14).

"For if ye live after the flesh, ye shall die: but if ye through the Spirit do mortify the deeds of the body, ye shall live" (Rom. 8:13).

"This I say then, Walk in the Spirit, and ye shall not fulfil the lust of the flesh. For the flesh lusteth against the Spirit, and the Spirit against the flesh: and these are contrary the one to the other: so that ye cannot do the things that ye would. But if ye be led of the Spirit, ye are not under the law. Now the works of the flesh are manifest, which are these; Adultery, fornication, uncleanness, lasciviousness, idolatry, witchcraft, hatred, variance, emulations, wrath, strife, seditions, heresies, envyings, murders, drunkenness, revellings, and such like: of the which I tell you before, as I have also told you in time past, that they which do such things shall not inherit the kingdom of God. But the fruit of the Spirit is love, joy, peace, longsuffering, gentleness, goodness, faith, meekness, temperance: against such there is no law. And they that are Christ's have crucified the flesh with the affections and lusts. If we live in the Spirit, let us also walk in the Spirit" (Gal. 5:16—25).

For believers to walk after the flesh and cultivate friendship with the world is to yield to the influence of the flesh and the world, automatically weakening our allegiance to Christ and denying our divine calling as saints. For believers to display any relationship to the world, the flesh, and the things offered by the world, is to deny by our actions our divine relationship to Christ, and will cause us to suffer the loss of our spiritual birth-right—which is abundant life, abundant peace, and joy unspeakable and full of glory. By such conduct we will also suffer loss of reward at the judgment seat of Christ. It is a grand and glorious privilege to be a believer, a "saint by calling" – but it is also a grave responsibility. We are sons of God, we are His representatives on this earth, and if we stand in the way of sinners and sit in the seat of the scornful we will suffer loss—here and hereafter. Not the loss of our *soul*, but the loss of spiritual joy *here*, and eternal reward at the end of life's journey.

". . . Called to be saints, with all that in every place call upon the name of Jesus Christ our Lord, both their's and our's." The last part of this verse is to be closely connected with the preceding clause. All who call upon the name of the Lord are "sanctified" and "called to be saints," and all who call upon the name of the Lord Jesus Christ acknowledge His authority as Lord. This does not mean just the believers in Corinth. This teaching is applicable to ALL believers in all churches. (Read carefully I Corinthians 4:17; 7:17; 11:16; and 14:33.)

To call upon the name of the Lord is to bow to His divine authority. The use of the term "call upon the name of the Lord" (in Scripture) indicates an act of worship and humble submission. The full title "Lord Jesus Christ" is used four times in the first ten verses of our present chapter, and in the form *"Jesus Christ our Lord"* in verses 2 and 9. This is very significant in the introduction of an epistle addressed to a church in which the authority of Christ at that time was disregarded and largely disowned.

You will notice that Paul uses the plural of the possessive pronoun, "OUR'S." The fact that he uses the plural is significant for two reasons:

First — out of the kindness and tender love of his heart he identifies himself with the believers in the church at Corinth, for they were his converts.

Second — it provides a hint as to the divisions in the church at Corinth and an implied admonition as to unity. Paul longed for unity in the church which was made up of his own children in the Lord.

It is of deepest interest and spiritual value that Paul connects the message of this epistle with the entire field of Christian profession. The message the Holy Ghost gave Paul in I Corinthians applies to believers today in many respects.

Verse 3: "Grace be unto you, and peace, from God our Father, and from the Lord Jesus Christ."

These words of greeting are used by Paul in all of

30

his epistles, with the exception of I Thessalonians,
where he says, "Grace unto you, and peace . . . ." In
I Timothy he adds *"mercy."* Grace is God's free, unmerited, unearned favor toward men. To those who respond to God's grace, peace is the result. God's grace
brings peace to the heart. Grace and peace come equally
from the Father and from the Lord Jesus, the Son of God's
love. The fact that grace comes from God the Father
and the Lord Jesus Christ is a definite divine testimony
to the deity of Christ.

Verse 4: "I thank my God always on your behalf,
for the grace of God which is given you by Jesus Christ."

After the address and greeting, Paul does not immediately mention the grievous matters, but everything
in which he can find praise and thanks has precedence.
Were they not his own children in the faith? He says
he always thanks God "for the grace of God which is
given you by Jesus Christ." That Paul should write
thus to the church in Corinth may be surprising to some.
The believers in Corinth were suffering severely because
of fleshly wisdom and worldliness, and it is true that
the Corinthian church was grievously out of line—but the
occasion of Paul's thanksgiving was the grace of God
bestowed on them in virtue of Christ Jesus. The evils
that had sprung up among the Corinthians had not caused
Paul to lose sight of the effects of the grace of God in
them. Paul is not speaking here simply of the grace
that brought salvation to their hearts; he is also referring
to the fuller operations of the grace of God in the earthly
life of the assembly of believers. The preposition used
here is *huper,* which is actually "concerning," and means
"on behalf of." It signifies an interest taken in whatever is mentioned or whatever precedes. The believers
in Corinth were "in Christ Jesus," and Paul was thankful
in his heart that they had been saved. In spite of their

weaknesses and shortcomings as having to do with their duties TO God, Paul was thankful that they were IN Christ Jesus.

The believer's position in grace is the result of the finished work of Christ and is fully entered the moment we receive Christ by faith. The moment we believe, we become sons of God. Condemnation is lifted, we are redeemed, and our names are placed in the Lamb's book of life. The split second a person believes in the finished work of Jesus and places his trust in the shed blood of Jesus, he is just as redeemed as he will *ever* be redeemed. He is then just as much a child of God as he will ever be. However, as newborn babies we are commanded to desire the sincere milk of the Word, that we may *grow*. We are commanded to work out our own salvation with fear and trembling, and to present our bodies a living sacrifice unto God and our members as instruments of righteousness. In so doing, we become stronger in the Lord; but becoming stronger makes us no better redeemed, because when Jesus redeems us the redemption is perfectly performed and we are as *completely* redeemed as it is possible to BE redeemed. When a person is saved, he is but a babe in Christ—and normal babies grow and develop. The same should be true in the spiritual life. However, the weakest, most insignificant, most ignorant, feeble, unnoticed believer has precisely the same relationship in grace as does the most outstanding saint in the church.

We do not *grow into* salvation; we do not grow into the family of God. We are *instantaneously born* into God's family . . . *instantaneously we are saved*. Salvation is not a *process*. We are saved by God's grace through faith, and that not of ourselves—"not of works, lest any man should boast. For we are His workmanship, created in Christ Jesus . . . ." We are born of God;

redemption is the work of God, entirely apart from the ability or the work of man. The believers in Corinth were carnal, they were divided. Some were sick, some were feeble, and some were dead. But Paul thanked God for the grace of God, given to the believers in Corinth by Jesus Christ.

Verse 5: "That in every thing ye are enriched by Him, in all utterance, and in all knowledge."

Writing to the believers at Philippi, Paul thanks God for their fellowship in the Gospel. Writing to the believers in the church at Colosse, he thanks God for their faith and their love. Writing to the believers in Thessalonica, he thanks God for their faith, labour of love, patience, and their hope.

Verse 5 here is a continuation of thanks to God for the work of grace in the Corinthian church. There was real, God-given enrichment in the saints in Corinth as having to do with their "utterance" and their display of "all knowledge." While these two things were highly esteemed among the Greek people, it seems that Paul is intimating that in the church they had proved a hindrance and danger to the spiritual condition of the believers in Corinth. Evidently their unusual ability in utterance and their unusual knowledge had not benefitted them in spiritual matters. (Study carefully I Corinthians 1:20,22,26; 2:12,13; 13:1,2,8; 14:37.)

The enrichment referred to here is very definitely spiritual. The Corinthian believers were enriched "IN HIM," and that enrichment had to do with utterance and knowledge. But seemingly, they were placing more emphasis on "utterance" than upon "knowledge." Utterance is the *outward expression* (literally speech, discourse); knowledge is the *inward comprehension* of the truth. It is altogether possible for a minister to be unusual and extraordinary in utterance, and yet not place emphasis upon the truth as he should, not possessing the knowledge he should possess to preach the full Gospel or give the church a well-rounded spiritual diet.

Verse 6: "Even as the testimony of Christ was confirmed in you."

How the testimony of Christ was confirmed in the believers in the church at Corinth was probably in the gifts they manifested as well as in their attitude toward the Lord's return for His children. Greek scholars tell us that the verb *"confirm"* used here was a technical term in the Greek commercial law, and denoted a warrant or a guarantee of title. The meaning therefore may be that these effects displayed in the believers at Corinth were a warrant or guarantee of the validity of the message they had heard through the Apostle Paul, which message they had received, thus becoming believers.

"How shall we escape, if we neglect so great salvation; which at the first began to be spoken by the Lord, and was confirmed unto us by them that heard Him" (Heb. 2:3).

"For they themselves shew of us what manner of entering in we had unto you, and how ye turned to God from idols to serve the living and true God; and to wait for His Son from heaven, whom He raised from the dead, even Jesus, which delivered us from the wrath to come" (I Thess. 1:9,10).

"When He shall come to be glorified in His saints, and to be admired in all them that believe (because our testimony among you was believed) in that day" (II Thess. 1:10).

In the fifteenth chapter of our present epistle Paul testified, "Moreover, brethren, I declare unto you the

Gospel which I preached unto you, which also ye have received, and wherein ye stand; by which also ye are saved, if ye keep in memory what I preached unto you, unless ye have believed in vain. For I delivered unto you first of all that which I also received, how that Christ died for our sins according to the Scriptures; and that He was buried, and that He rose again the third day according to the Scriptures: And that He was seen of Cephas, then of the twelve: After that, He was seen of above five hundred brethren at once; of whom the greater part remain unto this present, but some are fallen asleep. After that, He was seen of James; then of all the apostles. And last of all He was seen of me also, as of one born out of due time" (I Cor. 15:1–8).

Paul did not present the Gospel to the Corinthians with excellency of speech or wisdom. He said, *"For I determined not to know any thing among you, save Jesus Christ, and Him crucified"* (I Cor. 2:2). His speech and his preaching was not with enticing words of man's wisdom, but in the demonstration of the Spirit and power—and we know that the Gospel is "the power of God unto salvation to everyone that believeth."

Verse 7: "So that ye come behind in no gift; waiting for the coming of our Lord Jesus Christ."

The attitude of the believers in the church at Corinth concerning the return of the Lord Jesus was a sure sign that they had been truly born again. In our present verse the verb in the Greek (rendered *"come behind"*) signifies "to be lacking in, or to come short." The "gift" (gift of grace) is a term apparently used here for all spiritual endowments. That is, the Corinthians were endowed with many gifts. They were not lacking in ANY gift. Grace had bestowed upon them unusual gifts in every phase of spiritual living and testimony.

The Greek word here translated *"waiting for"* conveys earnest expectancy. These believers were expecting Jesus at any moment. And the word "coming" literally means "uncovering or unveiling." They were looking for the return of the Lord to receive His saints unto Himself in the Rapture. Paul had taught the Corinthians concerning the glorious day when Jesus will descend from heaven with a shout and with the voice of the archangel. The dead in Christ will be raised incorruptible, and we who are alive shall be changed, and together we will be caught up in the clouds to meet the Lord in the air. And the believers in Corinth were expecting that revelation, that unveiling, at any moment.

A person who does not believe in the second coming of Jesus Christ has no right to testify that he has been saved. We are clearly taught in the Word of God that ALL believers are expecting Jesus. We have the proof in Paul's letter to Titus:

"For the *grace of God* that bringeth salvation hath appeared to all men, *teaching us* that, denying ungodliness and worldly lusts, we should live soberly, righteously, and godly, in this present world; *looking for that blessed hope, and the glorious appearing of the great God and our Saviour Jesus Christ*; who gave Himself for us, that He might redeem us from all iniquity, and purify unto Himself a peculiar people, zealous of good works. These things speak, and exhort, and rebuke with all authority. Let no man despise thee" (Titus 2:11–15).

One of the outstanding reasons the devil hates and tries to hinder the preaching of the second coming of Jesus Christ is the fact that it is not only the blessed, happy hope, but it is the *purifying* hope:

"Beloved, now are we the sons of God, and it doth not yet appear what we shall be: but we know that, when

He shall appear, we shall be like Him; for we shall see Him as He is. And every man that hath this hope in Him purifieth himself, even as He is pure'' (I John 3:2,3).

A believer who expects Jesus at any moment, earnestly and anxiously awaiting His coming in the clouds to catch us up to be with Him, will be very careful how he lives, where he goes, what he does, and the company he keeps.

There are two messages the devil despises with all the hatred hell can provide: (1) The shed blood of Jesus Christ, without which there is no remission, no cleansing, no salvation. (2) The precious truth concerning the Rapture of the Church—a truth that brings comfort, joy, and consecration to believers who find and embrace this glorious truth with all of their hearts.

No church will ever climb higher than their pastor leads them. The pastor is the undershepherd of the flock, and it is his grave responsibility to lead believers into the deep truths of the Word of God as having to do with our sojourn here upon this earth and the glorious things that are in the future for all believers.

To live in earnest expectation of the Lord's return is a sure, positive means of promoting growth and spiritual progress in the life of that believer, and also enrichment in the knowledge of God and spiritual power: "Seeing then that all these things shall be dissolved, what manner of persons ought ye to be in all holy conversation and godliness, looking for and hasting unto the coming of the day of God, wherein the heavens being on fire shall be dissolved, and the elements shall melt with fervent heat?" (II Pet. 3:11,12).

Three Greek words are used in Paul's epistles in connection with the return of the Lord Jesus:

1. Parousia. This word means "personal presence." Paul uses it in referring to the coming of Stephanas (I Cor. 16:17). He also uses it concerning the coming of Titus (II Cor. 7:6,7), and in referring to his own coming to Philippi (Phil. 1:26). It is used in connection with the return of the Lord as having to do with His appearing for the saints and the blessing of the saints (I Cor. 15:23; I Thess. 4:14–17). It is also used in connection with the destruction of the Man of Sin when Jesus comes in the Revelation (II Thess. 2:8).

2. Apokalupsis. This word means "the unveiling, or revelation." It is used to emphasize the visibility of the Lord's return—that is, when every eye shall see Him and all the kindreds of the earth shall wail because of Him (Rev. 1:7). The same word is used of the Lord in II Thessalonians 1:7 and in I Peter 1:7,13; 4:13. It is used referring to the sons of God in connection with the return of Jesus (Rom. 8:19). It is used referring to the coming of the Man of Sin, the Antichrist (II Thess. 2:3,6,8). This Greek word always implies visibility. When Jesus comes in the Rapture, all will not see Him; but when He comes in the Revelation, *every eye will see Him.* The first word (*Parousia*) has to do with the Rapture; the second (*Apokalupsis*) has to do with the Revelation.

3. Epiphaneia. This word means "appearing." It is translated "brightness" in II Thessalonians 2:8. It is also translated "manifestation," and it means "to manifest, or appear." It is used referring to the advent of the Saviour when the Word became flesh (II Tim. 1:10) and in connection with both the Rapture AND the Revelation—the time when Jesus comes FOR His saints, and the time when He returns WITH His saints (I Tim. 6:14; II Tim. 4:1–8; II Thess. 2:8; Tit. 2:13).

We are admonished to study and rightly divide the Word of truth. If we do not study, comparing spiritual things with spiritual and rightly dividing the Word of truth, the Bible will become a book of confusion; but when we study diligently, comparing Scripture with Scripture and rightly dividing the Word in the fear of God as the Spirit leads, the Bible becomes a revelation.

Many have wondered why one Scripture refers to the return of Jesus as a thief in the night, while another declares that "every eye shall see Him." The answer is clear when we study and rightly divide the Word. He is coming for His saints as a thief in the night; and then when He returns to destroy the enemies of God and the Antichrist, He will come "and every eye shall see Him."

Verse 8: "Who shall also confirm you unto the end, that ye may be blameless in the day of our Lord Jesus Christ."

We have the same meaning here as in verse 6. The phrase "unto the end" may express degree (to the utmost), as in John 13:1: "Now before the feast of the passover, when Jesus knew that His hour was come that He should depart out of this world unto the Father, having loved His own which were in the world, He loved them *unto the end.*" It may refer to a period of time, or to the *end* of a period of time—either the end of our earthly course, or until the Rapture of the Church. Paul is saying here, "The Lord Jesus who saved you will also confirm you unto the end—whether it be death or the Rapture."

Scriptural truth concerning the believer is that He who has begun a good work in the heart of the believer is able to perform it unto the end—or until the time when we stand face to face with the Lord Jesus who saved us, to receive our just rewards for the deeds done in the body.

He who saves, KEEPS. Paul had unshakeable assurance; he declared, *"I know WHOM I have believed,* and am persuaded that *He is able to keep* that which I have committed unto Him against that day." He also declared, *"We are more than conquerors* through Him that loved us."

To the Hebrew believers, Paul said, ". . . He (Jesus) hath said, I will never leave thee, nor forsake thee. So that we may boldly say, The Lord is my helper." It is the spiritual birthright of every believer to enjoy unshakeable assurance in the saving and keeping power of our Christ.

It will be a happy day in the lives of many Christians when they realize that Jesus is more concerned about their spiritual success than they themselves. Jesus wants us to be good examples of faith. He wants us to be "living epistles, read of men." He wants us to present our body as "a living sacrifice" and live in such a way as to create a desire in the heart of unbelievers to know Christ. Therefore, He who saves shall also confirm the believer unto the end, that the believer may be unreprovable in the day of our Lord Jesus Christ.

The words *"that ye may be blameless"* signify "free from reproach." That is, we are to live blameless, and stand blameless before God in that day. We are not to be conformed to this world, but transformed by the renewing of our minds. We are to conform to the leadership of the Holy Spirit and acknowledge Him in all of our ways:

"To the end He may stablish your hearts unblameable in holiness before God, even our Father, at the coming of our Lord Jesus Christ with all His saints" (I Thess. 3:13).

"And the very God of peace sanctify you wholly; and I pray God your whole spirit and soul and body be preserved blameless unto the coming of our Lord Jesus

Christ" (I Thess. 5:23).

In other epistles we find expressions similar to *"the day of our Lord Jesus Christ"* used here: ". . . the day of the Lord Jesus" (I Cor. 5:5; II Cor. 1:14); ". . . the day of Jesus Christ" (Phil. 1:6); ". . . the day of Christ" (Phil. 1:10; 2:16). In each of these instances, the term refers to the Rapture—the time when the saints will be caught up into the air to be with the Lord Jesus. When Jesus comes in the Rapture He will not set foot upon this earth. He will descend into the heavens, He will shout, and the trumpet will sound. The dead in Christ will be raised first, then we which are alive shall be caught up together with them in the clouds to meet the Lord in the air. The Rapture is the time when Jesus comes in the first heaven above us and calls the Church up where He is.

In "the day of the Lord Jesus Christ" the saints will be made manifest. They will stand before the judgment seat of Christ to receive the things done in the body, according to the stewardship of the individual believer—whether good or bad; and here it is of that solemn hour that Paul is speaking. *"The day of our Lord Jesus Christ"* is not to be confused with *"the day of the Lord,"* at which time God will judge in the affairs of the *world*— not the Church. *The day of the Lord* is the time when God will overthrow Gentile power:

"Behold, the day of the Lord cometh, cruel both with wrath and fierce anger, to lay the land desolate: and He shall destroy the sinners thereof out of it. For the stars of heaven and the constellations thereof shall not give their light: the sun shall be darkened in his going forth, and the moon shall not cause her light to shine. And I will punish the world for their evil, and the wicked for their iniquity; and I will cause the arrogancy

41

of the proud to cease, and will lay low the haughtiness
of the terrible" (Isa. 13:9–11).

"For it is the day of the Lord's vengeance, and the
year of recompences for the controversy of Zion" (Isa.
34:8).

When *the day of the Lord* has run its course and God
has delivered the Jews from Gentile oppression, He will
set up the kingdom of righteousness on earth: "Yet have
I set my king upon my holy hill of Zion" (Psalm 2:6).

"The day of the Lord" and "the day of our Lord
Jesus Christ" are not one and the same. *"The day of
the Lord"* will be a day when fierce judgment and wrath
will be poured out upon this earth and upon the wicked.
In Joel 2:31, Malachi 4:5, and I Thessalonians 5:2,3 we
read of this horrible judgment. But the *"day of the Lord
Jesus Christ"* is the time when the bride will be caught
up to meet the bridegroom and the marriage supper of the
Lamb will be observed in the first heaven just above the
earth. At this time believers will be rewarded for their
faithful stewardship and will return to earth to reign with
Jesus for one thousand glorious years!

Paul was assuring the Corinthian believers that the
God who had so abundantly bestowed His grace upon them,
saving them and planting in their hearts such extra-ordinary
gifts, would also KEEP them to the end, that they might
be unreproveable in the day when they should be judged—
not as to whether they were saved or lost, sons of God
or sinners, but for their stewardship — whether their works
were gold, silver, precious stones; or wood, hay, and
stubble.

Verse 9: "God is faithful, by whom ye were called
unto the fellowship of His Son Jesus Christ our Lord."

"God is faithful!" Have you ever paused to give

thanks for the faithfulness of God the Father? It is He who calls the sinner to repentance. It was He who commended His love toward us in that while we were yet sinners, *Christ died for us.* Salvation was born in the heart of "God who is faithful."

Jesus said, "No man can come to me, except the Father which hath sent me draw him: and I will raise him up at the last day" (John 6:44). Paul mentions the faithfulness of God many times in his epistles, as in I Thessalonians 5:24: *"Faithful is He that calleth you, who also will do it."* The Old Testament writers declare that God is faithful: "Know therefore that the Lord thy God, He is God, *the faithful God*, which keepeth covenant and mercy with them that love Him and keep His commandments to a thousand generations" (Deut. 7:9).

For further study concerning the testimony of the Word of God to the faithfulness of God, read and study all of these Scriptures: Psalm 36:5; 40:10; all of Psalm 89; Psalm 92:2; 119:75, 90; 143:1; Isaiah 11:5; 49:7; Lamentations 3:23; Hosea 2:20; II Timothy 2:13; Hebrews 10:23; I John 1:9.

Believers are *"called unto the fellowship of His Son Jesus Christ our Lord."* "Fellowship" denotes *partnership or communion.* It also means "to have in common" . . . that is, we are partners with Christ, we commune with Him:

"That which was from the beginning, which we have heard, which we have seen with our eyes, which we have looked upon, and our hands have handled, of the Word of life; (For the life was manifested, and we have seen it, and bear witness, and shew unto you that eternal life, which was with the Father, and was manifested unto us;) That which we have seen and heard declare we unto you, that ye also may have fellowship with us: and truly our fellowship is with the Father, and with His Son Jesus Christ. And these things write we unto you, that your joy may be full" (I John 1:1-4).

From these tremendous verses we know that John is well acquainted with the One of whom he speaks. He saw Him, he heard Him, he touched Him — and he makes these truths known to us in order that *we* might fellowship with God the Father and God the Son, that we might enjoy our spiritual birthright of "full joy." The partnership with Jesus, to which we are called, involves rejection by the world. The world did not know Jesus, and if we walk with Him the world will not know US. Partnership with Jesus involves *suffering* with Him — but if we reject the world and suffer with Christ, we will share His glory!

"Searching what, or what manner of time the Spirit of Christ which was in them did signify, when it testified beforehand the sufferings of Christ, and the glory that should follow" (I Pet. 1:11).

"For even hereunto were ye called: because Christ also suffered for us, leaving us an example, that ye should follow His steps" (I Pet. 2:21).

"Beloved, think it not strange concerning the fiery trial which is to try you, as though some strange thing happened unto you: But rejoice, inasmuch as ye are partakers of Christ's sufferings; that, when His glory shall be revealed, ye may be glad also with exceeding joy" (I Pet. 4:12,13).

"But the God of all grace, who hath called us unto His eternal glory by Christ Jesus, after that ye have suffered a while, make you perfect, stablish, strengthen, settle you" (I Pet. 5:10).

Notice the titles in the last part of verse 9 of our

present chapter: "His Son". . . "Jesus". . . "Christ". . . "Our Lord." Each of these titles has a special meaning concerning the fellowship between the Saviour and the believer. Each refers respectively to the dignity of the relationship (God's own Son), to His humility, His exaltation in glory, and His authority over the life of the believer. When one becomes a Christian, that one is no longer his own; he is bought with a price; he is the bond-slave of Jesus Christ, called to become partners with Him, to commune with Him, and to share His reproach and suffering at the hands of unbelievers — and, at the end of life's journey, to share His glory. Believers are "heirs of God and joint heirs with Jesus."

I suppose no earthly man ever suffered more than Paul; yet he said, "For I reckon that the sufferings of this present time are not worthy to be compared with the glory which shall be revealed in us" (Rom. 8:18).

Verse 10: "Now I beseech you, brethren, by the name of our Lord Jesus Christ, that ye all speak the same thing, and that there be no divisions among you; but that ye be perfectly joined together in the same mind and in the same judgment."

"Now I beseech you" — that is, "I earnestly plead with you, I earnestly beg you, my brethren . . ." (and note that Paul is pleading in the name of *"OUR Lord Jesus Christ"*).

We see here an urgent entreaty, set in contrast to the thanksgiving poured forth from his heart in the opening verses of the chapter. Paul reminds the Corinthian believers of the bond of their mutual relationship in the Lord Jesus, as against their divided state in the local church, and then he offers an urgent entreaty concerning these divisions among them. He makes a strong appeal in the name of the Lord Jesus Christ who had saved them and God the Father who had called them into this fellowship. Because of the love, grace, and tender mercy of Jesus, Paul expressed his deep concern over the ugly divisions in the church at Corinth.

He first begged, *"that ye all speak the same thing."* Certainly this suggests that they were NOT all speaking the same thing; they did not have uniformity of utterance. Later in the epistle, we learn that they each had their own song, their own tongue, and their own little word which they felt they must sound out every time the assembly met.

Paul is not suggesting that they all say the same thing every time they speak in the assembly — certainly not! He is pleading for *unity in testimony*, based upon a common acceptance of the truth he had declared unto them but which they were not practicing in their meetings.

Next, Paul besought the Corinthian believers *"that there be no divisions among you."* The Greek word here translated "divisions" is *schisma* . . . literally a *rent* (Matt. 9:16). It is rendered "schism" in I Corinthians 12:25, and in I Corinthians 11:18 the same word is translated "divisions."

Schisma is different from a similar word, *hairesis* — a Greek word which means "a faction, or sect," and denotes a more complete division, separation, or lack of unity. *Schisma* is a weaker word than *hairesis*. There was dissension among the believers in Corinth, and Paul knew that such dissension would soon lead to a division in the church. Such differences would develop into a schism, and from thence into a sect (*hairesis*)—a division that has come to maturity and is established in the hearts of the divided, bringing about a sect or cult. Paul knew the need for believers to be alert at all times, the need for watchfulness against the beginning of strife: *"The beginning of strife* is as when one letteth out water:

therefore leave off contention, before it be meddled with"
(Prov. 17:14).

These dear believers in the church at Corinth were
Paul's children in the Lord. He did not *save* them—but
he preached the Gospel *through which they were begotten
unto salvation*, and he loved them with a deep love that
few men, apart from Jesus Christ, have ever known.

*"But that ye be perfected together in the same mind
and in the same judgment."* The Greek word *katartizo*
(perfect) used here means "to render fit, complete, or
perfectly joined." The same word is used in Matthew
4:21 and in Mark 1:19 in connection with the fishermen
mending their nets. In Galatians 6:1 the same word is
translated "restore." This word is not always applied
to something that has been damaged; however, that is
the case here regarding the assembly at Corinth. It is
pointing out the damage being caused by dissension and
division in the church.

". . . In the same mind and in the same judgment."
The mind is the faculty by which truth is grasped; judgment is the opinion formed concerning truth. Paul here
pleads that the believers in Corinth be perfectly joined
together in mind, that each and every one of them grasp
the pure truth of the grace of God and the blessings bestowed upon them by grace, and that their judgment be
in unity, not divided concerning the truth that had set
them free.

There can be — there *should* be — unity even where
there is variety, as in the members of the human body.
In I Corinthians chapter 12 the church is compared to
the human body. An assembly can be used and blessed
of God in the way He wants to use and bless the local
church *only when that assembly is possessed of unity*,
when the members live in harmony, honestly and sincerely

seeking the welfare of one another.

When believers display oneness of mind and of judgment they are equipped for testimony and conflict. Conflict will come, but the assembly—and individuals IN the assembly—are prepared to meet the enemy when they walk in unity and testify to the goodness of God and the saving power of His grace. Jesus said, *"In the world ye shall have tribulation*: but be of good cheer; I have overcome the world" (John 16:33b).

The oneness of Christ and His people is clearly set forth in many places in the Word of God. The prayer of intercession recorded in John 17 declares, "And now come I to thee; and these things I speak in the world, that they might have my joy fulfilled in themselves. I have given them thy Word; and the world hath hated them, because they are not of the world, even as I am not of the world. I pray not that thou shouldest take them out of the world, but that thou shouldest keep them from the evil. They are not of the world, even as I am not of the world. Sanctify them through thy truth: thy Word is truth. As thou hast sent me into the world, even so have I also sent them into the world. And for their sakes I sanctify myself, that they also might be sanctified through the truth. Neither pray I for these alone, but for them also which shall believe on me through their word; that they all may be one; as thou, Father, art in me, and I in thee, that they also may be one in us: that the world may believe that thou hast sent me. And the glory which thou gavest me I have given them; that they may be one, even as we are one: I in them, and thou in me, that they may be made perfect in one; and that the world may know that thou hast sent me, and hast loved them, as thou hast loved me" (John 17:13–23).

"For both He that sanctifieth and they who are

sanctified are all of one: for which cause He is not ashamed to call them brethren" (Heb. 2:11).

"God is faithful, by whom ye were called unto the fellowship of His Son Jesus Christ our Lord" (I Cor. 1:9).

"Herein is our love made perfect, that we may have boldness in the day of judgment: because as He is, so are we in this world" (I John 4:17).

"And we know that the Son of God is come, and hath given us an understanding, that we may know Him that is true, and we are in Him that is true, even in His Son Jesus Christ. This is the true God, and eternal life" (I John 5:20).

The Corinthians Were Following Human Leaders — Thus Dividing the Body of Christ

Verse 11: "For it hath been declared unto me of you, my brethren, by them which are of the house of Chloe, that there are contentions among you."

Who "the household of Chloe" was is not disclosed here, and we need not speculate as to their identity. The fact that the name is mentioned here implies willingness on the part of that household to be known as the informants. Paul did not hesitate to identify the persons who had provided sufficient evidence to let him know that there were contentions in the church. He did not write his letter to the Corinthians because of some tale-bearer who asked that his name not be mentioned. The information had come from God-fearing people who wanted this matter handled in the right way, in godly fear—and in making known the need of the church they were willing to allow their names to be used.

Surely it must have grieved those of the house of Chloe to have to make known to Paul the unsatisfactory conditions existing in the assembly. The burden undoubtedly rested heavily upon their hearts; they were not tale-bearers dealing in idle gossip. In many churches today there are those who seem to find a great deal of self-satisfaction in criticizing, backbiting, and gossiping about other church members and church leaders. Such a practice will divide the church, hinder its effectiveness for Christ, and will certainly prove a hindrance in bringing about a cure for whatever ills may exist in the local assembly!

Verse 12: "Now this I say, that every one of you saith, I am of Paul; and I of Apollos; and I of Cephas; and I of Christ."

The verb *"lego"* ("to say") sometimes signifies "to mean," and the dictionary says that is the case here . . . "now this I mean." What Paul meant by *"every one of you"* was that *each one* was at fault. It seems that every member of the church had allied himself with one or another of these respective groups. The phrase "every one of you" recorded here is to be understood much in the same way as that in I Corinthians 14:26, where Paul declared, "How is it then, brethren? When ye come together, *every one of you* hath a psalm, hath a doctrine, hath a tongue, hath a revelation, hath an interpretation. . . ." It represents a general condition existing in the church as a whole, and in which ALL were to blame.

In I Corinthians 4:6 we read, "And these things, brethren, I have in a figure transferred to myself and to Apollos for your sakes; that ye might learn in us not to think of men above that which is written, that no one of you be puffed up for one against another." This verse does not necessarily mean that certain groups were actually attaching themselves to Paul or to Apollos. Paul mentions his name and that of Apollos to illustrate a principle as applied to what was going on in the church. Other names he did NOT use, lest he hurt the cause and hinder the work of the Lord in the assembly at Corinth.

In verse 12 of our present chapter we clearly see that there were four distinct sects, respectively using Paul, Apollos, Cephas, and Christ as the leaders of their group. Those claiming Paul probably did so because he was the one used of God to begin the church in Corinth — but they would certainly find no sympathy or special favors on his part toward themselves. He would treat everyone alike.

True, the Lord used Paul to plant the seed of the Corinthian church — but He used Apollos in watering. Apollos—born at Alexandria, an "eloquent man and mighty in the Scriptures" (Acts 18:24)—would have appealed strongly to the Corinthians and could easily have caused some of them to form a sect (or group) around him—which, of course, would be contrary to the Holy Spirit and against the teaching of the Apostle Paul.

From II Corinthians 10:10 we know that there were certain factions in the church who were bitterly antagonistic toward Paul: "For his letters, say they, are weighty and powerful; but his bodily presence is weak, and his speech contemptible."

". . . *And I (am) of Cephas* . . . ." In speaking of the Apostle Peter, with the exception of Galatians 2:7,8, Paul always used the name *Cephas*. *Cephas* was an Aramaic name; *Peter* was a Greek name.

This sect, in a Greek city, using the name of Cephas, seems to suggest that the leading men in this little group were Jews. No doubt they stressed the fact that Cephas was pre-eminent among the twelve, and that he was the leader and spokesman. Perhaps his conduct at Antioch had given them the idea that Cephas, not Paul, should be the leader in the church. Thus, although there is no evidence that Cephas ever visited Corinth, this group had chosen to cast their lot with him.

"*. . . And I (am) of Christ.*" It may have been that the leaders in this group thought they were superior to those in the church who claimed to be followers of Paul, Apollos, and Cephas.

"Do ye look on things after the outward appearance? If any man trust to himself that he is Christ's, let him of himself think this again, that, as he is Christ's, even so are we Christ's" (II Cor. 10:7). This group no doubt professed a very special experience, a relationship to Christ which gave them a special position in Christ, and therefore superiority in the church. We have the same groups today under other names. One such group preaches long and loud that if you are not baptized by one of their ordained ministers in their church, you will not be taken in the Rapture. They do not consign us to hell if we have not been baptized by their particular group, but they declare that we will be *servants and guests* at the marriage of the Lamb, not seated at the marriage supper. The group who composed the "Christ party" in the Corinthian church perhaps taught some such doctrine.

Church groups have failed to heed the warning in this passage—warning against the evils of using the names of men, or other means, to establish churches. There are scores of sectarian groups in our land today. Surely the Holy Ghost gave the facts recorded in our present Scripture as a giant beaconlight shining out against the danger of these parties (sects), known today as "denominations."

In the next verse Paul asks a solemn question:

Verse 13: "Is Christ divided? was Paul crucified for you? or were ye baptized in the name of Paul?"

"IS CHRIST DIVIDED?" It seems that this question is directed not only to the "Christ Party" but to all the other groups. The Greek word *merizo* comes from the Greek *meros*, which means "a part, or a share." It seems that Paul is asking the Corinthians, "Have you received Christ in parts, or in shares? Has a part of Christ been apportioned to you?" The same word is used in I Corinthians 7:17, translated "distributed." It is used in Romans 12:3 and is translated "hath dealt." It is used again in Hebrews 4:12, translated "dividing." The Church of the Lord Jesus Christ is NOT divided; the Church is one body (I Cor. 12:12,13,27).

Party-forming tears the members of the church asunder, divides them, and thus brings about disunity and allows Satan to hinder the work of the Holy Spirit—not only in the church, but in the *community*, where the church represents all that Jesus died for. And this is what Paul is dealing with here — sectarianism under party leadership, rather than error.

The Lord Jesus Christ had saved and sanctified the Corinthian believers, and it was because of HIM that their discord and factions were so gravely serious. Paul was jealous for the honor of the Lord Jesus Christ. He was brokenhearted and sick in his soul that the believers in Corinth could place so much emphasis upon the names of *men* in rival groups, when they had come to know *the Son of God*, the Rose of Sharon, the "fairest of ten thousand"! How could these Christians set up *men* as head of their respective groups, when Paul had so clearly taught them that Jesus Christ is the head of the Church and Saviour of the body?

"*WAS PAUL CRUCIFIED FOR YOU?*" Here Paul

implies his own insignificance. What he is asking is simply this: *"Was it Paul* who died on the cross for you? Did Paul shed his blood for the remission of sin? Could the work of redemption be attributed to Paul—or to Apollos, or Cephas, or to any other man?"

By contrast Paul is pointing out that Christ, who is NOT divided, is the *one Saviour,* the only One who CAN save. This is the first mention in this epistle of the fact that the death of the Lord Jesus Christ is the only way to correct evils in the church. Regardless of what *man* may do, or say, or think, there is *only one message* that will correct evil—in the local church or in the life of an individual—and that message is the finished work of the Lord Jesus, accomplished in His death, burial, and resurrection. He now sits at the right hand of God the Father to plead our case and to make intercession for us (I Tim. 2:5; Heb. 1:1–3).

". . . Or were ye baptized in the name of Paul?" To the believer, baptism speaks of the death, burial, and resurrection of the Lord Jesus Christ. Immersion in water is the believer's testimony of devoted response to the sacrifice of the Saviour.

The unbeliever hears the Gospel of the grace of God — (and that Gospel is the death, burial, and resurrection of Jesus "according to the Scriptures"—I Cor. 15:1–4). Hearing the Gospel brings faith to the unbeliever, who then, *by faith,* appropriates the benefits of the sacrificial death of Jesus Christ; and this appropriation is to be followed by *outward expression* of that *inward* appropriation in the symbolic acts of identification with Christ in His death, burial, and resurrection. Such is the true picture of water baptism in this day of grace.

Baptism follows conversion. It does not *precede* faith in the finished work of Jesus Christ; it *follows* the experience of grace in the heart of the individual. Water baptism does not save us nor does it *add to* our salvation; but it DOES testify to a gainsaying world that we are *crucified* with Christ, *buried* with Christ, and *raised* with Christ to walk in newness of life (Rom. 6:1—10).

The Greek word used here for the preposition "in" is *eis*, and signifies "entrance into communion with and recognition of the authority of another." For Paul to conceive of such communion and authority centering in himself as rival to the Lord Jesus Christ was utterly repulsive to the Apostle Paul — he who counted all things loss that he might gain Christ. Paul desired that Christ have the pre-eminence in all things, and testified to the Colossians, "Ye are complete in Him." Paul was extremely jealous for Jesus . . . not jealous for himself, but for the Lord Jesus Christ whom he met on the road to Damascus and whom he loved with all of his heart, soul, and strength.

Verses 14 and 15: "I thank God that I baptized none of you, but Crispus and Gaius; lest any should say that I had baptized in mine own name."

The Scripture does not tell us why Paul baptized so few people. It may be that he feared their looking to *him* rather than to the Lord Jesus who saved them. We do know that in verse 17 we read, *"FOR CHRIST SENT ME NOT TO BAPTIZE, but to preach the Gospel!"* The fact that he baptized a few persons is evidence that Paul did not neglect the ordinance—and because he baptized so few he had given no occasion for the converts to use his name as a party watchword. Certainly a pastor should want the love, respect, and esteem of his people—but it is gross sin for believers to get their eyes on God's undershepherd instead of on *the Chief Shepherd*, the Lord Jesus Christ.

Paul said God sent him not to baptize, but to *preach*. Servants of God should fulfill only the service for which they receive guidance through the Holy Ghost. They should cooperate with others, make room for others—and not try to do everything themselves, nor try to get all the glory. If ministers would follow the leading of the Holy Ghost instead of following religious leaders, denominations, or their own desires, they would save themselves much trouble (and would probably receive a much greater reward at the end of their earthly ministry). Ministers are flesh, just as all believers are; they are not immune to the temptations of selfishness, pride, and other sins of which the flesh is capable.

Who was *Crispus*? "And Crispus, the chief ruler of the synagogue, believed on the Lord with all his house; and many of the Corinthians hearing believed, and were baptized" (Acts 18:8). Crispus was an outstanding personality—chief ruler of the synagogue. Could it be that Paul felt Crispus to be one of his prize converts, and thus baptized him? The same verse tells us that many of the Corinthians believed, but seemingly at this time Paul baptized only Crispus.

Who was *Gaius*? We read of him in Romans 16:23: "Gaius mine host, and of the whole church, saluteth you." It seems that Gaius was very close to the Apostle Paul.

We do not know who *Stephanas* was nor what he did. We simply know that Paul baptized his entire household:

Verse 16: "And I baptized also the household of Stephanas: besides, I know not whether I baptized any other."

The fact that Paul baptized entire households has been used by some to suggest that he baptized *babies*, but there is no scriptural ground for such a suggestion. It is recorded that during Paul's entire ministry he baptized three households: The household of Lydia (Acts 16:15); the household of the Philippian jailer (Acts 16:33); and the household of Stephanas, referred to in our present verse.

All who believed were baptized — and certainly infants could not believe. In John 4:53 we read that the entire household of the nobleman believed. This is also true of Crispus (Acts 18:8) and of Cornelius (Acts 10:2). We know that faith, joy, and the fear of God cannot be said to apply to babies—for *they* cannot fear God, nor can they exercise faith and display the joy of knowing that their sins are forgiven. *These qualities* come from believers who are old enough to know that God IS, and that "the wages of sin is death." They confess their sin, they believe on the Lord Jesus Christ, they are saved by God's grace through faith — and salvation brings joy unspeakable and full of glory.

Infants need no baptism; they are innocent, and *God takes care of the innocent.* There is nothing wrong in dedicating babies to God, even at the altar of a church— but to sprinkle or pour a few drops of water on a baby's head certainly adds nothing to the dedication! It is perfectly in order for parents to come forward in the assembly and have the minister pray with them as they dedicate their baby to God, but there is no place in the Bible where infant baptism is suggested. The Greek word for "baptize" means "to dip or plunge" — and certainly no minister would be guilty of putting a baby under the water!

"Besides, I know not whether I baptized any other." This does not suggest that these words are not inspired. Some have even suggested that the statement be stricken from the Word of God; but the Holy Spirit dictated these words to Paul just as truly as He dictated the rest of the epistle. The Holy Ghost did not deem it needful to give a record of all the converts Paul had baptized

(if there *were* others), because baptism has nothing to do with redemption.

Those whom the Apostle Paul baptized, he did so — *not that they might be saved* — but to testify that they *were saved* by the shed blood of Jesus Christ. Baptism is not of such significance or importance that Paul should keep a record of each and every person whom he baptized.

Verse 17: "For Christ sent me not to baptize, but to preach the Gospel: not with wisdom of words, lest the cross of Christ should be made of none effect."

Some dear ministers and teachers never use this verse as a text. They preach long and loud that unless you are immersed in water in the name of Jesus Christ, you will surely burn in hell — but such preaching is not inspired of God; it is not of the Holy Spirit. Baptism has nothing to do with regeneration: Baptism *follows* regeneration.

Paul declared, *"Therefore we conclude that a man is justified by faith without the deeds of the law"* (Rom. 3:28). Faith has nothing to do with water in a baptistry or a river: ". . . Faith cometh by hearing, and hearing by the Word of God"—not by being immersed in water. We are saved by grace, *entirely by grace*, apart from anything else.

Grace SAVES us — but FAITH brings saving grace. Hearing the Word brings faith: "In the beginning was the Word (Jesus), and the Word was with God, and the Word was God. . . and the Word (Jesus) was made flesh." Jesus is the heart and soul of redemption; He IS our redemption. Redemption is "Christ in you, the hope of glory" — not "you in the baptistry." I believe God's preachers should preach baptism, but Paul declared that Christ did not send him to baptize, *"but to preach the Gospel."*

Greek scholars tell us that the statement "to preach the Gospel" gives us our word *"evangelize."* In other words, Paul is saying here, "Christ commissioned me to evangelize, to preach the Gospel of the death, burial, and resurrection of Jesus and to point weary sinners to the finished work of Christ. I am commissioned to evangelize—not to baptize."

Baptism is honorable. It is a beautiful symbol, and undoubtedly it brings great joy to the heart of a pastor to put newborn babes in Christ into the watery grave and raise them up in the name of the Father, Son, and Holy Ghost. But to point sinners to salvation and see them born into the family of God is the greatest joy that can come to a pastor, an evangelist, a missionary, or a layman. It is honorable to baptize — but it is much more honorable to direct men to the "fountain filled with blood drawn from Immanuel's veins," telling them that "sinners plunged beneath THAT flood lose all their guilty stains"! The blood of Jesus Christ, God's Son, cleanses from ALL sin; the water in the baptistry cannot cleanse from ANY sin. Therefore, Paul declared in concise, understandable words, "Christ sent me not to baptize, but to preach the Gospel."

"Not with wisdom of words, lest the cross of Christ should be made of none effect." What Paul is saying here is this: "Christ did not commission me to preach with wisdom of speech—beautiful phrases, well-constructed sentences, in a religious manner; I was commissioned to preach in words easily understood, words that spell out salvation—the gift of God by grace through the blood of Jesus."

Paul is striking hard at the teachers in Corinth who were displaying their ability to speak great swelling words and preach outstanding sermons from the standpoint of construction, instead of employing the power of the Holy Ghost in the message. The Greeks admired a display of oratory. They judged the value of a discourse more by external exhibition than by the inward power of the message. The assembly in Corinth, as a whole, was in grave danger from the influence of superficial preaching. They were in danger of becoming an organization run strictly as a business, rather than allowing the Holy Ghost to speak through the teachers and leaders in the assembly.

Paul is not suggesting here that the minister should walk unprepared into the pulpit and expect God to give him a message. It was Paul who commanded, "Study to show thyself approved unto God, a workman that needeth not to be ashamed, rightly dividing the word of truth." It was also Paul who admonished, "Give attendance to reading." A minister should study and seek to find acceptable words that will present the greatest depth of truth in the simplest language possible. It is down-to-earth preaching that brings the greatest glory to God and the most people to the saving knowledge of Jesus Christ.

Paul wanted the assembly at Corinth to understand clearly that his message was the message of the cross, and he absolutely refused to allow anything—worldly wisdom, baptism, the ability to speak great, swelling words—to draw his attention away from the cross. In Paul's day the cross was "a stake or a beam," to which slaves and the lowest type of criminals were nailed to die. Death on a cross was the lowest, vilest, most horrible and despicable death possible.

Speaking here of the cross, Paul describes the death of Christ in its extreme depth of humiliation. Jesus took the place of the lowest criminal, He died the death of the vilest, that the lowest and vilest might be made sons of God and their black hearts washed white as the snow, in the blood of His cross!

The statement *"should be made of none effect"* denotes "to make empty" or "to make void." All through the writings of Paul he cries out, "The cross . . . *the cross . . . THE CROSS!"* He preached Jesus Christ, the virgin-born Son of God—crucified, buried, risen, seen of men, *"according to the Scriptures."* He determined not to allow *anything* or any person to come between him and the clear message of the cross of Christ.

Verse 18: "For the preaching of the cross is to them that perish foolishness; but unto us which are saved it is the power of God."

"The preaching of the cross" is literally "the Word, that which is of the cross." The Word is set in contrast to "wisdom OF words." The word here means the preaching about the cross, or what is said about the cross.

The preaching of the shed blood of Jesus Christ on the cross "is to them that perish, *foolishness* — but unto us who are saved, it is *the power of God."* We are told that the Greek word *moria* here translated "foolishness" is not used anywhere in the New Testament except in I Corinthians. It is found again in verses 21 and 23 of our present chapter, again in chapter 2 verse 14, and in chapter 3 verse 19. It means "that which is regarded as stupid, silly, or worthless."

The Greek verb used here (and in our King James version translated "perish") does not denote annihilation or extinction; it means "ruin—or loss of well being." (The unbeliever is *in the process* of perishing.)

We find this word again in chapter 15, verse 18, and also in II Corinthians 2:15: "For we are unto God a sweet savour of Christ, in them that are saved, and in them

that perish." The same word is used in II Corinthians
4:16.

The full force of the word as used in our present
verse expresses that which is certain . . . in other words,
*there is absolutely no forgiveness of sins apart from the
preaching of the cross.* Without the shedding of blood
there is no remission, no cleansing, no salvation—and any
person who looks upon *the preaching of the cross* as
"stupid, silly, or worthless" is sure to perish; his eternal
damnation is certain!

"Unto us which are saved" points to the initial deliverance in the experience of the believer when he receives Jesus by faith. This truth is set forth in Ephesians
2:5–9:

"Even when we were dead in sins, hath quickened
us together with Christ, (by grace ye are saved;) and hath
raised us up together, and made us sit together in heavenly places in Christ Jesus: That in the ages to come He
might shew the exceeding riches of His grace in His kindness toward us through Christ Jesus. For by grace are
ye saved through faith; and that not of yourselves: it is
the gift of God: not of works, lest any man should boast."

The word "saved" describes the present course of
the believer's life here upon this earth, and it points to
the final and permanent deliverance of the believer at
the coming of the Lord Jesus for His saints in the Rapture.

The preaching and the message of the cross received
by the sinner saves him from all past sins. He who receives the message of the cross *is being saved* moment
by moment, and thank God he who possesses the message
of the cross in his heart will BE saved when Jesus comes
in the Rapture! The blood of Jesus Christ saves us from
the *penalty* of sin, from the *power* of sin—and eventually,
from the *presence* of sin.

The pronoun "US" is in a position of emphasis, suggesting the joy in the benefit bestowed upon the writer (Paul) and the reader (the believers in the assembly at Corinth, as well as you and me). Paul does not say "to THEM that are saved," but "to US," thus making himself *one with the believers* in Corinth, and also one with believers of today.

"*The power of God*" is set in contrast to *foolishness*. What Paul is saying here is simply this: "Since the cross of Jesus exceeds the limits of human understanding, the death of Christ (to the natural man in his natural wisdom) seems insufficient to accomplish its purpose— the salvation of the soul. Therefore, to the natural man, the preaching of the cross is foolishness."

There are many ministers in pulpits around the world today, as well as in our own land, who never mention the blood of Jesus Christ. They never preach the crucifixion—*a divine necessity for salvation*. They call the message of the cross a "butcherhouse" message, and declare that in this enlightened age it is not needed— (nor accepted by thinking people).

These are of the same stock as the crowd in Paul's day who declared that the preaching of the shed blood of the Lord Jesus Christ on the cross for the remission of sin was a "stupid, silly, worthless" message. But the fact still remains that from Genesis to Calvary there is a stream of blood — a scarlet thread runs through the entire Old Testament; and since Calvary, we have the solemn, divine truth that "*without shedding of blood is no remission*" (Heb. 9:22). Jesus on the cross is God displaying His best for man's worst. The cross is a divine imperative, declared before the foundation of the world (I Pet. 1:18ff).

"But the natural man receiveth not the things of the

Spirit of God: for they are foolishness unto him: neither can he know them, because they are spiritually discerned'' (I Cor. 2:14).

Verse 19: ''For it is written, I will destroy the wisdom of the wise, and will bring to nothing the understanding of the prudent.''

We have here proof of the statements in verse 18. Through the inspired pen of the Apostle Paul, the Holy Spirit here quotes part of Isaiah 29:14: ''Therefore, behold, I will proceed to do a marvellous work among this people, even a marvellous work and a wonder: for the wisdom of their wise men shall perish, and the understanding of their prudent men shall be hid.''

There is only one change in the quotation: In Isaiah we read that the understanding of the prudent ''shall be *hid*,'' and in our present verse the Apostle says the understanding of the prudent shall be *''brought to nothing''*— which means ''to set aside, or reject.'' This same word is found in Psalm 33:10: ''The Lord bringeth the counsel of the heathen to nought: He maketh the devices of the people of none effect.''

All Scripture is given by inspiration and is profitable to us (II Tim. 3:16). The Holy Ghost goes back to the Old Testament many times, bringing forward its truths to incorporate them into the New Testament, thus proving that the Bible is God-breathed, and that the Old Testament is just as truly God's Word as is the New.

The verse quoted here is taken from the prophecy of Isaiah and has to do with Sennacherib's invasion of Judah. The leaders of Judah, instead of relying upon their God, sought to rely upon Egypt for assistance in the conflict. From the human and political standpoint this seemed an act of wisdom; but from the spiritual standpoint and in the sight of God it was an insult, an act of rebellion. Therefore, God brought Judah's policy to nought and allowed her to be chastened to a condition of utter helplessness, so that His people would depend upon Him alone.

The reason for the Old Testament quotation here is to emphasize point for point that salvation cannot be accomplished by man's wisdom, schemes, and efforts. Every effort put forth by man to save himself or to produce salvation is futile; man must come to accept the fact that it is vain folly for him, through his own wisdom, understanding, might or power, to attempt to produce his own salvation. He must learn that salvation is of the Lord, wholly apart from man or anything man can do. When the unbeliever faces this fact, he is ready to receive the Lord Jesus Christ and be saved.

The Gospel is "the power of God unto salvation to every one that believeth; to the Jew first, and also to the Greek. For therein is the righteousness of God revealed from faith to faith: as it is written, THE JUST SHALL LIVE BY FAITH" (Rom. 1:16,17). There are many passages in the Old Testament which present beautiful pictures of redemption. Salvation is entirely of God. Man can do nothing to save himself but receive the finished work of the Lord Jesus Christ by faith.

According to our present verse, he who exercises only the human quality of understanding will be brought to nothing. Permit me to use a term here which I often use in the pulpit: "God deals *below the collar button.*" It matters not how much wisdom and understanding one may boast of, except big men be converted and become as little humble children, they will in no wise enter into the kingdom of God. Later in this chapter we learn that the wisdom of the world is foolishness to God because the foolishness of God is wiser than men, and the weakness of God is stronger than men.

One of the most difficult things for me to do as an evangelist is to get people to see their utter helplessness, and then persuade them to exercise faith in the finished work of Jesus, simply trusting in HIM—*minus works!* The flesh wants to DO something, BE something, LIVE something — but according to the infallible Word of God, ". . . by grace are ye saved through faith; and that not of yourselves: it is the gift of God: not of works, lest any man should boast" (Eph. 2:8,9).

The fear of the Lord is the beginning of knowledge, and until one fears God from the heart, he has not begun to learn. Right wisdom comes only from God: "If any of you lack wisdom, let him ask of God, that giveth to all men liberally, and upbraideth not; and it shall be given him" (James 1:5).

Verse 20: "Where is the wise? where is the scribe? where is the disputer of this world? Hath not God made foolish the wisdom of this world?"

Again the Holy Spirit makes use of Old Testament truth. Even though it is not quoted verbatim, this seems to be a quotation from Isaiah 33:18: "Thine heart shall meditate terror. Where is the scribe? Where is the receiver? Where is he that counted the towers?" The powerful Assyrian warrior and conqueror came with gigantic armies and a staff of clerks and inventory takers to register the spoils; but utter destruction of the Assyrian host testified to the power of God and at the same time set at nought the worldly-wise councils of the Jewish rulers. We might call this an illustrated sermon from God—to testify to them that He is God, and that He will have no other Gods before Him. In connection with this, study the entire 33rd chapter of Isaiah.

In our present verse God condemns all and sundry who would dare substitute anything for, or add anything to, God's complete, finished way of salvation. Just before Jesus literally gave His spirit back to God the Father, He said, *"It is finished!"* And to the Colossians Paul said, "Ye are complete in HIM."

"Where is the wise?" This is perhaps directed to the Gentiles in Corinth. In verse 22 we read, "For the Jews require a sign, and the Greeks (Gentiles) seek after wisdom."

"Where is the scribe?" This undoubtedly points to the Jewish students who studied and interpreted the Old Testament Scriptures.

"The disputer" refers to both the Greeks and the Jews: "Then certain philosophers of the Epicureans, and of the Stoicks, encountered him. And some said, What will this babbler say? Other some, He seemeth to be a setter forth of strange gods: because he preached unto them Jesus, and the resurrection. And they took him, and brought him unto Areopagus, saying, May we know what this new doctrine, whereof thou speakest, is? For thou bringest certain strange things to our ears: we would know therefore what these things mean. (For all the Athenians and strangers which were there spent their time in nothing else, but either to tell, or to hear some new thing.)" (Acts 17:18–21).

As for the Jews, we read, "As I besought thee to abide still at Ephesus, when I went into Macedonia, that thou mightest charge some that they teach no other doctrine, neither give heed to fables and endless genealogies, which minister questions, rather than godly edifying which is in faith: so do. Now the end of the commandment is charity out of a pure heart, and of a good conscience, and of faith unfeigned: from which some having swerved have turned aside unto *vain jangling*; desiring to be teachers of the law; understanding neither what they say, nor whereof they affirm'' (I Tim. 1:3–7).

The word translated *"world"* is *aion*, which means "age" and "signifies a period of indefinite duration, or time viewed in relation to what takes place in the period. The force attaching to the word is not so much that of the actual length of a period, but that of a period marked by spiritual or moral characteristics" (Expository Dictionary of N. T. Words–by Vine). Since the Fall of Adam this age, or world, has been in spiritual darkness (Eph. 6:12) and subject to the power of darkness (Col. 1:13); and Satan, the god of this world, has blinded the minds of men so that they will not heed the glorious Gospel of Christ (II Cor. 4:4).

"Hath not God made foolish the wisdom of this world"? In Romans 1:22 Paul said about those who professed the wisdom of this world, "They became fools." In the passage in Romans, Paul, through the Holy Spirit, is showing how God rendered the wisdom of this world foolish by the development of its own corrupt and lewd tendencies. Read Romans 1:18–32 and you will see where the wisdom of man led him.

In our present passage (verses 21–25) the Holy Ghost shows us, through the pen of the Apostle Paul, how God has rendered the wisdom of the world foolish by the preaching of the cross of the Lamb of God.

In God's wisdom ends the world's wisdom:

Verse 21: "For after that in the wisdom of God the world by wisdom knew not God, it pleased God by the foolishness of preaching to save them that believe."

Tremendous is the blow which the Apostle Paul here deals the wisdom of the world! When man fell in the

Garden of Eden by eating the forbidden fruit and thereby obtaining the knowledge of good and evil, IN THE WISDOM OF GOD Jehovah God determined that man, through his own intellect and the way which his intellect would lead him, would prove an utter failure in knowing God. However, God did not leave man to himself without giving him a plain revelation which from the first held out to the eye of faith the Seed of the woman, who should bruise the serpent's head:

"And I will put enmity between thee and the woman, and between thy seed and her seed; it shall bruise thy head, and thou shalt bruise His heel" (Gen. 3:15).

But this plan did not suit fallen man, who had come to know good and evil and who then had knowledge. Fallen man assumed that he was competent, and that he could work out his own religion without the grace of God and without the necessity of the power of God; but the record in Genesis declares plainly that men grew worse, and worse, and worse—until corruption and violence became so unbearable that it was imperative for God to send the flood and sweep off the guilty race in a terrible deluge!

But even after the flood, in spite of the tremendous judgment of God upon mankind, man again became more ungodly and evil than *before* the flood. In Romans chapter 1, Paul minutely describes the conditions on earth during the process of evil which finally brought heathenism throughout the universe. Paul declares that when people knew God they glorified Him not AS God. They were not thankful, they were vain in their imaginations, their foolish hearts were darkened. They professed to be wise, but they became fools and changed the glory of the incorruptible God into an image "made like to corruptible man, and to birds, and fourfooted beasts, and creeping things." And because they did this, God gave them over to uncleanness, to the lusts of their own hearts, "to dishonour their own bodies between themselves."

But man did not stop there. He changed the truth of God into a lie; men worshipped and served the creature more than the Creator; and because of this, God gave them up to vile affections. But they went even further: They did not like to retain God in their knowledge—and because of this God gave them over to a reprobate mind, "to do those things which are not convenient."

They were not only filled with all species of unrighteousness and ungodliness, but knowing the judgment of God on such, they not only committed these terrible sins, but also *had pleasure* in them that did commit such hideous sins against the great God of heaven, the Creator of all things.

Their religion itself corrupted them, the symbols of that religion being identified with every species of moral iniquity and vice; and their *wisdom* bound them to slavery — slaves to lust and all kinds of unrighteous practices — morally and religiously. There is nothing which man is so slow to acknowledge as his own ungodliness and wickedness. During my many years of evangelistic meetings, the most difficult thing for me to do has been to convince men that they are sinners and need a Saviour. When a minister, through the Word of God, convinces a sinner that he is lost, unrighteous and ungodly, it is not difficult then to lead that sinner to the Saviour; but the most difficult part of winning souls is GETTING THE SINNER LOST in order to get him saved.

"For God hath concluded them all in unbelief, that He might have mercy upon all. O the depth of the riches both of the wisdom and knowledge of God! How unsearchable are His judgments, and His ways past finding out! For who hath known the mind of the Lord? or who hath been His counsellor? Or who hath first given to Him, and it shall be recompensed unto him again? For of Him, and through Him, and to Him, are all things: to whom be glory for ever. Amen" (Rom. 11:32—36).

". . . *The world by wisdom knew not God.*" Through the wisdom of the world it is utterly impossible for man to come to know God. Such a process is a divine impossibility.

". . . *It pleased God by the foolishness of preaching to save them that believe.*" The meaning here is that *God was well pleased and willing to save any and all who would believe on His Son.* We must not overlook the wording "it pleased God," which stresses the willingness and liberty of God to save the lost through the preaching of the Gospel. We have the same truth set forth in Luke 12:32: "Fear not, little flock; for it is your Father's good pleasure to give you the kingdom." God has no pleasure in the death of the wicked; it is not His will that any should perish, but that all should come to repentance.

The disciples asked Jesus on one occasion if they should call down fire from heaven and devour their enemies. Jesus rebuked them kindly by declaring that He had not come into the world to destroy men's lives, but to save them. And in spite of the fact that man, through his own wisdom, ability, understanding and power, attempted to set up his own salvation; and in spite of the insult he has hurled into God's face, God is still willing and takes great pleasure and joy in saving all who believe the preaching of the Gospel — and the Gospel, as we will learn later in this epistle, is the death, burial, resurrection, and ascension of Jesus Christ "according to the Scriptures."

The word here rendered "preaching" denotes not necessarily what is preached, but the *proclamation* of the message, the telling forth of the good news. The same word is used in I Corinthians 2:4. It lays stress upon the presentation of the message that will cause men to believe on the Lord Jesus Christ and trust in His finished work.

The phrase "them that believe" literally reads "the believing ones, or believers." Here it points to the initial act of faith in those who have exercised faith unto salvation. It means those who are saved through the Gospel delivered by human lips—a message which man's highest wisdom declares worthless, foolish, and futile. By saving men through such a message, God has displayed the folly of man's wisdom and the infinite power of His saving grace.

Verse 22: "For the Jews require a sign, and the Greeks seek after wisdom."

Here we have the marks of the two great representatives of human wisdom. This points to two classes—Jews and Gentiles—but is not necessarily speaking of individuals.

"For the Jews require a sign . . . ." The Jews sought after miracles or external evidence of the power of God — and especially were they looking for the world to be subject to Him as King. "A wicked and adulterous generation seeketh after a sign; and there shall no sign be given unto it, but the sign of the prophet Jonas . . ." (Matt. 16:4). "Then said Jesus unto him, Except ye see signs and wonders, ye will not believe" (John 4:48).

"And the Greeks seek after wisdom." The Greeks put much emphasis on oratory, and they were a very ambitious people. In religion they were of a speculative character, always seeking after some new doctrine. Paul declared this in his sermon on Mars Hill. In Acts 17:19—21 we read, "And they took him, and brought him unto Areopagus, saying, May we know what this new doctrine, whereof

thou speakest, is? For thou bringest certain strange things to our ears: we would know therefore what these things mean. (For all the Athenians and strangers which were there spent their time in nothing else, but either to tell, or to hear some new thing.)"

Verse 23: "But we preach Christ crucified, unto the Jews a stumblingblock, and unto the Greeks foolishness."

"But WE preach . . . ." Stress is laid on the pronoun *WE*, which is representative of all ministers who proclaim the pure Gospel. The subject of Gospel preaching is a Person—CHRIST. Christianity is not a theory *about* Christ; it is not a series of ethical statements proceeding *from* Christ; it is not a system built upon *the concepts OF Christ*. Christianity IS Christ! Christianity is not a cold, dead organization; it is a living organism, and it could not survive if Christ were removed from it, because He is the head and the foundation of it. Christianity cannot be compared with other religions; Jesus Christ is not to be compared with any other person: He is the *incomparable One*.

The basis for Christianity is the Word of God, and the Word of God is Christ. From Genesis through Revelation *the Word of God presents the Lord Jesus Christ*. He is the heart of the Scriptures—both the Old and the New Testaments. On the road to Emmaus (Luke 24:27), He preached to the disciples as they journeyed. He began with Moses, the prophets, and the Psalms, and opened unto them the Scriptures concerning Himself. The entire plan of salvation is summed up in a Person—*Christ*. God the Father wrought our redemption and obtained our pardon in Jesus, the Son of His love.

In Christianity, wherever one may turn, wherever one may look, Christ is the inevitable One. He is forever inseparable from the faith once delivered unto the saints.

Apart from Christ, all is loss; but in Him we have salvation. Apart from Christ, all is dark; but in Him we have light. Apart from Christ, all is death; but in Him we have life. *In HIM all things consist.* To the Colossians Paul said, "Ye are complete in HIM" (Col. 2:9,10). The person of Christ is the subject of all Bible preaching.

". . . We preach not ourselves, but Christ Jesus the Lord . . ." (II Cor. 4:5). "And He shall send Jesus Christ, which before *was preached* unto you" (Acts 3:20). The person of Christ was the subject of the message of the prophets of old.

"And daily in the temple, and in every house, they ceased not to teach and preach Jesus Christ" (Acts 5:42).

The person of Christ was the message of the apostles: "Now when they had passed through Amphipolis and Appolonia, they came to Thessalonica, where was a synagogue of the Jews: And Paul, as his manner was, went in unto them, and three sabbath days reasoned with them out of the Scriptures, opening and alleging, that Christ must needs have suffered, and risen again from the dead; and that this Jesus, whom I preach unto you, is Christ" (Acts 17:1–3).

The person of Christ was the message Paul delivered to his own people, the Jews. It was not the message they *wanted* (they hated Christ); but it was the message they *needed*. Therefore Paul preached Jesus to the Jews.

The person of Christ was the message preached to the Samaritans: "Then Philip went down to the city of Samaria, and preached Christ unto them" (Acts 8:5).

Paul preached the person of Christ to the Gentiles: "To reveal His Son in me, that I might preach Him among the heathen; immediately I conferred not with flesh and blood" (Gal. 1:16).

The person of Christ is the message WE are commanded to preach to all the world today: "And He said unto them, Go ye into all the world, and preach the Gospel to every creature" (Mark 16:15). ". . . Separated unto the Gospel of God . . . concerning His Son Jesus Christ" (Rom. 1:1–3).

What did the Holy Spirit say through the Apostle Paul concerning any man who deviates from the pure Gospel and preaches any other gospel? Galatians 1:6–9 answers:

"I marvel that ye are so soon removed from Him that called you into the grace of Christ unto another gospel: which is not another; but there be some that trouble you, and would pervert the Gospel of Christ. But though we, or an angel from heaven, preach any other gospel unto you than that which we have preached unto you, let him be accursed. As we said before, so say I now again, If any man preach any other gospel unto you than that ye have received, let him be accursed!"

These are solemn words, cutting words—words that should burn their way into the heart of every preacher. Every false witness is accursed. There is no favoritism. God deals alike with all false prophets. Paul said, "Though WE . . . ." Then he went further to say, ". . . or an *angel from heaven* . . . ." Then he put the capstone on the pyramid by saying, ". . . If *any* man . . . ." All are included; not one is excluded. NO man has any right to pervert the Gospel of the grace of God.

To the Corinthians Paul declared, ". . . I delivered unto you first of all that which I also received, how that Christ died for our sins according to the Scriptures; and that He was buried, and that He rose again the third day according to the Scriptures" (I Cor. 15:1–4). "If any man preach any other gospel, let him be accursed!" (Gal. 1:8,9). If any man defames the cross, the resurrection,

75

the Lord's return, let that man be accursed!

Paul cried out, "WOE IS ME IF I PREACH NOT THE GOSPEL" (I Cor. 9:16).

"... *Unto the Jews a stumblingblock* ...." Because of the cross, it was utterly impossible for the Jews to accept the claim that Jesus was their Messiah, their King. They were expecting a victorious Messiah—one who would come and deliver them from the rule of the Romans. They expected great signs and wonders. They expected Him to establish a kingdom here on earth, and the preaching of the cross of Jesus Christ was definitely a stumblingblock to them.

The word "stumblingblock" denotes anything that becomes a hindrance to others, or causes them to fall. Such was the case with the Jews. They were not looking for a *suffering* Messiah. They had read Isaiah many times, but their eyes were nevertheless blinded to the Lamb of God who was to be slain for sinners. They did not see the crown of thorns before the crown of glory. They did not see Christ's sufferings before His glorification.

"... *And unto the Greeks, foolishness.*" According to the Greeks' standard of wisdom, it was an utter impossibility that a king should wear a crown of thorns and be nailed to a cross. Some of their men of wisdom who wrote shortly after the crucifixion of Jesus declared that the Christian faith was foolish and absurd because the Christians actually "worshipped a dead man!" They ruled out the divine power of God and the miracle of the bodily resurrection of Christ.

Throughout His public ministry, Jesus declared that He would go into Jerusalem, that He would be arrested, put to death and buried—but would rise again the third day. The Greeks' reasoning was from the standpoint of man's wisdom, and thus by their own standards they could not accept the death, burial, and resurrection of the Son of God. The greatest bombshell ever to explode in the face of an unbelieving world was the bodily resurrection of the Lord Jesus Christ.

Verse 24: "But unto them which are called, both Jews and Greeks, Christ the power of God, and the wisdom of God."

"But unto them which are called" is literally "TO THE CALLED THEMSELVES." This corresponds to the pronoun "US" in verse 18, and implies that the called know the fact in their own experience. They know what happened to them when they believed on the Lord Jesus Christ. In this verse the word "called" is used in connection with the divine call through the Gospel, to partake of the blessings of redemption through the shed blood of Jesus Christ. It is through the preaching of the Gospel that God calls men unto salvation. Jesus declared, "Verily, verily, I say unto you, He that heareth my word, and believeth on Him that sent me, hath everlasting life, and shall not come into condemnation; but is passed from death unto life" (John 5:24).

We are saved by God's grace, and God's grace becomes ours by faith. There is only one way for faith to come—and that is by hearing God's Word: "So then faith cometh by hearing, and hearing by the Word of God" (Rom. 10:17).

"But unto them which are called, both Jews and Greeks . . . ." This simply means that whether Jew or Greek, those who hear the Gospel, who believe and receive the Gospel, are saved—and that they KNOW what happens in their own hearts.

". . . *Christ the power of God, and the wisdom of God."* Christ is the power of God. He is God's power in the salvation of the soul, because it is on the ground of His incarnation, death and resurrection that God can be just and yet justify the unbeliever (Rom. 3:24—26). *Christ is salvation* (Jonah 2:9).

Christ is God's *wisdom* because, IN Christ, God revealed and carried out His plan of redemption, foreordained before ever the universe was formed. In I Peter 1:18 and following, we learn that Jesus Christ was foreordained as a lamb without spot or blemish to shed His blood for the remission of sin. Therefore, Jesus IS God's wisdom.

Jesus is *more* than a sign for the Jews; He is more than wisdom for the Gentiles. Notice the order of these qualities: First, *power.* Then, *wisdom.* This is very significant. When we recognize God's power, we recognize God's wisdom. God's power and God's wisdom are set in contrast to human weakness and ignorance. It was because of that human weakness and ignorance that man fell. It is because of God's power and wisdom that man can be saved.

Verse 25: "Because the foolishness of God is wiser than men; and the weakness of God is stronger than men."

The literal reading of the Greek here is "*the foolish thing of God.*" That is, foolish in man's estimation, referring here specifically to the crucifixion of Christ. The wisdom of man sees the crucifixion as a foolish thing on the part of God. In other words, the wisdom of man reasons, "If God be God, then why was it necessary for Jesus to die the horrible death of the cross? If God is omnipotent, sovereign, could He not have worked out some other way?" Thus reasons the unregenerate man.

"*The foolishness of God . . . the weakness of God*" does not suggest that anything God does is lacking in wisdom nor in power. These phrases are ironical and are

used to point out the weakness and foolishness of man.
In each of the two clauses, "men" stands for all that
characterizes mankind insofar as he is mentally able or
physically strong.

The cross of the Lord Jesus Christ is the fullest
display of God's judgment of sin, and also the fullest
display of God's love for the sinner. What men declared
as foolishness and weakness (the Incarnate Word, suffering on a cross) proves man's utter ruin and God's saving
mercy. The Saviour endured the judgment of sin, that
the unbeliever might believe and be saved. Is this not
proof that God is wiser and stronger than men? Does
not the fact of the bodily resurrection of Jesus Christ
prove that the Gospel message is the power of God unto
salvation? No other religion even *suggests* a risen Saviour. There are many great men who have lived, died,
were buried—and their bones remain in their sepulchres
until this day; but the tomb of Jesus was borrowed for
seventy-two hours, and returned to Joseph of Arimathea
in perfect condition, as good as new. Jesus used the
tomb for three days and three nights, and then walked
out, leaving nothing save His grave clothes.

Did not the resurrection prove the power and wisdom
of God, and does not the Gospel proclaim this marvelous
truth? Indeed it does!

Paul Points Out to the Corinthian Believers
That They Were Not of the Wise and Noble

Verse 26: "For ye see your calling, brethren, how
that not many wise men after the flesh, not many mighty,
not many noble, are called."

This verse is additional proof that the truth set forth
in verse 25 is indisputable. *"Not many"* points to the
fact that there were a few wise, mighty, and noble called —
for instance, Erastus (Rom. 16:23), the centurions mentioned

in Luke 7:2 and Acts 10:1, and others through the centuries. Paul is not saying that because a man is wise, mighty, or noble he cannot be saved . . . the Gospel message is to "whosoever will." But the fact remains that wise men after the flesh, mighty men after the flesh, and the general rule of nobility, ignore the grace of God and the need of a Saviour. Those who heard and followed Jesus were just plain, ordinary folk. Not many wise, mighty, or noble cared for the humble Nazarene.

". . .*After the flesh*" has to do with each of the three classes. Here the word "flesh" refers not to the baser element in man, but to his natural attainments and human qualities, as set forth in II Corinthians 10:2,3.

Verse 27: "But God hath chosen the foolish things of the world to confound the wise; and God hath chosen the weak things of the world to confound the things which are mighty."

"*The foolish things of the world*" points out that God has chosen things foolish in the estimation of the world; that is, from the standpoint of man's wisdom the things God chooses to use are foolish. Men and women whom the world declares to be fools are frequently chosen of God to shake communities and (in the past) continents for God. Education, intellect, wealth, and nobility are valuable in God's sight—but only when completely and entirely consecrated to Him. These things do not spell success, but many times the opposite—because they have a tendency to make men self-satisfied and independent of God, hence keeping them from accepting the Gospel.

The Psalmist declares, "A little that a righteous man hath is better than the riches of many wicked" (Psa. 37:16); and Paul states clearly that we are fools for Christ's sake.

It has pleased the God of all grace to choose foolish things to confound the wise, and weak things in the eyes of the world to confound those that are mighty. The word "confound" here means "put to shame."

Verse 28: "And base things of the world, and things which are despised, hath God chosen, yea, and things which are not, to bring to nought things that are."

The Greek word *agenes*, here translated "base," means "ignoble—literally of low birth," here pointing out those who are of no repute so far as the world estimates man.

"Things that are despised" means "to regard as nothing, to utterly despise, to treat with utter contempt." In Luke 23:11 and in Romans 14:10 the same word is translated "to set at nought."

"Yea, and things which are not, to bring to nought things that are." "Things which are not" . . . things which by comparison are non-existent — things which, by the side of things of higher importance in our human eyes, appear to us as nothing. Yet in the counsels of God these things of unimportance change places with the things that are highly regarded in the sight of men. The down-to-earth truth which Paul is setting forth here is simply that the God of all creation—*sovereign God*—does not need the wisdom of man, the might of man, the nobility of man, nor the strength of man to carry out His plan and program of salvation, and eternal redemption of all creation.

Verse 29: "THAT NO FLESH SHOULD GLORY IN HIS PRESENCE."

This statement has a universal application, but there is no doubt that Paul is pointing the finger of accusation at the evil in the church at Corinth (note chapter 3, verse 21). Paul was pointing out the purpose of God's selection of objects and things of His choice as described in verses 26, 27, and 28. *"Flesh"* in verse 29 stands for man in his human nature—apart from Christ.

For man to glory in anything *he* is able to produce because of his own attainments, power, or wisdom is to *substitute self* for God; and to substitute self for God is to call down wrath upon mankind and invite God to put man to open shame and bring him to nought. God will not allow flesh to glory in His presence: He resists the proud—but He gives grace to the humble.

Verse 30: "But of Him are ye in Christ Jesus, who of God is made unto us wisdom, and righteousness, and sanctification, and redemption."

Here is introduced a contrast between the wise, the strong, the noble from the standpoint of the world, and those who have *true* wisdom and nobility—those who have been exalted to the position of sons of God, seated in heavenly places in Christ Jesus, having come into possession of the exceeding riches of His grace and divine nature through the miracle of the new birth. Great stress is upon the "YE." Paul is reminding the Corinthians that they were just plain, ordinary folks, once alienated from God but now *sons* of God, *heirs* of God, and *joint-heirs with Jesus Christ.*

It is of God that true believers directly receive their spiritual relationship and position "in Christ Jesus." Hebrews 2:11 tells us, "For both He that sanctifieth and they who are sanctified are all of one: for which cause He is not ashamed to call them brethren." In I John 5:19 we read, "And we know that we are of God, and the whole world lieth in wickedness."

The worldly wise and the nobility of the big city of Corinth might look upon the Christians as fools and non-entities, but in actuality, they were *somebody*—strangers and pilgrims on earth, but having citizenship in heaven and seated in heavenly places in Christ Jesus. They were sons of God, and they had a right to glory in the right way.

Christ Jesus is made unto us *"wisdom, and right-eousness, and sanctification, and redemption."* The true Greek translation here is not "was made," but *"became"* — that is, by His incarnation, His death on the cross, His resurrection from the grave according to the Scriptures, Christ *became* our wisdom, righteousness, sanctification, and redemption.

Christ is "THE WISDOM OF GOD" (verse 24). In that verse stress was laid upon the fact that Jesus Christ is *"the divine expression of the divine attribute of wis-dom."* Jesus was the wisdom of God in flesh. Here (verse 30) what He is to believers as such is the point in view. He reveals and imparts God's wisdom to all who will believe on His name and trust in His finished work. Divine wisdom comes from God — but Jesus brought God's divine wisdom down to man . . . and what a contrast to the puny wisdom about which the Corinthians were boasting!

In James 1:5 we read, "If any of you lack wisdom, let him ask of God, that giveth to all men liberally, and upbraideth not; and it shall be given him." In I Corinthians 2:14 we are told, ". . . The natural man receiveth not the things of the Spirit of God: for they are foolishness unto him: neither can he know them, because they are spiritually discerned."

It is a solemn Bible fact that it is utterly impossible for man to know God *apart from* the gift of wisdom *bestowed* upon man by God, who loved sinners so much that He set forth Jesus, the wisdom of God in flesh—*very God.* As believers we must recognize the fact that the wisdom through which we made Christ our Saviour by exercising faith in His finished work, was bestowed upon us by God Almighty, in Jesus Christ.

The natural man (unregenerate man) will not receive the things of the Spirit of God because to him they are foolish, empty, and vain; but God sent Jesus who, in a body, brought down to man the wisdom and righteousness of God, and presented God to man in an understandable form.

Witnessing to the Samaritan woman at the well, Jesus declared, "God is a Spirit . . ." (John 4:24); and this is true. The mind of man cannot comprehend an eternal Spirit—a Spirit with no beginning, *having always been.* There was never a time when God was NOT. But we *can* comprehend the man Christ Jesus, who was truly God in flesh, equal with God in every respect.

Before the unregenerate man can receive salvation, justification, righteousness, or sanctification, he must first accept the Word of God AS God's Word, the wisdom of God which was spoken in order that we might hear and have faith in the finished work of Jesus Christ, who was God in flesh.

Not only is Christ made unto us wisdom — He is also made (He became) the *righteousness* of God. "Righteousness" is the quality of the believer who has heard the Word and received the Lord Jesus Christ . . . and *because* he heard and believed, he has been made *right and just* in the sight of a holy God.

Here, righteousness expresses the character of the justified believer. He is *justified*—cleared of all guilt and disobedience before God. He then stands before God just as though he had never committed a sin—but *only because* God the Father made Christ the Son to be righteousness for us. Through the finished work of Christ, the believer becomes, in the sight of a holy God, *what God requires one to be*—a state which man could never attain within himself.

". . . We are all as an unclean thing, and all our righteousnesses are as filthy rags; and we all do fade as a leaf; and our iniquities, like the wind, have taken us away" (Isa. 64:6).

"For He (God) hath made Him (Jesus) to be sin for us, who knew no sin; that we might be made the righteousness of God in Him" (II Cor. 5:21).

Apart from Jesus Christ, all men are helpless, hopeless, and hell-bound. We have all sinned, we have all gone astray, there is none righteous—no, not one; BUT GOD placed on Jesus the iniquity of us all!

"Surely, shall one say, in the Lord have I righteousness . . ." (Isa. 45:24).

"But now the righteousness of God without the law is manifested, being witnessed by the law and the prophets" (Rom. 3:21).

"I do not frustrate the grace of God: for if righteousness come by the law, then Christ is dead in vain" (Gal. 2:21).

"Now to him that worketh is the reward not reckoned of grace, but of debt. But to him that worketh not, but believeth on Him that justifieth the ungodly, his faith is counted for righteousness" (Rom. 4:4,5).

"Not by works of righteousness which we have done, but according to His mercy He saved us, by the washing of regeneration, and renewing of the Holy Ghost" (Tit. 3:5).

"Even as David also describeth the blessedness of the man, unto whom God imputeth righteousness without works" (Rom. 4:6).

Every believer possesses the righteousness of God NOW. It is God's righteousness imputed to the believer; and *because* of God's imputed righteousness—apart from the law, apart from works, and apart from flesh—the believer is saved! God's righteousness becomes ours through

Christ, through grace, through faith in Christ's blood. It is imputed to us — it is not attained through human wisdom, might, power, or nobility.

Christ has become unto us wisdom, righteousness, *"and sanctification." Justification* involves the removal of the *guilt* of sin, while *sanctification* is the effect of the death of Christ on the relation of a believer to God — the believer is separated unto God, translated out of the kingdom of darkness into the kingdom of light (Col. 1:12,13). The unbeliever is a child of the devil, and when the unbeliever is made righteous he becomes a son of God; therefore he is taken out of the family of the devil and placed into the family of God.

The divine fact that Christ is made sanctification to the believer denotes the truth that believers are set apart to God in contrast to their condition as unbelievers, at which time they were alienated from God. When an unbeliever exercises faith unto salvation, he becomes a new creation (II Cor. 5:17). Sanctification here is not a process, a gradual attainment—but *an instant fact*! Christ is made (HAS BECOME) sanctification to the believer. The split second one believes on Jesus Christ, that one is sanctified *positionally*; however, *experimental* sanctification takes place day by day, hour by hour, moment by moment.

To be sanctified is to walk in the paths of righteousness, separated from sin and the world. If any man love the world and practice the things thereof, the love of God is not in him. Christ is our sanctification, and positionally this occurs the moment we receive Jesus; but in the Lord's prayer of intercession recorded in John's Gospel, Jesus prayed for His children: "Sanctify them through thy truth: thy Word is truth" (John 17:17). Many believers are afraid of the word "sanctification," but it is a good

Bible word and is not to be ignored simply because it has been abused by some.

Righteousness is the quality of being right (or just). Sanctification is being separated to God. But Christ is also made unto us *"redemption."* The Greek word used here is *apolutrosis*, and means "to release, to deliver." Christ is made unto us deliverance from guilt, condemnation, damnation, sin. The wages of sin is death. He took our place, He died for us. The same word is used in Romans 3:24, Ephesians 1:7, and Colossians 1:14. However, it is not limited only to the redemption which we received when we were saved; it also points to the deliverance experienced by believers day by day, and the future deliverance from the *presence and power* of sin.

I would point out that when a person is redeemed, he is *totally and wholly* redeemed. If you have been saved for fifty years, you are no more fully redeemed now than you were fifty years ago when you first put your faith and trust in the shed blood of Jesus Christ. But Christians grow in grace and in faith. There are many graces mentioned in the New Testament—such as love and sacrifice—and we should strive to grow in these graces; but *we do not grow in redemption*. We are redeemed from sin instantaneously when we put our faith and trust in Jesus Christ. It is then that we are delivered from the *guilt* of sin. We are delivered from the *power* of sin day by day as we live for Christ.

Redemption also points to the Rapture and the first resurrection, when believers will be delivered from the *presence of sin*. In redemption we have deliverance from the penalty of sin, the power of sin, and eventually from the presence of sin. These bodies of corruption will be delivered:

"For we know that the whole creation groaneth and

travaileth in pain together until now. And not only they, but ourselves also, which have the firstfruits of the Spirit, even we ourselves groan within ourselves, waiting for the adoption, to wit, the redemption of our body" (Rom. 8:22,23).

"Which is the earnest of our inheritance until the redemption of the purchased possession, unto the praise of His glory" (Eph. 1:14).

"And grieve not the holy Spirit of God, whereby ye are sealed unto the day of redemption" (Eph. 4:30).

Job said, "For I know that my Redeemer liveth, and that He shall stand at the latter day upon the earth" (Job 19:25).

We have redemption through the blood of Jesus Christ: "In whom we have redemption through His blood, the forgiveness of sins, according to the riches of His grace" (Eph. 1:7).

"Forasmuch as ye know that ye were not redeemed with corruptible things, as silver and gold, from your vain conversation received by tradition from your fathers; But with the precious blood of Christ, as of a lamb without blemish and without spot" (I Pet. 1:18,19).

In Christ we have redemption, and that redemption is eternal: "Neither by the blood of goats and calves, but by His own blood He entered in once into the holy place, *having obtained eternal redemption for us*" (Heb. 9:12).

Believers are redeemed from all iniquity: "Who gave Himself for us, that He might redeem us from all iniquity, and purify unto Himself a peculiar people, zealous of good works" (Tit. 2:14). Our bodies WILL BE redeemed (Rom. 8:22,23).

Verse 31: "That, according as it is written, He that

glorieth, let him glory in the Lord.''

We find these words repeated in II Corinthians 10:17. In these words we have a confirmation of the whole argument set forth in verses 18 through 30. The quotation is from Jeremiah 9:23,24.

We are to glory in none save the Lord Jesus Christ. To glory in the Father is to glory in the Son: *"And whatsoever ye shall ask in my name, that will I do, that the Father may be glorified in the Son"* (John 14:13). God the Father so loved us that He gave God the Son. God the Son so loved us that He willingly bore our sins in His own body on the cross. When we glory in the Father we glory in the Son. When we glory in the Son we glory in the Father. They are inseparable as having to do with our salvation.

Believers are indebted to the Lord for every good thing, and we should never glory in self, regardless of what we may be, do, or attain. We should say with Paul, "I am what I am by the grace of God." Every good and perfect gift cometh from the Lord. The sunshine and rain, health and strength, food and raiment, the air we breathe. All that we have and all that we are or hope to be is of God, and the most outstanding thing for which we should be thankful and in which we should glory in the Lord, is our salvation!

God forbid that I glory, save in the cross—or that I ever take credit for anything I have ever done or will do. All that I have, all that I am, all that I have ever done or ever will do for good, I owe to the grace of God. God loved me while I was yet unlovely. When I was yet without strength Jesus died for me; and if God so loved me that He gave Jesus to die for me, if Jesus willingly took my place in death, then the least that I can do is surrender to Him—soul, spirit, and body—and allow Him to lead me where He would have me go, show me what He would have me do—and then go where He leads and do what He bids to glorify His name, and His name only.

The work of salvation is totally of God. Man had nothing and *has* nothing to do with it. Jesus said, "It is finished." Paul said, "Not of works, lest any man should boast." The believers in Corinth, like many since, were inclined to take some credit to themselves. Paul reminds them to whom all credit is due. *In Christ* we live and move and have our being. Those of us who are saved must always say, "I am what I am by the grace of God."

CHAPTER TWO

1. And I, brethren, when I came to you, came not with excellency of speech or of wisdom, declaring unto you the testimony of God.

2. For I determined not to know any thing among you, save Jesus Christ, and him crucified.

3. And I was with you in weakness, and in fear, and in much trembling.

4. And my speech and my preaching was not with enticing words of man's wisdom, but in demonstration of the Spirit and of power:

5. That your faith should not stand in the wisdom of men, but in the power of God.

6. Howbeit we speak wisdom among them that are perfect: yet not the wisdom of this world, nor of the princes of this world, that come to nought:

7. But we speak the wisdom of God in a mystery, even the hidden wisdom, which God ordained before the world unto our glory:

8. Which none of the princes of this world knew: for had they known it, they would not have crucified the Lord of glory.

9. But as it is written, Eye hath not seen, nor ear heard, neither have entered into the heart of man, the things which God hath prepared for them that love him.

10. But God hath revealed them unto us by his Spirit: for the Spirit searcheth all things, yea, the deep things of God.

11. For what man knoweth the things of a man, save the spirit of man which is in him? even so the things of God knoweth no man, but the Spirit of God.

12. Now we have received, not the spirit of the world, but the spirit which is of God; that we might know the things that are freely given to us of God.

13. Which things also we speak, not in the words which man's wisdom teacheth, but which the Holy Ghost teacheth; comparing spiritual things with spiritual.

14. But the natural man receiveth not the things of the Spirit of God: for they are foolishness unto him: neither can he know them, because they are spiritually discerned.

15. But he that is spiritual judgeth all things, yet he himself is judged of no man.

16. For who hath known the mind of the Lord, that he may instruct him? But we have the mind of Christ.

Paul Reminds the Corinthian Believers That Christian Revelation Owes Nothing to Human Wisdom

Having proved that the marvelous Gospel of the grace of God, while not relying upon human wisdom, is nevertheless the instrument of God—God's power unto salvation and the manifestation of His wisdom — Paul now goes on to show that the character of his preaching, teaching, and conduct in Corinth was one hundred percent consistent with the essential character of the pure Gospel, with the purpose of God in his own life, and with the purpose of the preaching of the Gospel.

Paul did not use human wisdom. Although he was not a believer until he met Jesus on the road to Damascus, he was an educated man, a Pharisee of the Pharisees, having had much experience in religion. But he did not magnify his own ability from the standpoint of education and training.

Verse 1: "And I, brethren, when I came to you, came not with excellency of speech or of wisdom, declaring unto you the testimony of God."

Paul here begins to justify his preaching. The Greek word translated "excellency" strictly denotes "that which is superior or pre-eminent, or something that overhangs." The word is used in I Timothy 2:2, where it is translated "authority." Paul is saying that he did not use superior language—language which would render the preaching of the cross and the shed blood secondary to the demonstration of his own wisdom and ability. His preaching was not that of one skilled in the fashionable argumentation of the day in which he lived, and the *reason* he did not use the ability he possessed was *"that no flesh should glory" in the presence of God.* Paul was jealous for the message of the cross, and he determined not to preach anything nor act in any way that would *detract* from that message.

". . . The testimony of God" – or as some translations read, "the mystery of God." Paul is speaking here of his testimony *concerning* God, the witness that he gave to God's combined love, mercy, and justice, manifested to this world in and through the life and death of the Lord Jesus Christ.

In the New Testament, a mystery does not denote something mysterious, as the English word suggests, but rather "that which is outside the range of unassisted natural understanding." The mysteries in the Bible are made known only by divine revelation, at a time and in a manner appointed by Almighty God, and are revealed to men who are illumined by the Holy Spirit, as in Colossians 1:26: "Even the mystery which hath been hid from ages and from generations, but now is made manifest to his saints."

Among the ancient Greeks "the mysteries" were religious rites and ceremonies practised by secret societies into which any one who so desired might be received. Those who were initiated into these "mysteries" became possessors of certain knowledge, which was not imparted to the uninitiated, and were called "the perfected." Cp. I Cor. 2:6–16 where the Apostle has these "mysteries" in mind and presents the Gospel in contrast thereto; here "the perfected" are, of course, the believers, who alone can perceive the things revealed.*

---

* Expository Dictionary of New Testament Words — W. E. Vine.

Therefore, to Paul the mystery of the Gospel was "made known, unveiled, or made to be understood," and he proclaimed the mystery that was hidden from the beginning but which was definitely revealed to him—the minister ordained of God and sent to the Gentiles.

Verse 2: "For I determined not to know any thing among you, save Jesus Christ, and Him crucified."

Paul had come to the city of Corinth on a singular mission: To deliver a testimony concerning God, and that testimony must needs result in the humiliation of man. Paul was to make known the divine truth that God had revealed Himself in Christ. . . "*God was in Christ*, reconciling the world unto Himself" (II Cor. 5:19).

Paul did not judge it to be right to extend the subject of his preaching beyond Jesus Christ and Him crucified. The heart and soul—the very essence—of the Gospel message was Jesus Christ—crucified, buried, and risen again *according to the Scriptures*. Had Paul had the spirit of some ministers today, he would have broadened the scope of his message and ministry in order to avoid attack upon himself by those (both Jews and Greeks) who were prejudiced against the message of the shed blood as the only recourse for the remission of sin. But not so with the Apostle Paul—nor should it be so with any minister of the Gospel. (It is NOT so with GOD'S ministers.)

From the standpoint of crowds and receiving the things of this world, it is always easy, attractive, and profitable for a minister to court popularity; but such a ministry does not and cannot win the approval of God. It will fail to achieve the purpose of God in the preaching of the Gospel. Paul was determined to preach Christ crucified, to preach His humiliation, that the foolishness of his preaching might be doubly foolish and the weakness doubly weak.

The incarnation was a stumblingblock—to both the Jews and the Greeks; but if the *incarnation* was a stumblingblock, *the crucifixion and the shed blood were doubly so!* Such doctrine was foolish and absurd beyond man's imagination — but the shed blood is the only message that brings cleansing from sin and salvation unto God.

Paul had been called and commissioned to deliver a testimony concerning God, and that testimony was that Jesus, in His humanity, humbled Himself and became obedient unto death—yea, the most disgraceful death that any person could die in that day: He died the death of the cross. And Paul knew no message save that of the death, burial, and resurrection of Jesus—not according to some man-made doctrine, but *"according to the Scriptures."*

Verse 3: "And I was with you in weakness, and in fear, and in much trembling."

"And I was with you in weakness" undoubtedly had to do with the physical weakness of the Apostle: "And lest I should be exalted above measure through the abundance of the revelations, there was given to me a thorn in the flesh, the messenger of Satan to buffet me, lest I should be exalted above measure" (II Cor. 12:7).

If Paul had any eloquence, it was that of deep conviction concerning the message God had ordained him to deliver. He had no self-confidence; he had nothing but self-mistrust and the deepest sense of personal unworthiness. This was combined with the infirmity of his body, which infirmity was a great trial to him and of which he made frequent mention. (Study carefully II Corinthians 10:10; 11:30; 12:5,7,9,10; Galatians 4:13,14.)

Then too, his bodily presence was not that of an athlete or soldier: "For his letters, say they, are weighty and powerful; but his bodily presence is weak, and his speech contemptible" (II Cor. 10:10). Many believe that Paul's "thorn in the flesh" was "chronic ophthalmia, inducing bodily weakness and a repulsive appearance." We have no proof of his physical appearance, but we do know that he referred to his weakness and infirmities many times, thus indicating that they weighed heavily upon his heart.

". . . *And in fear, and in much trembling.*" This statement receives light from the comforting night vision of Acts 18:9,10: "Then spake the Lord to Paul in the night by a vision, Be not afraid, but speak, and hold not thy peace: For I am with thee, and no man shall set on thee to hurt thee: for I have much people in this city." "In fear and trembling" means exactly what it says. It is when we feel the reality of our own weakness that we are able to rely solely upon the power of the Lord.

Paul could have boasted of many things: He was well educated; he sat at the feet of Gamaliel; he was a Pharisee of the Pharisees and no doubt was a member of the Sanhedrin – but he gloried in none of these things. He had a deep determination to preach Jesus Christ— humiliated, crucified, buried, and risen again "according to the Scriptures." And when he delivered this message he did not demonstrate his ability to use swelling words and high-sounding phrases: He delivered the message with great humility, and in fear and trembling.

Verse 4: "And my speech and my preaching was not with enticing words of man's wisdom, but in demonstration of the Spirit and of power."

The Greek word here translated "speech" is frequently translated "word." In our present verse it signifies Paul's discourse, referring to the manner of his setting forth the Gospel, the manner of his preaching. "Preaching" points to the contents of the message. The true minister of God will not try to show forth his wisdom and ability, but will heed the exhortation, "As every man hath received the gift, even so minister the same one to another, as good stewards of the manifold grace of God. If any man speak, let him speak as the oracles of God; if any man minister, let him do it as of the ability which God giveth: that God in all things may be glorified through Jesus Christ, to whom be praise and dominion for ever and ever. Amen" (I Pet. 4:10,11).

"*. . . But in demonstration of the Spirit and of power.*" The word here translated "demonstration" signifies a showing forth — not just an exhibition, but positive proof. It indicates that which carries conviction—not by human ability or power, but by the power of God through the operation of the Holy Spirit.

Verse 5: "That your faith should not stand in the wisdom of men, but in the power of God."

Paul wanted his converts to put their faith in God— not in man. He was careful lest through his speech or his manner of preaching he might lead his followers to put their faith and trust in man's ability, rather than trusting in God through the Lord Jesus Christ; for it was Christ who took upon Himself the form of man, and in the flesh did for man what the law could never have done, thereby satisfying the heart of God. He paid the penalty of sin in full, and made it possible for God to be just and yet justify those who should rightfully burn in hell. (Study Romans 3:21–28.)

Paul had not come to Corinth for the purpose of setting forth an argument. *He had come to declare the truth.* Saving faith is the gift of God—the outcome of the power of God, who so loved the world that He gave *Jesus*. Faith comes by hearing, and hearing by the Word of God. Jesus was the Word of God in flesh. (Read John 1:1,14; 3:16; Romans 10:17.)

Saving faith produces the experience that not only delivers us from the penalty of sin, but also places us in the Son, thereby giving us a personal relationship with Him *in whom* we exercise saving faith. When we analyze salvation from beginning to end and then from the end back to the beginning, we discover the truth of Hebrews 12:2. Jesus IS the author and the finisher of our faith. He IS the Alpha and the Omega—the beginning and the end. *He is the all in all.*

Salvation *begins* in Jesus, *continues* in Jesus, and *will be finished in Jesus* when we stand before Him on that glorious resurrection morning. In other words, He HAS saved us, He IS saving us, He WILL save us. He saved us from the *penalty* of sin the moment we put our trust in His shed blood. He saves us daily from the *power* of sin when we trust and obey. He WILL save us from the very *presence* of sin when He comes in the Rapture.

The Gospel message was not given for the purpose of imparting wisdom; but to believers who grow in grace and in faith, the Word of God *does* impart the very *highest* wisdom—wisdom that has been hidden from the rulers and the wise men of this world, as we will see in the following verses of our present chapter. *True wisdom* is revealed by the Holy Spirit to those who exercise saving faith in the shed blood and the finished work of the Lord Jesus, and becomes ours through the operation of the Holy Spirit.

In chapter 1, verse 30, we learned that God has made Jesus wisdom unto us. A little later in our present chapter, we will learn that the natural (the unregenerate) man cannot know nor understand the things of God, and he cannot receive the things of God in the natural aspect. The very ability to *receive* God is a gift FROM God. The wisdom to receive the Word of God (through which saving faith becomes ours) is also a very definite gift from God.

When we hear the Word, allowing the Holy Spirit to operate in our thinking; when we think *right* about the Word of God, believing that it IS the Word of God, then we believe that God IS, and that He rewards those who honestly, sincerely, and diligently seek Him.

"But without faith it is impossible to please Him: for he that cometh to God must believe that He is, and that He is a rewarder of them that diligently seek Him" (Heb. 11:6). Truly, Christ is made unto us wisdom, righteousness, sanctification and redemption, and *we are complete in Him*!

"The fear of the Lord is the beginning of knowledge: but fools despise wisdom and instruction" (Prov. 1:7).

Verse 6: "Howbeit we speak wisdom among them that are perfect: yet not the wisdom of this world, nor of the princes of this world, that come to nought."

". . . *Them that are perfect.*" The Greek word used here for "perfect" means "that which has attained its end." It denotes the full-grown, the mature, in contrast with "babes" (I Cor. 3:1). The same word is used in I Corinthians 14:20, where it is translated "men," and in Ephesians 4:13, meaning "fully grown."

"But strong meat belongeth to them that are of full age, even those who by reason of use have their senses exercised to discern both good and evil" (Heb. 5:14).

It is the spiritual birthright of every believer (and the purpose of God concerning every believer) that sons of God develop spiritually to full-grown maturity. It is not the purpose of God that any believer should remain immature, having spiritual faculties undeveloped or crippled because of improper spiritual diet. Things that hinder spiritual development should be removed from the church (I Cor. 3:3). Paul declares that it is his desire and aim to "present every man perfect in Christ Jesus" (Col. 1:28). Paul wanted all of his converts to become full-grown in the grace of God. The Lord God Almighty has made full provision for the spiritual growth and development of His children: "As newborn babes, desire the sincere milk of the Word, that ye may grow thereby" (I Pet. 2:2).

"*. . . Yet not the wisdom of this world, nor of the princes of this world . . . .*" The word for "world" in this verse is *aion*, meaning "age." The "princes" or rulers of this world are those whose policy is occupied solely with the affairs of this present world period—or *man's day*, during which time mankind is in darkness, alienated from God and under the power of "the prince of this world," the prince of darkness.

We have enlightening words on this subject in I John 5:19: "And we know that we are of God, AND THE WHOLE WORLD LIETH IN WICKEDNESS." (One outstanding commentator translates the latter part of this verse to read, "'*The whole world lieth in the lap of the wicked one,*' just as Samson was lying in the lap of Delilah when he lost his power."

"*. . . That come to nought.*" The literal rendering is, "which are coming to nought" and means "to render inactive." The policies of human rulers, the plans of human leaders, the preaching of liberal ministers – all these are destined to become ineffective. They are empty and void in their message; they can never accomplish the redemption of mankind—nor will they ever be able to bring about universal peace, prosperity, safety, and freedom from fear.

What do we hear today on the radio? What do we read in the newspapers and magazines? The rulers of the world are preaching long and loud, "Peace, peace, peace!"-

when there IS no peace. They are preaching equality of mankind, the Fatherhood of God, the brotherhood of man. They promise peace, they promise to wipe out poverty and bring prosperity. They promise to deliver mankind from fear and bring about a world in which there will be peace and plenty, and where all men will be safe. But you may rest assured that, according to the Scriptures, they are "coming to nought."

One day Jesus Christ will sit on the throne of David in Jerusalem and reign, and the knowledge of the Lord will cover this earth as the waters now cover the sea. *Then* there will be peace on earth, good will toward men— but the man Christ Jesus, not human rulers, will bring this lasting peace with its prosperity and safety.

Verse 7: "But we speak the wisdom of God in a mystery, even the hidden wisdom, which God ordained before the world unto our glory."

This verse stresses *God's wisdom*, in contrast to *"the wisdom of this world"* in the preceding verse. *"The wisdom of God"* is primarily the singular message Paul declared he would deliver—"Christ, and Him crucified, according to the Scriptures" . . . and this message is the essence of the Gospel; it is the hub of the wheel of salvation. The crucified Christ is the center to which all aspects of the Gospel point, and without Jesus there would be no Gospel, no salvation, and no wisdom.

The phrase *"in a mystery"* signifies that the wisdom is in a mystery owing to the fact that it had been kept hidden for so long. (See discussion of mystery on verse 1.) The mystery *remains* hidden from those who refuse to receive the Gospel—and when we say "the Gospel," we speak of those who refuse to receive the truth concerning the virgin-born, crucified, buried, risen, ascended and coming-again Saviour.

". . . *Which God ordained before the world* . . . ."
The word "which" points to "God's wisdom." The verb
"ordained" used here means "to mark out beforehand,
to determine before." It does not mean simply "ordain";
it means something predestined and determined before
the world was spoken into existence. The same word is
used in Acts 4:28; Romans 8:29,30; Ephesians 1:5,11.

God's love for sinners, God's grace extended to sinners, God's wisdom as having to do with the Gospel of
His grace, was not brought about because of circumstances
or changed conditions upon the earth. It was all predetermined by Him before time began.

Peter sheds light on this divine truth in his first
epistle: "Forasmuch as ye know that ye were not redeemed
with corruptible things, as silver and gold, from your
vain conversation received by tradition from your fathers;
but with the precious blood of Christ, as of a lamb without
blemish and without spot: Who verily was foreordained
before the foundation of the world, but was manifest in
these last times for you. Who by Him do believe in God,
that raised Him up from the dead, and gave Him glory;
that your faith and hope might be in God" (I Pet. 1:18—21).

How refreshing to the soul to know that before God
ever made one thing, before He created the dust out of
which He made man, He planned and perfected salvation
in Jesus Christ, through His finished work. The wisdom
of God thought and planned our redemption, and it was all
complete before anything else was created.

". . . *Unto our glory.*" The word "glory" sometimes
signifies "praise" or "honor," but here it stands for
redemption—the salvation of the believer. When we are
converted we become sons of God, saved and completely
redeemed from the penalty of sin. "Unto our glory" also
stands for the growth of the believer, as we grow to maturity

in the spiritual aspect, becoming increasingly conformed to the character of Christ. It also points to that state of blessedness, completeness, and glory which begins with conversion and has its consummation in the Rapture and the first resurrection, when believers will be brought into His full likeness. Every believer is predestined to be conformed to the image of God's dear Son. Study I Corinthians 15:43–49; Romans 8:18–23; Philippians 3:21; and I Peter 5:1–11.

In God's great love for us, He extended His rich mercy to us even when we were dead in sins: "But God, who is rich in mercy, for His great love wherewith He loved us, even when we were dead in sins, hath quickened us together with Christ, (by grace ye are saved;) and hath raised us up together, and made us sit together in heavenly places in Christ Jesus: THAT IN THE AGES TO COME HE MIGHT SHEW THE EXCEEDING RICHES OF HIS KINDNESS TOWARD US THROUGH CHRIST JESUS" (Eph. 2:4–7). God forgives and saves sinners—but only for Christ's sake (Eph. 4:32b).

Verse 8: "Which none of the princes of this world knew: for had they known it, they would not have crucified the Lord of glory."

The rulers in the days of Jesus—the men who actually crucified Him—are here spoken of as representative of ALL rulers who are antagonistic to Christ and the Gospel of Christ. This verse presents the contrast between the shame of the cross and "the majestic glory of the crucified."

Jesus did not enjoy the cross . . . He *endured* the cross, despising its shame (Heb. 12:2), because He saw the glory on the other side. The wisdom of men sees only the shame and disgrace of the cross; but the wisdom of God sees beyond that to the glorified Lord sitting at the right hand of God the Father, making intercession for us, until one day He will sit on a throne in Jerusalem, reigning over this earth in peace, bringing the glories of the Millennium. The wisdom of God sees beyond the cross to where, finally, in the Pearly White City with the spotless bride on display, He will show forth the exceeding riches of His grace!

Had there been no cross, there could be no grace. Had there been no shame, there could be no glory. The wisdom of this world sees only cruel sinners nailing the Saviour to a cruel cross; but on the other side of the cross is the crown and the glory!

Spiritual Verities, Truths, or Facts Are Not Discoverable By Human Wisdom

Verse 9: "But as it is written, Eye hath not seen, nor ear heard, neither have entered into the heart of man, the things which God hath prepared for them that love Him."

"But as it is written . . . ." This phrase refers to Isaiah 64:4: "For since the beginning of the world men have not heard, nor perceived by the ear, neither hath the eye seen, O God, beside thee, what He hath prepared for him that waiteth for Him." The Holy Spirit here gives us a distinction between things perceived by the senses (the eye and the ear) and things apprehended by the understanding. Thus we find the significance of *"the heart"* in our present verse, as also in Matthew 13:15. (In Ephesians 1:18 Paul speaks of "the eyes of (our) understanding being enlightened," referring to the understanding of the heart.)

". . . The things which God hath prepared for them that love Him." This includes the benefits of God's grace (made known through the preaching of the Gospel and enjoyed in this present life), and also the things which are to be enjoyed *hereafter* because we have trusted

Jesus and received the grace of God. "The things which God hath prepared for them that love Him" include *all the benefits of His love*—from the beginning of time throughout all eternity. It is God who gives every good and perfect gift (James 1:17).

". . . *For them that love Him.*" This carries the same truth found in James 1:12 and 2:5, and in Romans 8:28—a verse beloved by all believers. The same Greek word is used in each verse and signifies deep love, expressed not only in affection but also in *action*. God not only *declared* His love for us, He *proved* it by giving His only begotten Son. Even when we were yet without strength—sinners, ungodly, enemies to God—Christ died for our sins! And having loved His own, He loved them to the end. God proved His love by action.

God Reveals Things of the Spirit to Dedicated Men

Verse 10: "But God hath revealed them unto us by His Spirit: for the Spirit searcheth all things, yea, the deep things of God."

"*God hath revealed them UNTO US.*" The emphasis here is on "unto US," in contrast to "the rulers of this world." The revelation that comes through the Holy Spirit unto us who believe is impossible to the attainment of the natural mind. No matter how intelligent, well educated or well trained the human mind may be, it is only through the work of the Holy Spirit that the things of the Spirit are made known. It is impossible for the unregenerate man to understand the things of the Spirit of God, as we will learn a little later in this chapter.

The things of God are not discovered through eye and ear alone, nor through earthly wisdom. The things of God become ours when we exercise childlike faith in "Thus saith the Lord," and the Holy Spirit bears home to our hearts the truth and blessing that only God can make known to man. "For the Spirit searcheth ALL things, yea, the deep things of God."

In our present verse we clearly see the personality of the Holy Spirit. We also see a definite distinction between the Holy Spirit and God the Father. The Holy Spirit searches the deep things of God—which He could not be described as doing were He identical with the Father. Because of His perfect knowledge of the mind of God, the Holy Spirit is likened unto the spirit of man (which is one of the elements of man's being). Paul speaks of the one as "the spirit of man which is in him," and of the other as "the Spirit which is from (or as the Greek reads, 'proceeds out of') Jehovah God." The Holy Spirit is the Revealer of spiritual truth. He alone imparts the knowledge of God and of the Word of God to the individual believer.

"For the Spirit searcheth . . . the deep things of God." This does not mean that the Spirit investigates for the purpose of acquiring knowledge, because the Holy Spirit KNOWS the deep things of God (verse 11). He penetrates their depth, shedding His light upon the deep things of God and making them known to those whom He indwells. What is stressed here is the operation of the Holy Spirit of God in the heart of the believer: "And He that searcheth the hearts knoweth what is the mind of the Spirit, because He maketh intercession for the saints according to the will of God" (Rom. 8:27).

"The deep things of God" are the counsels of God, His purposes, and *all* things that pertain to His nature and attributes: "O the depth of the riches both of the wisdom and knowledge of God! How unsearchable are His judgments, and His ways past finding out!" (Rom. 11:33). The deep things of God can be known and received

106

by the believer only as the Holy Spirit reveals them and the believer receives them by faith.

"For the prophecy came not in old time by the will of man: but holy men of God spake as they were moved by the Holy Ghost" (II Pet. 1:21).

"But ye have an unction from the Holy One, and ye know all things" (I John 2:20).

"But the anointing which ye have received of Him abideth in you, and ye need not that any man teach you: but as the same anointing teacheth you of all things, and is truth, and is no lie, and even as it hath taught you, ye shall abide in Him" (I John 2:27). The best teacher of the Word of God is the Holy Spirit.

Verse 11: "For what man knoweth the things of a man, save the spirit of man which is in him? Even so the things of God knoweth no man, but the Spirit of God."

"For what man knoweth the things of a man . . . ." The Greek verb for "knoweth" is *oida*, which means "to perceive from observation."

". . . *Save the spirit of man which is in him?"* The *spirit* here stands for the element in man by which he perceives or reflects. Man is definitely a trinity—soul, spirit, and body. The *soul* is that part of man which is the seat of emotion—love or hate, as the case may be. The *spirit* of man is that part of him which reasons—the mind. The *body* is the tabernacle in which the soul and spirit dwell. In I Thessalonians 5:23 Paul prayed, "And the very God of peace sanctify you wholly; and I pray God your whole *spirit*, and *soul*, and *body* be preserved blameless unto the coming of our Lord Jesus Christ." In connection with this please study Hebrews 4:12; I Corinthians 15:44; Matthew 26:38; 11:29; and John 12:27.

When Jesus stood at the tomb of Lazarus, He groaned

in His spirit; He wept. He was thinking with two broken-hearted sisters. But in the Garden of Gethsemane, when His perspiration was stained with His precious blood, He cried out, "*My soul* is exceeding sorrowful, even unto death!" In the Garden, He was loving a whole world, and paying the awful sin-debt *because* of that love.

"*Even so the things of God knoweth no man, but the Spirit of God.*" The Greek word translated "knoweth" in this part of the verse is *ginosko* and signifies "discerneth." This word is set in contrast to *oida*, used in the previous part of the verse in reference to the spirit of man. The Dictionary of New Testament Words gives this enlightening explanation of these two words, both translated "knoweth": "The distinction is that *oida* refers to 'the knowledge of facts, and ideas in themselves,' while *ginosko* suggests the *understanding* of these things in their relations and bearings"—that is, the natural man, in his natural mind, cannot know the things of God.

The very ability to understand enough Gospel to exercise faith unto salvation is a gift from God, and is included in grace. Because of the grace of God, Jesus was allowed to taste death for every man – and in His death, burial, and resurrection, He is made unto us—first, *wisdom*; then *righteousness*; third, *sanctification*; and *redemption*. The natural man cannot know God in, through, or by his own wisdom or natural ability. The natural man, through his own wisdom, ability, and power, can no more save himself than the leopard can change his spots or the Ethiopian change the color of his skin! Salvation is from without; it is the gift of God, and can be received only after the natural man has heard the Word which brings saving faith; and faith exercised in the finished work of Jesus places the natural man in the position to be born into the family of God by the Holy Spirit (John 3:5,7).

We have noted that in verses 10 and 11 the personality of the Holy Spirit is set forth, distinguishing the Holy Spirit from the Father. The fact that the Spirit searches the deep things of God certifies that He is not identical with the Father, but rather that He is the third Person of the Trinity. The Holy Spirit has perfect knowledge of the mind of God.

Verse 12: "Now we have received, not the spirit of the world, but the spirit which is of God; that we might know the things that are freely given to us of God."

"*The spirit of the world*" speaks of the predominating spirit operating in the unregenerate man, who is alienated from God; and "*the spirit which is of God*" points to the Holy Spirit bestowed upon us as a gift, and who takes up His abode within us the moment we believe. "If any man have not the Spirit of Christ, he is none of His" (Rom. 8:9). ". . . Except a man be born . . . of the Spirit, he cannot enter into the kingdom of God" (John 3:5). "That which is born of the flesh is flesh; and that which is born of the Spirit is spirit" (John 3:6).

"*We have received*" is literally "*we received*," denoting that we received the Spirit when we became Christians. Salvation does not come to us at *one* time, and then at a later time the Spirit take up His abode within us. When the unbeliever receives Jesus, the Holy Spirit immediately comes into the heart of that unbeliever.

". . . *That we might know the things that are freely given to us of God.*" The same Greek word for "know" used in verse 11 is used again here, signifying perception and realization. The things "that are freely given" speaks of the same time as that referred to in verse 12 when "*we received*" the Holy Spirit. The word could have been translated "graciously given," denoting that we have received redemption, righteousness, the Holy Spirit, because of the grace of God by the undeserved favor of God.

"... *The things that are freely given to us of God*" are of course enjoyed in this life; but they are also things eternal, and we will comprehend their fullness in much greater measure when we see Jesus face to face. However, we rob ourselves of our spiritual birthright if we do not seek to understand all we possibly can about these "things freely given to us of God" while we are here upon this earth in our terrestrial body, even though we will never *fully* understand until we see Him and are like Him.

To be wholly consecrated to God and be spiritually minded is to live in the suburbs of Paradise. Very few believers enjoy their spiritual birthright because they are not fully surrendered to the Spirit. The Spirit of God draws us TO God, convicts us of sin, "borns" us into the family of heaven, indwells us, leads us — and when we allow Him, He FILLS us (Eph. 5:18). Thank God for the third Person of the Trinity!

Revealed Things Are Taught in Words Given by the Holy Spirit

Verse 13: "Which things also we speak, not in the words which man's wisdom teacheth, but which the Holy Ghost teacheth; comparing spiritual things with spiritual."

"*Which things also we speak ....*" What Paul is saying to the believers in Corinth is that God has given to His servants the ministry of telling forth the truth of the very things that God has freely given but which can be received only as the Holy Spirit convicts, draws, and enlightens. Such things are not received nor taught by man's wisdom; they are not found or known by searching. They are ours only as the Holy Spirit searches the deep things of God and makes them known to us as we yield to Him!

Paul says, ". . . *We speak*," pointing to all preachers who are called and anointed of God to preach the Gospel — and there IS but *one Gospel*: all else is error!

". . . *Not in the words which man's wisdom teacheth* . . ." — or taught by man's wisdom. Paul was no ordinary man, even before he was converted on the road to Damascus. He sat at the feet of Gamaliel, he was a Pharisee of the Pharisees — but he wanted it clearly understood that in spite of his natural ability and his extensive training, he was teaching—not by man's wisdom, but in words taught by the Holy Spirit of God. In chapter 13 of our study Paul clearly sets forth the divine fact that all of man's ability is futile and vain apart from God the Father, God the Son, and God the Holy Spirit.

". . . *Comparing spiritual things with spiritual*." The best commentary on the Bible IS *the Bible*—a book (singular) made up of sixty-six *books* (plural); and each book is necessary if we would understand the program of God from beginning to end. There is not a verse of Scripture in all the Bible but what another verse somewhere in the Scriptures will shed light on that which appears hard to understand. The best way to understand the Bible is to compare Scripture with Scripture, spiritual things with spiritual. We should never take Scripture out of its setting and use it to prove a denominational or religious point. We should never add to it what we think, and we should never take away from it to make it say what we want it to say. We should study and rightly divide the Word of Truth as the Holy Spirit leads us. If we will do this we will keep ourselves free from much trouble and misunderstanding in our teaching and preaching.

If the devil cannot make a liberal of a minister, he will push that minister out on a religious limb or drive him down a denominational blind alley; and if he can cause a preacher to begin riding a religious hobbyhorse, he is happy, because that preacher's ministry is then rendered ineffective.

To the believers in Rome, Paul said, "Let God be true, but every man a liar." If we will allow the Word of God to speak, if we will preach *"Thus saith the Lord,"* we will deliver the message that will bring men to Christ; but if we argue points instead of preaching the Gospel, we will please the devil, not the Lord Jesus.

Denominations, religions, and preachers have done a good job of confusing people. God is not the author of confusion; neither is the Word of God the author of religious question marks. The Bible is the Word of God, dictated by the Holy Ghost to holy men of old, and the Holy Ghost is the best Teacher of the Word. If we will yield to HIM and study in the Spirit, comparing spiritual things with spiritual—not spiritual with carnal or spiritual with the wisdom of men—we will be able to help men and women find Jesus as Saviour and become spiritually minded as they feed on the milk and the meat of the Word. Human learning, skill, and wisdom are utterly unsuited to and incompetent for the setting forth of divine truth as laid down in God's holy Word. We must keep the wisdom and skill of man out of our preaching.

Revealed Things Are Spiritually Discerned

Verse 14: "But the natural man receiveth not the things of the Spirit of God: for they are foolishness unto him: neither can he know them, because they are spiritually discerned."

The natural (unregenerate) man rejects the things of the Spirit of God—first, because they are unintelligible to him, he cannot understand them, he cannot reason them out through his own ability; and in the second place, the things of God are distasteful and unattractive to the natural man because his nature craves the things of the world. Therefore, the natural man cannot receive the things of the Spirit of God.

It is utterly impossible for any man to understand anything about the spiritual things of God until he is born of the Spirit. To be born again, all the unbeliever need know is that Christ died for sinners "according to the Scriptures," that He was buried and rose again the third day "according to the Scriptures," and that He was seen of men, He ascended back to heaven, and now sits at the right hand of God the Father to make intercession for us. All the sinner need know and do in order to be saved is to know that Christ died for sinners, and believe from the heart that God raised Him from the dead: "That if thou shalt confess with thy mouth the Lord Jesus, and shalt believe in thine heart that God hath raised Him from the dead, thou shalt be saved" (Rom. 10:9).

". . . *For they are foolishness unto him: neither can he know them, because they are spiritually discerned.*" The unregenerated man cannot "*get to know*" the things of the Spirit of God from a study of the Word purely for argumentative purposes. Unregenerate man cannot discern the things of God. In spite of all the searching and studying he may do, his spirit will not allow the soul to form an opinion of God that will cause the natural man to *seek* God. Before the unregenerate spirit will seek God, he must hear the WORD of God with an open mind and an open heart and allow the Holy Spirit to convict him of sin and draw him to God.

In John 6:44 Jesus said, "*No man can come to me, except the Father which hath sent me draw him*: and I will raise him up at the last day."

It is impossible for the unregenerate to form the right opinion in regard to spiritual things apart from the divinely imparted spiritual faculties that only the Holy Ghost can give in answer to faith, or as a result of faith. The perception of the natural man does not and cannot extend beyond the region of the *intellect*, and we will never come to know God through intellect. We know God through the *heart*, not through the mind.

Verse 15: "But he that is spiritual judgeth all things, yet he himself is judged of no man."

"He that is spiritual" points to the man who has been born of the Spirit. He possesses divine nature; he is indwelt and energized by the Holy Spirit. The Holy Spirit is the dominating element in his being. Consequently, because the dominating element of his being is spiritual, his spiritual faculty enables him to examine all things in their relative proportion—that is, things divinely revealed as he studies the Word and yields to the Spirit, and things that are human and natural.

When a man is born again, he possesses two natures— the flesh and the spirit—and these are contrary one to the other. Only the spiritual man can examine and sift things in their right light in order that he may accept the good and shun the evil. Such a man cannot be subject to examination and judgment by unbelievers. The born again, blood-washed, Spirit-indwelt man is a riddle to unbelievers; they cannot understand his actions, motives, or his purpose in life.

This does not mean that every born again believer is above criticism — far from it! It is altogether possible for a believer to become carnal, as we will see later on in our study (I Cor. 3:1). There are some believers who, though born again, do not grow. They yield no fruit, and they become *spiritual dwarfs* when *the desire of God* for all believers is that they become spiritual *giants*, full-grown and strong in the Lord—good soldiers of the cross.

John asked, "Who is he that overcometh the world, but he that believeth that Jesus is the Son of God?" He then teaches us that we overcome by faith; and when we exercise faith in the saving grace of God, God puts within us the Holy Spirit, and He leads us in the paths of righteousness. As many as are led by the Spirit of God, they are the children of God. Therefore, he that is spiritual judgeth all things, receiving that which will benefit, rejecting that which will tear down the spiritual man. And only spiritually minded believers *can* judge all things, for the carnally minded believer (*because* of his carnality) will see no wrong in many things. But when the Holy Spirit controls the soul as well as the members of the body, then the judgment pronounced upon the things of the world will be altogether different, because it will be in the light of the revealed truth of God as the Holy Ghost makes known to us the things of God and how we should live, and walk, and act—before the Church and the world.

Verse 16: "For who hath known the mind of the Lord, that he may instruct Him? But we have the mind of Christ."

Here we have a quotation from Isaiah 40:13: "Who hath directed the Spirit of the Lord, or being His counsellor hath taught Him?" We find part of the same verse in Romans 11:34: "For who hath known the mind of the Lord? *or who hath been His counsellor?*"

In the quotation from Romans, Paul is arguing concerning the unfathomable character of God's wisdom, knowledge, and judgments—God's ways in view of the nature and effects of the Gospel, together with the futility and utter hopelessness of human merit, ability, or effort; whereas in our present verse we have the shorter quotation because Paul is simply pointing to the futility of the

115

natural, unregenerate man as contrasted with the discernment imparted by the Spirit of God to the spiritual man. The mind is "the seat of reflective consciousness comprising the faculties of perception, understanding, and judgment." The *mind* of the Lord Jesus Christ must be perceived if His WAYS are to be understood. It is utterly impossible for the natural man to understand the ways of God apart from the operation of the Spirit of God. It is He (the Holy Spirit) who imparts to the born again believer the mind of Christ; the believer possesses the mind of Christ because of the *indwelling* of Christ: ". . . Christ in you, the hope of glory" (Col. 1:27b).

"There is therefore now no condemnation to them which are in Christ Jesus . . ." (Rom. 8:1).

"For ye are dead, and your life is hid with Christ in God" (Col. 3:3).

"(Who) hath raised us up together, and made us sit together in heavenly places in Christ Jesus" (Eph. 2:6).

"Let this mind be in you, which was also in Christ Jesus" (Phil. 2:5).

(Here we have proof of the deity of Christ, for *"the mind of Christ"* is used as the equivalent of "the mind of the Lord"—and *the mind of the Lord* in the Old Testament speaks of the mind of Jehovah: "And because ye are sons, God hath sent forth the Spirit of His Son into your hearts, crying, Abba, Father"—Gal. 4:6.)

"But ye are not in the flesh, but in the Spirit, if so be that the Spirit of God dwell in you. Now if any man have not the Spirit of Christ, he is none of His" (Rom. 8:9).

The Bible speaks of "the Spirit of GOD" and of "the Spirit of CHRIST." The tragedy of this hour is that more emphasis is being placed on brains in the ministry than on the teaching of the Holy Ghost. I believe in education. I believe that a call from God—whether it be to the ministry, to missions, or to some other full-time Christian service—is also a call to study and prepare for that service; but one should yield mind, soul, and body to the Holy Spirit to be *led* as he studies. Higher learning should never be allowed to discredit the Word of God in any way, and when prime authority is in question, the Bible should always be the Book to which we turn.

Today we have too much "as it were . . . in my humble opinion" preaching. We need more dogmatic Gospel preaching where God's man steps into the pulpit, opens the Word of God, and without fear, favor, or apology declares *"Thus saith the Lord!"* God's minister should never enter the pulpit until he has untiringly studied the message the Holy Ghost has laid upon his heart, *searching* as the Spirit leads, feeding his own heart from the deep things of God in order to feed those to whom he ministers. He must be fed before he can feed others. He must be led before he can lead others. May God help us to get back to the Word and to Holy-Ghost-inspired, empowered preaching!

God's preacher need never apologize to any group of parishioners or church members for preaching the message bidden by the Holy Ghost as the preacher studies and prepares the message to his church.

CHAPTER THREE

1. And I, brethren, could not speak unto you as unto spiritual, but as unto carnal, even as unto babes in Christ.

2. I have fed you with milk, and not with meat: for hitherto ye were not able to bear it, neither yet now are ye able.

3. For ye are yet carnal: for whereas there is among you envying, and strife, and divisions, are ye not carnal, and walk as men?

4. For while one saith, I am of Paul; and another, I am of Apollos; are ye not carnal?

5. Who then is Paul, and who is Apollos, but ministers by whom ye believed, even as the Lord gave to every man?

6. I have planted, Apollos watered; but God gave the increase.

7. So then neither is he that planteth any thing, neither he that watereth; but God that giveth the increase.

8. Now he that planteth and he that watereth are one: and every man shall receive his own reward according to his own labour.

9. For we are labourers together with God: ye are God's husbandry, ye are God's building.

10. According to the grace of God which is given unto me, as a wise masterbuilder, I have laid the foundation, and another buildeth thereon. But let every man take heed how he buildeth thereupon.

11. For other foundation can no man lay than that is laid, which is Jesus Christ.

12. Now if any man build upon this foundation gold, silver, precious stones, wood, hay, stubble;

13. Every man's work shall be made manifest: for the day shall declare it, because it shall be revealed by fire; and the fire shall try every man's work of what sort it is.

14. If any man's work abide which he hath built thereupon, he shall receive a reward.

15. If any man's work shall be burned, he shall suffer loss: but he himself shall be saved; yet so as by fire.

16. Know ye not that ye are the temple of God, and that the Spirit of God dwelleth in you?

17. If any man defile the temple of God, him shall God destroy; for the temple of God is holy, which temple ye are.

18. Let no man deceive himself. If any man among you seemeth to be wise in this world, let him become a fool, that he may be wise.

19. For the wisdom of this world is foolishness with God. For it is written, He taketh the wise in their own craftiness.

20. And again, The Lord knoweth the thoughts of the wise, that they are vain.

21. Therefore let no man glory in men. For all things are your's;

22. Whether Paul, or Apollos, or Cephas, or the world, or life, or death, or things present, or things to come; all are your's;

23. And ye are Christ's; and Christ is God's.

Carnality Prevents Spiritual Growth

Having laid down the principles which guided his ministry and characterized his message, Paul now returns to the subject of the divisions existing in the church at Corinth, the divisions already mentioned in chapter one, verses 11 through 13.

Since the wisdom which is revealed by the Spirit of God can be understood only by spiritually-minded believers, the spiritual condition of those who would read Paul's letter proved a hindrance to his ministry. Where there is partisanship and prejudice, the Holy Spirit is hindered in producing and maintaining unity in the church, and in using the servants of God to teach the Word, build up the saints, and cause unbelievers to be born again.

They were divided, they were not living in unity. They had forgotten that they were human instruments of God, appointed by Him to a specific ministry. They were recipients of what the Lord had given them, and although their services differed in character, they were *"one"* in Christ and in their relationship to Him (verse 8).

It is God alone who gives the increase and who will reward each faithful servant for his labor; but because of the attitude and factions in the Corinthian church, God could not bless as He desired to—and *as He would have blessed* if the saints had been dwelling in harmony, working in unity, directing their every effort to the glory of God.

Verse 1: "And I, brethren, could not speak unto you as unto spiritual, but as unto carnal, even as unto babes in Christ."

"*And I, brethren, could not speak unto you as unto spiritual . . . .*" In chapter two, Paul emphasized the superiority of the wisdom which is the result of spiritual illumination. He now warns the Corinthians that though they are *brethren*, born again—they are only babes in Christ. They have entered the door of salvation, but they are still standing at the threshold.

All believers receive the Holy Spirit when they are saved. We are *born* of the Spirit, we are *indwelt* by the Spirit, and we are *sealed* by the Spirit; *but spiritual development and growth* depend upon the measure in which we submit ourselves TO the Holy Spirit to be led and controlled by Him. Paul pleaded with the Romans to present their bodies a living sacrifice and their members as instruments of righteousness. He admonished the Ephesians to be *filled* with the Spirit. It is a Bible fact that one can possess the Spirit, and yet the Holy Spirit not possess that believer.

". . . *But as unto carnal, even as unto babes in Christ.*" The word "carnal" signifies "partaking of the nature of the flesh."

In verse 3 of our present chapter Paul uses another word for "carnal," which is a much more severe term in the Greek. It signifies "sensual . . . under control of the fleshly nature instead of being governed by the Spirit of God." While the believers in Corinth were not *anti*-spiritual, they were not making spiritual progress. They were truly born again, they were sons of God — but they were spiritual babies.

The word used in verse 3, indicative of their jealousy and strife, suggests that they were guilty of yielding to the lust which originates in man's corrupt and fallen nature. They were immature Christians, lacking in spiritual understanding and power. It is clear that they were IN CHRIST, and thus (because they *were* in Christ) they could grow and develop if they would only hear the warning and obey the leadership of the Holy Spirit.

I have heard it said, "There is no such thing as a carnal Christian." To make this statement is to advertise Bible ignorance and spiritual stupidity. It is a Bible fact that one can be a believer, although possessing carnal tendencies. The unregenerate person is lost, and possesses only one nature—that of the natural man.

Paul said to the Ephesians, "In time past . . . ye were *by nature* the children of wrath"; but the born again person possesses *two* natures—the flesh and the Spirit—and these two are constantly warring against each other. There is no excuse, however, for the believer allowing the flesh to get the upper hand, for *"we are more than conquerors"* through the Lord Jesus; and all that we need in order to live a dedicated, consecrated, victorious, spiritual life is provided in our salvation.

Verse 2: "I have fed you with milk, and not with meat: for hitherto ye were not able to bear it, neither yet now are ye able."

By using the illustration, *"I fed you with milk,"* Paul here stresses the fact that the Corinthian Christians were infants, spiritually speaking. Certainly physical babies could not eat meat, and Paul declared that he could not give them the *spiritual meat* of God's Word because they were spiritual infants, still needing to be "bottle-fed." (Acts 18:11 tells us that Paul stayed in Corinth for a year and six months, teaching the Word of God among them.)

"Therefore leaving the principles of the doctrine of Christ, let us go on unto perfection; not laying again the foundation of repentance from dead works, and of faith toward God" (Heb. 6:1).

"For when for the time ye ought to be teachers, ye have need that one teach you again which be the first principles of the oracles of God; and are become such as have need of milk, and not of strong meat" (Heb. 5:12).

". . . *For hitherto ye were not able to bear it, neither yet now are ye able.*" Paul fed the believers at Corinth with spiritual *milk* because they were not able to bear spiritual *meat*. They had not developed spiritually to the place where they could receive the deeper things of God, and since Paul was a skillful teacher he knew that they must receive elementary instruction before they could receive the deeper truths of the Word and the things of the Spirit. They were standing in the way of their own development, hindering their own growth.

Verse 3: "For ye are yet carnal: for whereas there is among you envying, and strife, and divisions, are ye not carnal, and walk as men?"

". . . *For whereas there is among you envying, and strife, and divisions . . . .*" *Envy* desires to deprive another person of what he possesses, while *jealousy* desires to have *the same sort of thing* the other person has. Either jealousy OR envy will cause strife and contention. I am afraid that if God should send a new epistle to the churches on earth today, it would be necessary for Him to again give warning against jealousy and envy among believers. These are two of the ugliest sins prevalent today among Christians.

". . . *Are ye not carnal, and walk as men*?" The phrase is literally "*according to man,*" according to the practices of fallen humanity. Instead of following the Holy Spirit they were walking according to human standards. They were following men—even unregenerated men. I repeat: Religions and ministers have done a thorough job of confusing people — and dear reader, if you listen to *all* preachers, if you follow the idea that "there is a little good in all religions" and you attempt to pick out the little good, add it all up and make it your religion, you are in for a sad, heartbreaking experience!

You cannot give heed to all who claim to be ministers of the Gospel. In II Corinthians 11:13—15 we learn that the devil has ordained ministers who are under his power and leadership. Such are NOT the ministers of God, but ministers of Satan. We cannot follow the dogma and doctrines of men. We cannot serve God according to human standards; *we MUST follow the Spirit.*

Verse 4: "For while one saith, I am of Paul; and another, I am of Apollos; are ye not carnal?"

". . . *I am of Paul . . . I am of Apollos.*" Because of this division among the Corinthians, Paul asked, "Are you not carnal? Are you not acting on a purely human level? Those of you who are following me and those who are following Apollos lack spiritual discernment. You are not walking in the Spirit."

The believer who sets his mind "on things above, not on things on the earth" (Col. 3:2) will enjoy fellowship with the Father and with the Son, and such fellowship will enable him to understand the things of the Spirit of God. Paul did not want the converts to get their eyes on HIM; he was jealous for Jesus and for the grace of God, and he always pointed men to Jesus—never to himself. It was a divine imperative that he rebuke the Corinthian believers and show them that even though he was God's minister, he was only a man, and if they were following him they were walking as men and not on a spiritual level.

Only GOD Is Anything in Christian Service

Verse 5: "Who then is Paul, and who is Apollos, but ministers by whom ye believed, even as the Lord gave to every man?"

"*Who is Paul? Who is Apollos?*" One characteristic of Paul's epistles is that he asks many questions—and then gives the answers. In this instance, he answers his questions by pointing out that these men were only servants of Christ who preached the Gospel, through whose message the Corinthians had believed unto salvation. In other words, Paul is saying, "I am nothing, Apollos is nothing—insofar as your *salvation* is concerned. We simply revealed to you the truth of the death, burial, and resurrection of Jesus. You *believed* the message, and the Lord gave you everlasting life *because* you heard and believed the message of His ministers."

". . . *Even as the Lord gave to every man.*" I cannot emphasize too strongly the fact that *the very ability to* BELIEVE unto salvation is the gift of God. Regardless of who is preaching the Gospel when an unbeliever is saved, regardless of how great or outstanding the minister may be, it is not the *man* who is important, but the *message*—the message which God gives him, and which he in turn gives to the unbeliever. When the sinner hears the message, God gives him the ability to believe, to trust in the shed blood of Jesus for the remission of sin. Salvation is from without; it is never generated from within.

124

By faith we receive the finished work of Jesus; and when we exercise faith in His finished work He comes into our hearts in the Person of the Holy Spirit. Paul wants it clearly understood that he and Apollos (and all of God's preachers) are nothing more than God's anointed servants; and that insofar as giving salvation to the unbeliever is concerned, the minister is nothing. It is the Lord who gives salvation.

Verse 6: "I have planted, Apollos watered; but God gave the increase."

"I have planted, Apollos watered." The verbs used here are in the past tense, summing up the initial work of Paul (he first came to Corinth and preached the Gospel), and then the subsequent work of Apollos, who came later.

". . . *But God gave the increase.*" The literal translation is "God *was giving* the increase," signifying "something going on all the time." God was giving the increase moment by moment, day by day, as the preached Gospel was watered and new seed were being sown all the time.

"And when they were come, and had gathered the church together, they rehearsed all that God had done with them, and how He had opened the door of faith unto the Gentiles" (Acts 14:27).

"And a certain woman named Lydia, a seller of purple, of the city of Thyatira, which worshipped God, heard us: whose heart the Lord opened, that she attended unto the things which were spoken of Paul" (Acts 16:14).

God's Word will not return unto Him void; on the contrary, it continues *increasingly.* Paul planted the incorruptible seed of the Word, Apollos watered the seed planted by Paul; but it was God who gave the increase

125

and saved them for Christ's sake. It was God who was continually saving any and all who would yield to the Spirit. It was God who was continuing to keep them, strengthen them, and permit them to grow. If you will study Acts 18:1–18, and Acts 18:24 through the entire 19th chapter, you will find the work of Paul and of Apollos recorded.

There are instances in many churches where a faithful pastor has ministered for years, preaching the Word of God. Through his consistent spiritual living and teaching he has sown seed for many years — and then an evangelist comes in for eight days, a great harvest of souls is reaped, and the evangelist brags that he led that great number of souls to Christ during his meeting there. God forgive such a man!

I am an evangelist — yet sometimes I wonder if I have been used of God to win even one soul to Jesus apart from the assistance of my fellow ministers—pastors, evangelists, and missionaries. Through interpreters I have preached to the heathen and have seen many of them saved; but I could not come home and boast that I had led them to Christ. The dear missionaries who daily labored there had the greater part in such a harvest of souls. God have mercy on proud, boastful preachers who put emphasis on the number of converts, instead of humbly giving God the glory for whatever is accomplished!

As I reflect upon my own salvation, I realize that only the dear Lord knows how many people contributed to it. When I preach and unbelievers are saved at the close of the message, only God knows how many others prayed for them, witnessed to them, and in various ways sowed the seed which God used me to water, or from which I may reap a harvest.

Verse 7: "So then neither is he that planteth any

thing, neither he that watereth; but God that giveth the increase."

What Paul is saying here is simply, *"GOD is everything!"* The emphasis is upon GOD. The minister of the Gospel needs to fully realize his own insignificance and inability, his own insufficiency, and recognize his total dependence upon God if he hopes for fruit to God's glory. We who are His ministers need to learn to give God all the glory for the results in our services. When we sow seed, or when we water where someone else has sown, we are simply doing our duty as ministers of God. God saved us, God calls, ordains, and commissions us, and God empowers us. Where then is our glory? We are recipients of God's grace. I can personally say with Paul, "I am what I am by the grace of God." I am preaching God's Word, but the very strength to deliver the message is a gift from God. So wherein is MY glory? I am nothing; *God is everything!*

Verse 8: "Now he that planteth and he that watereth are one: and every man shall receive his own reward according to his own labour."

". . . *He that planteth and he that watereth are one . . . .*" In this statement Paul is pointing out to the Corinthian believers that he and Apollos are *ONE in the ministry.* The same is true of Paul and Peter. They were not rivals, not mere theologians, not founders of separate sects. God's preachers are one in Christ and one in the ministry; they are one in interest, one in aim and operation; and for the believers in Corinth to consider these men as rivals of each other was unscriptural and signified their ignorance of the Word and work of the Lord.

". . . *Every man shall receive his own reward according to his own labour.*" There is but one true Church. Jesus is the head and the foundation of that Church, every born again, blood-washed believer is a member of it, and each member of the Church will receive his or her own reward. The Scripture does not teach that all believers will share and share alike in eternity — far from it! Each believer will receive a reward for "the things done in his body, according to that he hath done, whether it be good or bad" (II Cor. 5:10).

Salvation is wholly of the Lord; but *rewards are earned* by and through faithful service. If we are faithful servants we will receive a full reward; if we are unfaithful we will suffer *loss* of reward. In II John, verse 8, we are warned, "Look to yourselves (be careful), that we lose not those things which we have wrought, but that we receive a full reward." John is not speaking of losing our salvation, but of losing *"the things which we have wrought"*—that is, our stewardship and faithful labor. Whether our service be planting or watering, whether it be much or little, it is not the *amount* of service that counts, but *"of what sort it is."*

Christian Stewardship and Rewards

Verse 9: "For we are labourers together with God: ye are God's husbandry, ye are God's building."

". . . We are labourers together with God . . . ." Paul is here showing how the unity mentioned in verse 8 is brought about. All of God's ministers are fellow workers, engaged in the same endeavor — servants of God.

"Ye are God's husbandry, ye are God's building." Here Paul uses two descriptions of the local church:

First, he uses an illustration from agriculture. *Husbandry* denotes tillage of the ground, cultivation of crops and vineyards. It suggests labor—daily, diligent toil. The agricultural illustration points out that if a field or vineyard is not tilled and cultivated, grass and weeds will curtail the crop and hinder its growth. God's ministers are His co-laborers, and the Church is God's husbandry. So the minister plants the seed, waters the planting, and tills the ground.

Second, Paul uses an illustration from *architecture*; he refers to the building—or "God's house in building." In verses 10 through 17 he develops this illustration. In Jeremiah 18:9 we read, "And at what instant I shall speak concerning a nation, and concerning a kingdom, *to build and to plant it.*" Jeremiah 24:6: "For I will set mine eyes upon them for good, and I will bring them again to this land: and *I will build them*, and not pull them down; and *I will plant them*, and not pluck them up."

Ezekiel 36:9 and 10 tells us: "For, behold, I am for you, and I will turn unto you, and ye shall be *tilled and sown*: And I will multiply men upon you, all the house of Israel, even all of it: and the cities shall be inhabited, and the wastes shall be *builded*."

Verse 10: "According to the grace of God which is given unto me, as a wise masterbuilder, I have laid the foundation, and another buildeth thereon. But let every man take heed how he buildeth thereupon."

"*According to the grace of God which is given unto me.*" Paul is here referring to the grace bestowed upon him for the special work of founding the local church in the city of Corinth, not to his *salvation by grace* through faith nor to his service in general, but to the assembly in Corinth in particular.

". . .*As a wise masterbuilder* . . . ." Paul is speaking here to a group of Christians who were putting too much emphasis on worldly wisdom, and upon individuals. He points out in clear, understandable language that *the grace of God* has been given to him, rendering him capable of being a wise masterbuilder. He is not an overseer; he is not a superintendent. GOD is the superintendent, and God gave Paul the blueprints, the plans, and the knowledge for the work he had been called to do. He wanted the Corinthians to understand that only because of God did he have the skill and qualifications to lay the foundation for the local assembly there.

"*. . . I have laid the foundation, and another buildeth thereon.*" Paul's mention of another builder does not refer to Apollos only, but to any and all who might follow in the ministry of the Gospel in Corinth or around the world, even to this present hour—for the plans Paul used are the singular plans that God has for every one of His ministers, missionaries, or evangelists.

Yes, Paul was God's *masterbuilder*. God called and anointed him a minister to the Gentiles. When God told Ananias to go into "the street called Straight" and enquire for Paul, He said to Ananias, ". . . (Paul) is a chosen vessel unto me, to bear my name before the Gentiles, and kings, and the children of Israel: For I will shew him how great things he must suffer for my name's sake" (Acts 9:15,16).

Later, when Paul was giving his testimony before King Agrippa in Acts 26, he declared that God had given him a heavenly vision and had promised to deliver him from those who would seek to take his life because of his ministry and his plain preaching. In Romans 11:13 Paul said, "For I speak to you Gentiles, inasmuch as I am the apostle of the Gentiles, I magnify mine office."

God revealed to the Apostle Paul the mystery that had been hidden from the beginning—the mystery of the Incarnation. He said to young Timothy, "And without controversy great is the mystery of godliness: God was manifest in the flesh, justified in the Spirit, seen of

130

angels, preached unto the Gentiles, believed on in the world, received up into glory" (I Tim. 3:16).

Writing to the Ephesians Paul said, "For this cause I Paul, the prisoner of Jesus Christ for you Gentiles, if ye have heard of the dispensation of the grace of God which is given me to you-ward: How that by revelation He made known unto me the mystery; (as I wrote afore in few words, whereby, when ye read, ye may understand my knowledge in the mystery of Christ) which in other ages was not made known unto the sons of men, as it is now revealed unto His holy apostles and prophets by the Spirit; That the Gentiles should be fellowheirs, and of the same body, and partakers of His promise in Christ by the Gospel: Whereof I was made a minister, according to the gift of the grace of God given unto me by the effectual working of His power. Unto me, who am less than the least of all saints, is this grace given, that I should preach among the Gentiles the unsearchable riches of Christ; and to make all men see what is the fellowship of the mystery, which from the beginning of the world hath been hid in God, who created all things by Jesus Christ: To the intent that now unto the principalities and powers in heavenly places might be known by the Church the manifold wisdom of God, according to the eternal purpose which He purposed in Christ Jesus our Lord: In whom we have boldness and access with confidence by the faith of Him" (Eph. 3:1-12).

There is a testimony in verse 10 of our present chapter, for Paul here testifies that he is *all that he is* by the grace of God. Grace brought salvation, by grace he was a minister of the Gospel, by grace he was a wise masterbuilder; by the grace of God he laid the foundation for the church in Corinth, and Apollos and others were building on that foundation. He gave God all the credit, all the praise, all the honor and glory — and then he warns:

"*But let every man take heed how he buildeth thereupon!*" This is a warning to those engaged in the formation of the assembly that makes up the local church. The Holy Spirit is here pointing out the solemn, divine responsibility for the character of the work put into the building of this, *God's building.* Those who engage in this construction should be very careful, always keeping in mind the judgment seat of Christ. There is danger of marring or scarring the temple (building), the holy character of which is pointed out.

The One Foundation

Verse 11: "For other foundation can no man lay than that is laid, which is Jesus Christ."

The emphasis in this verse is on "*foundation.*" As having to do with Paul's work in Corinth, all question concerning any other foundation was ruled out. There is only one true Gospel: "I marvel that ye are so soon removed from Him that called you into the grace of Christ unto another gospel: Which is not another; but there be some that trouble you, and would pervert the Gospel of Christ" (Gal. 1:6,7). There is only one Gospel, there is only one salvation—one Way, one Name, one Door, one Church, one Foundation, one Head, one body.

"*Than that is laid*" suggests that the site of the foundation was chosen by God, under the direction of the Holy Spirit, and that the laying of the foundation was therefore God's operation. The foundation stone is God's, wholly and absolutely, and is where He placed it. There are many builders, but the ground upon which the New Testament Church is built is God's ground, appointed by Him. The foundation is His, and the Chief Cornerstone is the stone which the builders disallowed.

The *one Foundation* of the New Testament Church is Jesus Christ, the Person—He who came forth from the heavenly Father and became man; He who was despised and rejected of men, yet through His death, burial, resurrection, and ascension (now being seated at the right hand of God the Father) He is the Saviour —the ONLY Saviour of men, the only Foundation of the New Testament Church.

In Matthew 16:18 this divine statement is recorded: ". . . Upon this rock I will build my Church; and the gates of hell shall not prevail against it!" The occasion for this statement was that Jesus had asked His disciples, "Whom do men say that I the Son of man am?" And they replied, "Some say that thou art John the Baptist: some, Elias; and others, Jeremias, or one of the prophets." Then Jesus asked them, "But whom say YE that I am?" And Simon Peter answered, *"THOU ART THE CHRIST, THE SON OF THE LIVING GOD!"*

Jesus assured Peter that the statement he had just made was not the result of his own wisdom or ability: "Blessed art thou, Simon Bar-jona: for flesh and blood hath not revealed it unto thee, but my Father which is in heaven." God the Father had given Peter the revelation that Jesus was truly the Son of God, God Incarnate, God wrapped up in flesh; and upon that Rock (Christ Jesus)—not on the pebble (Peter)—Jesus said, "I will build my Church, and the gates of hell shall not prevail against it." Jesus settled the divine fact that He is the Rock, the Chief Cornerstone, the one Foundation. There is no other.

There are various and sundry ideas about the Rock, the Foundation, and the Church; but if we will let the Word of God speak and we keep silent, comparing spiritual things with spiritual, we will have no trouble understanding the Gospel truth concerning the Church of the living God, and we will have no difficulty in discerning who is the head and the foundation of the one true Church.

For instance, in the New English Bible, published by Oxford University Press and Cambridge University Press, 1961 edition, in Matthew 16:17 we read, "And I say this to you: You are Peter, the Rock" (*Rock* is capitalized, indicating a personal name); "and on this rock I will build my church, and the forces of death shall never overpower it!"

Dearly beloved, do you see the subtleness of this translation? Peter is NOT the rock upon which Jesus is building the Church. It is true that the Greek for Cephas means "a little stone, or a little pebble," but the foundation of the New Testament Church is not a pebble. It is not Peter — *it is the Lord Jesus Christ.*

In the King James Bible, Matthew 21:44, we read, "And whosoever shall fall on this stone shall be broken: but on whomsoever it shall fall, it will grind him to powder." The Stone is Jesus. The Revised Standard Version (the Bible owned and copyrighted by the National Council of Churches of Christ of America) omits this verse in its entirety. The revisers removed it from the text, but in a footnote at the bottom of the page we read, *"Other ancient authorities add verse 44."* If ancient authorities added it, why did the modern revisers remove it? If you will read that verse and study the Stone, you will know why they removed it: The Stone is Jesus — and liberals and modernists do not teach that one must fall on Jesus to be broken and saved! If we fall on Jesus for mercy, our hearts are broken and we are saved, made vessels meet for the Master's use. If we do NOT fall on Jesus for mercy, then the Stone will fall on us in judgment. That verse of Scripture tells of the Stone that saves or condemns, as the case may be; and no one has a right to remove it from God's Holy Word.

This is the Stone of Daniel 2:34, cut out of the mountain without hands. This is the Stone mentioned throughout the Scriptures—Jesus Christ, the Chief Corner-stone, the foundation of the Church. Regardless of what the New English Bible says about it, or what the Revised Standard Version says about it, Jesus is still the one foundation that IS LAID—not *"being laid,"* not *"going to be laid."* It was laid before the foundation of the world. It was *foreordained of God* that Jesus should die on the cross to save sinners. The Church of the living God is made up of born again people, with Jesus as the foundation — and there is none other; there can never be another foundation.

Two Kinds of Stewardship and Their Results

Verse 12: "Now if any man build upon this foundation gold, silver, precious stones, wood, hay, stubble . . . ."

It must be remembered that it is not primarily Christian conduct of which Paul is speaking here, but the doctrine of teachers and ministers. We must not overlook the fact, however, that the principles laid down here are applicable to all Christian conduct and Christian service. The materials mentioned here are comprised of two classes: those that will *endure* fire, and those which fire will *consume.* Generally speaking, the different materials mentioned here represent a variety of teaching and works by the builders on God's foundation. In the divine estimate their teaching and ministry either *adds to the building* and its value, or else it is *worthless.*

Gold, silver, and precious stones are costly and valuable, while wood, hay, and stubble are practically worthless. The doctrines of Christianity center in Christ, and pure doctrine serves to form the character of those who make up the local church. Pure doctrine produces believers who conform to Christ. The minister and teacher who rightly divide the Word of Truth will produce this effect in edifying the believers in the local assembly. The value and results of such preaching or teaching is represented here as gold, silver, and precious stones.

There is no doubt that the gold sets forth the character and moral attributes of the Godhead — and the fullness of the Godhead dwells in Christ. Please read Exodus 25:11,17–20 and Colossians 2:9,10.

Silver represents the redemption wrought by God in and through the Lord Jesus Christ, while the precious stones represent truths which set forth the righteousness, the glory, the excellencies of the person and character of Christ. (See Revelation 4:3 and 21:11.) The Greek word used in these verses for "light" is really *light-giver*. Jesus is the pearl most precious, the ruby beyond compare, the diamond which sparkles and gives forth light. He is the Light-Giver. *He is the Light of the World.*

Wood, hay, and stubble are but *imitations* of pure Bible doctrine. These materials, instead of rightly dividing the Word of Truth, symbolize the persuasive words of man's wisdom: "From which some having swerved have turned aside unto vain jangling; desiring to be teachers of the law; understanding neither what they say, nor whereof they affirm" (I Tim. 1:6,7).

"If thou put the brethren in remembrance of these things, thou shalt be a good minister of Jesus Christ, nourished up in the words of faith and of good doctrine, whereunto thou hast attained. But refuse profane and old wives' fables, and exercise thyself rather unto godliness" (I Tim. 4:6,7).

"He is proud, knowing nothing, but doting about questions and strifes of words, whereof cometh envy, strife, railings, evil surmisings, perverse disputings of men of corrupt minds, and destitute of the truth, supposing that gain is godliness: from such withdraw thyself.

"But godliness with contentment is great gain. For we brought nothing into this world, and it is certain we can carry nothing out. And having food and raiment let us be therewith content. But they that will be rich fall into temptation and a snare, and into many foolish and hurtful lusts, which drown men in destruction and perdition. For the love of money is the root of all evil: which while some coveted after, they have erred from the faith, and pierced themselves through with many sorrows.

"But thou, O man of God, flee these things; and follow after righteousness, godliness, faith, love, patience, meekness. Fight the good fight of faith, lay hold on eternal life, whereunto thou art also called, and hast professed a good profession before many witnesses. I give thee charge in the sight of God, who quickeneth all things, and before Christ Jesus, who before Pontius Pilate witnessed a good confession; that thou keep this commandment without spot, unrebukeable, until the appearing of our Lord Jesus Christ: Which in His times He shall shew, who is the blessed and only Potentate, the King of kings, and Lord of lords; Who only hath immortality, dwelling in the light which no man can approach unto; whom no man hath seen, nor can see: to whom be honour and power everlasting. Amen.

"Charge them that are rich in this world, that they be not highminded, nor trust in uncertain riches, but in the living God, who giveth us richly all things to enjoy;

That they do good, that they be rich in good works, ready to distribute, willing to communicate; Laying up in store for themselves a good foundation against the time to come, that they may lay hold on eternal life.

"O Timothy, *keep that which is committed to thy trust, avoiding profane and vain babblings, and oppositions of science falsely so called*" (I Tim. 6:4—20).

Wood, hay, and stubble symbolize anything subversive to the truth—doctrinally or in works. A program set up through the wisdom of men, worldly ways and carnality, tends to detract from the power of the Word of God, which is the power of the Gospel that brings salvation.

We are kept by the power of God; we overcome by faith, faith comes by hearing, and hearing by the Word of God. Therefore if Satan can substitute the wisdom and ways of men and the methods of the world for the Word, he will not only damn souls who are not born again, but he will also render worthless the believer who remains a babe in Christ, never growing in grace and in the knowledge of the Lord and Saviour—for such a Christian will never become a vessel unto honor nor a good soldier of the cross.

Wood, hay, and stubble here have nothing to do with salvation as pertaining to the individual. That which corresponds to wood, hay, and stubble will be *burned* at the judgment seat of Christ, and we know that this could not apply to a child of God. The truth of this passage concerns those who teach and live doctrine that is pure and edifying as contrasted with those who teach the wisdom of men, and who, through the enticing words of man's wisdom, lead believers away from pure doctrine that would cause them to become strong, profitable servants of God in the Church. The verse has nothing to do with salvation insofar as redemption is concerned. It deals with rewards, as we will clearly see in the following verses.

Verse 13: "Every man's work shall be made manifest: for the day shall declare it, because it shall be revealed by fire; and the fire shall try every man's work of what sort it is."

"Every man's work shall be made manifest." This points out that each servant of God has an individual responsibility, and the material contributed, the service rendered, and the works performed by the individual will be revealed in their true character at the judgment seat of Christ.

God keeps perfect books. Not even a cup of cold water is overlooked when it is given in His name, and two mites dropped into the treasury by a poor widow brought words of commendation from the greatest Giver of all. Every minute detail of stewardship, right or wrong, is kept on record—whether it be gold, silver, and precious stones, or wood, hay, and stubble.

". . . *For the day shall declare it . . . .*" The *day* mentioned here is the same as that described in chapter 1, verse 8, as "the day of our Lord Jesus *Christ.*" It is not the *day of the Lord* mentioned in II Thessalonians 1:8 and 2:2. *The day of the Lord* is the day when Jesus will come in flaming fire, "taking vengeance on them that know not God" (referring to unbelievers); but in our present verse it is not *individuals* who are burned and consumed, but their *works.* Fire here suggests the testing of character. The word *declare* signifies "to make plain, to bring out into the open, to make evident," in the same way that the sunlight of the natural day brings what has been obscure in the night out into the open where it can be clearly seen. Jesus is the Light of the world — but He is also a consuming fire.

". . . *Because it shall be revealed by fire.*" The Greek reads, "It is revealed *IN fire.*" What is revealed in fire is not the *day*, but the *work*. The Bible often mentions the fire of God's judgment. Fire is one of His attributes. It is true that God is love (I John 4:8); but in Hebrews 12:29 we are told that He is also a consuming fire. (Read also Deuteronomy 4:24 and 9:3; Malachi 3:2; and II Thessalonians 1:8.) Fire thoroughly searches out and destroys all that is in its path, as in the judgment *God* will thoroughly search out and destroy all that is vile. Nothing that defiles shall enter the city of God; but only that which is thoroughly genuine and durable. Works of gold, silver, and precious stones will not be destroyed, but will only be the brighter *for having come through the fire.*

To the Romans Paul said, "As I live, saith the Lord, every knee shall bow to me, and every tongue shall confess to God" (Rom. 14:11). Each of us will stand before Jesus—He whose countenance is as the sun shining full strength and whose eyes are described in Revelation 1:14: "His head and His hairs were white like wool, as white as snow; *and His eyes were as a flame of fire.*"

Fire always separates the destructible from the indestructible, and such will be true at the judgment seat of Christ. All that we teach, preach, perform, give, or live that is not for the sole purpose of glorifying the Lord Jesus Christ will be burned.

". . . *And the fire shall try every man's work of what sort it is.*" This has nothing to do with the doctrine of purgatory. It has nothing to do with discipline as applied to character. No such thing is taught regarding the circumstances that surround the judgment seat of Christ. Only born again, blood-washed believers will be present at the judgment seat of Christ. (The wicked will be judged at the great White Throne Judgment described minutely in Revelation 20.) It is not the *character* of the person that will be judged at the judgment seat of Christ, but his work and stewardship will be tested.

It is altogether possible for a teacher or a preacher to produce results here on earth which appear to be excellent and of substantial quality, and yet at the judgment seat of Christ that work may be found worthless. God judges in righteousness; we judge by appearance. At the judgment seat of Christ only faithfulness—not popularity—will count. Only quality—not quantity or bigness—will count. Faithfulness and quality are the two essentials of stewardship that will bring reward.

The *quality* of stewardship is determined by the measure in which the steward magnifies and glorifies the Lord Jesus Christ, by the scriptural truth of his teaching, and by the influence of a pure, sanctified, holy life. There will be many surprises at the judgment seat of Christ. Some people whom we thought would occupy the "front seats" will be on the back row, and some whom we surely expected to see in the back seats will occupy places of honor at the front. It will indeed be a day of revelation when the Lord God Almighty passes out the crowns and trophies!

It is not always the man who makes headlines on earth who makes headlines in heaven. Sometimes the most powerful, most valuable member of the congregation never gets his or her name in the church bulletin, may never be called on to pray, may never sing a solo nor teach a class; but dedicated soul, spirit, and body to God, that one *prays* while others play, and *gives* while others rob God. But God keeps the record straight, and He will reward in righteousness.

It is not to be thought that the Lord Jesus Christ

needs to test one's stewardship in order to estimate the value of it. The estimate lies already within His perfect knowledge and will be made known in the "proving" of works tested by fire. Man looks on the outward appearance— the bigness and glamor of it; but God looks on the heart—as in the case of the widow who gave two mites, or the disciple who may give only a cup of cold water in Jesus' name. It is not "How *much* are you doing? How *big* is your ministry?" What counts with God is the SORT of ministry carried out.

Verse 14: "If any man's work abide which he hath built thereupon, he shall receive a reward."

"*If any man's work abide . . . .*" The Greek verb here translated "abide" indicates the enduring character of stewardship — it undergoes consuming fire, yet is not burned up. The statement has nothing to do with salvation and eternal life, which become ours the moment we believe on the Lord Jesus Christ and trust Him as our Saviour. Those who build gold, silver, and precious stones on the one foundation will share in the honor and dignity of service rendered to Him here on earth by sharing His authority in His eternal kingdom. This truth is clearly taught in the following Scripture:

"To him that overcometh will I grant to sit with me in my throne, even as I also overcame, and am set down with my Father in His throne" (Rev. 3:21).

"And there shall be no night there; and they need no candle, neither light of the sun; for the Lord God giveth them light: and they shall reign for ever and ever" (Rev. 22:5).

". . . *He shall receive a reward.*" If we suffer with Christ, we will reign with Him. If we are faithful in little, He has promised to make us rulers over much. This divine fact should be an incentive to us to be constantly on guard against the enemy, to be faithful in our devotion to the Lord Jesus Christ and in our stewardship. *Whatever we do*, we should do it all to the glory of God. We should, like Paul, count all things loss that we might gain Christ and follow in His steps.

Verse 15: "If any man's work shall be burned, he shall suffer loss: but he himself shall be saved; yet so as by fire."

". . . *He shall suffer loss*" of the reward—an eternal loss. The Greek verb here rendered "shall suffer loss" is used in the Hebrew in Exodus 21:22 and is translated "he shall pay" (or, "he shall be *fined*"). In Paul's day, in the Greek contracts if a workman put out inferior work, he was fined; part of his expected pay was taken away—and this is the picture set forth in verse 15.

In II John 8 we read, "Look to yourselves, *that we lose not those things which we have wrought, but that we receive a full reward.*" The devil's primary desire is to damn the soul of every individual and cause those souls to be tormented forever in the lake of fire; but when a person becomes a Christian and the devil recognizes the fact that he has lost the first desire of his murderous heart, he does not give up: He does everything in his diabolical power to cause the believer to become a vessel unto dishonor, not meet for the Master's use.

Beloved, if the devil cannot damn your soul he will do his utmost to rob you of your spiritual birthright and your eternal reward! What it will mean to be snatched as a brand from the burning and enter heaven without a reward, I do not know; but there will be some whose works will be burned and they will suffer eternal loss of reward. God grant that you and I will not be in that number. May we be found good, faithful stewards for Christ.

". . . *But he himself shall be saved; yet so as by (through) fire.*" Failing in stewardship does not involve loss of salvation. The born again, blood-washed believer will not suffer loss of his soul. There is, again, no question of purgatorial fire; the picture here is not that of a purifying process, nor even the punishment of the individual. His bad works are consumed in the testing, but he himself is saved—but only as one who has passed through fire (Job 23:10). This Scripture concerns works and stewardship—not the burning of souls, but the burning of works.

Much damage has been wrought by ministry carried on in the wisdom of men instead of in the demonstration of the Spirit. Earlier in this study I mentioned the belief of some that all will share alike in heaven, which erroneous belief is not taught in the Word of God. Each believer will enjoy the reward earned through his faithful stewardship — or he will suffer loss because of *unfaithful* stewardship. We are sending up material daily by the way we live, the things we do, the company we keep, and the way we represent Christ in this world. The record is being kept day by day, and our stewardship will be revealed at the judgment seat of Christ. If it is gold, silver, and precious stones, *we will receive a reward*; if it is wood, hay, and stubble, *our works will be burned*. But those who are true believers will be saved, even though it be as a brand snatched from the burning and their reward be completely lost.

Verse 16: "Know ye not that ye are the temple of God, and that the Spirit of God dwelleth in you?"

"*Know ye not . . . .*" This is the first of a series of appeals in this letter. You will find the same appeal in chapter 5, verse 6; in chapter 6, verses 2, 3, 9, 15, 16, and 19; in chapter 9, verse 24; and also in Romans 6:16

and 11:2. The verb "know" used here means "to know by perception, or by observation." Paul's appeal in each of the passages is to a fact which was either acknowledged by the believers in the church at Corinth, or certainly should have been obvious to them. If they did not know that they were the temple of God, it was certainly not his fault, because he had so taught them.

"*. . . Ye are the temple of God . . . .*" Every believer is God's temple. The Greek word is *naos,* meaning "sanctuary," and when used pertaining to the temple in Jerusalem it always denotes the *inner sanctuary*, the holy of holies, in contrast with the rest of the building. The word corresponds to the inner part of the tabernacle where the ark with the mercy seat rested.

In the figurative applications *naos* is always used, whether he is speaking of the entire Church (as in Ephesians 2:21) or of a local assembly—as in our present verse and also in II Corinthians 6:16. He also uses it in speaking of the individual's body (I Cor. 6:19). The word is used throughout the book of Revelation.

Any reference to an assembly (in the way in which Paul points out that we are the temple of God) is always referring to *a company of believers set apart to God . . .* a place of worship made up of a group of believers who are characterized by holiness, by righteous living, and by the manifestation of the glory of Christ as seen in an individual life and testimony. Certainly the divided, carnal group in the church in Corinth was not such an assembly.

"*. . . And that the Spirit of God dwelleth in you?*" If these believers did not know that the Holy Spirit dwelt in them, they certainly *should have known*, for Paul had taught this truth among them, and it was not his fault if they did not know it. A born again Christian who does not know that he possesses the Holy Spirit the moment he is born again is displaying gross spiritual ignorance. It is the ministry of the Holy Spirit to glorify Christ: "He shall glorify me: for He shall receive of mine, and shall shew it unto you" (John 16:14). The Holy Spirit can glorify Christ through each believer—but only as we allow Him to possess us, fill us, and lead us. We are God's temple, we are God's sanctuary; He dwells in us in the Person of the Holy Spirit. Since this is true, we should glorify the Lord Jesus in every minute detail of our living. Paul emphasizes the fact that even though these people were babes in Christ—carnal, divided—the Holy Spirit nevertheless dwelt in each of them.

Verse 17: "If any man defile the temple of God, him shall God destroy; for the temple of God is holy, which temple ye are."

In the original language the same word is used for "defile" and "destroy" and would read thus: "If any man *destroyeth* the temple of God, him shall God *destroy.*"

". . . *Him shall God destroy.*" This does not mean that God will destroy the spirit and soul of the believer who may dishonor the temple of God through faulty stewardship or unfaithful Christian living. The Greek verb is *phtheiro* and means "to destroy by corrupting." It is used here first (*"If any man destroyeth the temple"*) as having to do with marring and scarring an assembly by unprofitable, impure teaching which leads to a partisan spirit thus causing divisions in the assembly, and also leads believers away from holiness into carnality.

Secondly, the word is used to point out the marring of the offender by God through divine retribution: (*"Him will God destroy"*).

Hebrews 12:5—11 reveals that God chastens and scourges every son whom He receives, and if we are without chastisement we are not God's sons — we are illegiti-

146

mate and have never been born of the Spirit.

In the eleventh chapter of our present study, Paul rebukes the believers in Corinth for misbehaving at the Lord's table and tells them that *because* of that misbehavior some were sick, some were weak, and some were dead. Then he declares, "For if we would judge ourselves, we should not be judged. But when we are judged, we are chastened of the Lord, *that we should not be condemned with the world*" (I Cor. 11:30–32).

God chastens the child who will not follow Him in daily living; He chastens in order to correct. If we would judge ourselves and repent, we would not BE chastened; but if we refuse to repent, then we are judged and cut off; the body is destroyed but the spirit is saved. We will see this clearly pointed out in chapter 5.

Paul is not telling us in verse 17 that God will destroy us and damn us in the lake of fire if we do something unbecoming to a Christian, something which dishonors God instead of honoring Him. The same truth is pointed out here as in verse 15, concerning a man's stewardship being burned but his spirit saved. One outstanding Greek authority translates this verse thus: "If any man do hurt to the temple of God, to him shall God do hurt."

". . . *For the temple of God is holy, which temple ye are.*" *Hagios* ("holy") primarily signifies *separated*— "hence in Scripture in its moral and spiritual significance, means 'separated from sin and therefore consecrated to God, sacred.'" The Holy Spirit places strong emphasis upon the personal pronoun "YE." Those of us who teach and preach the Word of God should tremble at the very thought that we might unintentionally injure the very structure we are seeking to build. It is extremely important that we think, pray, study, and rightly interpret the Word of God, lest we who would bring men TO Christ should drive them away from Him through error or half-truth.

147

Verse 18: "Let no man deceive himself. If any man among you seemeth to be wise in this world, let him become a fool, that he may be wise."

The remaining verses in this chapter give solemn warning against human estimate of the servants of God who minister His Word. We must be on guard against the tricks and pitfalls of the devil which might cause a true minister to be placed on the shelf. God's preacher must never become self-complacent, supposing himself to be wise. He must never glory in men, nor preach to please mankind.

"Let no man deceive himself." This refers not to the assembly, but to each individual IN the assembly. There were those in the church at Corinth who professed to be teachers—very, very wise; yet they were the originators of the party spirit which had divided the church. But the minister of God who is *really* wise is, in the eyes of the world, a *fool*. (Notice chapter 1, verses 18–25.)

In the eyes of the natural man, the minister who depends on God's Word and the leadership of the Holy Spirit to supply him with the message and the ministry needed in his church is looked upon as a fool. The wisdom of the world is always asking "Why?" and wanting to *"see,"* just as the Pharisees on many occasions demanded a sign from Jesus; but "the just shall live by faith . . . whatsoever is not of faith is sin," and when the minister of God, knowing that he is called of God, fails to depend upon God for the message he is to deliver, that minister actually is becoming foolish. (Of course, if he depends on God and delivers "Thus saith the Lord," the *world* will brand him a fool.) A bit later in our study Paul testifies, "We are fools for Christ's sake. We are weak, we are despised." Such is true in the life of the dedicated, Spirit-filled minister, insofar as the world and the natural man are concerned.

Verse 19: "For the wisdom of this world is foolishness with God. For it is written, He taketh the wise in their own craftiness.

In this verse Paul sums up what he taught in I Corinthians 1:22—25, where he applied the teaching to the subject now under consideration.

"For it is written . . . ." Paul is here referring to a statement in Job 5:13: "He taketh the wise in their own craftiness: and the counsel of the froward is carried headlong." Here we have God's true estimate of human wisdom. God deals in faith, and the wisdom of man has no place in His great program.

"In the beginning, *God . . . .*" ALL things were created by Jesus Christ and FOR Jesus Christ. The fear of the Lord is the beginning of knowledge, and if any man lack wisdom, let him ask of God. Without God, we can do nothing; IN Him we have all that we need. Christ is our sufficiency; in Him we are complete; but without Him we *are* nothing, we can *do* nothing. Regardless of how popular we may be, or how wise (insofar as education and ability are concerned), if we do not possess the grace of God and His wisdom and power, at the close of life's journey we will depart this world—helpless, hopeless, and *hell-bound*!

The wisdom of man is foolishness with God. A person is a fool to try to run his own life, leaving God out of his daily routine, making his own plans, laying out his own program. In the twelfth chapter of Luke, Jesus describes such a man, to whom God said, "Thou fool! This night thy soul shall be required of thee: then whose shall those things be which thou hast provided?"

"He taketh the wise in their own craftiness." The Greek verb translated "taketh" is *drassomai*, which means "to grasp or grip," and carries with it the suggestion of a firm grip on a slippery object.

"Craftiness" is literally "all-working"—that is, doing

everything in an unscrupulous way. It denotes unscrupulous conduct, and the same word is used in Luke 20:23, II Corinthians 4:2, and in Ephesians 4:14.

"The wise" refers to those who make use of the wisdom of this world to obtain their own selfish desires and accomplish their own ends. These "wise" men in Corinth were drawing groups unto themselves; they were engaged in party-making in the assembly, thus going against the leadership of the Holy Spirit. They employed the wisdom and ability of man, instead of depending upon the Spirit of God to lead them in the things they were doing.

Verse 20: "And again, The Lord knoweth the thoughts of the wise, that they are vain."

The word "vain" signifies "void of effect." Practically the same word is used in I Corinthians 1:17 and 9:15 and means "to make of no effect—or void of real value." Those who depend upon the wisdom of the world and trust in their own ability are building wood, hay, and stubble. Some of these people are truly *born again*; but they are carnal, babes in Christ, and they will lose their reward. They are not true ministers of the Gospel.

Verse 21: "Therefore let no man glory in men. For all things are your's."

"Let no man glory in men." This is a comprehensive exhortation. Paul not only has reference to the party leaders in the church at Corinth; he also includes himself and Apollos—and ALL men through the Church Age. To glory in men implies a self-satisfied assurance of one's own estimate of a leading brother, and this should not exist in the local assembly. We are all ONE, we are laborers together; and although we do not all have the same ministry, each ministry is a *divine essential* if the Church is to go forward as God would have it move—ever onward and outward, carrying the Gospel to the whole wide world, even "to every creature."

In the last statement of this verse, Paul makes clear why we should not glory in men: "FOR ALL THINGS ARE YOUR'S."

Verses 22 and 23: "Whether Paul, or Apollos, or Cephas, or the world, or life, or death, or things present, or things to come; all are your's; and ye are Christ's; and Christ is God's."

"All things are yours." This statement strikes a death blow to the partisan idea of belonging to a special group or following a special leader, regardless of how great that leader might be. True ministers are God's gifts to the local church. They are to be valued and esteemed very highly—but in a very humble way. Paul always testified that he was a bondslave—not the king, not the superintendent, but *God's slave.* Then, too, the minister whom God places in the local assembly as His undershepherd is God's gift to the entire assembly—not to just a select group of a party made up of selfish babes in Christ.

"All things are yours" is a divine fact for born again believers; but even though all things *belong* to the believers, this does not mean that they can use the things of the Lord as they choose in their own wisdom or for their own gratification. God allows us to appropriate and enjoy His blessings only in the light of our relationship to Christ. "No good thing will He withhold from them that walk uprightly," and if we seek first the kingdom of God and His righteousness, all other things will be added. If we present our bodies a living sacrifice, holy and acceptable unto God, we may then rest assured that "all things work together for good to them that love God, to them who are the called according to His purpose."

It is only as we belong to Christ that all things are ours. Believers are members of Christ, and all things are under His authority and control: ". . . Jesus spake unto them, saying, *All power is given unto me in heaven and in earth*" (Matt. 28:18). "For to this end Christ both

151

died, and rose, and revived, *that He might be Lord* both of the dead and living" (Rom. 14:9). "For He hath put *all things* under His feet. But when He saith all things are put under Him, it is manifest that He is excepted, which did put all things under Him" (I Cor. 15:27).

Regardless of what may befall a believer, no matter how adverse the circumstances may be, if that believer is in the right relationship with God, whatever happens to him is for his good and God's glory.

"And ye are Christ's." This makes it clear that believers belong to the Lord Jesus—not to Paul, Apollos, nor Cephas. All believers are the purchased possession of Christ. He redeemed us at the tremendous price of His blood. God is no respecter of persons, and whether one be *minister or custodian* in the local assembly, all believers belong to Christ.

"And Christ is God's!" This statement does not suggest that Jesus Christ is inferior in regard to the Godhead. The oneness of Christ with the Father is clearly taught in the Scriptures. Jesus said, *"I and my Father are one"* (John 10:30). In Philippians 2:6 Paul clearly teaches the equality of the Godhead. Jesus became man — but in flesh He was the *GOD-man*, and in flesh He was entirely surrendered to the Father's will. He said, "And He that sent me is with me: the Father hath not left me alone; for I do always those things that please Him" (John 8:29).

In His prayer of intercession, Jesus said, "I have glorified thee on the earth: I have finished the work which thou gavest me to do. And now, O Father, glorify thou me with thine own self with the glory which I had with thee before the world was" (John 17:4,5). Jesus was with the Father "in the beginning." In the fullness of time He was born of a woman (Gal. 4:4); He took a body of flesh in order that He might taste death for every man (Heb. 2:9) and destroy the devil who had the power of death (Heb. 2:14). He conquered the world, the flesh, and the devil (Matt. 4:1–11). He conquered death, hell, and the grave (Rev. 1:18). And when He had by Himself purged our sins, He ascended to the Father, and He is now seated at the right hand of God to make intercession for us (Heb. 1:1–3; I Tim. 2:5).

Christ is God's gift to the sinner; and on the grounds of His sacrificial death, He acts as Mediator between God and men. Believers should follow HIM—not human leaders; and the only way to keep an assembly in perfect unity and harmony is for each believer IN the assembly to have a single eye, fixed on the Lord Jesus Christ at all times. We dare not take our eyes off of Him.

CHAPTER FOUR

1. Let a man so account of us, as of the ministers of Christ, and stewards of the mysteries of God.

2. Moreover it is required in stewards, that a man be found faithful.

3. But with me it is a very small thing that I should be judged of you, or of man's judgment: yea, I judge not mine own self.

4. For I know nothing by myself; yet am I not hereby justified: but he that judgeth me is the Lord.

5. Therefore judge nothing before the time, until the Lord come, who both will bring to light the hidden things of darkness, and will make manifest the counsels of the hearts: and then shall every man have praise of God.

6. And these things, brethren, I have in a figure transferred to myself and to Apollos for your sakes; that ye might learn in us not to think of men above that which is written, that no one of you be puffed up for one against another.

7. For who maketh thee to differ from another? and what hast thou that thou didst not receive? Now if thou didst receive it, why dost thou glory, as if thou hadst not received it?

8. Now ye are full, now ye are rich, ye have reigned as kings without us: and I would to God ye did reign, that we also might reign with you.

9. For I think that God hath set forth us the apostles last, as it were appointed to death: for we are made a spectacle unto the world, and to angels, and to men.

10. We are fools for Christ's sake, but ye are wise in Christ; we are weak, but ye are strong; ye are honourable, but we are despised.

11. Even unto this present hour we both hunger, and thirst, and are naked, and are buffeted, and have no certain dwelling-place;

12. And labour, working with our own hands: being reviled, we bless; being persecuted, we suffer it:

13. Being defamed, we intreat: we are made as the filth of the world, and are the offscouring of all things unto this day.

14. I write not these things to shame you, but as my beloved

sons I warn you.

15. For though ye have ten thousand instructers in Christ, yet have ye not many fathers: for in Christ Jesus I have begotten you through the gospel.

16. Wherefore I beseech you, be ye followers of me.

17. For this cause have I sent unto you Timotheus, who is my beloved son, and faithful in the Lord, who shall bring you into remembrance of my ways which be in Christ, as I teach every where in every church.

18. Now some are puffed up, as though I would not come to you.

19. But I will come to you shortly, if the Lord will, and will know, not the speech of them which are puffed up, but the power.

20. For the kingdom of God is not in word, but in power.

21. What will ye? shall I come unto you with a rod, or in love, and in the spirit of meekness?

Judgment of the Servants of Christ Is Not Committed to Men

In this chapter, Paul continues his admonition against human estimation of God's ministers and servants. Ministers of God are called BY the Lord God, their responsibility is entirely to Him as their Lord and Master, and He alone is their Judge. It is He who will declare the true value of service at the judgment seat. The Lord Jesus Christ is the Judge of the living and the dead, for the Father has committed all judgment to the Son.

Verse 1: "Let a man so account of us, as of the ministers of Christ, and stewards of the mysteries of God."

". . . *As of the ministers of Christ* . . . ." Here the Greek word *huperetes* is used, referring to the ministers of Christ, and the dictionary gives this meaning: "Properly an under rower (*hupo*, under, and *eretes*, a rower); hence the word came to denote any subordinate acting under another's direction." Thus the minister is God's undershepherd. If Paul, Apollos, and Cephas belonged to the saints in the assembly at Corinth, as suggested in chapter 3, verse 22, they belonged to them only because, as undershepherds, they were acting for Christ *the Chief Shepherd.*

". . . *And stewards of the mysteries of Christ.*" The

Greek word used here for "stewards" means "the manager of a household or state, one acting for his master." That is the picture of every true minister of the Gospel and every steward of the spiritual things of God. We are acting for the Lord Jesus Christ. We are stewards of God's mysteries, and our duty to the household of God is to furnish meat in due season, the pure Gospel of the grace of God.

We are not our own; we are bought with His blood, called into the ministry by His grace, and empowered by His Spirit. Therefore we have nothing of which to boast. All that we are and have, all that we are able to do that will be gold, silver, and precious stones, is because of Him, and Him alone.

". . . *The mysteries of God.*" This simply means the good news that God, through His infinite wisdom, through His unknowable and indescribable love and power, has made possible *salvation for sinners* who should be consigned to hell; but because of God's love and mercy, grace has been brought down. In I Timothy 3:16 Paul gives us a clear statement concerning the mysteries of God:

"And without controversy great is the mystery of godliness: God was manifest in the flesh, justified in the Spirit, seen of angels, preached unto the Gentiles, believed on in the world, received up into glory."

When we read of the mysteries of God in the New Testament, it does not mean something that cannot be known today, but something that was *hidden in the ages behind us* and made known through the appearing of the Lord Jesus Christ and through the teaching of the Holy Spirit, who abides in the bosom of every believer.

Verse 2: "Moreover it is required in stewards, that a man be found faithful."

ANY man or ALL men who are stewards are required to be found faithful; and the fact that he is *required* to be faithful suggests that he must give an account to his master. We know the Bible clearly teaches that every believer is a steward of that which has been intrusted to him by the Lord and because of the grace of God: "As every man hath received the gift, even so minister the same one to another, as good stewards of the manifold grace of God" (I Pet. 4:10).

The Lord Jesus knows NOW whether or not we are faithful, but the issues will be *made manifest* at the judgment seat of Christ. Our reward will not be according to our success, but according to our faithfulness; not according to the bigness or the amount of what we do, but the faithfulness with which we DO it.

"And that servant, which knew his lord's will, and prepared not himself, neither did according to his will, shall be beaten with many stripes. But he that knew not, and did commit things worthy of stripes, shall be beaten with few stripes. For *unto whomsoever much is given, of him shall be much required:* and to whom men have committed much, of him they will ask the more" (Luke 12:47,48).

Verse 3: "But with me it is a very small thing that I should be judged of you, or of man's judgment: yea, I judge not mine own self."

A true and faithful minister of the Lord Jesus Christ will not be perturbed by the unfavorable opinion of others, whether they be unbelievers, or carnal babes in Christ; nor will a faithful minister of Christ desire praise of men or be elated by their applause. The true minister seeks only to please God and glorify HIM, knowing that God Himself will reward at the appointed day.

". . . *With me it is a very small thing . . . .*" In other words, "What you think about me or how you judge me counts for very little. It is the Lord Jesus who will judge in righteousness, and it is HIS judgment that counts— not the judgment of man."

Man cannot judge in righteousness. The judgment of the natural man is warped and perverted because he is alienated from God. Every believer—especially a minister and servant of God—should be extremely careful how he lives. Believers should conduct themselves every moment of every day in such a way that any criticism or harsh judgment that may be heaped upon them, either by *unbelievers* or by carnal Christians, would be false. Thus when we are falsely accused or unfairly judged, we can rejoice (Matt. 5:11,12). Jesus was criticized, persecuted, and falsely accused; and if the world persecuted HIM they will certainly persecute US and bring false accusations against us (John 15:18; 17:14).

Paul said to Timothy, "Yea, and all that will live godly in Christ Jesus shall suffer persecution" (II Tim. 3:12). But if we are not guilty of that of which we are accused, if we are not guilty of things that would bring reproach upon the name of Jesus, then we need not be sad or despondent because of what others think of us, even though we must remember that *we are ALL exposed to the danger of being unduly influenced* by what others think or say about us.

"Yea, I judge not mine own self." Paul did not mean that he was free from self-reproach. He simply meant that in his own heart he was assured that his ministry was to the glory of God, his motives were right, and he was yielded completely to the Lord Jesus Christ. He confessed that he was human, with human frailties, and therefore if he DID judge himself his judgment would be inadequate to either condemn or acquit. Knowing that he would give an account for his stewardship, he looked forward to the day when he would receive his just reward at the judgment seat of Christ. Even believers who are unreservedly dedicated to the Lord are not capable of judging in themselves the things which only the Spirit of God can reveal in truth and verity. (Contrast this verse

with I Corinthians 11:31. There is no contradiction. Here the judging of stewardship is in view; in 11:31 the judging of known sin in the life.)

Verse 4: "For I know nothing by myself; yet am I not hereby justified: but He that judgeth me is the Lord."

"For I know nothing by myself . . . ." God help us who name the name of Jesus to recognize the fact that *an unaccusing conscience* does not, within itself, necessarily imply freedom from guilt. It is possible for a believer's conscience to be calloused. Paul is saying here, "Insofar as I am capable of knowing, I have a clean conscience. I know more about myself than anyone else knows, and in my own heart I have no knowledge of neglecting my duty. Yet—though I have a clear conscience and know nothing against myself in conduct or practice of life—this does not justify."

We are justified by faith in the shed blood of Jesus Christ, and that is the *only way* a sinner CAN be justified in the sight of God.

"But He that judgeth me is the Lord." Regardless of what the *believers* in Corinth thought about him, regardless of what the *unbelievers* thought about him, and regardless of what he knew about *himself,* Paul confessed, "MY JUDGE IS THE LORD." And He is your judge, and mine. He will judge the living and the dead at His appearing, and He will judge in righteousness. He is the only One who can judge in righteousness. Therefore we are admonished, "Judge nothing before the time."

Verse 5: "Therefore judge nothing before the time, until the Lord come, who both will bring to light the hidden things of darkness, and will make manifest the counsels of the hearts: and then shall every man have praise of God."

Paul is here admonishing believers not to pass judgment upon others, for there will be a season of judgment *when all will be judged* by the Righteous Judge. This

159

refers to the time when the Lord Jesus will come for His saints in the Rapture, as promised in John 14:3 and described in detail in I Thessalonians 4:13—18. The next great event in store for believers is the Rapture of the Church, when living saints will be caught up, changed "in the twinkling of an eye," and the saints who have died will be raised incorruptible, to meet the Lord Jesus in the air. We will sit at the marriage supper in the sky and all believers will be rewarded for their stewardship.

When Jesus comes, He will *"bring to light the hidden things of darkness, and will make manifest the counsels of the hearts."* The "hidden things of darkness" may signify things which darkness holds, or things whose nature is dark. We know that the statement refers to that which has been kept secret in one's life—whether the person's own conscience be ignorant of it, or whether it be purposely kept secret by the individual. These "secret things" our neighbors cannot know or see — but before the eyes of Him who will judge us, *all things* are even now naked and laid open, and at the judgment seat of Christ will be made manifest in their true character: "For there is nothing covered, that shall not be revealed; neither hid, that shall not be known. Therefore whatsoever ye have spoken in darkness shall be heard in the light; and that which ye have spoken in the ear in closets shall be proclaimed upon the housetops" (Luke 12:2,3). The only way to be rid of secret sins is to confess them to Jesus and get them under His atoning blood.

". . . And then shall every man have praise of God." Each individual will receive the praise that is rightfully his, whether it be great or small, much or little. There were those in the church at Corinth who were receiving praise of men, praise that was empty and vain; and in contrast to this, Paul sets the praise *God* will give to each believer. According to verse 4, the Lord Jesus will be the Judge, and the praise will come from God, which

makes it clear that the judgment exercised by the Lord Jesus Christ is in accord with God's judgment.

Verse 6: "And these things, brethren, I have in a figure transferred to myself and to Apollos for your sakes; that ye might learn in us not to think of men above that which is written, that no one of you be puffed up for one against another."

Having stated the principles whereby the local assembly could arrive at the right estimate of Apollos and himself, Paul reminds the believers of the application of these principles to others. The divisions and the party spirit that existed in the Corinthian assembly were due to the inflated regard of the believers for party leaders, and Paul makes a strong appeal against this existing spirit.

"And these things, brethren, I have in a figure transferred to myself and to Apollos . . . ." The Greek word translated *transferred* means "to change in appearance or form." The same verb is used in Philippians 3:21 where it has reference to the transformation of the bodies of believers at the Rapture. The same verb is used in describing the false appearance of Satan and his ministers in II Corinthians 11:13–15.

In our present verse Paul uses it by way of veiled allusion to those who were actually responsible for the factions and divisions in the church. He does this tactfully, not using their names, but naming himself and Apollos only as examples. He was tactful, yet positive, in his instruction. Whatever opinions the believers in Corinth may have formed or expressed about himself and Apollos, it was the unnamed carnal party leaders in whom the divisions and factions had originated and spread among the believers in the assembly.

". . . That ye might learn in us . . . ." That is, "That in us you may find an object lesson which could be applied to the actual conditions in the local church. Paul was using himself and Apollos in an attempt to get

161

the believers to see what was really taking place.

"*. . . Not to think of men above that which is written, that no one of you be puffed up for one against another.*" Paul is probably referring to what has been said in chapter 1, verses 19 through 31, and in chapter 3, verses 19 and 20. He is warning the teachers not to go beyond the terms of the commission intrusted to them. No teacher or preacher has any right to go beyond the light and instruction received from the Word of God—diligently studied, rightly divided, under the leadership of the Holy Spirit. (Read I John 2:27.)

Believers must be on guard at all times against the tendency toward an attachment to some particular person who is a leader in the assembly—one whose natural qualifications and influence make a special appeal to certain individuals and consequently lead to the formation of religious cliques. We have entirely too many such cliques today, where two or three families—sometimes more—band together in the church as in social and business life. This should not be.

We may have a warm spot in our hearts for the person who led us to Jesus or was instrumental in our becoming a Christian. We may have an especially warm affection for some evangelist, Bible teacher, or Sunday school teacher who has proved to be a special and peculiar blessing to us. But such appreciation should not lead us to develop undue estimation of that person's gifts or think of him more highly than we ought. There is grave danger of idolatry in such a practice, and we need to keep our eyes and hearts centered on Jesus Christ. We should give honor to whom honor is due, but individuals bless US only because THEY are blessed of the Lord. Therefore, the glory and honor should be directed to HIM, not to the person who is the vessel through which God works. In the life of a spiritually minded Christian there is no room for a puffed-up spirit.

Verse 7: "For who maketh thee to differ from another? and what hast thou that thou didst not receive? Now if thou didst receive it, why dost thou glory, as if thou hadst not received it?"

". . . *Who maketh thee to differ . . .* ?" The meaning here is to make a distinction as having to do with superiority. Paul is saying here, "Who has given you the superior discriminating power to exalt one believer and disown another, both of whom belong to the same body?" Those who display such a spirit automatically advertise their self-conceit. Certainly the Holy Spirit has nothing to do with such an attitude on the part of a believer.

"*What hast thou that thou didst not receive?*" Even if a believer *does* possess such superiority over another, the gift is from God and therefore self-glory is ruled out. One who is a recipient of blessings and graces bestowed upon him by God should never boast as if he himself were the *source* of blessings and power. Such boasting is nothing less than the extreme height of self-conceit. Such a person may be saved, but he is certainly behaving like a babe in Christ, not as one who has developed spiritually. Paul's testimony was consistently, "I am what I am by the grace of God!"

Verse 8: "Now ye are full, now ye are rich, ye have reigned as kings without us: and I would to God ye did reign, that we also might reign with you."

In this verse Paul passes from the individual and the party leaders, going on to the entire assembly. He proceeds to deal a further blow to the Corinthian vanity, and this of the keenest irony: "*Now ye are full, now ye are rich . . . .*" This phrase would be clearer rendered "*Already* (before the time) ye are full. *Already* (before the time) ye are rich!"

This suggests the premature nature of their supposed fulness and enrichment. They were acting as spiritual kings and giants, capable of teaching and instructing, when what they really needed was that they *themselves* be taught. They were indicating that they *already possessed* the spiritual fulness which can be granted only in the coming day when Christ reigns. At that time we shall indeed be at ease and of the fullest satisfaction. But now is the time to deny self, to take up the cross and follow Jesus. (Compare this with the Lord's rebuke to the Laodiceans described in Revelation 3:17.)

"*. . . Ye have reigned as kings . . . .*" Here Paul is rebuking the believers who were puffed up and acting as though they were already in possession of the fullness of spiritual blessings, as though they were already in the Millennium, *reigning*, instead of being humble stewards and servants of God as they should be in the local church and in the community.

"*. . . Without us . . . .*" Paul places special emphasis on this fact. It was through him that the Corinthians had heard the Gospel message that brought the new birth (verse 15), and Paul here sets about to show them the drastic difference between themselves and the ministers who had brought the Gospel to them—the Gospel through which they had received salvation and spiritual blessings. How foolish they were to imagine *themselves* more favored and exalted than were the servants of God who had brought them the Gospel and whose manner of life had been an example to them!

"*I would to God ye did reign, that we also might reign with you.*" There is no irony or sarcasm in this statement, for Paul truly declares his desire and longing for the time when believers *will* dwell in unity, when the saints *will* reign with Christ, when the knowledge of the Lord will cover the earth as the waters now cover the sea and there will be no schism among the people of God.

Paul declared to the Romans, "If . . . we suffer with Him, that we may be also glorified together"—but the Corinthians were not suffering; they were behaving as kings, not as servants or bondslaves of Christ. II Timothy 2:12 *also* clearly sets forth that reigning with Christ is conditional upon suffering with Him. Paul wanted the believers at Corinth to abandon their pride, conceit, and carnality, and walk in the footsteps of Jesus in the path of suffering. Paul had set the example, but they were not following him.

It will be wonderful just *to be in the kingdom* with Christ, but it will be a higher, happier, and nobler experience to *reign* with Him in His kingdom. Remember, fellow believer, it is altogether possible for a believer to lose his reward. Wood, hay, and stubble will burn; gold, silver, and precious stones will endure. I ask myself, "What kind of works am I sending on before me? Is my stewardship gold, silver, and precious stones? Or is it wood, hay, and stubble?" I want some crowns to cast at the blessed feet of Jesus when we crown Him Lord of all!

Paul Points Out the Apostolic Example of Humility, Patience, and Suffering

Verse 9: "For I think that God hath set forth us the apostles last, as it were appointed to death: for we are made a spectacle unto the world, and to angels, and to men."

". . . *God hath set forth us* . . . ." Here Paul presents himself and his fellow missionaries in contrast with the conceited, self-satisfied members of the assembly at Corinth. To "set forth" literally means "to show forth," and is suggestive of the exhibition of the gladiators in the arena in Rome as the final act of a day of entertainment—that which provided the most thrilling spectacle of the day for the onlookers.

"*As it were appointed unto death* . . ." or "men doomed to death." The Holy Spirit employs the phrase here in describing God's apostles: they were *men doomed to death.*

165

". . . *We are made a spectacle unto the world, and to angels, and to men.*" The word rendered "spectacle" is literally "theatre." While frequently the word is used of a place (a building, or an arena), it is here used of the *persons* exhibited—God's apostles. They were a spectacle "unto the world, and to angels, and to men." The picture set forth here corresponds to the multitudes of spectators who gathered around the arena in the amphitheatres in Rome.

All young men who feel God's call to the ministry and all young women who feel God's call to the mission field should study these verses carefully, ponder them prayerfully, and search deeply into their meaning. Salvation is free—the gift of God; but apostleship is costly and many times calls for much suffering—sometimes to the sealing of a testimony with one's lifeblood.

Verse 10: "We are fools for Christ's sake, but ye are wise in Christ; we are weak, but ye are strong; ye are honourable, but we are despised."

"*We are fools for Christ's sake . . . .*" In this and following statements Paul sets forth in detail the contrast between the true servant of God who suffers because of his stand for the Gospel, and the condition then existing in the assembly at Corinth. The apostles were "fools" on account of Christ and their stand for the Gospel. Because of their preaching and their manner of daily living for Christ, they were looked upon as being stupid, "*fools — for Christ's sake.*" With this verse compare chapter 1:21–23 and II Corinthians 4:11.

". . . *But ye are wise in Christ.*" There is no doubt of the irony in this statement, and of a note of sarcasm. These individuals whom Paul is rebuking were so conceited and filled with self-esteem that even in the virtue of their union with Christ they regarded themselves as possessed of wonderful, extraordinary powers of discernment and wisdom.

166

One who *truly* possesses the wisdom of Christ does not show conceit nor strive for self-glory. The Lord Jesus Christ was the most humble person who ever walked upon the face of this earth, and true believers are admonished to follow in His steps.

"We are weak, but ye are strong . . . ." What Paul is saying is, "We apostles suffer infirmity amidst all we experience in our service for the Lord Jesus Christ, whereas you act with vigor and advertise a 'supposed' spiritual strength." But the Corinthians were deceived. They were neither strong nor wise.

"Ye are honourable, but we are despised" . . . or the literal rendering, "Ye are glorious, but we are without honor." The Word of God declares, "Woe unto you, when all men shall speak well of you" (Luke 6:26). Jesus Christ did not receive honor and glory from all men; the masses rejected Him; only the minority received Him. The same is true with the minister of the Gospel. There are preachers who had rather have the praise of men than to have the honor of God upon their ministry. They choose to compromise and stand in well with the masses rather than to preach the pure Gospel of the grace of God and endure the persecution that comes with such a ministry, even though they are winning souls to the Lord Jesus Christ.

The masses followed Jesus as long as He fed them loaves and fishes, healed their sick, opened the eyes of the blind and raised the dead; but when He fell beneath the cross, it was necessary for the soldiers to compel Simon the Cyrene to bear the cross the rest of the way for Him. The masses have *always* followed the line of least resistance; it is the minority who prove faithful — a friend indeed.

Not all who say "Lord, Lord," will enter heaven; but those who do the will of the heavenly Father; and it is the will of God that we believe on His Son Jesus Christ

167

and put our faith in His finished work and shed blood—not in the ability of men seeking glory and honor from other men.

Verse 11: "Even unto this present hour we both hunger, and thirst, and are naked, and are buffeted, and have no certain dwellingplace."

"*Even unto this present hour . . . .*" Practically this same statement is repeated at the close of verse 13, used there with great emphasis. The time phrase mentioned at the beginning of this verse signifies that Paul *had* suffered and *was suffering*, even as he wrote the epistle to the believers in Corinth.

". . . *We both hunger, and thirst, and are naked, and are buffeted . . . .*" The Greek word translated "naked" literally means "to be scantily clothed," and it is used only *here* in the New Testament.

The word "buffeted" means "to strike with clinched hands, to buffet with fists." The same word is used to describe the treatment given to the Lord Jesus as recorded in Matthew 26:67 and Mark 14:65. It is also used to describe treatment given slaves in I Peter 2:20.

While the believers in Corinth were living as though they were kings—reigning, proud of their honor, power, and glory—Paul was suffering for the sake of the Gospel. While they were boasting and glorying in their wisdom and honor, he was at that time in the same position as that of a slave.

"*And have no certain dwellingplace*" means "to wander about as a vagabond." The meaning is not that of instability, but rather of having no permanent home. Paul had no permanent home on earth — he spent about as much time in a jail cell as he spent in any other place! When he went into a city to conduct services, they did not need to make reservations for him in the hotel or the inn, for he knew that sooner or later he would be spending his nights in jail. Probably no person save the Lord Jesus Christ ever suffered for the sake of the Gospel quite so much as Paul suffered.

Those who suffer for the sake of Christ and the Gospel can claim the promise of God's provision of "some better thing": "And others had trial of cruel mockings and scourgings, yea, moreover of bonds and imprisonment: They were stoned, they were sawn asunder, were tempted, were slain with the sword: they wandered about in sheepskins and goatskins; being destitute, afflicted, tormented; (Of whom the world was not worthy:) they wandered in deserts, and in mountains, and in dens and caves of the earth. And these all, having obtained a good report through faith, received not the promise: *God having provided some better thing for us, that they without us should not be made perfect*" (Heb. 11:36—40).

Verse 12: "And labour, working with our own hands: being reviled, we bless; being persecuted, we suffer it."

". . . *Labour, working with our own hands . . . .*" The Greek word *kopiao* used here is suggestive of "labor that causes weariness." Paul was not simply earning a living — he was undergoing hardship in doing so. In I Thessalonians 2:9 he speaks of "labour and travail . . . labouring night and day." We know that Paul did not work twenty-four hours a day, but his labor was a daily task, continuous—not spasmodic, part-time work—and such labor caused much weariness.

In his youth he had been taught the trade of tentmaking: "And because (Paul) was of the same craft, he abode with them, and wrought: for by their occupation they were tentmakers" (Acts 18:3). The tents were made of goats' hair, and the weaving was hard work. Manual labor was dishonorable and despised among the Greeks; and the fact that Paul did such labor in Corinth caused some misunderstanding among the believers: "Have I committed an offence in abasing myself that ye might be exalted, because I have preached to you the Gospel of God freely?" (II Cor. 11:7). Also read Acts 20:33—35.

The Word of God clearly teaches that the laborer is worthy of his hire (Luke 10:7). "Even so hath the Lord ordained that they which preach the Gospel should live of the Gospel" (I Cor. 9:14). I believe that when it is possible, a church should pay the pastor a living salary in order for him to be free to spend his time looking after the flock—visiting on the field, winning souls in the home, preparing for services in the assembly. But it is a matter of historical record that Paul and his fellow ministers labored to support themselves while they ministered in Corinth. It is not a disgrace for a minister to do secular work or manual labor, even if it is "labor and travail" that brings much weariness, if circumstances render it necessary or advisable in order to further the Gospel and win souls. Paul said, "I become as all men are, that I might win some." We should be willing to follow his example to the glory of God, and for the sake of souls finding Jesus as their Saviour.

"Being reviled, we bless; being persecuted, we suffer it." Because the Greeks considered it a disgrace to do manual labor, they abused the disciples, heaped contempt upon them, and aroused prejudice against them. But Paul and his helpers were acting in conformity with instructions given by the One who had called them, ordained them, and sent them to preach the Gospel:

"But I say unto you, Love your enemies, bless them that curse you, do good to them that hate you, and pray for them which despitefully use you, and persecute you. . . . Love your enemies, do good to them which hate you" (Matt. 5:44 and Luke 6:27).

Verse 13: "Being defamed, we intreat: we are made as the filth of the world, and are the offscouring of all things unto this day."

". . . We intreat . . . ." The Greek word used here has several meanings, but in this instance it seems to signify "to beseech" (not *beg*); to request cessation of

the slander. This humble, gentle way of meeting such treatment is contrary to the flesh and can be practiced only by spiritually minded believers. The flesh cries out, "Fight back! An eye for an eye!" — but the truly spiritual believer, like Stephen, prays, "Lay not this sin to their charge." Such a spirit on the part of an individual finds its source in the grace of God—and ONLY in grace.

"We are made as the filth of the world . . . ." Paul and his co-laborers were regarded as scum, rubbish—the offscouring and refuse of the world. Among the Greeks in Paul's day, such language was applied to victims sacrificed in expiation, and also to describe criminals who were kept at public expense until they could be thrown into the sea or put to death in some other manner. Sacrifices were offered in this manner when there was an outbreak of pestilence, with the thought that it would cleanse away the defilement of the nation. It was in this spirit that the refined, cultured Greeks looked upon Paul and his fellow ministers. The meaning of the Greek language here signifies refuse that must be removed or done away with, and in the eyes of the Greeks Paul and his helpers must be disposed of in one way or another. They were royally hated and despised.

". . . And are the offscouring of all things . . . ." The Greek word used here is a synonym to that rendered "filth," meaning "that which is wiped off or removed from amidst humanity." If the believers in Corinth took Paul's words to heart, the description he gives here must have been a severe rebuke to the self-conceit and pride of those who read the epistle.

". . . Unto this day . . . ." This is a repetition of the statement in verse 11 and emphasizes the fact that Paul at that very moment, while writing the epistle, was suffering persecution and was looked upon as filth.

Verse 14: "I write not these things to shame you,

but as my beloved sons I warn you."

In spite of Paul's sternness in the preceding verses, we see tenderness here. He wanted his children in the faith to enjoy their spiritual birthright, and he knew that as long as they gave way to pride, self-esteem, and conceit, as long as they succumbed to the flesh and the wisdom of the world, as long as they allowed religious cliques and a partisan spirit in the church, they could not have full joy, which was their spiritual birthright.

The New Testament teaches discipline, and discipline is *necessary*; but it should always be carried out in love. The motive should always be for the glory of God, and to the end that those who undergo discipline should come out stronger in the Lord. Disciplinary measures should never be carried out with the spirit of "getting even," and believers who are fully consecrated will not harbor such a spirit.

The Corinthian believers were Paul's children in the Lord, for he had preached the Gospel which led them into the knowledge of salvation. He loved the Corinthian saints as a father loves his children. He knew they were living in God's *second best* while he wanted God's very *best* for them! They were not pleasing God in stewardship.

Verse 15: "For though ye have ten thousand instructers in Christ, yet have ye not many fathers: for in Christ I have begotten you through the Gospel."

The Greek word used here for *instructer* literally means "child leader." The reference here is to the pastor, rather than to the teachers; those who *cared* for the saints, not those who taught them.

Paul was not referring to instructions, but to the *duty* of the pedagogue of the household, who exercised a general supervision over a child. Therefore, the "wise," self-esteemed teachers at Corinth were, after all, nothing more than guardian slaves. If they were true teachers, they were *appointed by God* and they were His bondslaves.

Paul's position, however, was altogether different. A spiritual relationship had been established between the apostle and the saints through the Gospel he had preached to them—the Gospel which they had received, through which they were saved, and in which they were standing (I Cor. 15:1—4).

"For in Christ Jesus I have begotten you through the Gospel." In Galatians 4:19 we read, "My little children, of whom I travail in birth again until Christ be formed in you." The believers in Corinth had received the new birth through Paul's ministry "in Christ Jesus." This expresses spiritual relationship, for all believers are "IN Christ" (Col. 3:3). Notice that in the first part of the verse Paul says, *"in CHRIST,"* but here the name "Jesus" is added, which stresses Paul's living union with the Lord in his ministry. The name "Jesus" means *Saviour:* "And she shall bring forth a son; and thou shalt call His name JESUS: *for He shall save His people from their sins"* (Matt. 1:21).

Verse 16: "Wherefore I beseech you, be ye followers of me."

The meaning here is that Paul wanted the believers in Corinth to feel toward him as a child feels toward its father. He wanted them to follow him as he followed Jesus. He had set an example for them through humble, dedicated living and true Gospel preaching. Study Ephesians 5:1 and Philippians 3:17.

Every minister of the Gospel, whether pastor, evangelist, or missionary, should be an example of the grace of God to the people to whom he ministers. His life should be a living testimony, a living epistle read of men. He should never participate in anything that would bring reproach upon the Gospel or upon the name of Jesus. *Paul was that kind of minister*, and for that reason he could beg his children in the faith to imitate him and follow in his steps, as he followed in the steps of Jesus.

Verse 17: "For this cause have I sent unto you Timotheus, who is my beloved son, and faithful in the Lord, who shall bring you into remembrance of my ways which be in Christ, as I teach every where in every church."

". . . *Timotheus, who is my beloved son . . . .*" Timothy was Paul's son in the Lord, and in relationship stood as did the believers in Corinth insofar as spiritual things were concerned. However, Timothy was a *faithful* son, while the saints at Corinth, even though likewise beloved, were not.

". . . *And faithful in the Lord . . . .*" The phrase "in the Lord" is to be distinguished from "in Christ." *In Christ* points to our heavenly position — we sit together in heavenly places in Christ Jesus (Eph. 2:6), while *in the Lord* denotes His authority over us, and is consequently connected with our circumstances, activities, and relationships on earth. In the first part of Ephesians we find the phrase "in Christ" where our heavenly position is dealt with. In the latter part, which deals with earthly matters, "in the Lord" is prominent (Eph. 4:1,17; 6:1,10, 21). Timothy was Paul's beloved and faithful child in the Lord; he recognized the Lordship of Jesus and was fully surrendered to Him. He followed Jesus, not men, and Paul longed to see the believers in Corinth dedicated to the Lordship of Jesus as Timothy was.

". . . *Who shall bring you into remembrance of my ways which be in Christ . . . .*" It seems that the Corinthians had forgotten the ways in which Paul ministered among them. He had lived the life of a true minister, for Jesus was not only Paul's *Saviour* — He was also Lord of his life; and the Apostle had not evidenced self-conceit, pride, nor worldly wisdom. On the contrary, he had never advertised himself as an outstanding person, but as "the least of the apostles." He had preached Jesus Christ—crucified, buried, risen, ascended, and coming again. Now he was sending Timothy to remind them of these things, and to point out how they were abusing the spirit in which Paul had taught them while he was with them.

". . . *As I teach every where in every church.*" This indicates that Paul was consistent in his preaching wherever he went. (Compare chapter 7:17, 11:16, and 14:33 with this statement.) This assures us that the teaching found in I Corinthians was not directed solely to the church at Corinth, but was also given for OUR admonition, even in this present day.

There Is Such a Thing As Apostolic Authority

Verse 18: "Now some are puffed up, as though I would not come to you."

This testifies that it had been reported to Paul that they were angry, as though he would not visit them for one reason or another, and suggested that at that particular time he was sending Timothy because he dared not visit them himself.

Verse 19: "But I will come to you shortly, if the Lord will, and will know, not the speech of them which are puffed up, but the power."

The Lord willing, Paul's plans were to visit the assembly in Corinth. (Servants of God who obey the Spirit will operate as the Lord leads and go where He directs.) Study Acts 16:7; 18:9; and James 4:15. It was under the authority of the Lord Jesus that the apostles ministered and directed their movements from one assembly to another. But subjection to the Lord in no way enfeebles the conduct of His servant.

". . . *And will know, not the speech of them which are puffed up, but the power.*" Paul had the Holy Spirit dwelling within, and if these who claimed so much were all that they claimed to be, *he would know it*—not through their words, but through the power evidenced in their

175

preaching and exercised in their lives. He would know if they were building gold, silver, and precious stones and bringing forth fruit to the glory of God, or if they were building only wood, hay, and stubble. The true servant of God cannot be confused or confounded (I Pet. 2:6).

Paul's preaching was not in the flesh nor through the wisdom of man: "And my speech and my preaching was not with enticing words of man's wisdom, BUT IN DEMONSTRATION OF THE SPIRIT AND OF POWER" I Cor. 2:4). If these powerful preachers and dynamic leaders were all they claimed to be, Paul would have no trouble seeing it in the results they were producing.

Verse 20: "For the kingdom of God is not in word, but in power."

This is a clear, understandable statement: The energy of the kingdom of God is not external — it is not in words; it is in the heart, *in the inner man.* The activities of the kingdom are produced by and through the Holy Spirit, and *"the fruit of the Spirit* is love, joy, peace, longsuffering, gentleness, goodness, faith, meekness, temperance: against such there is no law" (Gal. 5:22,23).

When one possesses the Holy Spirit, the presence and power of the Spirit will be manifested in the life lived and the activities performed. The essential evidences of a Spirit-controlled life are "righteousness, and peace, and joy in the Holy Ghost" (Rom. 14:17). The fruit of the Holy Spirit is not conceit, pride, vainglory, and self-praise. It is not difficult for a spiritually-minded person to readily recognize another believer who is controlled and permeated by the Spirit; and by the same token it is not difficult to detect a counterfeit profession.

Here Paul uses "the kingdom of God" in a general way, meaning *the realm of God's rule.* Just now, the earth is in rebellion against God; but the sphere in which God rules is acknowledged by individual believers who have entered the kingdom of God by way of the new birth (John 3:3,5). At this present time the kingdom of God "cometh not with observation" (Luke 17:20). The kingdom of God is not made manifest at this time as it will be when Jesus sits on the throne of David in Jerusalem—His King upon His holy hill of Zion (Psalm 2:6). When Jesus sits on the throne in Zion, the kingdom of God on earth will be in glorious and universal manifestation (Matt. 25:31—34; Rev. 11:15).

To be in the kingdom of God at this present time brings reproach, persecution, and suffering (Acts 14:22; II Thess. 1:5). Individual believers who are faithful in bearing the cross and suffering with Christ will share in the eternal reward for endurance and faithfulness (II Tim. 2:12; Rev. 3:21).

In the Gospel of Matthew we read concerning "the kingdom of heaven," literally *the heavens*. The Kingdom of *Heaven* will be upon this earth, as promised to Abraham and Israel. There will be one thousand years of righteous government on earth, and the Church will reign with Christ over the millennial earth.

The Millennium is promised primarily to Israel, and God will keep His promise. When Gabriel announced to Mary that she would bring forth a Son, he also announced that the Son would sit on the throne of His father David in Jerusalem, and this will literally come to pass.

The model prayer given to the disciples in Matthew will no doubt be prayed again in the Kingdom Age here upon this earth. The disciples were taught to pray, "Thy kingdom come, thy will be done in earth, as it is in heaven," and this will literally take place in the future. The Kingdom of *God* is within man, a spiritual kingdom; but the Kingdom of *Heaven* will be here upon this earth for one thousand years during the period of time known as the Millennium.

Verse 21: "What will ye? Shall I come unto you with

a rod, or in love, and in the spirit of meekness?"

"The rod" here stands for rebuke or discipline. *"In love"* conveys the thought of parental love between parent and child. Paul's desire was not to come to the Corinthians with a rod, but that they repent and be obedient Christians so that he could come to them in love: "But we were gentle among you, even as a nurse cherisheth her children" (I Thess. 2:7). It was for them indeed to decide *how* he was to come, for this was the real question — not *whether*, nor *when*, but *HOW:* with a rod, or with love and meekness.

". . . *And in the spirit of meekness.*" The word "meekness" does not signify mildness. It does not indicate that Paul would come to them helpless, or as we would say, a weakling or "jellyfish." He could be severe; he could exercise power; such was the meekness of the Lord Jesus. God is love — but He is also a consuming fire. He is slow to anger — but He is furious in judgment. He calls, He stretches out His hand; but when man refuses to regard the hand of the Lord or hear His call, then God declares, "I also will laugh at your calamity; I will mock when your fear cometh" (Prov. 1:26).

What Paul is saying to the believers in Corinth is, "The decision rests with you as to whether I come to you with a rod, to chasten you as a father would chasten his child, or come in love and meekness. If you will repent and become obedient to the Spirit, then I will come to you as I long to come—in love and meekness; but if you rebel and continue in your disobedience, I have authority from God to bring a rod of chastening, even though I do not desire to do so."

Someone has said that a good undershepherd *feeds* the sheep, *leads* the sheep—and *shears* the sheep. All three procedures are necessary if the flock is to be healthy and profitable. They cannot be fed all the time without being led into green pastures beside the still waters; and if the sheep are only *fed*, they are of no profit, for the shearing yields the wool that pays dividends. "For whom the Lord loveth He chasteneth, and scourgeth every son whom He receiveth" (Heb. 12:6). "Now no chastening for the present seemeth to be joyous, but grievous: nevertheless afterward it yieldeth the peaceable fruit of righteousness unto them which are exercised thereby" (Heb. 12:11).

CHAPTER FIVE

1. It is reported commonly that there is fornication among you, and such fornication as is not so much as named among the Gentiles, that one should have his father's wife.

2. And ye are puffed up, and have not rather mourned, that he that hath done this deed might be taken away from among you.

3. For I verily, as absent in body, but present in spirit, have judged already, as though I were present, concerning him that hath so done this deed,

4. In the name of our Lord Jesus Christ, when ye are gathered together, and my spirit, with the power of our Lord Jesus Christ,

5. To deliver such an one unto Satan for the destruction of the flesh, that the spirit may be saved in the day of the Lord Jesus.

6. Your glorying is not good. Know ye not that a little leaven leaveneth the whole lump?

7. Purge out therefore the old leaven, that ye may be a new lump, as ye are unleavened. For even Christ our passover is sacrificed for us:

8. Therefore let us keep the feast, not with old leaven, neither with the leaven of malice and wickedness; but with the unleavened bread of sincerity and truth.

9. I wrote unto you in an epistle not to company with fornicators:

10. Yet not altogether with the fornicators of this world, or with the covetous, or extortioners, or with idolaters; for then must ye needs go out of the world.

11. But now I have written unto you not to keep company, if any man that is called a brother be a fornicator, or covetous, or an idolater, or a railer, or a drunkard, or an extortioner; with such an one no not to eat.

12. For what have I to do to judge them also that are without? do not ye judge them that are within?

13. But them that are without God judgeth. Therefore put away from among yourselves that wicked person.

Immorality in the Church:
Paul Rebukes the Believers for Lack of Discipline

Paul now begins to deal with the *second* ugly evil

in the assembly at Corinth. There is no doubt that the divided condition which existed in the church had been influential in creating the careless attitude the believers had taken toward the gross sin and ugly conduct of one of their own members. Pride and self-importance lay at the root of these evils in the church.

Paul again reminds them that they are "puffed up." He was leading up to the mention of this terrible sin in the church when he spoke of the *rod* in verse 21 of chapter 4, trusting and hoping that they would do something about it before he arrived in Corinth. The fact that they had allowed such an ugly case of immorality to occur in the church was grave enough, but their attitude toward this terrible sin and those who had committed it made matters much worse! Paul is here reminding them that they must immediately take the necessary steps to correct this situation, even in his absence.

Verse 1: "It is reported commonly that there is fornication among you, and such fornication as is not so much as named among the Gentiles, that one should have his father's wife."

"It is reported commonly . . ." — or, "It is *actually* reported." This existing sin in the church was "commonly reported"—that is, seemingly everyone knew about it. The Greek wording suggests that it was not only reported *to Paul*, but was talked about among the members of the assembly. At any rate, it was well known that fornication was being practiced by one of the members of the Corinthian church and was the subject of conversation among other believers. This should not be in the Church. "But fornication, and all uncleanness, or covetousness, let it not be once named among you, as becometh saints" (Eph. 5:3).

". . . And such fornication as is not so much as named among the Gentiles, that one should have his father's wife." From the verb "have" (which in the original is "hath"), it appears that this relationship had been entered

181

into as something permanent and lasting, as though those who were guilty of fornication were not just guilty of an *act*, but were *united*, as in marriage. Some Bible authorities suggest that II Corinthians 7:12 indicates that the father was still living:

"Wherefore, though I wrote unto you, I did it not for his cause that had done the wrong, *nor for his cause that suffered wrong*, but that our care for you in the sight of God might appear unto you."

The fact that the word "fornication" is used, and not "*adultery*," suggests that there had been a separation or a divorce. Paul does not mention the woman involved; he speaks only of the man. Evidently the woman was not a member of the assembly, but was one of "those without, whom God judgeth" (verse 13). The act referred to here was forbidden—not only by the law of Moses, but also by Roman law.

"The nakedness of thy father's wife shalt thou not uncover: it is thy father's nakedness" (Lev. 18:8).

"A man shall not take his father's wife, nor discover his father's skirt" (Deut. 22:30).

There are instances where the natural conscience of an unregenerated person is more sensitive and acts on a higher moral level than the *seared* conscience of a carnal believer. There is only one possible way to explain what had happened in this case — and I offer this explanation as a *suggestion*, not a fact: If the one guilty of fornication had taken "his father's wife," it is only reasonable to suppose that the woman was not the boy's own mother, but his stepmother. I further suggest that the father of the man who was guilty of fornication had probably married a woman much younger than himself, and the son had stolen the affection of his stepmother. Evidently when the father discovered this illicit affair between his wife and his own son, he divorced the woman and the son then took her. *Whatever* had happened was well known in the church, but the assembly had done nothing about it and Paul was disturbed beyond measure when it was made known to him. He gave definite instruction concerning the matter.

Indifference to Evil in the Church Was the Result of Divisions

Verse 2: "And ye are puffed up, and have not rather mourned, that he that hath done this deed might be taken away from among you."

"And ye are puffed up, and have not rather mourned . . . ." The assembly at Corinth was in a sad spiritual state indeed. They were self-complacent and proud, they were wise in their own eyes, self-willed and conceited; and these factors had brought about such carnality in their thinking that the scandal in their midst had not only wrought terrible damage among outsiders, but had also damaged *the entire assembly!* Yet this had not disturbed them. They were "puffed up," they had not mourned, their consciences were calloused and seared and they could not realize the seriousness of this sin that existed among them. What had happened was to the destruction of God's glory in the church.

Where such sin is known and unjudged it is plain that the Holy Ghost is either ignored or forgotten; for no believer will deliberately say that he is a partner to iniquity— and *this he must be* if evil is known and unjudged in the church where Christ dwells.

The Laodicean spirit of self-satisfaction was prevalent in the church at that time: "Because thou sayest, I am rich, and increased with goods, and have need of nothing; and knowest not that thou art wretched, and miserable, and poor, and blind, and naked" (Rev. 3:17). Such a spirit in any assembly will result in evil and the loss of spiritual power and effective testimony.

". . . *He that hath done this deed might be taken away from among you.*" It is suggested here that if the assembly had judged this evil as they should have done, if they had mourned as they should have and had the proper attitude toward this sin, the erring one might have been removed by divine judgment—and if *not* by divine judgment, then certainly they themselves would have removed him from among their number. But because of their laxity in spiritual things, they had done absolutely nothing about the situation beyond making it the subject of conversation throughout the assembly and possibly the entire community.

Verse 3: "For I verily, as absent in body, but present in spirit, have judged already, as though I were present, concerning him that hath so done this deed."

Here we see Paul's deep concern about this matter. He could not be present in body, but he was there in spirit and had already judged in his own heart what he *would have done* had he been there in person. Certainly the situation would have been dealt with in the very beginning. Any dear minister who knowingly covers and condones sin in his congregation is not doing what the Lord would have him do as laid down in the Word of God.

There are instances where known sin is being practiced by members of the church, but rather than hurt or offend anyone or cause the guilty party—and probably his family and friends—to leave the church, the pastor allows the practice to go on and on, unjudged. Sin in the local assembly is to be dealt with immediately—and if the person leaves the church, even if other influential members leave *with* him, the church is far better off, because, as we will learn in verse 6 of this chapter, "*a little leaven leaveneth the whole lump!*"

Paul was deeply concerned because his children in the faith had been so lax and unconcerned about so grave a matter. He loved the believers in all the churches which God had used him to establish; he loved to rejoice with

them, and to know that *they* were rejoicing: "For though
I be absent in the flesh, yet am I with you in the spirit,
joying and beholding your order, and the stedfastness
of your faith in Christ" (Col. 2:5).

Verse 4: "In the name of our Lord Jesus Christ,
when ye are gathered together, and my spirit, with the
power of the Lord Jesus Christ."

"In the name of our Lord Jesus Christ . . . ." Not
in the name of *the Lord*, nor in the name of *Jesus*, but
"in the name of our Lord Jesus Christ." When the Son
of God is thus named, the name is indicative of character.
For instance, John 17:6 speaks of His *rank*, Hebrews 1:4
speaks of His *power*, John 17:11 and 12 speak of His
authority, and the same is true in this present reference.
Here "the Lord Jesus" is associated with both the gathering together of the saints in the assembly, and "to deliver
such a one unto Satan." Paul is instructing the church
at Corinth to call a meeting – and personally, I think the
suggestion is that they call a special meeting to deal
with this matter *immediately.*

*". . . When ye are gathered together, and my spirit,
with the power of our Lord Jesus Christ . . . ."* This
statement indicates that the Apostle Paul, in his capacity
as the anointed minister of Almighty God, was endowed
with special authority in such a matter; but the one essential was that it must be done both on the *authority*
of the Lord Jesus Christ, and also by His *power.* (Notice
that the verse begins, "In the NAME of our Lord Jesus
Christ," and ends with "the POWER of our Lord Jesus
Christ.")

Paul, being the founder of the Corinthian church,
used of God to bring these people into the knowledge of
salvation, had the authority to send the urgent declaration
that this matter be attended to immediately—but *only in the*

name of the Lord Jesus Christ and through the *power* of the Lord Jesus Christ.

Verse 5: "To deliver such an one unto Satan for the destruction of the flesh, that the spirit may be saved in the day of the Lord Jesus."

The statement *"to deliver such an one unto Satan"* means simply to put the offender out of the local assembly and place him in the sphere of the world, among "those who are without," where God's authority is not acknowledged and where Satan is "the god of this world." This would seem to suggest severe physical affliction. If flesh had been indulged shamelessly, flesh must be galled and broken to pieces under the adversary's hand, but for good at any rate — *"that the spirit may be saved."*

It seems clear that in the day of the Apostle Paul these men who had been specially appointed by God during the transition period actually did have such gifts of apostolic authority, to deliver the offender to Satan (I Tim. 4:14). "Of whom is Hymenaeus and Alexander; whom I have delivered unto Satan, that they may learn not to blaspheme" (I Tim. 1:20).

I have often said that the number-one desire of Satan is to damn every individual he possibly can; but if that individual is born again, then the adversary is ever seeking to destroy the testimony of the child of God. He does this through tempting the believer to turn aside from the right ways of the Lord, and embrace the things of the flesh. The devil is a master craftsman in the art of laying snares for believers.

"Moreover he must have a good report of them which are without; lest he fall into *reproach and the snare* of the devil" (I Tim. 3:7).

"And that they may recover themselves out of the

snare of the devil, who are taken captive by him at his will" (II Tim. 2:26).

The Corinthian assembly was to deliver to Satan the one guilty of fornication, "FOR THE DESTRUCTION OF THE FLESH." The Greek word used here is *olethros*, which means *"ruin"*—not destruction or total annihilation. The word means the ruin of well-being, ruin insofar as the *purpose* of what is referred to is concerned. Such ruin and destruction is definitely the work of Satan, but in a case such as that under discussion here, God *permits* it as an act of judgment upon the unfaithful believer.

There are some who teach that this verse has to do with the destruction of the soul and spirit, and thus such a person would be lost forever: but it is very clear that the *destruction* referred to here has nothing to do with eternal life nor with the spiritual part of the believer:

". . . *That the spirit may be saved in the day of the Lord Jesus."* Jesus said to Nicodemus, ". . . That which is born of the Spirit is spirit" (John 3:6b). Such a person as the young man described here, guilty of taking his father's wife, can be turned over to Satan for the destruction of the flesh (the body), but the soul and spirit are not affected; and in the resurrection such a person will have a glorified body, as will all believers. Satan is never allowed to touch the soul of a born again, blood-washed believer!

". . . *The day of the Lord Jesus"* is the period immediately after the Rapture of the Church. Each believer will appear at the judgment seat of Christ to receive a reward for things done in the body: "So then every one of us shall give account of himself to God" (Rom. 14:12). "For we must all appear before the judgment seat of Christ; that every one may receive the things done in his body, according to that he hath done, whether it be good or bad" (II Cor. 5:10).

"If any man see his brother sin a sin which is not unto death, he shall ask, and he shall give him life for them that sin not unto death. There is a sin unto death: I do not say that he shall pray for it" (I John 5:16).

The *sin unto death* is committed by believers. (This is the death of the *body*, not of the soul.) The *unpardonable sin* is committed by unbelievers (Matt. 12:31,32). Any person who blasphemes the Holy Spirit cannot be forgiven—either in this life or in the life to come; but a believer who commits the sin unto death will be destroyed *physically* and saved spiritually. He will, of course, suffer great loss of reward, but his spirit will be saved "in the day of the Lord Jesus." There are well-meaning born again people who refuse to accept this Bible fact. Nevertheless, it is clearly set forth in our present verse—and anyone who refuses to receive this truth does so simply because he has a closed mind and is married to a denomination or a religion, instead of obeying the Spirit, rightly dividing the Word, and allowing the Word of God to speak while man keeps silent.

Verse 6: "Your glorying is not good. Know ye not that a little leaven leaveneth the whole lump?"

"*Your glorying is not good.*" This points back to verse 2, where Paul reminds the Corinthians that they are "puffed up." They have no right to *glory*; they have nothing whereof TO glory. With the Corinthian church in the state it was in at the time of the writing of this epistle, the believers there should have been *weeping*, they should have been on their faces before God, repenting in sackcloth and ashes, instead of reigning as kings, advertising their own wisdom and glorying in their own ability.

"*Know ye not . . . .*" This statement is used in

I Corinthians 3:16, it is used five times in chapter 6 and twice in chapter 9. These believers had advertised their wisdom, but in action they demonstrated gross ignorance concerning spiritual matters, and utter lack of the wisdom that comes from God.

"Know ye not that a little leaven leaveneth the whole lump?" The stress is on "little." A very small amount of leaven spreads through a very large lump. In the same way, a seemingly small sin will continue to grow until it becomes very great; and that is what had happened in the assembly at Corinth. They had allowed *little* things to go unjudged—things such as jealousy, envy, conceit, partisan spirit—until now the leaven had grown into the gross immoral sin of fornication.

Writing to the Galatians, Paul uses the same statement: "A little leaven leaveneth the whole lump" (Gal. 5:9). In the Old Testament, leaven is referred to many times. In the New Testament we are told that leaven is symbolic of the power of evil: "Then understood they how that (Jesus) bade them not beware of the leaven of *bread,* but of the *doctrine of the Pharisees and of the Sadducees"* (Matt. 16:12). The first reference to leaven in the Bible is found in Genesis 19:3, where Lot served *unleavened bread* to his heavenly guests.

Verse 7: "Purge out therefore the old leaven, that ye may be a new lump, as ye are unleavened. For even Christ our passover is sacrificed for us."

The reference here is to the Jewish household that was commanded to remove all leaven from the house in preparation for the Passover (Ex. 12:18—20 and 13:6,7). Removing all leaven from Jewish homes in preparation for the Passover signified that they had completely broken with the old manner of life in Egypt, and that their entrance upon the new life was designed to enjoy the fellowship that only God could give. The Jewish family who refused to obey that command and remove all leaven from the home could not enjoy the fellowship with God that could be theirs when they *obeyed* His command.

Paul is here attempting to show the believers in Corinth that if they refused to remove the leaven from the assembly, they could not expect the blessings of God upon either the fellowship or the testimony of the church there. The assembly at Corinth was NOT an unleavened assembly; evil existed there, and that evil must be put away if they hoped to experience the blessings of God and enjoy *fellowship* with God—blessings and fellowship that were theirs if they would only humble their hearts, repent of their carnality, and deal with the fornicator within their membership.

"For even Christ our passover is sacrificed for us." The literal Greek reads, "For our passover also hath been sacrificed, even Christ." The Greek word for Passover used here is *pascha*, the same word used in Matthew 26:2 of the Passover Feast. It is used frequently in John's Gospel; also in Acts 12:4 and in Hebrews 11:28. The Passover Lamb is Christ Himself, and the original language places great emphasis upon the word *"Christ."* The Greek verb is in the past tense, indicating a definite act *already performed*, with abiding results. The Passover Lamb, without spot or blemish, "HATH BEEN SACRIFICED."

Verse 8: "Therefore let us keep the feast, not with old leaven, neither with the leaven of malice and wickedness; but with the unleavened bread of sincerity and truth."

"Therefore let us keep the feast . . . ." *Heortazo*, translated "let us keep the feast," denotes the keeping of a festival. This is the only place where the word is found in the New Testament. It does not refer to the

Lord's Supper, nor does it refer to the Passover Feast. It points to "THE CONTINUOUS LIFE OF THE BORN AGAIN BELIEVER"—(the tense is present, *continuous*). It is important to realize that this does not mean only at the table of the Lord on Sunday, but every day. The seven days of the Jewish feast take in every day of the week and represent our whole Christian sojourn here on earth.

". . . *Not with old leaven, neither with the leaven of malice and wickedness.*" The statement "old leaven" is repeated from verse 7 and emphasizes the importance of purging ourselves, keeping ourselves free from moral and spiritual corruption. There might be new forms of evil besides those of old habits and associations. "Leaven" also symbolizes malice and wickedness.

"Malice" means *badness*, or anything that is vicious and injurious. Malice and wickedness together embrace anything that is displeasing to God, anything that pollutes the spirit and the soul, or blinds the spiritual mind and intelligence and proves to be detrimental to our stewardship and service for the Lord.

"*But with the unleavened bread of sincerity and truth.*" The Greek word used for "sincerity" here means "unalloyed, pure." It was used to describe an unmixed, singular substance without a trace of anything added. The Greek word used here for "truth" means "that which is consistent with reality." Therefore, the exhortation here having to do with our manner of life is based on two facts:

First, that sin, like leaven, will impart its nature to all with which it comes in contact. Therefore we must not allow it to come in contact with our lives. We must totally abstain from leaven in the spiritual sense.

In the second place, that the sacrifice of the Lamb

of God, without spot or blemish, demands and commands the believer to put away evil out of his life and have no part of anything that is evil.

The clear teaching is simply this: Regardless of how little or insignificant sin may seem, if it is allowed to come into our lives it will grow and continue to grow until it "leavens the whole lump." If we are born again and Jesus Christ is our Lord, the very fact that He has saved us and has become Lord of our lives demands that we put away all evil. We are commanded to abstain from the very *appearance* of evil, and to have no fellowship with the unfruitful works of darkness, but rather reprove them. We are commanded to love not the world, neither the things that are IN the world. We are admonished to seek first the kingdom of God and His righteousness, to present our bodies a living sacrifice, and *whatsoever we do*, we are to do it ALL to the glory of God! Since Jesus purchased us at the tremendous price of His own blood, and since He is Lord of our lives, *He has a right* to command us. It is ours to obey — and if we refuse, we will suffer loss.

Verse 9: "I wrote unto you in an epistle not to company with fornicators."

The important thing in this verse is the injunction against friendly company with fornicators on the part of the believers.

Verse 10: "Yet not altogether with the fornicators of this world, or with the covetous, or extortioners, or with idolaters; for then must ye needs go out of the world."

"Yet not altogether with the fornicators of this world . . . ." In this statement Paul makes it clear that they were not to keep company with fornicators under any circumstance. They were to withdraw themselves from the company of such—both in the assembly and out of it.

"The world" here stands for mankind—human society in contrast with believers. Born again people are children of God, strangers and pilgrims here, and this world is not our home. Even now we sit together in heavenly places in Christ Jesus. *Our* citizenship is in heaven; the citizenship of *unbelievers* is on earth. Believers are IN the world, but not OF the world. Unbelievers are in the world—and *they* are OF the world.

"*. . . Or with the covetous, or extortioners, or with idolaters . . . .*" The believers at Corinth were not to keep company with covetous people, extortioners, and idol worshippers. The Greek word rendered "covetous" means "*desiring to have and possess more* in an evil sense," and would apply to individuals who were greedy of gain and whose aim in life was governed by selfishness; those who desired to take advantage of others in order to bring gain to themselves.

Extortioners and idolaters are dealt with much more fully in chapters 8 and 10. Idolatry embraces much more than bowing down to a stone god. We will go into the deeper meaning of that practice later in our study.

"*. . . For then must ye needs go out of the world.*" The instruction given here has to do with fellowshipping *in the assembly* with idolaters, extortioners, and covetous people. However, to totally abstain from meeting these people they "must needs go out of the world" — that is, they would have to cease from all communication with unbelievers. What Paul is saying here is that it is not against spiritual living nor harmful to a good testimony for a Christian to deal with unbelievers *insofar as business and society are concerned,* so long as the standards of righteousness and dedicated spiritual living are upheld; but it IS wrong to bring these people into the assembly, or to knowingly allow them to remain there.

Believers must of necessity mix and mingle with society; if we participate in community affairs—many of which are honorable though not Christian—we will be associated with unbelievers. We cannot entirely divorce ourselves from such association, but we certainly are not to receive unbelievers into the local church and fellowship with them in a personal way if they are known to be fornicators, covetous, extortioners, or idolaters. The leaven must be purged from the assembly.

Verse 11: "But now I have written unto you not to keep company, if any man that is called a brother be a fornicator, or covetous, or an idolater, or a railer, or a drunkard, or an extortioner; with such an one no not to eat."

"But now I have written unto you." We have the same statement in verse 9. Paul may be referring to a former letter, or it is possible that he is referring to statements made in the earlier chapters of *this* letter.

"... *Not to keep company* ...." No one need misunderstand Paul's instructions here. What he is saying is simply this: "Anyone who professes to be a believer yet does not bear the fruit of the Spirit, by the ungodly character of his life disqualifies himself as a Christian brother."

"... *If any man that is called a brother be a fornicator, or covetous, or an idolater, or a railer, or a drunkard, or an extortioner* ...." Notice that Paul adds two characters to those given in verse 10—*railers* and *drunkards*. A railer (reviler) is a person who habitually uses abusive, violent language against another individual. Believers are not to keep company with such a person. The same is true of drunkards.

"With such an one no not to eat." Paul is here emphasizing the admonition given in previous verses. It is not the Lord's Supper that Paul is referring to. The Co-

194

rinthian Christians were not to invite these people into their homes for fellowship around the table, nor were they to *accept* social invitations from those who behaved in such manner. Such fellowship would serve as a practical acknowledgment of mere profession—a condoning of the evil life—and would identify the believer with it.

If a spiritually minded person visited an idolater for the specific and sole purpose of *witnessing* to him, that would be different from inviting the person for dinner in the home or for a social visit. Trying to win such people to Jesus through witnessing to them is not the point under consideration here, but simply fellowshipping socially, either in the home or in the assembly. Certainly Christians should do anything and all things honorably possible in an attempt to win even the most wicked person to Jesus. Paul said, "I become as all men are, that I might win some." He did not mean that he compromised by participating in their evil ways, but rather that he was willing to make any sacrifice by way of pointing people to Christ.

In my evangelistic campaigns I have often suggested that believers invite their unsaved loved ones and neighbors into the home for dinner, with the understanding that they would all attend the evangelistic services that evening; and there have been instances where this has resulted in unbelievers being saved. Certainly this is not against spiritual thinking or spiritual living; but to mix socially with unbelievers just for the sake of social contact is poor testimony.

Verse 12: "For what have I to do to judge them also that are without? Do not ye judge them that are within?"

What Paul is asking is, "What have I to do with judging them who are unbelievers, unregenerate?" In connection with this please read Mark 4:11, Colossians 4:5,

I Thessalonians 4:12, and I Timothy 3:7.

Through this statement Paul makes it clear to the believers at Corinth that he did not mean for them to avoid unbelievers to such extent that they refused to even be in company with them, for it would be utterly impossible to live in this world and NOT come in contact with unsaved people—in some instances the *vilest* of them; but we need not fellowship with them in their social events nor take part in their activities, in the home or otherwise. Christians should keep company with unbelievers only so long as they are attempting to point them to Jesus and through holy lives influence them to become believers.

"Do not ye judge them that are within?" This speaks of believers—children of God—as distinct and separate from the world. The assembly is responsible for those whom it receives, and if fellowship needs to be withdrawn from one of its members, the assembly is responsible for taking action and *excluding* that person from fellowship. Paul is simply pointing out the believer's responsibility in such cases.

Verse 13: "But them that are without God judgeth. Therefore put away from among yourselves that wicked person."

Those that are without (the unbelievers) are not under the jurisdiction of church judgment. God will deal with them in due time. The assembly is responsible only for the conduct of those who are *members* of the assembly. If one member so lives as to bring reproach upon the name of Jesus and upon the Gospel, *the entire assembly will suffer*; and if there is such a person in the church (like the young man who was guilty of fornication), it is the grave responsibility of the assembly to deal with that individual; and if they do not fulfill their duty, God will hold them accountable for that very fact.

GOD judges the unbeliever. We know that "whatsoever a man soweth, that shall he also reap." We know that "the wages of sin is death." (The final and complete wages of sin is *eternal* death.) This is clearly pointed out in the account of the Great White Throne Judgment when unbelievers will be judged, as recorded in Revelation 20.

"THEREFORE put away from among yourselves that wicked person." The Greek word translated "wicked" is *poneros.* It not only signifies that the person has bad character, but that he is also having a bad influence upon others. The case in question here is a sad one, because the young man guilty of fornication is not only destroying his own testimony — he is also destroying the testimony of the entire assembly insofar as "those who are without" are concerned. They would eventually lose all respect for the Church if this fornicator were allowed to continue in fellowship while he still lived in gross sin.

The quotation is from Deuteronomy 17:7, which commanded the punishment of death for idolatry and disobedience to parents: "The hands of the witnesses shall be first upon him to put him to death, and afterward the hands of all the people. So thou shalt put the evil away from among you." In Deuteronomy 21:21 we read, "And all the men of his city shall stone him with stones, that he die: so shalt thou put evil away from among you; and all Israel shall hear, and fear." In the local church a born again believer is not only a member of that assembly — he is also a member of the body of Christ; and his fellowship with God's people depends upon his fellowship *with God.* Those outside the Church—unbelievers, unregenerate—are referred to throughout the Bible as spiritually *dead.* Therefore, the believer who is excommunicated through true Bible discipline is placed in the company of the spiritually dead—until he repents or until the Lord removes him through physical death.

In the days when Israel was under law, a person could not be put to death except upon the testimony of two or three witnesses: "At the mouth of two witnesses, or three witnesses, shall he that is worthy of death be put to death; but at the mouth of one witness he shall not be put to death" (Deut. 17:6).

This indicates that in such cases, those who are responsible for chastening a person guilty of sin must be extremely careful. Those in authority in the assembly—the pastor, the deacons—must be careful in discipline because the believer who has erred and brought reproach upon the Church *is still a believer;* he is still a child of God, a member of the body of Christ. Discipline should therefore be carried out with but one end in view: To restore the erring one to fellowship—not to destroy him!

Grave responsibility rests upon the shoulders of a pastor. If he condones evil in the church, *he* will suffer and *the cause of Christ* will suffer; but if he mistreats a believer—either for selfish reasons or with the spirit of "getting even"—that minister will himself suffer for his ugly, un-Christian actions. The pastor should never knowingly allow sin to remain in the assembly.

Evil detected in the assembly calls for deep humiliation before God, on the part of the pastor *and* the entire church. Every member should seek God's face and know His will concerning the matter. We have the solemn warning that "a little leaven leaveneth the whole lump," and when evil is recognized in the assembly it is extremely important that corrective steps be taken immediately.

Paul was gravely concerned about the church at Corinth. These were his children in the faith and he loved them tenderly; but he could not allow the ugly sin that was in the church to continue. He wrote in love—but also in sternness, demanding that something be done immediately, even in his absence, to put a stop to this terrible thing that was going on in the assembly.

CHAPTER SIX

1. Dare any of you, having a matter against another, go to law before the unjust, and not before the saints?

2. Do ye not know that the saints shall judge the world? and if the world shall be judged by you, are ye unworthy to judge the smallest matters?

3. Know ye not that we shall judge angels? how much more things that pertain to this life?

4. If then ye have judgments of things pertaining to this life, set them to judge who are least esteemed in the church.

5. I speak to your shame. Is it so, that there is not a wise man among you? no, not one that shall be able to judge between his brethren?

6. But brother goeth to law with brother, and that before the unbelievers.

7. Now therefore there is utterly a fault among you, because ye go to law one with another. Why do ye not rather take wrong? Why do ye not rather suffer yourselves to be defrauded?

8. Nay, ye do wrong, and defraud, and that your brethren.

9. Know ye not that the unrighteous shall not inherit the kingdom of God? Be not deceived: neither fornicators, nor idolaters, nor adulterers, nor effeminate, nor abusers of themselves with mankind,

10. Nor thieves, nor covetous, nor drunkards, nor revilers, nor extortioners, shall inherit the kingdom of God.

11. And such were some of you: but ye are washed, but ye are sanctified, but ye are justified in the name of the Lord Jesus, and by the Spirit of our God.

12. All things are lawful unto me, but all things are not expedient: all things are lawful for me, but I will not be brought under the power of any.

13. Meats for the belly, and the belly for meats: but God shall destroy both it and them. Now the body is not for fornication, but for the Lord; and the Lord for the body.

14. And God hath both raised up the Lord, and will also raise up us by his own power.

15. Know ye not that your bodies are the members of Christ? Shall I then take the members of Christ, and make them the members of an harlot? God forbid.

16. What? know ye not that he which is joined to an harlot is one body? for two, saith he, shall be one flesh.

17. But he that is joined unto the Lord is one spirit.

18. Flee fornication. Every sin that a man doeth is without the body; but he that committeth fornication sinneth against his own body.

19. What? know ye not that your body is the temple of the Holy Ghost which is in you, which ye have of God, and ye are not your own?

20. For ye are bought with a price: therefore glorify God in your body, and in your spirit, which are God's.

Believers Should Never Go to Law Against Each Other

Paul now deals with a third evil in the Corinthian church—the evil of born again believers going to law against each other before Gentile courts which were made up of unbelievers. The practice of appealing to the courts of law had existed before the Gospel reached Corinth, and that practice still prevailed. Paul rebuked the Corinthian Christians for seeking to obtain judgment from men who, being judges in the world's courts, had no place in the assembly (verse 4). In consequence, there was a loss of spiritual power and a weakening of Christian testimony.

What these disputes were, we are not told; but we do know that they were petty in nature and could easily have been taken care of in the church if the love of God had prevailed. This is quite evident from what Paul says in verse 2: ". . . Are ye unworthy to judge the smallest matters?" In chapter 5, verse 12, he makes reference to judgment, and in chapter 6 he discusses the rules that believers should follow in such matters.

For Christians to appeal to the law courts of the land to settle a dispute *between Christians* was unscriptural—and still is. Born again believers should settle their differences in the church—not in courts of law. When trouble arises between two born again people in the church, those in authority should appoint a committee—in most cases the deacons or stewards—who would attempt in Christian love to settle any differences that exist between them.

Paul tells the Corinthian believers who were going to law one with another that it would be much better to be defrauded than to bring reproach upon the Church, or cause those *outside the Church* to lose respect for the children of God.

It is altogether understandable that born again believers may differ with each other, and they may even come to the place where they will need someone to help them *settle* their differences; but they should never go before a judge and seek legal settlement in the courts of the world where the grace of God is not known.

Paul wants the Corinthian believers to remember the life from which they had been delivered through the grace of God. They were to remember *what they had been*, in contrast to what they had *become* through God's grace, and live consistently—before the Church and before the world—knowing that the grace of God is sufficient to meet any and every need of the believer, regardless of what or how serious those needs may be.

Nothing can happen between born again brethren that could not be settled in prayer and by the Scriptures, through proper counsel and advice from qualified, spiritually minded persons. The believer is complete in Jesus, God's grace is sufficient, and we therefore need not look to the world or to the unregenerate for *anything*. May God help us to hear Paul's instructions and take them to heart.

Verse 1: "Dare any of you, having a matter against another, go to law before the unjust, and not before the saints?"

The Greek verb used here for "dare" means "bringing one's self to do anything." It has the same meaning as set forth in Romans 5:7. Paul is saying in simple language, "Is it possible that believers could bring themselves to the point of going to law against each other? It is absurd to think such a thing!"

Paul speaks in the singular here, but verse 6 in this same chapter clearly teaches that many were going to law one against the other; it was not just a singular instance. Even one such lawsuit would have been bad enough, but a *multiplicity* of such cases was outrageous and unthinkable among those who knew the grace of God.

". . . *Having a matter against another* . . . ." "*A matter*" is translated from the Greek word *pragma*, which carries with it the sense of a lawsuit. The Greek verb *krino* is translated "go to law," and means "the effort to get a judgment passed."

"*The unjust*" does not suggest that it would be impossible to obtain *a just verdict* in a court of law. The Apostle's own experience had proved differently: "And when Gallio was the deputy of Achaia, the Jews made insurrection with one accord against Paul, and brought him to the judgment seat, saying, This fellow persuadeth men to worship God contrary to the law. And when Paul was now about to open his mouth, Gallio said unto the Jews, If it were a matter of wrong or wicked lewdness, O ye Jews, reason would that I should bear with you: But if it be a question of words and names, and of your law, look ye to it; for I will be no judge of such matters. And he drave them from the judgment seat" (Acts 18:12–16).

Paul infers that it is simply unreasonable and absurd that one believer should attempt to get judgment against another believer in a Gentile court. Brothers in Christ should be able to settle their differences without going before the unrighteous to do so. It is a sinful disgrace when believers must hire lawyers and go to court against each other in order to settle their differences.

If an assembly is what it should be, there are no differences that could arise between two born again believers that could not be settled in the church if each believer involved were willing to obey the Lord and follow the Spirit. It certainly is a poor testimony for the Church and for Jesus Christ when two of God's children go to an unbeliever, a child of the devil, for help in settling their differences!

Verse 2: "Do ye not know that the saints shall judge the world? And if the world shall be judged by you, are ye unworthy to judge the smallest matters?"

"Do ye not know . . . ?" In this verse we are reminded of the high calling of believers, which calling the assembly at Corinth had failed to realize. If they had known it previously, they had become so carnal and careless as to forget that they were sons of God, possessors of the Holy Spirit, members of the body of Christ, having the mind of Christ in the Spirit.

". . . The saints shall judge the world . . . ." Paul is speaking here of the time when the Church will reign with Christ in the Millennium. The actual authority to judge will be given to faithful believers at that time — but only the faithful who have taken the cross and followed Jesus, confessing Him and suffering with Him, will receive this grand and glorious privilege:

"If we suffer, we shall also reign with Him: if we deny Him, He also will deny us" (II Tim. 2:12).

"And Jesus said unto them, Verily I say unto you, That ye which have followed me, in the regeneration when the Son of man shall sit in the throne of His glory, ye also shall sit upon twelve thrones, judging the twelve tribes of Israel" (Matt. 19:28).

The promise is to the overcomer—the believer who works diligently and untiringly to the glory of God; the believer who is willing to suffer and bear the reproach that goes with cross-bearing. It is to this faithful one that the promise is made: "And he that overcometh, and keepeth my works unto the end, to him will I give power over the nations" (Rev. 2:26). "And I saw thrones, and they sat upon them, and judgment was given unto them: and I saw the souls of them that were beheaded for the witness of Jesus, and for the Word of God, and which had not worshipped the beast, neither his image, neither had received his mark upon their foreheads, or in their hands; and they lived and reigned with Christ a thousand years" (Rev. 20:4).

Such glorious promises should stimulate and inspire us, and cause us to rejoice even in the face of temptation and persecution, "looking unto Jesus the author and finisher of our faith," He who endured such contradiction of sinners, who resisted unto blood striving against sin; who was tempted in all points as we are, yet without sin.

"*. . . If the world shall be judged by you, are ye unworthy to judge the smallest matters?*" What Paul is saying is that compared with the circumstances of the Millennial Age when the saints will reign with Christ here upon this earth and will judge with the righteous Judge, the small matters that concerned the Corinthian Christians at that particular time were insignificant. If the saints are to judge the world during the reign of Christ, surely they should be able to settle earthly matters among themselves now. In the light of the position of the saints in eternity, we should even now be able to give a true estimate of matters relating to our earthly life.

Then, too, we have the Holy Spirit to guide us. It is a grand and glorious opportunity to be a child of God, but it is also a grave responsibility; and we must give an account to God for the way in which we conduct ourselves before unbelievers. We must also give an account to God for our conduct toward *each other* as believers in this present world. All born again people belong to the same body, and we should settle our differences *within that body*—not before those who are without.

Verse 3: "Know ye not that we shall judge angels? How much more things that pertain to this life?"

". . . *We shall judge angels.*" The meaning here is clear: The saints will sit with the Lord Jesus and will be associated with Him in the judgment pronounced upon angels (probably the fallen angels—Jude 6) in that day of *final judgment.* Exactly what part believers will play IN that judgment is not revealed in the Word of God. The point set forth here by the Holy Spirit is that members of the body of Christ are the highest form of created beings and are therefore superior to angels, and that we will sit with Jesus and judge the angels. We should realize our eternal dignity, not only in respect to life beyond this earth, but in relation to correctly regulating the circumstances of this present life.

The phrase, *"that pertain to this life"* in the original language is one word—an adjective, *biotikos*, meaning "of this life." The Greeks often used this word in pertinence to business matters, and it is frequently in this field that believers have misunderstandings; but in this Scripture the word applies to any difficulty or misunderstanding that has to do with the daily life of the believer while traveling this pilgrim journey.

Verse 4: "If then ye have judgments of things pertaining to this life, set them to judge who are least esteemed in the church."

"IF . . . ye have judgments . . . ." Paul does not say "WHEN ye have judgments," but "IF ye have judgments" (or tribunals) dealing with matters of this sort, the "IF" implying that they ought not to have need of any such thing.

". . . Who are least esteemed"—or, "Who are of no account." Paul is saying, "Do ye set them to judge who are *of no account* in the Church? Do you go outside the assembly of believers to attain a verdict from those who are *unbelievers?* those who preside over Gentile courts? those who are of the world and do not even belong to the assembly?" That is, they are of no value to the Church because they are not spiritual, and the natural man cannot understand or receive the things of the Spirit of God. Such men are in line to be judged by the Lord God Almighty in that great judgment day and are therefore in no position to decide matters of difficulty that have arisen between born again people.

Paul is not speaking of any of the born again believers in the assembly as being *"least esteemed."* The reference to "a wise man" in the next verse makes this clear. Paul is not making a command; he is asking a question:

Verse 5: "I speak to your shame. Is it so, that there is not a wise man among you? no, not one that shall be able to judge between his brethren?

"I speak to your shame." Contrast this statement with chapter 4, verse 14. Paul shames the believers in this verse for acting as they did. He is asking, "Has it come to this? Have you reached such a degree of carnality that a wise man cannot be found in the entire assembly?"

What Paul is trying to get across to these carnal believers is the tragic situation that exists if there is not one man in the entire assembly who is spiritual enough to judge the matters that had been coming up between believers.

"No, not one that shall be able to judge between his brethren?" Was there not one person in the assembly who was spiritually minded enough to arbitrate between one believer and another? Paul intended this to be a very humiliating question. It should have humbled the proud Corinthians who had been advertising their great wisdom and who were conceited—both in their daily practice of life, and in the church.

Verse 6: "But brother goeth to law with brother, and that before the unbelievers."

It was a sad thing that there were divisions in the church and that believer had aught against believer. That was bad enough, but it was even worse for believers to carry their grievances before the courts of the Gentiles and discuss those grievances before the world. It certainly brought reproach upon the testimony of Christians. It was a disgrace to the Church of the living God that such should be going on between believers in the assembly at Corinth.

Verse 7: "Now therefore there is utterly a fault among you, because ye go to law one with another. Why do ye not rather take wrong? Why do ye not rather suffer yourselves to be defrauded?"

The Greek word translated "fault" is *hettema*, meaning "a defect, or a loss." Here it signifies the *spiritual* loss. Paul sets their loss in contrast to the fullness they should be demonstrating. Instead of going forward, they were slipping backward. Instead of gaining, they were losing. Because of their disputes and their habits of going to law before unbelievers, they had suffered a tremendous loss of respect from those who were without, and had suffered loss of spiritual power in the church. The evil that was present in the assembly not only marred the spiritual life of those who were involved in lawsuits against each other, but the word "utterly" indicates that it had also marred the spiritual life and testimony of the *entire assembly.*

"Why do ye not rather take wrong? Why do ye not rather suffer yourselves to be defrauded?" Paul is asking, "Since you are a believer and you know the Lord Jesus as your Saviour, why is it that you cannot suffer for Him—even though you may suffer unjustly? You may be injured wrongly, but why not suffer physical injury and financial loss rather than suffer loss of spiritual power and have your testimony damaged by the way you are acting?"

Jesus Himself set the example. He said, "Blessed are ye, when men shall revile you, and persecute you, and shall say all manner of evil against you falsely, for my sake. Rejoice, and be exceeding glad: for great is your reward in heaven: for so persecuted they the prophets which were before you" (Matt. 5:11,12).

We know that the world has never loved righteousness. We know that in the eyes of the world, all who live godly are foolish. But Paul said, *"We are fools for CHRIST'S sake."* It is shameful when a born again person cannot suffer a little reproach or a financial loss for the sake of the Christ who gave His lifeblood that we might have salvation!

Verse 8: "Nay, ye do wrong, and defraud, and that your brethren."

"Brethren" refers to other members of the assembly, fellow believers. There is emphasis upon "ye" and "brethren." The un-Christlike conduct of individual believers not only did injury and spiritual hurt to those who were acting thus; it also caused injury to their fellow believers.

It was not only *the individual* who suffered loss, but the entire Church — and why? Because the Church of the living God is one body, made up of born again individuals, and when one member suffers, ALL members suffer. We will see this clearly taught later in this epistle. Those who were going to law with each other were not willing to be defrauded, they were not willing to suffer injustice individually, but because of their un-Christlike actions they had defrauded the brethren and caused *them* to suffer.

The Sanctity of the Believer's Body; the Sanctity of Marriage

Verses 9 and 10: "Know ye not that the unrighteous shall not inherit the kingdom of God? Be not deceived: neither fornicators, nor idolaters, nor adulterers, nor effeminate, nor abusers of themselves with mankind, nor thieves, nor covetous, nor drunkards, nor revilers, nor extortioners, shall inherit the kingdom of God."

"Know ye not that the unrighteous shall not inherit the kingdom of God?" If the believers did not know that these who were guilty of the sins named and individually pointed out shall not enter into the kingdom of God, it was due to willing ignorance on their part. Certainly Paul had preached pure, unadulterated Gospel to them when they were converted. *"The unrighteous"* here means all who are not born again; there is no middle ground. We are either believers, or unbelievers. We are sons of God, or sons of the devil. We are righteous, or unrighteous, holy or unholy. God is light — He is never twilight; and we are either *for* Him or *against* Him. We are saved, or we are lost: *there can be no neutrality here.*

"The kingdom of God" has reference to the future eternal kingdom of our God (Gal. 5:21; Eph. 5:5; II Pet. 1:10,11).

"Be not deceived." Paul uses this term often in his epistles. There is no excuse for any believer becoming a victim of deception, for all believers possess the

Holy Spirit. I Peter 2:6 tells us plainly, "He that believeth on (Jesus) shall not be confounded (confused)." Believers have THE LIGHT, and if we will walk in that light as the Holy Spirit directs, we need not be deceived. We have the Word of God—a lamp unto our feet and a light unto our pathway (Psalm 119:105).

Paul names certain individuals who will not under any circumstance enter into the eternal kingdom of God's eternal glory. Certainly a book could be written here, but for the sake of time and space I will just mention the ten categories named:

"Fornicators" —meaning sexual immorality in general, but having a *primary* meaning—in Scripture the only grounds for divorce. Study Deuteronomy 24:1—4.

". . . *Nor idolaters* . . . ." Fornication and idolatry are frequently associated one with the other in Scripture. Many of the religions of idolatry practiced—and still practice—gross sexual immorality in the name of religion.

". . . *Nor adulterers* . . . ." Jesus sheds light on adultery in the Sermon on the Mount, declaring that if a man look upon a woman to lust after her, he hath committed adultery with her in his heart. (Man looks on the outward appearance, but God always looks upon the heart.) Much could be said about adultery; *one* thing MUST be said: *Ladies should be very careful how they dress and how they conduct themselves before men.* A well-meaning woman can be used of Satan to cause men to commit adultery, which could be the first step on the road that would eventually lead them into the lake of fire. We *are* "our brother's keeper" in this respect.

". . . *Nor effeminate* . . . ." This word is defined by Webster as meaning "wanting in manly strength or force; marked by weakness, softness, and love of ease." This was definitely not the quality described by Paul

211

when he said, "Thou therefore *endure hardness*, as a good soldier of Jesus Christ" (II Tim. 2:3).

". . . *Nor abusers of themselves with mankind.*" I am confident that this refers to the sin of sodomy. Please read Romans 1:18–32, paying special attention to verses 26 and 27.

". . . *Nor thieves* . . . ." One of the Ten Commandments is "Thou shalt not steal." There are many ways in which we can steal from our fellowman, but there is no place in heaven for a thief.

". . . *Nor covetous* . . . ." Another of the Ten Commandments is, "Thou shalt not covet." Covetousness is sin, and a covetous person—one who is always longing for what another has, simply for the satisfaction of the flesh and of the mind—cannot enter heaven.

". . . *Nor drunkards* . . . ." It is crystal-clear that drunkards cannot go to heaven. This does not mean only a man who is found lying drunk in the gutter, but one who *indulges* in strong drink. The Bible is very specific about this: "Look not thou upon the wine when it is red, when it giveth his colour in the cup, when it moveth itself aright" (Prov. 23:31). (This of course means fermented wine.) The Word of God also warns, "Woe unto him that giveth his neighbour drink, that putteth thy bottle to him and makest him drunken also . . ." (Hab. 2:15). It is definitely a sin to drink intoxicating beverages, and drunkards cannot enter heaven.

". . . *Nor revilers* . . . ." Webster's dictionary defines a reviler as "one who decries another with abusive or contemptuous language." This is certainly contrary to the admonition in Colossians 4:6: "Let your speech be alway with grace, seasoned with salt, that ye may know how ye ought to answer every man."

". . . *Nor extortioners* . . ."—those who get gain at

the expense of others, through extortion. This is an age when there are many extortioners, and I am afraid many of them belong to the local churches of our day.

After naming these ten groups Paul makes a bold, clear-cut statement: Those who are guilty of the sins named here *"shall not inherit the kingdom of God."* God help us not to follow this modern trend, but to hear the plain Word of God concerning sin!

Ministers today do not name sin as they should. I believe that when we preachers stand before the people we should name sin and declare that according to the Word of God *they who commit these sins* cannot and will not inherit the kingdom of God! There is too much "as it were" preaching; we need more emphatic, dogmatic, positive preaching that includes sin-naming. It is possible for one to belong to most churches today (not *all* of them, thank God) and commit a little of most any of the sins named in these ten categories. Regardless of what *man* thinks about sin, the question is settled in the Word of God; and woe be unto the preacher who fails to preach *"Thus saith the Lord!"* We need to cry aloud and spare not.

Verse 11: "And such were some of you: but ye are washed, but ye are sanctified, but ye are justified in the name of the Lord Jesus, and by the Spirit of our God."

"And such were some of you." According to these words, some of the believers in Corinth had been guilty of these sins—drunkards, thieves, fornicators—but that is now in the past. The practices named in verse 10 identify sinners; but the new birth changes all this, because when one becomes a believer the old sinful heart is replaced with a new heart (Ezek. 36:26), and "all things are become new" (II Cor. 5:17). Jesus said, "For from within, out of the heart of men, proceed evil thoughts, adulteries,

fornications, murders, thefts, covetousness, wickedness, deceit, lasciviousness, an evil eye, blasphemy, pride, foolishness: All these evil things come from within, and defile the man" (Mark 7:21–23). All evil, regardless of what it may be, originates in an unregenerate heart.

When an unbeliever accepts the Lord Jesus Christ through faith in His finished work, *divine* nature then replaces the old nature. This does not mean that the old nature is completely eradicated, because as long as we live in this flesh we will be tempted. *God is an eternal Spirit* and He cannot be tempted with sin (James 1:13); but as long as we remain in the flesh *we* can be tempted. It is not a sin to be tempted; the sin is in *yielding* to temptation — but *"we are more than conquerors through Him that loved us"* (Rom. 8:37).

"Who is he that overcometh the world, but he that believeth that Jesus is the Son of God?" (I John 5:5). *"He that believeth"* overcomes the world, and "this is the victory that overcometh the world, even our faith" — faith in Jesus who conquered the world, the flesh and the devil, death, hell and the grave, that we might be *"more* than conquerors!"

"But ye are washed." This does not refer to the baptistry. As the dear old song of the Church testifies,
"There is a fountain filled with blood drawn from Immanuel's veins;
And sinners plunged beneath that flood, lose all their guilty stains!"

The blood of Jesus Christ, God's Son, cleanses us from all sin — not from just a few sins, not just *partially clean*; but cleansed from ALL sin; and without the shedding of blood there IS no cleansing, no remission (Heb. 9:22).

These Corinthian believers were genuinely saved;

they did not just "join the church." Paul had preached the Gospel of the death, burial, and resurrection of the Lord Jesus Christ; he did not preach a social gospel, a message simply of religion; he preached the cross, the blood, the resurrection. They received his message, and were washed in the blood.

"But ye are sanctified . . . ." When an unbeliever receives Jesus and becomes a believer, through the operation of the Holy Spirit he is translated from the kingdom of darkness into the kingdom of light, removed from the kingdom of the devil and placed over into the kingdom of God (Col. 1:13). "And now, brethren, I commend you to God, and to the word of His grace, which is able to build you up, and to give you an inheritance among all them which are *sanctified*" (Acts 20:32).

The sanctification referred to here is not something the believer attains by good living, nor even by consistent Bible study, prayer, and service. The moment one becomes a Christian and is born into the family of God, *that very moment* this sanctification takes place. The instant the sinner exercises faith in the finished work of Jesus, the instant the unbeliever believes ON Jesus as Saviour—that instant God the Father takes him out of the kingdom of darkness and places him in the kingdom of light. He does this on the grounds of the finished work of Jesus. This sanctification is through God's grace—not by human merit: "Christ . . . is made unto us . . . sanctification" (I Cor. 1:30). This sanctification is the effect the death of the Lamb of God has on the relation of the born again believer to God the Father: "By the which will we are sanctified through the offering of the body of Jesus Christ once for all" (Heb. 10:10). "Wherefore Jesus also, that He might sanctify the people with His own blood, suffered without the gate" (Heb. 13:12).

The believer is separated FROM the world, separated UNTO the Lord. There is no middle ground: "Being then made free from sin, ye became the servants of righteousness. I speak after the manner of men because of the infirmity of your flesh: for as ye have yielded your members servants to uncleanness and to iniquity unto iniquity; even so now yield your members servants to righteousness unto holiness. For when ye were the servants of sin, ye were free from righteousness. What fruit had ye then in those things whereof ye are now ashamed? for the end of those things is death. But now being made free from sin, and become servants to God, ye have your fruit unto holiness, and the end everlasting life" (Rom. 6:18—22).

The work of grace is entirely God's part in our salvation; but after we are saved by grace and placed into the kingdom of God, it is the responsibility of the believer to maintain a holy walk and a separated, sanctified life by trusting in the finished work of Jesus, relying upon the leadership of the Holy Spirit, and studying the Word of God untiringly.

"Who hath saved us, and called us with an holy calling, not according to our works, but according to His own purpose and grace, which was given us in Christ Jesus before the world began" (II Tim. 1:9).

"But as He which hath called you is holy, so be ye holy in all manner of conversation; because it is written, Be ye holy; for I am holy" (I Pet. 1:15,16).

". . . *But ye are justified* . . . ." The Greek word used here for "justified" means "to declare to be right." Some great Bible scholar of the past has said, "To be justified in the sight of God is to be just as just as *Jesus* is just; to be just as though one had never committed a sin"—and this is true; because when we are

216

justified we stand before God *covered by the blood of Jesus*, possessing divine nature, indwelt by the Holy Ghost. When God looks at us He sees the blood, and when we are covered by the blood we are just as pure in the eyes of the Father as the blood of the Lamb that covers us!

When the death-angel passed through the land of Egypt, God said, "When I see the blood, I will pass over you." The same is true in essence today. It is the blood of Jesus that makes us fit for the kingdom of God—not works of righteousness which we may do, but *the finished work of Calvary*, the shed blood of the Lamb without spot or blemish. Justification takes place the split second we believe or exercise faith in the finished work of Jesus: "Therefore by the deeds of the law there shall no flesh be justified in His sight: for by the law is the knowledge of sin" (Rom. 3:20).

"And the Scripture, foreseeing that God would justify the heathen through faith, preached before the Gospel unto Abraham, saying, In thee shall all nations be blessed" (Gal. 3:8).

Justification brings peace; hostilities cease between the unbeliever and God: "Therefore being justified by faith, we have peace with God through our Lord Jesus Christ" (Rom. 5:1).

Justification is *"in the name of the Lord Jesus."* In I Corinthians 5:4 Paul says *"our* Lord Jesus Christ." There the pronoun "our" was used because of the special act of discipline with which the Apostle was dealing under the authority of Christ. But here, because the subject applies to *God's grace toward ALL believers*, the definite article "the" is used instead of the possessive pronoun. The title *"Lord Jesus Christ"* suggests both His authority and His character—both in God's grace in justification through the Lord Jesus Christ, and in the responding life of the believer because of his sanctification. It points to the *responsibility of the believer* because Jesus is not only our Saviour and keeper — He is also Lord of our life. We should therefore live a life of sanctification; we have no right to live any other way.

". . . *And by the Spirit of our God.*" (In the Greek it is "IN the Spirit of our God.") This refers to the Holy Spirit, and marked out here we have His work as the personal Agent through whose power we are washed, sanctified, and justified. This statement ("the Spirit of our God") is not found any other place in the New Testament. The Bible never refers to "God the Spirit," nor to "God the Son," as if there were three Gods. There is ONE GOD, manifest in three Persons. We should be very careful to use scriptural terms concerning the Trinity.

The subject of dealing with immorality began in chapter 5, but now Paul deals with it in a more general way. Fornication was prevalent in the city of Corinth (I Cor. 7:2; II Cor. 12:21), and the sad state of affairs was that the Corinthian Christians did not regard it in as serious a light as they should have. The idea of Christian liberty had been perverted and abused by some.

We learn here that Paul had been misquoted and misjudged (Rom. 3:8), and this fact had caused much misunderstanding among believers—not only in the church at Corinth, but in other places as well. As a matter of course, it is the work of the devil to cause God's preachers to be misquoted and misunderstood; but these people were practicing immorality *and declaring that Christian liberty gave them the right to do so*, since they were not under law, but under grace! In the next verse of our study, Paul clearly sets forth the significance and scope of true spiritual liberty in the Lord Jesus, and also the character and purpose of the *body* of the born again believer.

Verse 12: "All things are lawful unto me, but all things are not expedient: all things are lawful for me, but I will not be brought under the power of any."

"All things are lawful for me . . . ." Paul is not referring to things that are sinful and ungodly. There are many things which believers could do which would not harm us *individually* and would not be contrary to the laws of God and of spirituality; but *for the sake of other believers and those without the Church*, we dare not do those things.

I am not suggesting that just our feeling that some things are not wrong will make them right; but there are places where an individual believer could go which would have no ill effect on him — yet if another believer of different temperament, perhaps saved from a different background, should attend or visit the same place, it could bring to mind old sins and cause temptation that could be the means of the weaker brother's stumbling.

"All things are lawful unto me, *but all things are not expedient.*" Paul is saying here, "I am the bond-slave of Jesus Christ and I refuse to be brought under the power of anything except the grace of God and the Gospel of that grace." In this verse (as in chapter 10 verse 23 of this epistle and chapter 14 verse 20 of Romans) Paul is speaking in relation to himself — *and the subject is food.*

In Paul's day, animals were sacrifices to idols, and according to Jewish custom they were not supposed to eat the meat of an animal that had been offered to an idol. Paul knew that he was saved by the grace of God, and he knew that his salvation *depended* upon the grace of God, and not upon abstinence from meats; yet he said,

"If meat make my brother to offend, I will eat no flesh while the world standeth, lest I make my brother to offend" (I Cor. 8:13).

Paul's statement that all things were lawful unto him had been misunderstood and abused by those who wanted to practice habits of the old life. It was absurd for those who were lax in their moral living to think that Paul had suggested any such thing. Never man walked upon this earth who lived a more dedicated, consecrated, separated life than the Apostle Paul. He preached what he lived, and lived what he preached, and no one had any reason to think that he had suggested that Christian liberty relating to food made it lawful to be lax in moral matters.

The Greek word used for "expedient" is *sumphero*, the literal meaning of which is "to bring with, or together, to profit withal." It signifies that which is helpful to ourselves or to others. Christian liberty is ours only when beneficial to our individual lives, to the lives of other believers, and when it is not a hindrance to those who are not saved. No believer has a right to do something that he may consider to be innocent, if his action might prove detrimental to others. Everything about the believer's life must be regulated—not only from an ethical point of view, but from the standpoint of whether or not it is pleasing unto the Lord. Believers should never forget that He who is our Saviour also has the right to be Lord of our life, and all that we do should be done to His glory.

"All things are lawful for me; but *I will not be brought under the power of any*." This deals only with the *effect* upon the individual *himself*. Paul is saying here, "All things are *within* my power, but I will not put myself *under the power* of any of them!"

If the believer abuses his liberty it will lessen his

power of self-control; and if this happens, then what is supposed to be liberty will become bondage. Regardless of however lawful anything may be, if it occupies my time or energy in a way not to the glory of God and the edification of others, I am in grave danger of allowing myself to fall into bondage to it. Only by careful watchfulness and fear of the Lord in the heart can we prevent even *that which is legitimate*—business, amusements, dress, food, or even our family—from gaining dominion over us and enslaving us, instead of being the bondslave of Jesus Christ and a servant of our fellow believers. *Paul* said, ". . . I count ALL things but loss for the excellency of the knowledge of Christ Jesus my Lord: for whom I have suffered *the loss of all things*, and do count them but dung, that I may win Christ" (Phil. 3:8).

The Body of a Believer Belongs to the Lord

Verse 13: "Meats for the belly, and the belly for meats: but God shall destroy both it and them. Now the body is not for fornication, but for the Lord; and the Lord for the body."

The Greek verb used for "destroy" is *katargeo* and means "to render inactive." It is also used in I Corinthians 1:28 and 2:6. The meaning here is that the natural appetite belongs to the physical body and physical nature as God created it. Meats, foods, and digestion are matters that belong to our present state. This body is destined to return to dust, and these things will cease their operation at the death of the body—or when we are changed in the Rapture. Foods and digestion (denoted here by "meats for the belly") have no moral significance within themselves; they *acquire* moral significance in particular individuals under certain circumstances.

"Now the body is not for fornication, but for the Lord . . . ." We see here a contrast between the belly

221

and the body. The belly is for the body, but the body is the Lord's and in its glorified state will be eternal; but meats and appetites are NOT eternal — they will cease at death. In Luke 24:41–43 we read that Jesus in His glorified body asked His disciples, "Have ye here any meat? And they gave Him a piece of a broiled fish, and of an honeycomb. And He took it, and did eat before them." But it will not be *necessary* for the glorified saints to eat, whereas in this body of flesh it IS necessary for us to eat if the body is to remain alive.

The body is definitely a part of human personality, and the body of the *believer* is to be an instrument for God to use, through which He is to be glorified in all things. In our present verse Paul is pointing out that unchastity is not like food: *Meats* were lawful for him, but under no circumstance is *unchastity* lawful for any believer!

Through this reasonable argument and comparison, Paul deals with the dangerous argument which had been— and was being—used among the carnally minded Corinthians, that if the gratification of ONE natural desire is lawful, then *why not the gratification of another*? If meats were lawful, then why not adultery, fornication, drunkenness, etc.?

The believer should bear in mind at all times the fact that his body belongs to the Lord—the One who died to redeem the soul, spirit, AND body—and therefore believers should seek the will of God at all times concerning all things, allowing the divine purpose of God to be wrought in all activities of life. Whatever Christians do should be done to God's glory and to help others.

". . . *And the Lord for the body.*" Seemingly we often fail to realize the fact that this body is the tabernacle in which the Holy Spirit abides—and *will abide* until

222

the body returns to dust or is changed "in a moment, in the twinkling of an eye" at the Rapture. If a believer dies before the Rapture, his body will be raised incorruptible; if he lives until the Rapture, he will never die. But, *live or die*, the body belongs to the Lord who purchased us with His own precious blood — ". . . The Lord Jesus Christ: who shall change our vile body, that it may be fashioned like unto His glorious body, according to the working whereby He is able even to subdue all things unto Himself" (Phil. 3:21).

"Beloved, now are we the sons of God, and it doth not yet appear what we shall be: but we know that, when He shall appear, we shall be like Him; for we shall see Him as He is" (I John 3:2).

Verse 14: "And God hath both raised up the Lord, and will also raise up us by His own power."

The clear truth set forth here—that God the Father who raised the Lord Jesus, by the same power will raise us—is set in contrast with the natural elements which will be brought to nought (mentioned in the foregoing verse). Our *physical appetites* will cease when we depart this life, but our bodies will have part in the resurrection— for without the body we would not be our complete selves, and we are told that in that land that is fairer than day, we shall know even as we are known (I Cor. 13:12). I firmly believe that the fifteenth chapter of this epistle teaches that our glorified bodies will resemble these bodies of flesh in which we now dwell.

Paul assures us here that the power of God, which raised up the Lord Jesus Christ on the third day as promised, will just as surely raise *us*. We know that if this earthly tabernacle be dissolved, "we have a building of God, an house not made with hands, eternal in the heavens" (II Cor. 5:1). This mortal will one day put on immortality, and when we see Jesus, we will be like Him!

We have this assurance because we are in Christ and He is in us. We possess divine nature, because the body is the tabernacle of the Holy Spirit. We are dead— and our lives are hid with Christ in God. We sit together in heavenly places in Christ Jesus, and we know that the God who raised up Christ from the dead will also raise us by the same power. Therefore, as we sojourn here we should live in this body in such a way that *whatever* we do will glorify God. The present use of this body should be directed in every detail to bring honor and glory to the Lord God Almighty, who gave Jesus to die for us and who will raise us up in that glorious morning!

Verse 15: "Know ye not that your bodies are the members of Christ? Shall I then take the members of Christ, and make them the members of an harlot? God forbid."

Here, additional truth is added to that in verse 13. The body of the believer not only belongs to God and is for His use, but *the body of the believer is united TO Him.* This part of the personality of the individual believer is a member of the body of which Christ is the head. We will study this fully in chapter 12 of our present epistle.

In Romans 12:1 Paul begs us to present our bodies a living sacrifice, holy and acceptable unto God, which is our reasonable service. Ephesians 5:30 declares in unmistakeable language, "For we are members of His body, of His flesh and of His bones."

The relationship of the individual believer with Christ involves the divine fact that *the body of the believer* is the *instrument* through which the Lord works, in the ministry and activities committed to that person. The believer's body as a member of the body of Christ is a living organism, fitted and fashioned for the purpose of carrying out God's will and purpose through grace. Since this is true, how then can a born again believer "take away" that which is divinely united to Christ, rightfully *His*, and unite it with that which is unlawful and unholy, thereby robbing God of the instrument through which He is to be made manifest and glorified in the world?

These bodies of ours are instruments through which Jesus shows Himself to an unbelieving world. It has pleased God to dwell within individuals in the Person of the Holy Spirit; and a life controlled by the Spirit bears fruit that glorifies God, with no desire to be joined to a harlot nor to be a party to adultery, fornication, drunkenness, and other such practices. *"GOD FORBID"* that such be allowed to bring disgrace and reproach upon the Church, upon Christ—and upon the individual who would be guilty.

Verse 16: "What? Know ye not that he which is joined to an harlot is one body? for two, saith He, shall be one flesh."

I pointed out earlier that Paul asks and answers many questions in his epistles. This is true in this verse, the last part of which is quoted from Genesis 2:24: "Therefore shall a man leave his father and his mother, and shall cleave unto his wife: and they shall be one flesh." With this quotation Paul points directly to the decree made by God concerning husband and wife. The fact is also true of fornication—what has been done lives morally in both, whether in the case of husband and wife or in unlawful union. True, marriage in its moral value for born again believers involves the most intimate association between husband and wife—for the joint service of God and for the specific purpose of bringing up children to the glory of Him who is the Author of all life. The mere gratification of lust is the complete distortion of this and is detrimental to spirituality and will hinder spiritual growth.

There is nothing on earth more beautiful than marriage when two people are truly joined in holy matrimony. They are no longer two; they become one flesh, and the desires of their lives should be one. That desire should be to glorify the Lord and Saviour, Jesus Christ.

This Scripture teaches that if illicit sex practice is carried on between two individuals, they become one body, one flesh; and that which God intended to be high, noble, and beautiful becomes low, ugly, and degrading. There is nothing that will destroy an individual so quickly as promiscuous sex practice, whether it be fornication or adultery. The Holy Spirit here warns—not only the believers in Corinth—but all believers even unto this present hour and until we are caught up into Paradise to be with Jesus.

Verse 17: "But he that is joined unto the Lord is one spirit."

The spiritual union to which Paul refers here is the same as that set forth by the Lord Jesus in speaking to His disciples: "At that day ye shall know that I am in my Father, and ye in me, and I in you" (John 14:20). In John 15:4 and 5 Jesus said, "Abide in me, and I in you. As the branch cannot bear fruit of itself, except it abide in the vine; no more can ye, except ye abide in me. I am the vine, ye are the branches: He that abideth in me, and I in him, the same bringeth forth much fruit: for without me ye can do nothing."

We find a similar declaration in John 17:21–23: "That they all may be one; as thou, Father, art in me, and I in thee, that they also may be one in us: that the world may believe that thou hast sent me. And the glory which

thou gavest me I have given them; that they may be one,
even as WE are one: I in them, and thou in me, that they
may be made perfect in one; and that the world may know
that thou hast sent me, and hast loved them, as thou hast
loved me."

When the believer fully realizes the existence of
this union with Christ and allows the indwelling Spirit
of God to keep this fact uppermost in his thoughts, aims,
and activities, then that believer will conform to the
mind of Christ and to the will of God for his life; and
this can happen only when the individual knows and recognizes this clear fact and surrenders to it. When we
are saved by God's grace, we become part of Christ and
He becomes part of us. We then are members of His body
and He abides in our body. God help us to realize this
solemn fact and conduct ourselves accordingly.

Verse 18: "Flee fornication. Every sin that a man
doeth is without the body; but he that committeth fornication sinneth against his own body."

It has been previously pointed out in our study that
fornication was one of the outstanding sins in the city
of Corinth. Paul knew there was grave danger that some
of the believers would become careless enough to suc-
cumb to the immoral influences all around them; therefore
he gave clear command that they were to FLEE FORNI-
CATION.

The lust of the flesh is a savage, deadly master.
It is extremely dangerous to think on these things or to
be exposed to conversation centered around such subjects. The only way to deal with the sins of fornication
and adultery is to flee from them as we would flee from
any other danger, such as a poisonous snake, a deadly
plague, or a vicious beast.

Every *other* sin (lying, robbery, murder, etc.) is

"without the body." Fornication is singular in the catalog of sin; it is a sin against the body in that it makes the body itself (and thus the whole being) the very *motive for* as well as the *instrument of* sin. The practice of fornication will eventually bring about the complete destruction of the personality of an individual, and render the living organisms of the body helpless in the fulfillment of the Lord's design for the human body which He created to be devoted to His services. There is no other sin that will destroy personality, character, and vigor so quickly and completely as the sin of fornication.

Because God saw the loneliness of man, He created woman FOR man and gave her to him to make his life more complete; but neither man nor woman has any right to abuse the bodies to satisfy the lust of the flesh. Our bodies were created for the Lord, and if we as believers refuse to surrender our bodies to the Lord, holy and acceptable, and yield our members as instruments of righteousness, we will reap a harvest of corruption *in our bodies.* That does not mean that the soul will be damned; it simply means that the body will be destroyed because of "the sin unto death." Some of the Corinthians had already committed the sin unto death, and others were on the verge of it.

The Body of the Believer Is the Temple of the Holy Ghost

Verse 19: "What? Know ye not that your body is the temple of the Holy Ghost which is in you, which ye have of God, and ye are not your own?"

The Greek word *naos* used here for "temple" means "a sanctuary or shrine." The same word is used in chapter 3, verse 16 of this epistle. Jesus used it concerning His own body of flesh in John 2:19–21, and Paul uses the same word in referring to the local assembly in II Corinthians 6:16. It is used in referring to the Church (the mystical body of Christ) in Ephesians 2:21.

The "temple of God" is a place of worship—a place where God's honor dwells and where His glory is made manifest; and since the believer's body is the temple of God, we should guard the body accordingly. It is extremely important how a believer uses his body. It is a grave sin to destroy the temple of God.

". . . *Which is in you* . . . ." This stresses the fact that every born again believer possesses the Holy Spirit. The body is holy because the inner man is justified by the blood and indwelt by the Holy Spirit. It is absurd to be so willingly ignorant as to suppose that a person can be a child of God and not possess the Holy Spirit! It is the Holy Spirit who convicts us and draws us to God (John 6:44; 16:7–9). Every believer *possesses* the Holy Spirit (Rom. 8:9). Every believer is *led* by the Holy Spirit (Rom. 8:14). The Holy Spirit *assures* us that we are the children of God (Rom. 8:16). We are *sealed* by the Holy Spirit (Eph. 4:30). And in Ephesians 5:18 we are admonished to be *filled* with the Holy Spirit.

There is no such thing as being a child of God apart from the Holy Spirit, for it is He who convicts us and draws us to Christ. It is He who comes to abide in our hearts the moment we believe. It is He who teaches us, guides us, and directs us into spiritual pathways and the will of God. It is true that not all believers are *fully surrendered* to the Spirit, but all believers do *possess* the Spirit—and we will learn later (in chapter 12) that we are all *baptized into the body of Christ* by and through the Holy Spirit!

Jesus died on the cross to save us from sin. The moment we believe, we are saved, the soul is redeemed, and the body will be redeemed at the first resurrection. As pointed out earlier, we have the assurance that the

God who raised up Jesus will raise US up – there is no doubt about it. We need not fear, there need be no dread. Those of us who are redeemed know assuredly that we will be raised, for the purchase of this body was included in redemption. It will be sown in dishonor and raised in glory, to be like His glorious body.

Soul, spirit, and body, we belong to the Lord who purchased us: "For whether we live, we live unto the Lord; and whether we die, we die unto the Lord: whether we live therefore, or die, we are the Lord's. For to this end Christ both died, and rose, and revived, that He might be Lord both of the dead and living" (Rom. 14:8,9).

Verse 20: "For ye are bought with a price: therefore glorify God in your body, and in your spirit, which are God's."

Paul declared, "I determined not to know any thing among you, save Jesus Christ, and Him crucified" (I Cor. 2:2). Paul's message always was CALVARY–the death, burial, and resurrection of Jesus. Notice also I Corinthians 1:23 and 5:7. The shed blood of the Lord Jesus was the purchase price that brought about a change of ownership. Jesus said to His disciples, "I came not to be ministered unto, but to minister. I came not to be served, but to serve. I came to give my life a ransom for many!" And He did just that. He paid the ransom, paid the sin-debt, and made freedom and liberty possible for all who will exercise faith in His finished work. He purchased us completely; and when we stand face to face with Him in the glorious day of the first resurrection, *we will be like Him!*

Since it is a divine fact that we are "bought with a price," then it is only reasonable that we should glorify God in our bodies. We have a divine command to keep the body from unchastity–not only from *obligation*, but we should abstain from fleshly lusts for the purpose of glorifying God in our bodies, thus bringing glory to Him and having reward at the end of life's journey.

Since God loved us so much that He gave His Son to die on the cross, and since Jesus loved us so much that He willingly laid His life down for us and paid our ransom with His own precious blood, we should be thankful to such extent that we would allow Him to have preeminence in all things. The glorious privilege of being a Christian carries with it an equally grave responsibility. We should glorify God simply because of what He has done for us.

We are saved by the grace of God; but we should never take advantage of this liberty to satisfy selfish desires—whether small and seemingly innocent, or gross sin such as fornication. We should walk in the fear of God—not in the sense that we are afraid of something that would devour or crush us, but as little children fear and respect their parents. We are not to fear God from the standpoint of dreading the day we meet Him, but rather to the extent that the desire of our hearts should be to glorify Him in all that we do or say, since He has done so much to make it possible for us to escape the lake of fire.

I do not believe in requiring believers to sign a pledge regarding rules and regulations before allowing them to become a member of the local assembly, for such procedure is definitely unscriptural. If a person is saved by the grace of God and *led by the Spirit of God*, that person will live as he should. I realize that we will fall short of the glory of God, but spiritually-minded believers will not practice open sin, and one who has a *desire* to embrace sinful practices will not abstain from them simply because he has signed a pledge not to indulge!

Such pledge-signing is unscriptural. When we are

saved *we are set free* from the law of sin and death, and we have liberty in Jesus. We overcome the world because we ARE believers. By contrast, one who is NOT a believer finds it impossible to live a clean life regardless of how many pledges he may sign. He cannot overcome for the very simple reason that he is NOT a believer, saved by grace. (Study I John 5:1-5.)

Christians should have a deep desire to have a clean mind, clean soul, and a clean body—spiritually clean, and free from adultery, fornication, drunkenness, or any other lust of the flesh. Have YOU presented YOUR body a living sacrifice, holy and acceptable unto God, which is only your reasonable service? Have you yielded your members unto God as instruments of righteousness? If not, do it now!

CHAPTER SEVEN

1. Now concerning the things whereof ye wrote unto me: It is good for a man not to touch a woman.

2. Nevertheless, to avoid fornication, let every man have his own wife, and let every woman have her own husband.

3. Let the husband render unto the wife due benevolence: and likewise also the wife unto the husband.

4. The wife hath not power of her own body, but the husband: and likewise also the husband hath not power of his own body, but the wife.

5. Defraud ye not one the other, except it be with consent for a time, that ye may give yourselves to fasting and prayer; and come together again, that Satan tempt you not for your incontinency.

6. But I speak this by permission, and not of commandment.

7. For I would that all men were even as I myself. But every man hath his proper gift of God, one after this manner, and another after that.

8. I say therefore to the unmarried and widows, It is good for them if they abide even as I.

9. But if they cannot contain, let them marry: for it is better to marry than to burn.

10. And unto the married I command, yet not I, but the Lord, Let not the wife depart from her husband:

11. But and if she depart, let her remain unmarried, or be reconciled to her husband: and let not the husband put away his wife.

12. But to the rest speak I, not the Lord: If any brother hath a wife that believeth not, and she be pleased to dwell with him, let him not put her away.

13. And the woman which hath an husband that believeth not, and if he be pleased to dwell with her, let her not leave him.

14. For the unbelieving husband is sanctified by the wife, and the unbelieving wife is sanctified by the husband: else were your children unclean; but now are they holy.

15. But if the unbelieving depart, let him depart. A brother or a sister is not under bondage in such cases: but God hath called us to peace.

16. For what knowest thou, O wife, whether thou shalt save thy husband? or how knowest thou, O man, whether thou shalt save thy wife?

17. But as God hath distributed to every man, as the Lord hath called every one, so let him walk. And so ordain I in all churches.

18. Is any man called being circumcised? let him not become uncircumcised. Is any called in uncircumcision? let him not be circumcised.

19. Circumcision is nothing, and uncircumcision is nothing, but the keeping of the commandments of God.

20. Let every man abide in the same calling wherein he was called.

21. Art thou called being a servant? care not for it: but if thou mayest be made free, use it rather.

22. For he that is called in the Lord, being a servant, is the Lord's freeman: likewise also he that is called, being free, is Christ's servant.

23. Ye are bought with a price; be not ye the servants of men.

24. Brethren, let every man, wherein he is called, therein abide with God.

25. Now concerning virgins I have no commandment of the Lord: yet I give my judgment, as one that hath obtained mercy of the Lord to be faithful.

26. I suppose therefore that this is good for the present distress, I say, that it is good for a man so to be.

27. Art thou bound unto a wife? seek not to be loosed. Art thou loosed from a wife? seek not a wife.

28. But and if thou marry, thou hast not sinned; and if a virgin marry, she hath not sinned. Nevertheless such shall have trouble in the flesh: but I spare you.

29. But this I say, brethren, the time is short: it remaineth, that both they that have wives be as though they had none;

30. And they that weep, as though they wept not; and they that rejoice, as though they rejoiced not; and they that buy, as though they possessed not;

31. And they that use this world, as not abusing it: for the fashion of this world passeth away.

32. But I would have you without carefulness. He that is

unmarried careth for the things that belong to the Lord, how he
may please the Lord:

33. But he that is married careth for the things that are of
the world, how he may please his wife.

34. There is difference also between a wife and a virgin.
The unmarried woman careth for the things of the Lord, that she
may be holy both in body and in spirit: but she that is married
careth for the things of the world, how she may please her
husband.

35. And this I speak for your own profit; not that I may cast
a snare upon you, but for that which is comely, and that ye
may attend upon the Lord without distraction.

36. But if any man think that he behaveth himself uncomely
toward his virgin, if she pass the flower of her age, and need so
require, let him do what he will, he sinneth not: let them marry.

37. Nevertheless he that standeth stedfast in his heart, having no necessity, but hath power over his own will, and hath
so decreed in his heart that he will keep his virgin, doeth well.

38. So then he that giveth her in marriage doeth well; but
he that giveth her not in marriage doeth better.

39. The wife is bound by the law as long as her husband
liveth; but if her husband be dead, she is at liberty to be married to whom she will; only in the Lord.

40. But she is happier if she so abide, after my judgment:
and I think also that I have the Spirit of God.

God Established Marriage

Adam had finished the work God had given him to
do. He had named all of the animals — but in all of the
animal kingdom he had found none to be his helpmate
nor to add to his joy and happiness. The Lord God Almighty saw Adam's loneliness, and recognized that the
life of man was not complete. So He caused a deep sleep
to fall upon Adam, tenderly removed a rib from his side,
and from that rib created woman and gave her to Adam
to be his helpmate. "And Adam said, This is now bone
of my bones, and flesh of my flesh: she shall be called
Woman, because she was taken out of Man" (Gen. 2:23).

What God said, or how He performed that first marriage,

is not recorded; but God united the first couple in holy matrimony, and said to them, "You are no longer two, but one—*one flesh.* What God hath joined together, let not man put asunder." So began the first marriage, the first home; and surely until sin entered there, that home was a suburb of God's Paradise! That is the way God intended it to be, and it CAN be that way, even today in these bodies of flesh, marred and scarred because of sin. The home where mother and father are dedicated to God, with the children following in their footsteps, can be *what God intended the home to be.* Yes, God is the Originator of marriage and of the home.

Paul continues to answer questions that had arisen in the Corinthian assembly, and in this chapter he deals primarily with the subject of marriage.

Verse 1: "Now concerning the things whereof ye wrote unto me: It is good for a man not to touch a woman."

This is a very clear statement. Paul is not forbidding marriage, nor is he attempting to encourage believers NOT to marry. In the following verses he points out certain *advantages* in being unmarried, but he does not teach or imply that a single person is holier than one who is married. Please study I Timothy 4:1—4 and Hebrews 13:4.

Two verses from the Old Testament shed light on the word *"touch"*:

"And God said unto him in a dream, Yea, I know that thou didst this in the integrity of thy heart; for I also withheld thee from sinning against me: therefore suffered I thee not to touch her" (Gen. 20:6).

"So he that goeth in to his neighbour's wife; whosoever toucheth her shall not be innocent" (Prov. 6:29).

Verse 2: "Nevertheless, to avoid fornication, let every man have his own wife, and let every woman have her own husband."

Paul is saying here, "In spite of the fact that it is good for a man not to touch a woman, to avoid fornication let every man have his own wife." In the city of Corinth, where sin was rampant and temptation was great, Paul gave this exhortation concerning marriage—not as if it were the lesser of two evils, but as a safeguard *against* evil.

Even though it would be well for a man not to touch a woman, it is much better for men and women to marry than to be guilty of sin. Certain teachers in that day advocated that marriage was wrong, and some of the Jewish teachers taught polygamy; but Paul makes it very clear that every man should have his own wife, and every woman her own husband—*one* husband, *one* wife.

Verse 3: "Let the husband render unto the wife due benevolence: and likewise also the wife unto the husband."

The subject of the first two verses in this chapter leads Paul to give much-needed advice to those who were married. It is true that in many ways it is far better for a person to remain single. There are many advantages to single life—*provided the individual is strong enough to keep temptation from overcoming him.* However, it is man's God-given duty to replenish the earth by bringing forth children; therefore it is a duty for men and women to marry—if they are suited to one another and *IF they marry in the Lord.* (A bit later in our study, Paul warns against Christians being unequally yoked together with unbelievers.)

The Greek word translated *"render"* signifies—not the granting of a favor—but *"the discharge of an obligation—* here from husband to wife and wife to husband." Marriage is a serious matter. There should be much time and many discussions between the parties to be united in holy matrimony. A young woman who is selfish, unwilling to render to her husband that which is rightfully to be expected in marriage; or a young man who is not willing to render unto his bride that which is due her, should not marry. There are many men who could live to be a hundred years old and never need or want the love and devotion of a woman; and the same is true of some women. There are people who could live a lifetime and never be tempted to commit the sin of which Paul warns in these verses. But there are others who actually must have a mate; otherwise, they will be continually tempted and drawn away in lust and sin.

Marriage is a fifty-fifty proposition; and if the husband is not willing to give his wife the love, devotion, and attention due her because she IS his wife, then *he should never take a wife!* The same is true concerning the woman toward her husband. Married people cannot afford to be selfish; they must share, not expecting more of a mate than they are themselves willing to give in return.

Verse 4: "The wife hath not power of her own body, but the husband: and likewise also the husband hath not power of his own body, but the wife."

In this verse the wife is mentioned first—probably because she is mentioned *last* in the preceding verse and not because she owes her husband any more than he owes to her. These verses clearly teach the equality of the sexes (and in Paul's day, the woman was not looked upon as equal to the man). True, the Word of God does teach that woman is "the weaker vessel," but that does not suggest that in marriage she owes her husband any more than is due *her* as his wife.

The Greek verb translated *"hath not power"* signifies the exercising of authority in whatever matter may be under consideration—which in this case is the body of the husband and the body of the wife. Individual, separate ownership of one's self cannot exist in marriage. When we marry, we are no longer our own; a husband belongs to the wife, the wife belongs to the husband—and neither has any right to say to the other, "Is it not lawful for me to do what I will with mine own?" (Matt. 20:15a). The desire of either husband or wife should not be self-gratification. Selfishness must be removed from the mind and heart. The husband has a duty to fulfill toward the wife, and the wife has a duty to fulfill toward the husband.

Verse 5: "Defraud ye not one the other, except it be with consent for a time, that ye may give yourselves to fasting and prayer; and come together again, that Satan tempt you not for your incontinency."

Here we have *expressed negatively* what is *declared positively* in verse 3. The husband is NOT to defraud the wife, the wife is NOT to defraud the husband—unless it be:

1. With mutual consent and understanding between husband and wife.
2. Temporarily — and then only for a short time.
3. For the purpose of prayer—not pleasure.

This verse needs to be preached often in the Church today. No wonder divorce courts are grinding out divorces like water pours over Niagara Falls! Men and women work today with the husband on one shift and the wife on another. They take separate vacations, having their own personal automobiles and their own bank accounts. In fact, many marriages today seem to be largely an agreement that two parties will live under the same roof, though seldom seeing each other and having almost no fellowship as man and wife. Under such an arrangement they are separated more than they are together, and this *cannot* lead to a happy marriage.

When man and woman unite in marriage, they become

one flesh, and it is unscriptural for husband and wife to stay apart for extended periods of time for *any* reason. Please note that even in the case of fasting and prayer the separation is to be for only a short time. Many homes have been broken and divorces granted because the wife spent too much time in her natal home with her mother. In such cases, the wife should never have married and left the mother. Homes have also been broken (and divorces granted) because the husband spent more of his free time hunting and fishing—or with the "boys" at the club—than he gave to his wife and family.

When husband and wife agree to part from each other for a season of prayer, they are instructed, *"Come together again, that Satan tempt you not for your incontinency."* That is, lest the devil should make lack of self-control a means of temptation to commit evil—yes, even after a season of prayer and fasting.

Satan never takes a vacation; he is always alert and on the job. We must therefore put on *"the whole armour of God . . . taking the shield of faith,"* that we may be able to quench the fiery darts of the devil. We must not be unaware of his snares and pitfalls. I Peter 5:8 warns us, "Be sober, be vigilant; because your adversary the devil, as a roaring lion, walketh about, seeking whom he may devour."

Verse 6: "But I speak this by permission, and not of commandment."

The meaning of this verse is simply that Paul is giving the Corinthian believers good, sound, spiritual admonition and advice. It was not a commandment of God that a man touch not a woman and that the single person marry not; but since Paul was the spiritual father of those who made up the church in Corinth, he felt toward them as a father would feel toward his children and had a deep desire to see them live victoriously and enjoy their spiritual birthright. For that reason he gave this spiritual admonition and advice—but not as a commandment from the Lord God Almighty.

(That does not mean that these verses are not inspired; the Apostle gave a command only when it was received from God *as* a command; otherwise by the divine help of the Lord he counsels as a spiritual guide.)

It is not a command of God that a wife and husband defraud not each other except it be with consent for a time — but very few husbands and wives can afford to ignore Paul's advice in the matter, because *we are human and the devil is no respecter of persons*! It matters not who we are, we are not immune to temptation. We would do well to hear these words of admonition from the Apostle Paul.

Verse 7: "For I would that all men were even as I myself. But every man hath his proper gift of God, one after this manner, and another after that."

Paul was not a married man at the time of this writing, although many Bible scholars believe that he WAS married at one time. (He was a member of the Sanhedrin, and only married men, as a rule, were members of that body.) However, insofar as I have been able to determine, there is no positive proof that Paul was ever married. Certainly he was not married when he wrote this letter to the Corinthians.

Paul wanted all believers to possess the same power of restraint that *he* possessed, so that even though they were unmarried, they would not fall prey to temptation and become a fornicator. Some people who know nothing about temptation relative to the subject Paul is discussing are tempted through another avenue of evil, such as slandering their fellowman by making suggestions pertinent to things about which they do not know the whole truth. Such a slanderous person could ruin the testimony and completely wreck the usefulness of another believer in the church by speaking when he (or she) should keep quiet and pray for the other until the whole truth of the matter in question is brought to light.

The Apostle Paul clearly testifies that insofar as he was personally concerned, he did not need to marry because there was no danger of his becoming a fornicator.

"But every man hath his proper gift of God, one after this manner, and another after that." Paul is saying here that his own condition did not give grounds for him to decide the condition of others. The fact that *he* was not married certainly did not give him a right to command *others* not to marry. The Greek word here translated "gift" is *charisma*, meaning "a gift of grace." For reasons known to God, the gift of grace was abundantly bestowed upon the Apostle Paul to such degree that he could live through this life without the aid, comfort, love, and companionship of a wife.

Whether a believer is single or married, each is given a gift by the grace of God. Each believer has a ministry to carry out *to the glory of God*, and if each of us would seek and follow God's will for our lives, we would not have time to plan the lives of others — we would be too busy fulfilling that which God has ordained for us as His child. We are responsible to Him alone, and it is to Him that we must give an account. Paul's teaching does not suggest a *moral superiority* in the unmarried, but he *does* suggest an advantage of the unmarried state, in that there was power to be undivided in service for the Lord and the things of God.

Verses 8 and 9: "I say therefore to the unmarried and widows, It is good for them if they abide even as I.

But if they cannot contain, let them marry: for it is better to marry than to burn."

Paul names widows especially, that they might know the advice was intended for them, as well as for those who had never been married; and at the same time, "the unmarried" does not mean widows only, but includes *all who are unmarried.* (This will be discussed more fully in verses 25 through 28 of this chapter.)

Paul makes it plain to whom he is speaking, and then advises, "*It is good for them if they abide even as I. BUT if they cannot contain, let them marry . . . .*" In other words, "If they cannot *practice self-control*, let them marry."

"*. . . For it is better to marry than to burn.*" The Greek word here translated "burn" suggests an emotional struggle within, which of course would destroy the peace which the Lord gives, and which all believers are entitled to enjoy.

If an unmarried person is dedicated to the Lord to such degree that there is no longing for the companionship of a mate, no *desire* to be married, then it is better for that one to remain so. But when a desire for companionship burns within the bosom and that person lacks sufficient self-control, it is better to marry; for such desire will take away the peace and joy which the Christian should have, and that one's service to God will be rendered much less effective. Such a person by all means should marry. In connection with this, study I Timothy 5:11—15.

Instructions to the Married Among Gentile Believers

Verses 10 and 11: "And unto the married I command, yet not I, but the Lord, Let not the wife depart from her husband: But and if she depart, let her remain unmarried, or be reconciled to her husband: and let not the husband put away his wife."

243

The admonition and instructions given in these verses are without a doubt directed to husbands and wives where both are Christians. Evidently the question of divorce, in the event of believers separating, had been discussed in the church at Corinth. It is possible that some of the "wise" teachers had suggested that it was *perfectly in order* for believers to divorce each other, but the admonition given by Paul does not point to the possibility of divorce between believers. Certainly he does not advise it.

"... *Unto the married I command, yet not I, but the Lord* ...." Jesus laid down the commandment against divorce: "What therefore God hath joined together, let not man put asunder" (Mark 10:9). "Whosoever putteth away his wife, and marrieth another, committeth adultery: and whosoever marrieth her that is put away from her husband committeth adultery" (Luke 16:18).

Paul does not speak of a *special revelation* given to him by God concerning this matter, such as that in I Thessalonians 4:15. He is simply pointing out *the command of the Lord* as having to do with divorce: *The wife is not to depart from her husband* — but if, for some reason not pointed out here, she does depart, *she is to remain unmarried, or be reconciled to her husband*. There is no suggestion of divorce. Paul makes this very clear.

"... *And let not the husband put away his wife*." Dearly beloved, this may be hard doctrine, but it is scriptural: *There is absolutely no Bible ground for divorce among believers*! If husband and wife are both children of God, there is nothing that could happen between them that could not be settled on their knees in prayer before God. I repeat, this is surely a hard saying in these days of laxity and liberalism, when so many ministers preach to please men instead of delivering "*Thus saith the Lord*." But according to the Word of God as set forth here, there is no ground for a divorce between believers—and if they find it impossible to live together and choose to separate, they must remain unmarried or else be reconciled. The believer who leaves his or her mate has no right to marry another person. This is according to the Scripture.

Verses 12 and 13: "But to the rest speak I, not the Lord: If any brother hath a wife that believeth not, and she be pleased to dwell with him, let him not put her away. And the woman which hath an husband that believeth not, and if he be pleased to dwell with her, let her not leave him."

Paul is speaking here to those who marry before they are converted, and later one or the other of them is saved. Such cases are different from those addressed in verses 10 and 11, where he dealt with husband and wife who are both believers.

"But to the rest speak I, not the Lord." This does not mean that these words were not inspired — ALL Scripture is given by inspiration; and in these next verses, Paul gives scriptural and spiritual admonition to those who were in the condition described in the latter part of this verse:

"If a brother (a believer) *hath a wife that believeth not . . . ."* The only reasonable conclusion to be drawn here is that both husband and wife were unbelievers when they married; but the husband has been saved, and the wife remains unconverted. Yet, if the unbelieving wife be pleased to live with the believing husband, the husband should not put her away.

"And the woman which hath an husband that believeth not . . . ." We have the same picture here: Both husband and wife were unbelievers before they married, and *after* marriage the wife heard the Gospel and was born again but the husband remained unsaved. If the unsaved husband be pleased to dwell with the believing

wife, she should not leave him, even though he is a sinner and she is a Christian.

(It is well to note that there is no scriptural ground for a Christian *marrying* an unbeliever. Christians are commanded to marry Christians, and when a believer marries an unbeliever, trouble is sure to follow! There are rare instances where a Christian wife may lead an unsaved husband to Christ—or vice versa—but this is the exception rather than the rule. Usually there is much trouble and sorrow, and often there is a separation—because when the Christian mate desires to go to church, the sinner rebels. He has no interest in the house of God. Such a situation is bound to bring about unrest and friction.)

Verse 14: "For the unbelieving husband is sanctified by the wife, and the unbelieving wife is sanctified by the husband: else were your children unclean; but now are they holy."

The truth is clearly set forth here: The unbelieving husband is sanctified (set apart) by the believing wife, the unbelieving wife is sanctified by the believing husband. The Christian woman is part of the unbelieving man, and the Christian man is part of the unbelieving woman: for as already pointed out, when two are married *they become one flesh.* When two sinners are married, they become one flesh in the sight of God; and when one of them is converted, whether it be husband or wife, they are still one flesh — but thank God, the righteousness of the saved one is greater than the wickedness of the unsaved one, *and the born again believer sanctifies the unbeliever.*

This does not imply a change of the spiritual state in regard to God in respect to the unbelieving partner. He or she (as the case may be) is still a lost soul and needs to be saved by the blood of Jesus Christ. But through the natural union the unsaved mate receives a spiritual influence holding the possibility of actual conversion.

". . . *Else were your children unclean; but now are they holy.*" Again, this does not imply that the children are saved because they have a Christian mother or father. The words "sanctified" and "holy" are used in this verse in the same manner, and neither implies salvation.

If the home is broken up the unsaved wife or husband is removed from the privilege of spiritual influence and a place of sanctified relationship. This is also true of the children. As long as the home is not broken up the children are in the place of privilege and can be influenced for Christ.

In this verse we have a great contrast of the grace of Christianity and the rigor of Judaism. One of the ways Israel remained a holy people was in refusing to mix with the heathen in marriage. Those who took heathen wives were polluted, and their children were unclean. When they judged the sin they proved it by not only offering a blood sacrifice, but by putting away both children and wife (Ezra 10:3).

In the case of the Christian who was married to an unbeliever, Paul says that he does not have to put away his children — they were not unclean, but holy.

The born again husband can be the means of winning the unbelieving wife if he will remain with her, pray for her, and live a life of godliness, purity, and sincerity before her, claiming her for Jesus. The same is true of the born again wife and the unbelieving husband. We have the promise of John 15:7: "If ye abide in me, and my words abide in you, ye shall ask what ye will, and it shall be done unto you."

Verse 15: "But if the unbelieving depart, let him

depart. A brother or a sister is not under bondage in such cases: but God hath called us to peace."

"*. . . If the unbelieving depart, let him depart.*" Here Paul clearly tells us that if an unbelieving husband or wife departs from the mate who has been converted and is living a Christian life, "*a brother or a sister is not under bondage in such cases.*" That is, if the unbelieving one refuses to live with the believer, then the believer is not responsible for the departure of the unbeliever; and if the unbelieving mate departs and continues on in sin, dying without the Lord, the believing husband or wife is not responsible.

"*But God hath called us to peace.*" I firmly believe this to mean that it is better to allow the unbeliever to depart than for the believer and unbeliever to remain together where there is friction, argument, and quarreling between them. But if they CAN live together in peace and harmony, they should remain together; and the believer certainly has the promise from the Word of God that the unsaved mate *can be won* to the Lord. This should be a refreshing, comforting promise to dear wives who have unbelieving husbands, and to born again husbands who have unbelieving wives.

Verse 16: "For what knowest thou, O wife, whether thou shalt save thy husband? or how knowest thou, O man, whether thou shalt save thy wife?"

In this question Paul is simply asking, "Christian wife, if you remain with your unbelieving husband, do you not know that you may be able to save him?" This does not mean that the wife can forgive the sins of the husband; but through her prayers and godly living she may be *the means of his being saved* from the lake of fire. The same is true of the believing husband in relation to the unbelieving wife. GOD does the saving, in answer to the prayer and faithfulness of the born again companion.

You dear Christians who are now living with an unsaved mate, *do not despair*! If it is at all possible to live with that unbelieving companion, if life is not made unbearable for you—and especially if there are children in the home—stay with your husband (or wife, as the case may be); pray faithfully, live as God would have you live and set a Christian example in the home. Upon the promise of the Word of God, there is a good chance that you will be the means of leading that companion into salvation—and that will be worth all the heartaches and heartbreaks you have endured along the way.

Verse 17: "But as God hath distributed to every man, as the Lord hath called every one, so let him walk. And so ordain I in all churches."

Permission to separate from an unbelieving husband or wife is given only to meet the specific and special case wherein the *unbelieving partner* demands a separation. Paul here advises, "Remain in the condition in which you were called." That is, if you are married to a sinner, do not seek separation from him, but be faithful in the place where you find yourself when you are saved. That was his rule to his converts wherever he went, and in the following verses he gives remarkable illustrations of his principle—concerning the Jew and Gentile, slave and freeman, circumcised and uncircumcised.

Thus Paul shows that Christianity was not intended to bring about a violent revolution to society, but to sanctify existing relations between individuals until such time as these relations could be amended in peace, and bring about continuing unity—not division or separation. The true teaching of Christianity is simply that it interferes *indirectly*—not directly—with existing institutions upon this earth.

"And one of the company said unto Him, Master, speak to my brother, that he divide the inheritance with me. And He said unto him, Man, who made me a judge or a divider over you? And He said unto them, Take heed, and beware of covetousness: for a man's life consisteth not in the abundance of the things which he possesseth" (Luke 12:13–15).

Believers are to be "wise as serpents, and harmless as doves." Paul's teaching in our present passage is simply this: For a husband or wife who was converted from heathendom, a radical change was involved in the life *morally and spiritually*; but conversion from heathendom need NOT involve a radical change *externally*, to the extent that the believing partner take steps to bring about a separation from the unbeliever simply *because* the partner was an unbeliever.

The uppermost aim in the heart of the Christian should be to glorify God. A saved person is *in the light*, while the unbeliever is in darkness—the darkness of sin, his mind blinded by the god of this age. The believer can therefore bring honor and glory to God by remaining with the unsaved companion and leading him into the light of salvation. Some of the converts in Corinth had become restless because they had been converted and their mate had remained unsaved.

"And so ordain I in all churches." Paul makes it clear that this is not his teaching to the Corinthians only, but to all the churches where he had preached and taught.

Verse 18: "Is any man called being circumcised? Let him not become uncircumcised. Is any called in uncircumcision? Let him not be circumcised."

Paul first applied his principle to the undesirability of a drastic change in matters relating to married life, and now extends that principle to the subject of circumcision and conditions of slavery in his day. In this verse he gives us a statement of what is really the important thing in the life of the believer.

The individual converted as a Jew was not to change the external sign of his connection with God's chosen people. If he had been circumcised after the manner of the Jews, he was not to attempt to change this; nor was the converted Gentile to take steps to enter the Jewish community by being circumcised. Paul also deals with this matter in Galatians 5:6:

"For in Jesus Christ neither circumcision availeth any thing, nor uncircumcision; *but faith which worketh by love.*" Here he shows that in the Lord Jesus Christ, it is neither circumcision nor uncircumcision that produces spiritual results, but faith working through love—and love is the heart and soul of Christianity.

Verse 19: "Circumcision is nothing, and uncircumcision is nothing, but the keeping of the commandments of God."

That is to say, those who had been circumcised after the custom of Israel need not be ashamed of it; but by like token, those who were *uncircumcised* need not seek circumcision, because IN GRACE circumcision avails nothing. What matters in Christianity is obeying the Word of God, following *"Thus saith the Lord."* If we love God with all our heart, soul, strength, mind, and body, and love our neighbor as we should, "On these two commandments hang all the law and the prophets" (Matt. 22:40).

Christianity can be summed up in one word: *Obedience.* ". . . Behold, to obey is better than sacrifice . . ." (I Sam. 15:22). Christianity is not rituals and ceremonies, nor following the doctrines and traditions of men or of religion. Christianity is Christ in the heart—a new man, the inner man made new through the miracle of the grace of God; and obedience brings glory and honor to God.

Verse 20: "Let every man abide in the same calling wherein he was called."

Those of us who are not married to a religion or a denomination have no trouble seeing what this verse sets forth in this day of grace. In verse 17 the subject of circumcision was introduced. Here is repeated the exhortation of verse 17, introducing the subject of a bondslave or servant.

In verses 17 and 18, Paul dealt with religious distinction — i.e., *the outward performance does nothing for the inward possession*; but here he is dealing with social distinction. The calling referred to in this verse does not deal with the matter of one's vocation—whether he is called to be a minister, doctor, farmer, lawyer; but rather, it concerns the *circumstances* in which the calling took place — we might say it has to do with the condition in which the calling is found, as here we see it applied to circumcision or uncircumcision, married or unmarried, slavery or freedom. It certainly did not refer to earthly occupations, some of which would clash with God's Word, and offend a Christian conscience. A man making and selling whisky could not continue in his business after being converted. A change of heart in many instances would of necessity mean a change of one's earthly occupation.

When I was converted, I made restitution for many things; but there were some things I had done as a sinner for which it was *humanly impossible* to make restitution. I believe that when we are converted, we should set things right wherever possible. If we owe money, we should pay it; and if we cannot pay it, we should go to the one to whom the debt is owed, and explain that we cannot pay, but *will pay* as we can, little by little if need be.

If we have wronged someone, we should go to that person and make it right if it is at all possible to do so. There are, of course, some things that cannot be straightened out after conversion. In murder, for example, we know that no one can bring back the dead; and there are many other things that cannot be set to right, humanly speaking.

Two wrongs have never made a right. The only thing anyone can do after being born again is to pray, seek God's face, and follow the leading of the Holy Spirit. If we try to follow men, ministers, or religions, we will drive ourselves to frustration—perhaps even to insanity; but God is not the author of confusion. *He is the author of peace and assurance!*

God does not forgive *part* of our sins, and hold another part unforgiven until we make proper restitution. When God redeems us through the blood of Jesus, *we are completely redeemed!* One second after conversion, we are just as saved, just as much sons of God, as we will be if we live a Christian life for fifty years or more; but making restitution, setting old wrongs right insofar as is humanly possible, will bring satisfaction and spiritual strength.

Remember that "whatsoever we sow, we reap," and this does not necessarily mean that we will do our reaping in hell. We reap, at least partially, in this body and in this life; and those of us who sowed to the flesh in a terrible way while we were sinners are still reaping—and *will reap* until the day we die! Oh, yes, God forgives the sins; but I still suffer in my body for sins I committed long before I was saved. God made my spirit and soul whole, but my body has never been whole since God saved me, because I had almost destroyed my body with tobacco, alcohol, and other things that I will not name here. If a man gets drunk and loses an eye, an arm, or a leg while

in that condition, God will save his soul if he repents—
but the lost member of his body is not restored. This
body is destined to return to dust.

Verse 21: "Art thou called being a servant? Care not
for it: but if thou mayest be made free, use it rather."

"Art thou called being a servant?" If the believer
was a slave before his conversion, he is not to let that
fact trouble his mind *after* conversion. In Paul's day,
many born again people were slaves, and there were some
born again slavemasters. Explain this? I cannot; but the
Bible records it, and therefore we must face it. It is not
God's will that men should be slaves to other men, but
God allowed it, and there is no need for us to argue
about it.

". . . But if thou mayest be made free, use it rather."
If a converted slave is set free by his master, he should
accept his freedom and *use it to the glory of God.* Actually, the important thing is one's relationship to the
Lord. Whether slave or freeman, when a person is born
again *he is free in Christ.* He may be a slave physically—
but spiritually he is free; and "if the Son therefore shall
make you free, ye shall be free indeed!"

Paul's advice to those who were slaves was that if
their slavemaster were an unbeliever and refused to set
them free, they were to continue as slaves and not worry
or fret about it. They were free in Christ and one day
would go to be with Him, and after all, what really matters
is to know that we have spiritual freedom and a home with
Jesus in the life to come.

Verse 22: "For he that is called in the Lord, being a
servant, is the Lord's freeman: likewise also he that is
called, being free, is Christ's servant."

Here, "the call" refers to the time of conversion.
"In the Lord" means that the one who is called and who

becomes a believer *is immediately brought under the authority of the Lord Jesus Christ*; and even though he may be in bondage physically, his true Master is the Lord Jesus Christ.

Though a slave, the believer who is, by the grace of God, born into *the family of God* is thereby brought into subjection to Christ as His master, and spiritually he is a freeman because the Son of God has set him free. Under the law of the Romans in Paul's lifetime, a slave who had been freed was still under the protective guardianship of his master, who was thereafter called his "patron." But in the case of a Christian slave, Christ was not his *patron*; He was Owner, Master, and Lord. This is true of all believers. We have no right to anything, nor to any part of ourselves. We are bought with a price, and we are not our own.

Paul is pointing out the fact that even though a born again slave might *remain* a slave, *his spiritual freedom could not be destroyed by the slavemaster*. He might be kept in bondage to a physical master, but he could not be brought into bondage spiritually. He could rest assured that everything was controlled for him by the will of God, and though he be a slave, nothing could happen to him without God's permission.

"Likewise also he that is called, being free, is Christ's servant." In other words, the Christian slave is the Lord's freeman; the Christian freeman is the Lord's slave. Paul rejoiced to describe himself as the bond-slave of Jesus Christ. Study Romans 1:1, Philippians 1:1, and Titus 1:1. Believers should follow in his footsteps. We may not have been physical slaves—either before or after conversion; but we are not free to do the things we *like* to do simply *because* we are Christians. That is not grace at all. A true believer delights in the fact that he is a bondslave of Jesus Christ, and he joys in his

position AS a bondslave to Him who has done so much for US.

The name "Christ" speaks of grace and love such as only God could give; but *"Lord"* denotes ownership and authority. The name "Jesus" denotes the Saviour. Therefore, all who are saved because of God's love and grace should give Jesus Christ full authority in everything we do, in all avenues of life.

Verse 23: "Ye are bought with a price; be not ye the servants of men."

We read the same statement in I Corinthians 6:20, but the connection is different. There, the price speaks of the blood of Christ—the grounds for salvation—and the ground for the exhortation to remember that our bodies are temples of the Holy Spirit, and therefore are to be used to the glory of God. Christ lives in this tabernacle of flesh because He shed His blood and purchased redemption for us. We are redeemed through His blood.

But in our present verse, the Holy Spirit is speaking concerning the ground upon which, social distinctions apart, we are to remember that we are bondslaves of Christ, and having been freed from the slavery of sin and Satan, we are to serve the Lord Jesus with all of our heart, soul, and strength.

In Paul's day, among the Greeks a slave was freed through a fiction of legality, according to which the slave set free was purchased by "a god"—(*not Jehovah God*). The slave could not provide the money for his own freedom. His master paid the price, but he put it into the temple treasury, placing it there in the presence of a document drawn up—and on the document the words were written, *"For freedom."* After this transaction, no person could ever again enslave the one thus set free. He was the property of "a god," and therefore man could not buy or enslave him after he was set free in such a manner.

Believers were *slaves to sin*, children of the devil, and we could not pay the price of our redemption. But God paid the price through the blood of Jesus which cleanses us from ALL sin. We are now redeemed and hell cannot claim us. The Son of God has set us free and we are free indeed, because the offering He made was His own blood—an offering made once, forever, never to be repeated. Those who are covered by the blood are therefore perfected forever. (Please study the entire tenth chapter of Hebrews.)

Because we are set free through the purchase price of the blood of Jesus, we are admonished, *"Be not the servants of men."* Whatever our condition—slave or free-man—Christ died to make us His own. We should be at His disposal, listening always for His direction through the Spirit, and follow accordingly. We should consider ourselves His bondslaves.

The warning in this verse is also against ecclesiastical domination, and the enslavement of conscience to follow the judgments of men. *We are to follow God always*; we are not to follow the dictates of men nor allow them to dominate our lives. Ministers are God's undershepherds—not God's dictators. They are not lords over God's heritage. They are to *lead* the sheep, not *drive* them. Christians are not the servants of men, and if we fear men we are defeated spiritually that moment. We are to fear God, have faith in God, listen to the voice of God through His Word and the Holy Spirit, and stop our ears to what men may say. We are sons of God, servants of God, heirs of God, joint-heirs with Jesus Christ; and if God be for us, who can be against us? He has promised, ". . . I will never leave thee, nor forsake thee. So that we may boldly say, The Lord is my helper, and I will not fear what man shall do unto me'' (Heb. 13:5,6).

Verse 24: "Brethren, let every man, wherein he is called, therein abide with God."

This is a repetition of verse 20, with the added *"with God."* The believer is hid with Christ in God, God is ever looking down upon us, and that fact should dominate every intention of our lives. Regardless of our calling, regardless of family, social background, or any other circumstance, we must be always aware of the presence of God and do all that we do to His glory.

We are to be sanctified, meet for the Master's use, and we should not allow anything to come into our lives that would hinder our service for Christ. We must be good bondslaves, obedient servants, knowing that He is our Lord and Master—and rightly so, for He loved us and saved us by His grace. The believer who is constantly abiding with God enjoys perfect peace: "Thou wilt keep him in perfect peace, whose mind is stayed on thee: because he trusteth in thee" (Isa. 26:3). At God's right hand there are pleasures for evermore (Psalm 16:11). If we are abiding with God we shall not be unduly eager for change. Believers should permit the Lord to choose their way for them, and any change will come about only as He appoints and directs in it.

Advice Concerning the Unmarried

Verse 25: "Now concerning virgins I have no commandment of the Lord: yet I give my judgment, as one that hath obtained mercy of the Lord to be faithful."

This subject was introduced in verse 8, but here Paul deals with it a bit more fully. He gives his personal opinion, and then gives the principle that is divine and therefore *is superior* to his own opinion.

". . . *Concerning virgins, I have no commandment of the Lord* . . . ." This does not mean that this verse is not inspired; it is inspired just as much as any other Scripture. Paul clearly states, *"I give my judgment, as one that hath obtained mercy of the Lord to be faithful."* Remember, in Paul's lifetime the perfect law of liberty had not fully come; that which is perfect was not present. We now have the whole of the revealed truth of God, and we need no new epistles or commandments given upon the judgment of Spirit-filled, Spirit-controlled men. Paul was a special minister to the Gentiles, and God gave him revelations and the right to give out admonition as the Holy Ghost directed him.

Verse 26: "I suppose therefore that this is good for the present distress, I say, that it is good for a man so to be."

"I suppose" does not mean that Paul was uncertain. He was very sure of the soundness of the principle he was setting forth.

". . . *That this is good* . . . ." The Greek word *kalos* is used here for "good," signifying that which is *intrinsically good*—that is, something well adapted to its circumstances or ends; something good in character or beneficial in effect.

". . . *For the present distress* . . . ." The Greek word used here for "distress" means "that which arises from the pressure of external circumstances—as a result of which people tend to do what they would NOT do under some other condition or under ordinary circumstances." This could well refer to the distresses to which believers were then beginning to be subjected, making the married state less desirable than the single state.

". . . *For a man so to be.*" That is, "He should not change his condition." Most Bible scholars agree that the meaning here is that it is good for a man to remain as he is at the time of His conversion. Because of the severe persecutions the Christians were already under-going, any drastic or hasty changes socially could be detrimental rather than helpful to him as a believer.

God help every young Christian who reads these lines to know "that He which hath begun a good work in you will perform it until the day of Jesus Christ"—until that day when we stand face to face with Him. He who promised never to leave us nor forsake us will lead us into paths of right living and well-being. If we listen to *people*, they will take the joy out of our Christian experience; but if we listen to the Holy Spirit and follow Him, He will lead us beside the still waters, and we will enjoy our spiritual birthright of abundant life, with joy unspeakable and full of glory.

Verse 27: "Art thou bound unto a wife? Seek not to be loosed. Art thou loosed from a wife? Seek not a wife."

This verse is self-explanatory: If you are married, STAY married. If you are unmarried, do not seek a wife or a husband.

Verse 28: "But and if thou marry, thou hast not sinned; and if a virgin marry, she hath not sinned. Nevertheless such shall have trouble in the flesh: but I spare you."

"*. . . If thou marry, thou hast not sinned. . . .*" Some of the "wise" teachers (so-called) in Corinth had taught that it was a sin to marry; but Paul assures the believers that if they have married, they have not sinned in so doing; and if a *virgin* marries, she does not sin thereby. However, though a young lady be a virgin, or a young man be as clean as the morning dew, it is a proven fact that "*such shall have trouble* (or tribulations) *in the flesh.*"

"The flesh" here stands for more than the body of bone, blood, and sinew; *it stands for circumstances all around us*, circumstances which affect life. Paul is referring here to trouble that is sure to come, in various ways, in married life. Such trouble may be physical, or financial, or general—but *there will be* problems and heartaches in married life that single people know nothing about! Married life has its wonderful points, but it also has times of trouble and heartbreak. A single person is not without problems, but such problems as one encounters in single life are of a different nature to those found in marriage.

"But I spare you." Here the emphasis is upon *"I."* Paul is saying that insofar as he was concerned personally, acting as their spiritual adviser, he would spare them this trouble and tribulation in the flesh by advising them to remain unmarried.

Verse 29: "But this I say, brethren, the time is short: it remaineth, that both they that have wives be as though they had none."

"But this I say . . . ." refers to Paul's forthcoming advice and warning. He is making a declaration.

"The time is short." The Greek verb used here signifies "has been drawn so as to be little in amount," or "has been contracted." The word denotes a season, or a period providing an opportunity; it does not refer to length of time as such. Paul is here speaking of the time in which our life and circumstances are to be viewed and planned in the light of the imminent return of the Lord Jesus Christ. We know He is coming, but we do not know the day or the hour — He may come this moment. Therefore, we should occupy until He DOES come; and for you and for me as individuals, *the time IS short.*

"It remaineth . . . ." The Greek word here rendered "remaineth" means "henceforth," and is a very strong, emphatic word. It means "that which remains of our life here on earth." The admonition set forth here by the

Apostle Paul is that the believer is to avoid anything that will cause him to become a slave in the flesh—whether it be circumstances or relationships, marriage included. One who is about to be married is to weigh the matter—its circumstances and all that has to do with married life—in view of the eternity he faces. (Study II Corinthians 4:16,17 and Romans 13:11,12.)

". . . *That both they that have wives be as though they had none.*" The meaning here is not that a married man should cease to live with his wife as a married man should; but that a man who is married should make all of his plans and live his life in view of his relationship to God, allowing the Lord to have first place in heart, home, and business. He is not to allow anything—not even the relationship between himself and his wife—to cause him to be less obedient to Jesus Christ, the Lord of his life.

Verse 30: "And they that weep, as though they wept not; and they that rejoice, as though they rejoiced not; and they that buy, as though they possessed not."

". . . *They that weep . . . they that rejoice . . . .*" Believers are not to allow things that cause them to weep (or to rejoice, as the case may be) to come between them and their service to the Lord. If they weep, they are to live as though they wept not, giving their best to the Master, even through heartbreak and tears. If they are happy, rejoicing over many things, they are not to allow their rejoicing to take away or diminish their glorying in the Lord.

". . . *They that buy, as though they possessed not.*" The Greek verb *katecho* used here is translated "possessed," meaning "to securely hold fast to a thing or an object." What the believer "owns" here on earth is simply a trust, for "the earth is the Lord's, and the fullness thereof," and *everything that we have* belongs to

God. He has given us what we have—but only to hold in trust. It is not ours. We may brag that we need to tear down old barns and build new ones to store our goods and our material gain — but when we do that, we are playing the part of a fool. The very air we breathe is given to us by God who gives all good things (James 1:17).

This does not mean that a believer should have no desire to make progress in business, *but he is not to allow business to come between him and his service to God.* When a businessman is so busy that he does not have time to attend church, pray, and read his Bible, he is TOO busy! He is not gaining ground — he is losing.

Verse 31: "And they that use this world, as not abusing it: for the fashion of this world passeth away."

The Greek language here does not signify abuse, but implies "using to the utmost, or overmuch." The Greek verb is rendered, "used to the full." We are not to allow business, money, or any material interest to fill our time and our life. We are sons of God, bondslaves of Jesus Christ, and servants of our fellow believers to the glory of God.

"World" denotes the sum total of our temporal possessions, or of conditions around us. Born again believers are not to use any of the things of the world as though those things were the object of life. The Bible clearly teaches that if we love the world, the love of God is not in us (I John 2:15—17). To love the world means to allow the world to occupy in our lives the place that should belong to God and receive the love that should be directed only to Him.

". . . *The fashion of this world passeth away.*" The Greek word used for "fashion" means "outward appearance." Here, it indicates the manner of life, actions, and things in general. We should not allow the world to possess us, because these things will pass away.

In II Corinthians 4:18 Paul declares that "we look not at the things which are seen, but at the things which are not seen: for the things which are seen are temporal; but the things which are not seen are eternal." In I John 2:17 we read, ". . . The world passeth away, and the lust thereof: *but he that doeth the will of God abideth forever!*" A spiritually minded believer does not have the attitude, "I will get all I can out of life," but rather, "I will put into my stewardship anything and all things that will glorify God." That should be the desire of our hearts and lives.

Verse 32: "But I would have you without carefulness. He that is unmarried careth for the things that belong to the Lord, how he may please the Lord."

·"*But I would have you without carefulness.*" What Paul wants us to see here is that things around us are not the things of primary importance, because they will pass away. He wanted his children in the faith to live a life without care toward earthly things, seeking first the kingdom of God and His righteousness, knowing that all other necessary things would be added. This is the same thought contained in Matthew 6:28–30 when Jesus said to His disciples:

"And why take ye thought for raiment? Consider the lilies of the field, how they grow; they toil not, neither do they spin: And yet I say unto you, That even Solomon in all his glory was not arrayed like one of these. Wherefore, if God so clothe the grass of the field, which to day is, and to morrow is cast into the oven, shall He not much more clothe you, O ye of little faith?"

In Matthew 10:29–31 Jesus said, "Are not two sparrows sold for a farthing? and one of them shall not fall on the ground without your Father. But the very hairs of your head are all numbered. Fear ye not, therefore, *ye are of more value than many sparrows.*"

During times of burdens, distress, perplexities and anxieties, the believer becomes discouraged and is thus rendered less effective in God's service. It is not God's will that we give way to anxiety and worry; He wants us to trust Him for everything. He will supply our need, and He can make us content in whatsoever state we find ourselves. It is a sin to worry, for after all, *"If God be for us, who can be against us?"* Paul said, ". . . My God shall supply all your need according to His riches in glory by Christ Jesus" (Phil. 4:19). He will never leave us nor forsake us. Why should we worry, with such promises to lean upon?

"He that is unmarried careth for the things that belong to the Lord, how he may please the Lord." Paul is speaking here of matters in general. Naturally, a man who is married knows that it is his duty to supply the physical and material needs of his wife and family, and it is only reasonable that he would have less time for the things of the Lord. It is the duty of the head of a family to provide for those who depend upon him. In I Timothy 5:8 Paul said, "If any provide not for his own, and specially for those of his own house, he hath denied the faith, and is worse than an infidel!" A man who is married is duty-bound to care for his family; and in so doing, his service to God is automatically limited. But if he is unmarried he is free to go to the ends of the earth if the Holy Spirit so leads, and preach the Gospel in places where it would be physically impossible for him to go if he had a wife and children.

Verse 33: "But he that is married careth for the *things that are of the world, how he may please his wife.*"

This simply enlarges upon the last part of the preceding verse. Paul speaks of the natural tendency of men, not inferring that the married man is worldly-minded or less spiritual than the unmarried man; but simply that since he is married, life necessarily involves more attention to matters pertinent to his wife and family. Anyone who will be reasonable can see this. A single person has no responsibility except to himself — but a married man has a wife to care for—and, in most cases, *children*; and this makes a tremendous difference in many ways.

Verse 34: "There is a difference also between a wife and a virgin. The unmarried woman careth for the things of the Lord, that she may be holy both in body and in spirit: but she that is married careth for the things of the world, how she may please her husband."

As was true of *men* in verses 32 and 33, a single *woman* has more time for the Lord. Her whole soul, spirit, and body can be set apart to the Lord's service—on the mission field or at home; and the simple fact that she IS single enables her to give *her entire being* to the Lord in service and stewardship; whereas, if she is married, she must of necessity as a faithful wife, give special care and time to her husband—and in most cases, to her children.

This does not mean that she has failed to please God; but it is a certain fact that since she IS married, with husband, home (and probably children) to care for, those circumstances make it much easier to neglect prayer and Bible study, and also make it much more difficult to attend services regularly in the local assembly. We must face facts: *Those who are unmarried have the advantage in spiritual matters*, for they have only the Lord to please, while married people have a family to think of—and rightly so.

Verse 35: "And this I speak for your own profit; not that I may cast a snare upon you, but for that which is comely, and that ye may attend upon the Lord without distraction."

The Greek word used here for "profit" is *sumphoros*. It is found only twice in the New Testament—here, and in chapter 10, verse 33. It means, "That which makes for one's best interest." Paul is here giving advice for the good of the believers.

"Not that I may cast a snare upon you . . . ." The Greek word *brochos* means a noose, or halter, and literally reads, "throw a noose over you." This word occurs only here in our New Testament. It signifies a noose to catch an animal, depriving it of the liberty it enjoys, the liberty for which it was born.

Paul's object was to their advantage. In urging them to remain single, he had no intention of restraining their liberty. The figure is, "I do not wish to raise scruples to make you afraid to move lest you fall into a snare." The former explanation is preferable.

Paul did not wish to bring his readers into a state where they had no liberty. They were free to do what they pleased. There was no moral obligation upon them to remain single; there was no superior holiness in celibacy. He was only saying what was, *in his judgment*, best for them under the existing circumstances.

The Holy Spirit is saying, through the Apostle Paul, that a minister has no right to force anyone into a life for which he or she is not fitted. A minister has no right to tell any couple that they should marry, or that they should NOT marry. The same can be said concerning other matters. A minister has no right to tell a young lady that she should—or should not—go to the mission field. The Lord of our life is the One to lead us in the ministry, or in marriage, in business, in whatever has to do with our earthly sojourn.

"*. . . But for that which is comely . . . .*" The Greek word used here is *euschemon* and means "what is becoming." It signifies that which is worthy of the position and high calling of the born again believer. (In I Corinthians 12:24 the same word is used, having to do with parts of the body.) We should not allow anything to come into our lives that will hinder our testimony. Insofar as is possible, we should conduct ourselves in such manner and live under such conditions as will promote Christian stewardship at its highest, and lead us to do things that will glorify the Lord at all times.

"*. . . That ye may attend upon the Lord without distraction.*" The meaning of the statement here is that believers should not allow anything to come into their lives that would draw their attention, love, and service away from the Lord Jesus Christ. (The Greek word *aperispos* means "without distraction" and signifies "to apply oneself diligently to anything.) Spiritually, our eye is to be singled always on Jesus, our minds are to be stayed on Him, and all that we do, we are to do to His glory.

Verse 36: "But if any man think that he behaveth himself uncomely toward his virgin, if she pass the flower of her age, and need so require, let him do what he will, he sinneth not: let them marry."

Apparently, Paul had been asked a question pertaining to the duty of a father toward his daughter concerning marriage. If the girl had reached marriageable age ("*if she pass the flower of her age*") and yet was NOT married, what was the father's obligation to her? Should he insist that she find and marry a respectable young man? Should he ignore the whole situation? Or should he attempt to keep his daughter from marrying?

In Corinth, there was grave danger for a girl who was at an age for marriage. "*If need so require*" – if she desired to marry and the father refused to allow her to do so, she might disgrace her father and ruin her own testimony by marrying the wrong person. In that case, what God intended to be morally beautiful would become morally ugly and bring about a scandal in the church and in the community.

"... *Let him (the father) do what he will* ...." This simply means that a godly father should act in accordance with the convictions of his own heart. Some Bible commentators have suggested that this refers to a sort of spiritual betrothal between unmarried persons, but such teaching is not true and is to be rejected.

Verse 37: "Nevertheless he that standeth stedfast in his heart, having no necessity, but hath power over his own will, and hath so decreed in his heart that he will keep his virgin, doeth well."

Here we have presented a case where the father is convinced in his own heart that he is doing the right thing in refusing to permit his daughter to marry. "... *Having no necessity*" points out the absence of any reason whatsoever which would make it improper or wrong for him to withhold his consent to such a marriage. There are many circumstances which could bring about such a refusal.

"... *But hath power over his own will, and hath so decreed in his heart that he will keep his virgin* ...." This suggests that the father has the right to act according to his own conviction and purpose of heart — not necessarily that he has the control over his own will, but that there is nothing to interfere with his exercising of his right as a parent, as would be the case were he a slave.

What is true today was exactly the opposite in Paul's day. Customs in those days placed the disposal of a daughter wholly under the power and at the discretion of the father. He had a right to say "Yea" or "Nay" concerning her marriage. But even today, a believing father who has the welfare of his daughter at heart, and flatly refuses to go along with a wedding which he knows would not be to the glory of God or for the happiness and welfare of his daughter, "doeth well" if he takes a stand and exercises his authority.

Verse 38: "So then he that giveth her in marriage doeth well; but he that giveth her not in marriage doeth better."

The father who is willing to give up his virgin daughter in marriage to the right man *in the Lord*, "doeth well"; but the father who does NOT give his daughter in marriage *"doeth better."* The Holy Spirit is not contrasting between "well" and "better" as having to do with what is morally right or wrong. This has to do with what is expedient (or to the advantage of all parties concerned), always keeping in mind that we are dealing here with believers, not with sinners.

If he knows the man his daughter is about to marry is a sinner, it is the duty of any father to do everything in his power—in the right way and in a Christian attitude— to prevent the marriage. Paul has already pointed out that there is great advantage in being unmarried, insofar as service and stewardship to God are concerned; and always the one thing uppermost in his mind was "to do all to the glory of God." If young people can marry to the glory of God, "Amen!" If they cannot marry to the glory of God, then it is far better that they remain single.

If a parent can prevent a marriage that is not to the glory of God because of circumstances and the parties involved, that parent is doing service—to his daughter and to the Lord. We are responsible for our children and we should be gravely concerned about whom they marry.

Verse 39: "The wife is bound by the law as long as her husband liveth; but if her husband be dead, she is at liberty to be married to whom she will; only in the Lord."

The statement here is clear: Paul, having dealt with the subject of giving a *virgin* in marriage, now gives a bit of extra advice on the remarriage of widows. The subject has already been introduced in verses 8 and 34, and is also discussed in Romans 7:1—6 where the illustration has to do with law and grace.

In our present verse a wife is bound by law as long as her husband lives; but if her husband dies, she is at liberty to be married to whomsoever she will—but "ONLY IN THE LORD!"

The case here is different from that of virgins, for the widow must make the decision *in her own heart.* If she does marry a second time it must be in the Lord, and she must *seek the will of the Lord* in the matter.

This distinctly points out that a born again widow is not to marry an unbeliever, for such a marriage could not be "in the Lord." But the admonition given here goes further than that. It does not mean that the born again widow is free to marry anyone she chooses simply because she wants to marry, even if the man is a believer. First, the Lord's will must be wrought in her life if she hopes to have His blessing upon her marriage and upon her future. The responsibility of the widow is to the Lord—not to her own desires or her own wishes, regardless of how much she may feel the need of marrying again. She must first seek the will of the Lord; she must not marry simply for companionship, or to have a husband to supply her needs in this life.

Verse 40: "But she is happier if she so abide, after my judgment: and I think also that I have the Spirit of God."

This verse needs little comment. Paul was not

271

married, he did not know the companionship of a mate, and he could say, "I count all things loss that I might gain Christ; and in my judgment, one is happier if he or she abide in single state."

"And I think also that I have the Spirit of God." Paul never tried to force his opinions on others. He was a good undershepherd; he never tried to *drive* those under his ministry. But he always declared that his own views and opinions were of the Holy Spirit. He is not giving a command here; he is only advising in the Spirit, and this verse is just as much inspired as any other verse in the Bible. He presents the argument and evident fact that married people are responsible for their mates, they must expend time, concern, love, and energy on home and family, whereas one who is single can give more time, more love, and more service to the Lord.

Paul was a true servant of God, a true pastor, and he loved his children in the faith—those who had become believers because of his ministry. He wanted them to give their best to Jesus and enjoy their full spiritual birthright. So — even though it might have hurt him in the flesh, he spoke words of soberness and truth. He left no stone unturned, no sermon unpreached, that would make the believers in Corinth stronger in the Lord and help them to overcome the many hindrances that were there.

CHAPTER EIGHT

1. Now as touching things offered unto idols, we know that we all have knowledge. Knowledge puffeth up, but charity edifieth.

2. And if any man think that he knoweth any thing, he knoweth nothing yet as he ought to know.

3. But if any man love God, the same is known of him.

4. As concerning therefore the eating of those things that are offered in sacrifice unto idols, we know that an idol is nothing in the world, and that there is none other God but one.

5. For though there be that are called gods, whether in heaven or in earth, (as there be gods many, and lords many,)

6. But to us there is but one God, the Father, of whom are all things, and we in him; and one Lord Jesus Christ, by whom are all things, and we by him.

7. Howbeit there is not in every man that knowledge: for some with conscience of the idol unto this hour eat it as a thing offered unto an idol; and their conscience being weak is defiled.

8. But meat commendeth us not to God: for neither, if we eat, are we the better; neither, if we eat not, are we the worse.

9. But take heed lest by any means this liberty of your's become a stumblingblock to them that are weak.

10. For if any man see thee which hast knowledge sit at meat in the idol's temple, shall not the conscience of him which is weak be emboldened to eat those things which are offered to idols;

11. And through thy knowledge shall the weak brother perish, for whom Christ died?

12. But when ye sin so against the brethren, and wound their weak conscience, ye sin against Christ.

13. Wherefore, if meat make my brother to offend, I will eat no flesh while the world standeth, lest I make my brother to offend.

Meats and Christian Liberty

Paul now turns to the discussion of idols and idol sacrifices (meats offered to idols); and this continues through verse 1 of chapter 11. This was undoubtedly the next question in line in Paul's letter from the church at Corinth. There is much in common between this subject and that in chapter 7—namely, immorality as related to the worship of idols. The two were closely associated, and immorality and idol worship were common practices in heathen nations. Study Revelation 2:14—20.

The difficulty concerning idols, and sacrifices offered to idols, was twofold: First, to take any part in social life in the city of Corinth necessarily involved eating in public, in what was known as "common meals." These feasts were usually held in the temple, and on occasions there was a gala feast with more ceremony, which related to the worship of a pagan god.

In the second place, a great percentage of the meat sold in the marketplace had been offered to idols. Thus, two difficulties arose for believers.

Was it right for a born again believer to take part in such social activity? Was it right for a born again believer to eat meat which had been offered to idols? There were two opinions in the assembly in Corinth:

Some felt that the idols were dead and meaningless, and they therefore taught that it was harmless to take part in the temple feasts which were, to them, nothing more than a social function—or, as we would say today, "a community feed." Other believers felt that all such activities were inconsistent with Christian living and with the Christian faith they practiced, and they therefore believed that they should abstain from taking any part in these feasts.

Paul refers to the former group as "strong" and the

latter as "weak." In this and in the following chapters he gives instruction concerning such feasts, and how believers should feel toward them. In the first place, the principle of Christian love is 'that believers should not take part or participate in anything that might cause a weaker believer to stumble. Those of us who profess to be strong in the Lord should have proper regard for the conscience of weaker believers; and even though personally we may see no harm in certain things, for the sake of others we should not participate in them.

I stated earlier in this study that there are many things the believer could do which, insofar as the individual is concerned, would not harm *him*, but might be the means of causing someone else to stumble. "For none of us liveth to himself, and no man dieth to himself" (Rom. 14:7). In this sense, spiritually speaking, we are our brother's keeper, and if eating meat offends the weaker brother, we should not eat meat.

Paul uses himself as an illustration, and points out his own experience in the matter. (See chapter 9:1–23.) Then he sets forth the fact that in the life of the believer there should be constant self-discipline (chapter 9:24 through 10:13). He points out that the believer should always show fidelity to a Christian testimony—especially if it is in connection with the Lord's Supper. The believer should also show fidelity to the conscience of another. Whatever a believer participates in should be done to the glory of God — but it should also be for the profit, benefit, strengthening, and edification of all believers (chapter 10:14 through 11:1).

Verse 1: "Now as touching things offered unto idols, we know that we all have knowledge. Knowledge puffeth up, but charity edifieth."

Some of the believers in the assembly had been

advertising their wisdom, and Paul here indicates that they claimed to be enlightened regarding the true nature of idol worship. Paul frequently refers to this matter of knowledge—such knowledge as caused the Corinthian Christians to have a tendency to boast and brag: "Let no man deceive himself. If any man among you seemeth to be wise in this world, let him become a fool, that he may be wise" (I Cor. 3:18).

Some of the assembly seemed to regard knowledge as the paramount feature of the Christian faith. Of course, they knew there was nothing to a dead idol insofar as the stone or the wood was concerned — Paul does not deny that fact; but he does go further to show these wise believers that *knowledge* is not the main thing in Christian living, but that *love* must be the center and heart of our experience in all that we do. Whatever we do, we must do it because we love God and love the brethren. We must do nothing to hinder "those who are without," because we love them and want them to be saved. LOVE — not knowledge — must be the judge in what we do.

"Knowledge puffeth up, but charity edifieth." The Greek verb used here denotes "to blow up, or to inflate," and the Greek noun signifies "a pair of bellows." Throughout the New Testament this word is used in connection with pride. Knowledge has a tendency to "blow up," but love *"filleth up"*—that is, love builds up the believer in spiritual living and character and brings about the establishment of true union among those in the assembly. God resisteth the proud, but giveth grace to the humble. The way to advance in God's program is to be humble, not to be "blown up."

Verse 2: "And if any man think that he knoweth any thing, he knoweth nothing yet as he ought to know."

The meaning here is simply this: If any man thinks

in his own mind that he has fully acquired true knowledge, that man has not yet *begun* to know anything; he has not even learned how knowledge should be gained!

True knowledge is free from pride. The self-satisfied attitude of the Corinthian believers seemed to have made some of them feel that they had attained *complete* knowledge. They acted after the manner of what we would call a "know-it-all." They were attempting to teach when they needed to be taught. The believer who, in most cases, is ready to instruct others, has only superficial knowledge. (Notice again I Corinthians 3:18.) These believers in the Corinthian church are all dead, but we have some of the same kind of people in our churches today.

Verse 3: "But if any man love God, the same is known of him."

The love of God in one's heart never begets pride of knowledge. The more completely we are controlled by the Spirit of God and permeated by the love of God, the more humble we are. The love of God within us enables us to walk humbly before Him. Love is the essence of Christianity; knowledge is secondary. One who possesses *true knowledge* of God and of His Word loves God and His Word the more.

Verse 4: "As concerning therefore the eating of those things that are offered in sacrifice unto idols, we know that an idol is nothing in the world, and that there is none other God but one."

In the heathen festivals and sacrifices, portions were given to the priest who made the sacrifice to the idol. True believers recognized the fact that all of this was nothing but emptiness and vanity; but even though the believers in Corinth *knew* this, that did not settle the questions that were in their minds—questions which brought about divisions among the believers. *There IS but one God.*

An idol therefore *cannot* be an image of another god, because it stands to reason that an image cannot be made of a god that does not exist! Since there is but one true God, the sacrifices made to idols were but vain and empty nothings.

Verses 5 and 6: "For though there be that are called gods, whether in heaven or in earth, (as there be gods many, and lords many,) but to us there is but one God, the Father, of whom are all things, and we in Him; and one Lord Jesus Christ, by whom are all things, and we by Him."

Paul clearly teaches that there were supernatural powers behind the idols being worshipped in Corinth: "But I say, that the things which the Gentiles sacrifice, they sacrifice to *devils*, and not to God: and I would not that ye should have fellowship with devils" (I Cor. 10:20). Insofar as the idol was concerned, it was nothing; but the worship directed TO the idol was actually worshipping the devil (or demons).

"But to us there is but one God, the Father, of whom are all things . . . ."

"In the beginning God . . ." (Gen. 1:1).

"Hear, O Israel: The Lord our God is one Lord" (Deut. 6:4).

"For the Lord your God is God of gods, and Lord of lords, a great God, a mighty, and a terrible, which regardeth not persons, nor taketh reward" (Deut. 10:17).

"O give thanks unto the God of gods: for His mercy endureth for ever. O give thanks to the Lord of lords: for His mercy endureth for ever" (Psa. 136:2,3).

Paul maintains the eternal truth that God is *one God*. We believe in the Trinity, and in this verse we see the Trinity set forth; but Paul is reminding the Corinthians that in spite of all the gods man may make, set up, and

278

worship, there is still but one true God; and He is the Father of all things. His Fatherhood is a matter of revelation (Matt. 11:27; John 17:25). But the relationship is not universal (Matt. 13:38; John 8:23, 41, 44); it exists only for those who have been born anew (John 1:12,13). Before anything was created, "in the beginning − GOD!" God is an eternal Spirit; there was never a time when God was not; He had no beginning, He has no ending. "Lord, thou hast been our dwelling place in all generations. Before the mountains were brought forth, or ever thou hadst formed the earth and the world, even from everlasting to everlasting, thou art God" (Psa. 90:1,2).

In the beginning, God created the heaven and the earth, and in the process of creation, all things were created by Him − through the Lord Jesus Christ, and for the glory of God and Christ: "All things were made by Him; and without Him was not any thing made that was made" (John 1:3). "And as a vesture shalt thou fold them up, and they shall be changed: but thou art the same, and thy years shall not fail" (Heb. 1:12). "For by Him were all things created, that are in heaven, and that are in earth, visible and invisible, whether they be thrones, or dominions, or principalities, or powers: all things were created by Him, and for Him" (Col. 1:16).

The earth is the Lord's, and the fulness thereof. The universe (including the meats under discussion here) is OF God; and the redeemed are FOR God. Believers are God's children through faith in the shed blood and the finished work of Jesus Christ. We are set apart by the sanctifying power of the Holy Spirit—the third Person of the Godhead; and the purpose of our being set apart is for the use and the glory of God. We are workers *together WITH God*, and all that we do is to be done to His glory. "UNTO HIM" are the words that should be written upon the heart of every believer, and these words should be the controlling motive for all of our activities—small or great.

"*. . . And one Lord Jesus Christ . . . .*" The Greek word *kurios*, here translated "Lord," is also translated "master, or owner," and occurs in all the books of the New Testament except the epistle to Titus and the epistles of John. The Lord Jesus used this same word in referring to Himself in the solemn warning given in Matthew 7:21,22. He also used it in Matthew 9:38 and Matthew 22:41–45. It is used in Mark 5:19, Luke 19:31, and John 13:13. What Jesus meant by using the word was not fully understood by His disciples until after His crucifixion and resurrection—the ultimate proof of His deity.

On many occasions He had told them that He would arise from the dead on the third day — but they did not grasp the meaning of His words. After the crucifixion, Peter went fishing, and the other disciples followed him. *Thomas* doubted to the extent that he declared, "Except I shall see in His hands the print of the nails, and put my finger into the print of the nails, and thrust my hand into His side, I will not believe. . . Then saith (Jesus) to Thomas, Reach hither thy finger, and behold my hands; and reach hither thy hand, and thrust it into my side: and be not faithless, but believing. And Thomas answered and said unto Him, My Lord and my God!" (John 20:25,27, 28).

Jesus is the *Saviour* of all Christians, but He is not *Lord* of all Christians. Those who own Him as Lord are His faithful servants: "For he that is called in the Lord, being a servant, is the Lord's freeman: likewise also, he that is called, being free, is Christ's servant" (I Cor. 7:22). "Not with eyeservice, as menpleasers; but as the servants of Christ, doing the will of God from the heart" (Eph. 6:6).

As His servants, we must be obedient in all things: "And why call ye me, Lord, Lord, and do not the things which I say?" (Luke 6:46). When a believer unconditionally and completely surrenders to Jesus, looking to Him as Lord of life, Jesus then graciously admits that believer to His friendship: "Ye are my friends, if ye do whatsoever I command you. Henceforth I call you not servants; for the servant knoweth not what his lord doeth: but I have called you friends; for all things that I have heard of my Father I have made known unto you" (John 15:14,15).

"*. . . By whom are all things, and we by Him.*" The first part of this verse points to Christ's work in creation—including meats. The second part of the verse points to His work in the *new creation* whereby the believer becomes a new creature in Christ (II Cor. 5:17).

Christ is here set forth as Creator of both the natural and the spiritual, having brought all things into existence: "Who is the image of the invisible God, the firstborn of every creature: For by Him were all things created, that are in heaven, and that are in earth, visible and invisible, whether they be thrones, or dominions, or principalities, or powers: all things were created by Him, and for Him" (Col. 1:15,16).

Jesus was not just *present* at creation; He was not just a bystander. *He IS the Creator.* ALL things were created by Him: "And unto the angel of the church of the Laodiceans write: These things saith the Amen, the faithful and true witness, the beginning of the creation of God" (Rev. 3:14).

Christis "the beginning of the creation of God," and therefore creation owes its origin to Him. The wood, stone, silver, gold, or whatever substances the idol gods were made of, were created in the beginning by the ONE

GOD — the Father, and the Son, and the Holy Spirit. The dead stone gods were nothing; and the eating of meat that had been offered to them did not hurt the believer who was strong spiritually; but Paul makes it plain that in the spiritual aspect we are our brother's keeper and must do nothing to cause one of our weaker brothers to stumble.

Verse 7: "Howbeit there is not in every man that knowledge: for some with conscience of the idol unto this hour eat it as a thing offered unto an idol; and their conscience being weak is defiled."

What Paul is pointing out here is the fact that not all believers possess the knowledge necessary to understand that a believer could, without harming his conscience, eat meats that had been offered to idols. Not all of the Corinthian believers had grown to that point of spirituality.

"For some with conscience of the idol unto this hour eat it as a thing offered unto an idol." The Greek word here for "conscience" has the meaning "a custom or force of habit." Some of the believers in Corinth had not reached the place in spiritual thinking where they did not associate meat offered to idols with idol-worship; hence for them to eat the meat constituted the very act of idol-worship. They had not grown in grace and spirituality to the point where they recognized the liberty in Christianity, and when these weak believers ate meat offered to idols, *their conscience, being weak, was defiled.*

The defilement did not come through the meat, however, for eating food offered to an idol could not defile: "And (Jesus) saith unto them, Are ye so without understanding also? Do ye not perceive, that whatsoever thing from without entereth into the man, it cannot defile him; because it entereth not into his heart, but into the belly, and goeth out into the draught, purging all meats?" (Mark 7:18,19).

"And the Lord said unto him, Now do ye Pharisees make clean the outside of the cup and the platter; but your inward part is full of ravening and wickedness. Ye fools, did not He that made that which is without make that which is within also? But rather give alms of such things as ye have; and, behold, all things are clean unto you" (Luke 11:39–41).

It was not the eating of the meat itself that defiled these weaker believers, but doing that which the conscience regarded as evil: "And he that doubteth is damned if he eat, because he eateth not of faith: *for whatsoever is not of faith is sin*" (Rom. 14:23).

When a believer feels in his heart that he is doing something wrong, his act itself is wrong on the ground that he is wounding his God-given conscience. Yet when that same believer grows in grace and spirituality, receiving further light by studying the Word of God, the very thing that once wounded his conscience may no longer do so, and therefore to him it would not be wrong. A conscience that is defiled (or hurt) cripples spiritual enjoyment and hinders complete communion with God. A believer with a wounded conscience cannot have full joy, nor can he enjoy abundant life.

Verse 8: "But meat commendeth us not to God: for neither, if we eat, are we the better; neither, if we eat not, are we the worse."

The Greek word here translated "commend" denotes "to present for approval." Food itself will have no bearing upon the opinion or judgment of God concerning believers, for while man looks on the outward appearance, God looks on the heart. What matters is the pure heart, not undefiled food. The weak brother confuses the two.

There are many people today who refuse to partake of certain foods because they believe the eating of that food to be sinful. Those following some religions will eat no pork; others will eat pork every day in the week except Friday. Members of some cults refuse to drink carbonated beverages (soft drinks); but insofar as spirituality is concerned, food has nothing whatever to do with our being spiritual, or being carnal.

We should of course abstain from any food that is detrimental to our health. Christians should not eat or drink anything that harms us, tears down our body, or wrecks our health. Many people cannot eat hog meat because of high blood pressure, ulcers, or various other health problems, while others eat pork and are none the worse for it. Meats have nothing to do with spirituality, but they may have *much* to do with physical health; and it is sinful to destroy the body which is the temple of God.

"For neither, if we eat, are we the better; neither, if we eat not, are we the worse." The Greek reads, "If we *eat not*, do we *lack*? Or if we *eat*, do we *abound*?" Our refusal to eat does not cause God to think any more of us, nor any less; and by like token, if we eat we gain no advantage with God, nor do we bring about any *disadvantage* with Him. Eating meats, or not eating meats, has nothing to do with spirituality. It will not bring the blessings of God upon us, nor cause God *not* to bless us. It is the condition of the heart that counts with God. If the heart is right and if we walk uprightly, no good thing will He withhold from us.

Verse 9: "But take heed lest by any means this liberty of your's become a stumblingblock to them that are weak."

It is true that the Son has set us free and we are therefore free indeed; but this liberty which is ours must not become a stumblingblock to those who are weak. The Greek word here translated "liberty" is *exousia* and denotes liberty, or power, or right; so Paul is actually saying, "Lest this *right* which you assert should become a stumblingblock." Some of the believers in Corinth were taking their rights, even though it did hurt weaker Christians; and such liberty becomes evil. We have no right to do anything that will cause someone else to stumble.

The Greek word used here for "stumblingblock" is *proskomma*, meaning "an obstacle against which one may dash his foot." Paul uses the same word in Romans 14:13, meaning "spiritual hindrance to a weak brother by the selfish use of a strong brother's liberty."

I repeat: There are many things which believers could do which would not hurt them as individuals, but which might prove harmful to others. There are some places where Christians could go without harming their *own* spirituality, and yet if a weaker Christian saw them entering the place, that weaker brother could be hurt, caused to stumble, and perhaps be influenced to do something much worse! We must be very careful where we go, what we do, the language we use, and the attitude we display.

Verse 10: "For if any man see thee which hast knowledge sit at meat in the idol's temple, shall not the conscience of him which is weak be emboldened to eat those things which are offered to idols?"

"For if any man see thee which hast knowledge...." This refers to the strong brother's estimate of himself, and not to the weak brother's opinion of him.

". . . Sit at meat in the idol's temple . . . ." This speaks of the feast where the animals were sacrificed within the temple. Evidently some of the believers thought that it was perfectly all right for them to go into the idol

285

temple while the sacrificial feast was in progress and feast on the meat that was served there after the sacrifices had been killed and offered. Undoubtedly some of them had been attending these sacrificial feasts in the idol temple.

"*. . . Shall not the conscience of him which is weak be emboldened to eat those things which are offered to idols?*" The Greek word translated "be emboldened" is *oikodomeo* and means "to build up." The believing brother referred to as "weak" would be built up to do the thing that was contrary to his God-given conscience; and for a spiritually minded believer to set an example before a weak believer which violates that weak brother's conscience, is NOT building him up, but pulling him down in spiritual living and practice. Therefore, the strong brother who could eat the meat without any conviction of conscience must not participate for the sake of weaker brethren.

Verse 11: "And through thy knowledge shall the weak brother perish, for whom Christ died?"

The Greek verb here translated "perish" is *apollumi*. Many times in the New Testament it is translated "destroy." The meaning is "the loss of well-being" – in this case, speaking of the weak brother, the well-being of abstaining from doing that against which the conscience testifies. Therefore when the spiritually strong deliberately participate in things that may wound the spiritually weak, they are destroying him instead of building him up – not that his spirit will be damned or his soul be eternally lost, but if his conscience is wounded, he is losing ground spiritually instead of gaining.

And this one who is suffering hurt is "*the weak brother for whom Christ died.*" The argument Paul sets forth here is that the weak believer who suffers is a *brother*, not a stranger to the stronger believer; he is not "one of those without," but one for whom Christ died. Jesus loved him so much that He was willing to die for him while he was yet a sinner; but this strong brother deliberately eats meat that will offend the weak brother, knowing all the time that the weak are offended by the act in which he is participating.

Christ not only died to save the weak brother from hell, but to save him from all that would rob him of communion and abundant life: "But if thy brother be grieved with thy meat, now walkest thou not charitably. Destroy not him with thy meat, for whom Christ died" (Rom. 14:15).

It is the spiritual birthright of every believer to enjoy the fullness of the Spirit—abundant life, joy unspeakable and full of glory; and those of us who profess to be spiritually minded and strong in the faith have no right—even though we have liberty—to do anything that will cause a weak brother to stumble.

Verse 12: "But when ye sin so against the brethren, and wound their weak conscience, ye sin against Christ."

We see here that when we injure a fellow believer, the injury is to Christ Himself: "And he said, Who art thou, Lord? And the Lord said, I am Jesus whom thou persecutest: it is hard for thee to kick against the pricks" (Acts 9:4,5).

"Then shall He answer them, saying, Verily I say unto you, Inasmuch as ye did it not to one of the least of these, ye did it not to me" (Matt. 25:45).

In chapter 12 of this epistle we will learn that the Church is one body, made up of many members; and when one member suffers, the whole body suffers. In Ephesians 5 we learn that Jesus is the head of the Church and the Saviour of the body. Therefore when a weak Christian

287

is hurt, Christ is hurt. When a weak brother suffers because of the actions of the stronger brother, the conscience of the weak brother is *defiled* (verse 7); he is caused to *stumble* (verse 9); and in our present verse, he is *wounded*.

Verse 13: "Wherefore, if meat make my brother to offend, I will eat no flesh while the world standeth, lest I make my brother to offend.

The Greek word used here for "meat" is *broma*, and means "food"—not only meat that had been offered to idols, but *any* food, and is used by way of contempt, as in verse 8. Paul here speaks of his own conviction and determination. He does this to put to shame the brethren who claim to be wise and strong, contending for their rights and liberty even at the expense of defiling, wounding, and causing one to stumble who was not strong in the faith and in the Spirit.

Believers are certainly not to sacrifice their Christian liberty because of bigoted prejudice; but when a sincere believer is hurt or hindered by something we do or say, even though we do have liberty in Christ, we not only wound the weaker brother: *we wound our Saviour, too.* We are brothers in Jesus; we belong to the same body, and we are members of the Church of which Jesus is the head.

True believers should be willing and anxious to practice self-denial when it brings glory to God and strength to a weaker brother; but we should never compromise or surrender one iota of truth to please one who is prejudiced or bigoted. If we are led by the Spirit we can and will know when we are doing the right thing concerning habits of life and things that might cause a weak brother to be offended or to stumble.

The glorious thing about Christianity is that we have within us the Holy Spirit, the divine nature of God; and

He leads us into the paths of right living to the glory of God. "As many as are led by the Spirit of God, they are the sons of God," and he who believes on Jesus shall not be confounded or confused. When we seek the will of God concerning the habits of life—stewardship or anything else that has to do with our Christian testimony—He will lead us by the Holy Spirit; and "if we walk in the light, as He is in the light, we have fellowship one with another" (I John 1:7).

It would be utterly impossible for us to please all people. Paul is not setting forth such an idea. He is writing to the spiritually minded believers in Corinth concerning those who were truly born again, saved from paganism and idolatry, and yet had not grown spiritually to the place where they could appreciate Christian liberty.

We are never to use the liberty of grace to satisfy the lust of the flesh. We are never to enjoy the liberty of grace and salvation, at the expense of the spirituality and strength of other believers. *We are all members of one body*, and that body is Christ. We must therefore do all things—first of all, to glorify the Lord Jesus Christ, and then to strengthen the brethren in the faith. And "whatsoever is not of faith is sin" (Rom. 14:23).

CHAPTER NINE

1. Am I not an apostle? am I not free? have I not seen Jesus Christ our Lord? are not ye my work in the Lord?

2. If I be not an apostle unto others, yet doubtless I am to you: for the seal of mine apostleship are ye in the Lord.

3. Mine answer to them that do examine me is this,

4. Have we not power to eat and to drink?

5. Have we not power to lead about a sister, a wife, as well as other apostles, and as the brethren of the Lord, and Cephas?

6. Or I only and Barnabas, have not we power to forbear working?

7. Who goeth a warfare any time at his own charges? who planteth a vineyard, and eateth not of the fruit thereof? or who feedeth a flock, and eateth not of the milk of the flock?

8. Say I these things as a man? or saith not the law the same also?

9. For it is written in the law of Moses, Thou shalt not muzzle the mouth of the ox that treadeth out the corn. Doth God take care for oxen?

10. Or saith he it altogether for our sakes? For our sakes, no doubt, this is written: that he that ploweth should plow in hope; and that he that thresheth in hope should be partaker of his hope.

11. If we have sown unto you spiritual things, is it a great thing if we shall reap your carnal things?

12. If others be partakers of this power over you, are not we rather? Nevertheless we have not used this power; but suffer all things, lest we should hinder the gospel of Christ.

13. Do ye not know that they which minister about holy things live of the things of the temple? and they which wait at the altar are partakers with the altar?

14. Even so hath the Lord ordained that they which preach the gospel should live of the gospel.

15. But I have used none of these things: neither have I written these things, that it should be so done unto me: for it

were better for me to die, than that any man should make my glorying void.

16. For though I preach the gospel, I have nothing to glory of: for necessity is laid upon me; yea, woe is unto me, if I preach not the gospel!

17. For if I do this thing willingly, I have a reward: but if against my will, a dispensation of the gospel is committed unto me.

18. What is my reward then? Verily that, when I preach the gospel, I may make the gospel of Christ without charge, that I abuse not my power in the gospel.

19. For though I be free from all men, yet have I made myself servant unto all, that I might gain the more.

20. And unto the Jews I became as a Jew, that I might gain the Jews; to them that are under the law, as under the law, that I might gain them that are under the law;

21. To them that are without law, as without law, (being not without law to God, but under the law to Christ,) that I might gain them that are without law.

22. To the weak became I as weak, that I might gain the weak: I am made all things to all men, that I might by all means save some.

23. And this I do for the gospel's sake, that I might be partaker thereof with you.

24. Know ye not that they which run in a race run all, but one receiveth the prize? So run, that ye may obtain.

25. And every man that striveth for the mastery is temperate in all things. Now they do it to obtain a corruptible crown; but we an incorruptible.

26. I therefore so run, not as uncertainly; so fight I, not as one that beateth the air:

27. But I keep under my body, and bring it into subjection: lest that by any means, when I have preached to others, I myself should be a castaway.

Paul Defends His Apostolic Authority

In this chapter, Paul *illustrates* the appeal made in chapter 8, that the Corinthian Christians refrain from exercising their rights and using their Christian liberty, when to do so would hinder weaker brethren spiritually. This he does by using himself as an illustration, and gives them his own practice in the use of his apostolic rights. He points out in particular his reasons for refusing to be maintained by the church.

At the same time, he stresses his *right* to be taken care of by the church. It was not wrong that the assembly maintain him, but for the sake of the Gospel he *refused* their support. He points out that believers should be careful what they do, and that they should refrain from doing certain things, because we must all appear before the judgment seat of Christ to receive the reward for things done in this body.

Verse 1: "Am I not an apostle? Am I not free? Have I not seen Jesus Christ our Lord? Are not ye my work in the Lord?"

This chapter is devoted to Paul's defense of his apostolic authority. We must not miss the connection between this chapter and chapter 8, where Paul exhorted the Corinthian believers to sacrifice their own personal liberty in grace for the benefit of weaker brethren. In the last verse of that chapter, Paul declared that he was ready to act upon the principle he had set forth—that is, regardless of how much he loved meat, if eating meat caused his weak brother to stumble, then he would eat no meat so long as he lived.

Some probably said, "This is fine doctrine – but does Paul practice what he preaches?" Paul is about to give proof of his sincerity by referring to his sacrifice of self for the good of others. Some of the believers had even suggested that he was not an apostle at all. (We will see Paul's defense against this accusation a little later in the chapter.)

"Am I not an apostle? Am I not free?" Scholars tell us that this part of the verse should read, "Am I not free? Am I not an apostle? Am I not *YOUR* apostle?"

Some of Paul's enemies declared that he had no right to be called an apostle, because all the other apostles had seen the Lord in the flesh and had been associated with Him in His earthly ministry, while Paul had not. But Paul answers with another question:

"Have I not seen Jesus Christ our Lord?" Yes, Paul HAD seen the Lord. He saw Him on the Damascus road. Study Acts 9:3–17,26,27; 22:17–21; and Galatians 1:15–19. "Then spake the Lord to Paul in the night by a vision, Be not afraid, but speak, and hold not thy peace: For I am with thee, and no man shall set on thee to hurt thee: for I have much people in this city" (Acts 18:9,10).

Later in this epistle, Paul declares, "And last of all, He was seen of me also, as of one born out of due time" (I Cor. 15:8). Here Paul speaks of the experience he had on the road to Damascus when he definitely saw the Lord Jesus.

"Are not ye my work in the Lord?" Paul had been used of the Lord in founding the church at Corinth, and the Corinthian believers should have been the last people on earth to doubt that he was a true apostle. They should have needed no other proof of the genuineness of his mission. What Paul is saying here is simply this:

"If anyone wants to know whether or not I am a genuine apostle, I will show him you Christians in Corinth who were converted through my ministry. I will point out to him the divine proofs of my apostleship. First, you received my preaching, then you exercised faith in Christ, and were saved through the Gospel that I preached to you. God then poured out many and varied gifts of the Holy Ghost upon you."

What had happened in the individual lives of the believers at Corinth should have been proof enough to them that Paul was God's anointed apostle, for certainly no

MAN could have effected such a change in their lives as that which had occurred when they received Paul's message. It must have hurt the Apostle deeply when some of his own converts took sides with those who accused him of being *a counterfeit apostle.*

Verse 2: "If I be not an apostle unto others, yet doubtless I am to you: for the seal of mine apostleship are ye in the Lord."

The seal or signet is an emblem denoting ownership and security. The Greek word here translated "seal" stands for the *impression* made by the seal, and is used metaphorically of the believers in the assembly at Corinth, proving Paul's authentic apostleship.

It is true that at Corinth souls might have been converted through the preaching of others; but the church itself stood as a guarantee that the one whom the Lord had used to establish it and the one who was now writing this epistle to them was no ordinary preacher. God had called him, anointed him, empowered him, sent him to them — and through his preaching a tremendous miracle had occurred. The church in the wicked city of Corinth had been established; they were Paul's seal, his proof of truly divine apostleship.

Verse 3: "Mine answer to them that do examine me is this."

Without a doubt this verse points back to what has been said in verses 1 and 2. The word rendered "examine" means "critical investigation," pointing of course to Paul's enemies who claimed that he was not a divinely appointed apostle. Here it is used in the sense of a judicial investigation. The fact that the word is in the present tense points out that some in the church at Corinth were making a practice of suggesting that Paul was not a true apostle; but he simply points to his converts as divine proof that he was God's apostle, and that the believers in Corinth were converted because God had used him to bring the message of salvation which they had received, through which they were saved, and wherein they were standing (I Cor. 15:1—4).

Verse 4: "Have we not power to eat and to drink?"

What Paul is asking here is simply this: "Do we have no right to eat and drink at the expense of the church? Is it not right that they who preach the Gospel should live of the Gospel? Should not the believers feed us?" (Paul had helpers. Timothy, Titus, and others were with him.) This statement has nothing to do with the matter of eating as studied in chapter 8.

Verse 5: "Have we not power to lead about a sister, a wife, as well as other apostles, and as the brethren of the Lord, and Cephas?"

Here Paul declares that the ministers who were married had a right to expect the church not only to take care of them, but to also care for their wives and families. According to divine order, the local assembly is duty-bound to support the Lord's minister and his family.

Although Paul himself was not married, this verse indicates that most of the apostles were. We know that Peter was married, for the Bible speaks of his mother-in-law (Matt. 8:14; Mark 1:30; Luke 4:38).

". . . *The brethren of the Lord*" would almost certainly be the children of Joseph and Mary after the birth of Christ.

The reference to *Cephas* suggests that at least some of the critics belonged to the Cephas party (chapter 1, verse 2).

It was right (and scriptural) for the assembly to take care of the servants of God who ministered to them in spiritual things. Any pastor has a full time job, regardless of how small his church may be. It is honorable for young preachers to work in the business world to help support themselves while organizing a new work or helping a struggling church to get on its feet; but the moment the church is financially able to take care of the minister, he should be on the field full time. A pastor does not have time to work at secular work and take care of the affairs of the church and the community insofar as spiritual matters have to do.

Verse 6: "Or I only and Barnabas, have not we power to forbear working?"

The mention of Barnabas indicates that Paul is referring here to his first missionary journey. Barnabas made that journey with him, and no doubt they had agreed to take care of their own financial needs where it was advisable to do so. Otherwise, there were some localities where Paul would have been accused of preaching simply for money.

From the beginning of the Church, it has been a scheme of the devil to suggest that all ministers are out for money and that the ministry is a soft job with a big paycheck. This was not true in the lives of Paul and Barnabas, nor is it true in the lives of God's preachers today.

The pastor is worthy of a living wage, although he should be willing to live on the same level as the majority of his members live. He should not want to live above them, nor should a congregation expect the pastor to live *below* their standard of life. A church should take care of its pastor. I do not believe a pastor should expect more than the members of his assembly have for themselves, but many times God's dear preachers suffer for the very necessities of life, while those who compromise and preach a social gospel have an abundance of everything—and to spare!

We know that if a minister is faithful to the Word of God, God will supply his daily need. It may come in day by day, and he may not have all he would like to have; but his actual need will be supplied. Our God is able to supply all of our needs, and if we seek first His kingdom and His righteousness, these things will be added. God cannot and will not break His promise.

The Bible Plan:
He Who Preaches the Gospel Shall Live of the Gospel

Verse 7: "Who goeth a warfare any time at his own charges? Who planteth a vineyard, and eateth not of the fruit thereof? Or who feedeth a flock, and eateth not of the milk of the flock?"

In this verse, Paul uses three illustrations by way of explaining the work of a true minister or missionary:

"Who goeth a warfare any time at his own charges?" The soldier is in the business of making war against the enemy — and so is the servant of God. Christians are soldiers fighting against evil—yea, against Satan himself; against the rulers of darkness and against spiritual wickedness in high places.

"Who planteth a vineyard, and eateth not of the fruit thereof?" The husbandman plants the vineyard; by parallel, the servant of God is used of God to plant the local church. The minister sows the seed that produces converts—the fruit that makes the local assembly possible.

". . . Who feedeth a flock, and eateth not of the milk of the flock?" The shepherd cares for and feeds the flock. He leads the flock into green pastures where the grass is tender and the water is still and sweet. The pastor is God's undershepherd. It is *his business* to feed

the babes in Christ with the sincere milk of the Word, and
to feed the older Christians with bread and meat. He is
to also be watchful, that wolves do not get into the flock
to destroy the lambs and cripple the sheep.

A soldier, a planter of vineyards, and a shepherd of
the flock expect to receive their maintenance as the result of their labors, because a good soldier, a good planter,
and a good shepherd, do not have time to leave their post
of duty and go to other fields of service to earn a livelihood. They expect their living to come from that which
they serve. Paul is here pointing out that the same is
true concerning the ministers of the Word of God. They
have a right to expect to be taken care of by those to
whom they render spiritual service and minister the things
of the Lord. It is sinful and unscriptural for a church
to be negligent in providing for its pastor.

Verse 8: "Say I these things as a man? or saith not
the law the same also?"

What Paul is saying here (and the Greek language
makes it a little clearer) is this: "In accordance with
man's opinion, have these natural illustrations no spiritual application?" Since God feeds the shepherd from the
flock, does that same God not expect *His flock* to feed
His undershepherd—pastor, evangelist, or missionary? Since
the planter of the vineyard gathers fruit therefrom, does
not God expect the vineyard in which the pastor serves
to feed that pastor?

No doubt some were arguing that there was no scriptural instruction concerning the support of the Apostle
Paul, pointing out that the law of Moses did not specifically determine how the minister should earn his bread;
but Paul showed these critics that they were wrong:

Verse 9: "For it is written in the law of Moses, Thou
shalt not muzzle the mouth of the ox that treadeth out the

corn. Doth God take care for oxen?''

The Greek here reads *"while treading out the corn."* This speaks of the separation of the grain from the husk. The oxen were used to drag the threshing instrument over the grain, and while working in this manner the ox was unmuzzled; his mouth was left free in order for him to eat as he threshed the grain. The truth clearly set forth here is that those who produce food for others ought to share in it themselves. Paul fed the Corinthian believers the spiritual meat, bread, and milk, and it was only right in the sight of God that they take care of his earthly needs.

Paul quotes from Deuteronomy 25:4: ''Thou shalt not muzzle the ox when he treadeth out the corn.'' This statement from the law of Moses undoubtedly carried much weight with those Jews in the assembly at Corinth who were bitterly opposing Paul and his Gospel.

"Doth God take care for oxen?" Verse 10 continues this line of thought:

Verse 10: ''Or saith He it altogether for our sakes? For our sakes, no doubt, this is written: that he that ploweth should plow in hope; and that he that thresheth in hope should be partaker of his hope.''

The quotation from the law establishes the fact that the law of Moses was the voice of God speaking. This quotation also illustrates the fact that there are certain statements in the Word of God which, even though relating to the natural and the physical, are designed to convey spiritual truths that need to be seen and understood. We must be careful in making those spiritual applications, however, and the only safe way to make the *correct* application is to avoid adopting ideas which go beyond what is written. We must confine ourselves to the interpretations which are supported by the clear, understandable

Word of God. We should never speculate, nor take Scripture out of its setting, to prove a denominational point.

Paul is not suggesting here that God does not care for animals. God DOES care for the animal kingdom—a truth which Jesus taught in Matthew 6:26. Neither does Paul mean that God is not thinking of the oxen at all. The Greek word translated "altogether" in this verse signifies "as doubtless it is." That is, "There is no doubt that this is written for our sakes, to set forth the truth that he who ploweth should plow in hope, and he that thresheth in hope should be a partaker of his hope."

The same is true in the spiritual life. We who sow spiritual things, feeding the Church from the Word of God, should do so in hope and faith, trusting the Lord to take care of our physical needs *through those* to whom we minister. If *animals* are allowed to share in the food they help to produce, then surely God will take care of a minister whom He called, ordained, and sent as His undershepherd! Indeed, *He will* take care of His own.

Paul testifies, "I have learned, in whatsoever state I am, therewith to be content. . . My God shall supply all your need according to His riches in glory by Christ Jesus" (Phil. 4:11,19). God *will* supply our every need—through one source or another. Paul was trying to get the believers in Corinth to understand that if they did not give to the support of their ministers and supply their physical needs, the believers themselves would be losers—they would lose in rewards.

Verse 11: "If we have sown unto you spiritual things, is it a great thing if we shall reap your carnal things?"

Notice that Paul twice uses the plural pronoun *"we,"* denoting the ministers—Paul, Timothy, Titus and others who had sown *spiritual things* in the assembly. Then he uses *"YOUR carnal things,"* thus stressing the difference between the ministers and members of the assembly. He asks, *"Is it a great thing if we shall reap your carnal things?"* That is, "Can the necessities of the *body* be compared to the necessities of soul and spirit?" Jesus asked, ". . . What is a man profited if he shall gain the whole world, and lose his own soul? Or what shall a man give in exchange for his soul?" (Matt. 16:26). With such difference in value, we dare not compare spiritual things with carnal.

Verse 12: "If others be partakers of this power over you, are not we rather? Nevertheless we have not used this power; but suffer all things, lest we should hinder the Gospel of Christ."

The "others" to whom Paul refers here are probably the false teachers, Judaizers who were perverting the Gospel and attempting to put the believers partially back under the law of Moses. *"If others be partakers of this power* (or right) . . . ." This points out the fact that these Judaizers had taken the right (whether it was theirs or not) to be maintained by the believers in the assembly at Corinth. They HAD no right, but they had taken it, nevertheless.

Paul points out to the Corinthians that he and his fellow missionaries' rights were paramount in this respect, since they were the ones used of God to establish the church in Corinth, and it was they who preached the marvelous grace of God through which the believers had been saved from a life of sin and an eternity in hell. It was Paul and his helpers—not these conceited, self-appointed Judaizers—who were worthy of support.

"Nevertheless, we have not used this power; but suffer all things, lest we should hinder the Gospel of Christ." The true spirit of a God-called minister is set

forth in these words. A minister of the Gospel who is true to his calling will suffer lack of material things rather than bring reproach upon the Gospel. Many times, a minister could request various things that he needs for the comforts of life, but fearing that he may bring reproach upon the Gospel by having someone accuse him of preaching for money, he suffers the loss of these things and carries on without them.

Had Paul exercised his right as a divinely appointed minister of Jesus Christ, he might have been suspected of preaching the Gospel for filthy lucre. He would have gained financially, but would have lost morally and spiritually; because God called him to win souls—not to get ahead financially.

Verse 13: "Do ye not know that they which minister about holy things live of the things of the temple? and they which wait at the altar are partakers with the altar?"

Paul is again pointing back to the law of Moses and the temple as having to do with the minister and the things that are sacred. Please study Leviticus 6:16—26 and Numbers 18:8—19. These two passages have to do with the portion allotted by God to His appointed priest, and in Deuteronomy 18:1—4 we learn the Bible rule for the portion set aside by the Lord God for the Levites.

When the appointed priests of God made the peace offering on the altar, a portion of the offering was consumed on the altar and a portion of it was designated for the priests' own personal use. The Greek verb translated "wait upon" is *paredreuo*, and literally denotes "to sit constantly beside." In our present verse, the verb speaks of the priests' *presentation of themselves* at the altar—being constantly beside the altar to offer sacrifice. They were appointed by God just as Paul had been appointed; and if *they* lived of the things of the temple, why should not Paul be taken care of by those to whom *he* ministered? They were his own children in the faith, having been born again through the message he had delivered unto them.

Verse 14: "Even so hath the Lord ordained that they which preach the Gospel should live of the Gospel."

Just as the priest who served in the temple *lived* of the things of the temple, *"even so"* God has ordained that His *ministers* be taken care of by those to whom they minister. Just as God gave command concerning the priests and Israel, the Lord Jesus gave instructions concerning His servants:

"Provide neither gold, nor silver, nor brass in your purses, nor scrip for your journey, neither two coats, neither shoes, nor yet staves: for the workman is worthy of his meat" (Matt. 10:9,10).

". . . In the same house remain, eating and drinking such things as they give: for the labourer is worthy of his hire. Go not from house to house. And into whatsoever city ye enter, and they receive you, eat such things as are set before you" (Luke 10:7,8).

Paul was familiar with the teachings of Jesus concerning the livelihood of the servants of God. He clinches his whole argument concerning the maintenance of ministers by using the reference to the Lord, and to God, and to the priests in the Old Testament.

Verse 15: "But I have used none of these things: neither have I written these things, that it should be so done unto me: for it were better for me to die, than that any man should make my glorying void."

Paul repeats here what he said in verse 12. He had taken nothing from the *Corinthians*, but in his second epistle to them he testifies that this was the only church from which he did not accept gifts. Paul wanted these believers to clearly understand that he was not writing these things by way of suggesting that they give him material gifts. He declared that he had rather die than that man should make his glorying void.

The Greek word for "glorying" is *kauchema*, and here stands for "the ground of glorying." The word translated *"make void"* means "to empty, to make of no effect." Paul counted all things loss that he might gain Christ, testifying that he became as all men are, that he might win some. And to him, death would be much better than for his ministry to be made of no effect.

Verse 16: "For though I preach the Gospel, I have nothing to glory of: for necessity is laid upon me; yea, woe is unto me, if I preach not the Gospel!"

What a tremendous declaration! Paul had received a divine commission from the Lord God Almighty (Acts 9:15). He had been "laid hold of" (literally captured) against his previous will. He had been a Judaizer from the heart, sold to the religion of his fathers; but Christ called him, anointed him, and sent him to preach the Gospel: "As they ministered to the Lord, and fasted, the Holy Ghost said, Separate me Barnabas and Saul for the work whereunto I have called them" (Acts 13:2). "And He said unto me, Depart: for I will send thee far hence unto the Gentiles" (Acts 22:21).

To Paul, the ministry was an absolute necessity. The Gospel of the grace of God had been entrusted to him, even the mystery which had been hidden from the beginning had been revealed to him (Col. 1:26); and it was a divine imperative that he preach the message he had received. There was no ground for glorying, because what he was doing was done of necessity. He was a bondslave to Jesus Christ and could therefore claim nothing from his Master who had saved him by grace even though he was a persecutor of all who were in "the Jesus way."

"Woe is unto me, if I preach not the Gospel!" Paul points here to the account he must give to the Lord at the judgment seat for believers, if he failed to preach the message that had been entrusted to him. The testimony of the Prince of Apostles was always, "God forbid that I glory save in the cross of Jesus Christ, for I am what I am by the grace of God!"

Paul did not glory in himself, realizing that he was a vessel chosen of Almighty God to bear the good news of the grace of God to the people who were aliens to the commonwealth of Israel, strangers to the covenants, without God and without hope, but who, in the grace of God, could become a people of hope—yea, sons of God, created anew in Christ Jesus. Paul declared, "I will be a woeful creature indeed if I preach not this Gospel of grace!"

Verse 17: "For if I do this thing willingly, I have a reward: but if against my will, a dispensation of the Gospel is committed unto me."

If Paul had chosen the ministry and taken it up as a vocation or a business (and some in Corinth had done just that), then he would have his reward in the payment he received for his labors; but if he were preaching, not of his own will but of God's will and under God's appointment, then he could say, "A stewardship is entrusted to me." Paul's preaching was not of his own choosing, and accordingly he was not merely a steward—a servant doing service as steward in a rich man's house; but he was a *steward of God*, doing that which was his duty to his Master and Lord—Jesus, the Saviour.

". . . *A dispensation of the Gospel is committed unto me.*" The King James version of the Bible uses the word "dispensation," from the Greek word *oikonomia*. A clearer translation would be our English word "stewardship," which primarily means "the management of a household." In common usage it came to mean the management of property belonging to another. Thus, to the Apostle Paul, God had entrusted the Gospel, and the Gospel is God's Word— yea, *very God*. Paul was indeed a steward of God. (See also Luke 16:2–4.)

Verse 18: "What is my reward then? Verily that, when I preach the Gospel, I may make the Gospel of Christ without charge, that I abuse not my power in the Gospel."

We have here another of Paul's questions: *"What is my reward then?* Am I preaching for money? Or am I preaching for the Lord Jesus?" Then as was his custom, he answered his own question. In essence he said, "My reward is in the joy I receive in my heart in refusing that which I could rightfully claim—*gifts and money* from the believers, to take care of my daily necessities. I find great joy and reward in ministering to you—*free of charge!*"

Paul was only a vessel yielded to God for service. (All that WE do to please God and render stewardship to Him is really *His working in us and through us*.) All true ministry is the work of the Holy Spirit in us, yet the Lord God is pleased *in grace* to recognize the willingness and devotion of any of His servants who will allow the Holy Spirit to use them, and will reward these individuals for their *willingness* to be used. By contrast, if the Holy Spirit *does not* work through the minister, no good will be accomplished.

The fact that Jesus loved us while we were yet sinners and saved us from sin is sufficient to make us eager to do what He leads us to do, and to serve Him in complete devotion and with all of our might. Paul never sought glory for himself. He wanted all the glory and honor to be directed to the Lord Jesus, the One worthy of all honor, praise, and glory.

The Method and Reward of True Ministry

Verse 19: "For though I be free from all men, yet have I made myself servant unto all, that I might gain the more."

Paul was careful not to be brought into bondage by man; he was *free from ALL men* in that none could exercise compulsion over him or make demands of him. He depended on the Lord, not on men; but though he was free from all men, he had made himself *"servant unto all,"* that he might *"gain the more."*

How Paul made himself a servant to all men is explained in the next three verses. He had denied himself, he had denied his rights as an apostle, he had resorted to hard labor to obtain his livelihood. He had therefore obtained a greater result in the Gospel and in his stewardship.

Verse 20: "And unto the Jews I became as a Jew, that I might gain the Jews; to them that are under the law, as under the law, that I might gain them that are under the law."

"And unto the Jews I became as a Jew . . . ." This was illustrated in the fact that Paul allowed Timothy to be circumcised after the custom of the Jews: "Him (Timothy) would Paul have to go forth with him; and took and circumcised him because of the Jews which were in those quarters: for they knew all that his father was a Greek" (Acts 16:3).

"Then Paul took the men, and the next day purifying himself with them entered into the temple, to signify the accomplishment of the days of purification, until that an offering should be offered for every one of them" (Acts 21:26).

Paul himself was a servant of the Jews, but he did

not compromise with their demands upon the Gentiles: "But when I saw that they walked not uprightly according to the truth of the Gospel, I said unto Peter before them all, If thou, being a Jew, livest after the manner of Gentiles, and not as do the Jews, why compellest thou the Gentiles to live as do the Jews?" (Gal. 2:14).

". . . *To them that are under the law, as under the law.*" This refers to the whole Mosaic Law. This is not a mere repetition of the first part of the verse. The difference is that *"to the Jews I became as a Jew"* is referring to nationality, not religion. The Apostle was ready to yield at every side where Christ was not concerned. "Under the law" means that Paul took his position alongside the Jews by submitting to certain restrictions of the law in order that he might gain their confidence and preach the grace of God to them. He did not compromise with the law in that he mixed law and grace, as evidenced by the following passages from his writings:

Romans 6:14: "For sin shall not have dominion over you: for *ye are not under the law, but under grace.*"

Galatians 5:18: "But if ye be led of the Spirit, *ye are not under the law.*"

Romans 10:4: "For *Christ is the end of the law* for righteousness to every one that believeth."

Verse 21: "To them that are without law, as without law, (being not without law to God, but under the law to Christ,) that I might gain them that are without law."

"To them that are without law" does not mean that they were "lawless" or that they were transgressing the law. Paul here refers to those who were *outside law*, as he did in Romans 2:14: "For when the Gentiles, which have not the law, do by nature the things contained in the law, these, having not the law, are a law unto themselves."

". . . *As without law*" points to the Gentiles—those who were aliens from the commonwealth of Israel and strangers to the covenants. ". . . *Being not without law to God, but under the law to Christ.*" Paul's freedom from the law of Moses did not give him the right to live as he pleased, or to please himself. On the contrary, he always made it his aim to be in complete subjection to the will of God.

". . . *Under the law to Christ* . . . ." The Greek word translated "under law" is *ennomos*, the literal meaning of which is "in law." The deep meaning is not the condition of being subject to or under the power of a law, but rather suggests *intimacy*—a relationship or union established between Christ and the believer. We love Him because He first loved us. Since He loved us enough to die for us, now that we are believers *we love Him* with complete devotion—heart, soul, strength, and mind; *we are "in law" to Christ.* Christ is the end of the law for righteousness to everyone who believes. "For ye are dead, and your life is hid with Christ in God" (Col. 3:3).

Verse 22: "To the weak became I as weak, that I might gain the weak: I am made all things to all men, that I might by all means save some."

"*The weak*" were those who were disturbed by such things as eating meat—and many other frivolities that have nothing to do with the grace of God. Paul knew these things were unimportant in salvation, yet for the sake of others he abstained from things which the weak considered to be wrong.

"Him that is weak in the faith receive ye, but not to doubtful disputations" (Rom. 14:1). "We then that are strong ought to bear the infirmities of the weak, and not to please ourselves" (Rom. 15:1). "Who is weak, and I am not weak? Who is offended, and I burn not?" (II Cor. 11:29).

"I am made all things to all men . . . ." (The literal Greek reads, "I am *become* all things to all men.") These words do not in the least suggest a sacrifice of principle, or a compromise; but rather Paul's readiness to approach all men at all times on their most accessible side, that he might have the opportunity to point them to the Lord Jesus.

". . . That I might by all means save some." Paul believed in and practiced the use of any and all things permissible, any method which was honest and aboveboard that might cause men to stop and hear the Gospel, think on their way *and be saved.* He knew that even if he employed every permissible method and did everything within his power, if he sacrificed in every way possible, *only "some" would be saved*; the majority would continue to travel the broad road to destruction.

Verse 23: "And this I do for the Gospel's sake, that I might be partaker thereof with you."

The literal translation here is *"And I do all things for the Gospel's sake."* Paul's whole life was dedicated to the work of the Gospel, pointing men to the grace of God. The ministry of the Gospel, the telling forth of the good news of God's grace, meant more to Paul than anything else on earth—not only because of his delight in the Gospel and his joy in the grace of God, but because of the *effects* of the Gospel upon the lives of those who heard it. Paul also knew that all stewards will be rewarded according to their faithful stewardship, and he considered the effects of his ministry in the coming day of reward.

". . . That I might be a partaker thereof with you." (In the original text, *"with you"* is omitted.) Paul was not thinking of his partnership with the believers in the assembly at Corinth, but of his cooperation with the Gospel

of the grace of God in its activity. He is thinking of the great, eternal issues, and of the effects of taking *his share* of the work of the ministry—the telling forth of the good news of the grace of God to all. It was his divine duty to preach the Gospel; and wherever he went, in whatsoever he participated, he did so for the Gospel's sake, that he might be a joint partaker thereof (of the Gospel).

Verse 24: "Know ye not that they which run in a race run all, but one receiveth the prize? So run, that ye may obtain."

Paul is referring here to the public games that were held every three years, very close to the city of Corinth. The Corinthians were very familiar with these games. Such occasions were *more* than contests between athletes or racers — they were great national and religious festivals. Only free men could enter the games, and even then only if they satisfied the officials that they had undergone the appointed training and were physically equipped and trained to participate in the games.

Each participant was announced in a gala manner and the country he represented was named by the master of ceremonies. The victor in these games and races received a crown fashioned from ivy or pine leaves, and his family was highly honored. When the victor returned to his home town, a breach was opened in the wall of the city, and he was allowed to enter the city through the breach. This was a token that a place so honored needed no defending walls to protect it from the enemy. The name of the victor was then immortalized by some famous Greek poet.

Paul reminds the Corinthian believers that it is possible for *each* believer to receive a reward if in this life he fulfills the conditions required of a good steward of Jesus Christ; but it is also possible for a believer to *lose* his reward, or to receive only a *partial* reward.

311

"*So run, that ye may obtain.*" That is, "Be faithful, be dedicated, consecrated—that you may obtain the prize." Paul wanted his children in the faith to receive a full reward at the judgment seat of Christ. It is the spiritual birthright of every believer to enjoy abundant life here, with joy unspeakable and full of glory, and also receive a full reward at the end of life's journey.

Careless Christians will not receive a full reward. There are many, many verses in the New Testament which clearly teach that each believer will be rewarded according to his faithful stewardship—not according to the amount (how *much* he may do), but according to the faithfulness with which he discharged his duties as a good steward.

Verse 25: "And every man that striveth for the mastery is temperate in all things. Now they do it to obtain a corruptible crown; but we an incorruptible."

". . . *Temperate in all things* . . . ." The Greek verb translated "is temperate" is a word used figuratively in the Greek, referring to the rigid self-control practiced by athletes who participated in the games. Their rigid training took place over a period of many months before they were allowed to enter into the competition. Believers are *God's* runners, God's soldiers; and our training will last throughout our lifetime. Self-control should be practiced by all believers, and those who do *not* practice self-control will certainly suffer loss at the end of life's journey.

". . . *They do it to obtain a corruptible crown.*" The Greek word used for "corruptible" in this verse means "liable to decay." The runners and participants in the Grecian games went through rigid training and self-control for months, striving to win a wreath made of leaves—something which, at best, could last only a short while. History did not bother to record the names of those who won such crowns.

". . . *But we an incorruptible.*" Here is stated very clearly that rewards earned through faithful stewardship, given to the believers by Christ at the judgment seat, will never corrupt or fade away; they will last throughout eternity. In the light of this tremendous truth, how foolish it is for believers to be unfaithful, bring reproach upon the Lord's name, and dishonor Him in service, thus running the risk of losing that incorruptible, eternal reward. To those who are faithful in their responsibilities, God's Word promises "a crown of glory that fadeth not away" (I Pet. 5:4).

Verse 26: "I therefore so run, not as uncertainly; so fight I, not as one that beateth the air."

What Paul is saying here is that he is not running as one with no definite aim; he is not running without knowing why or whither he runs: "That I may know Him, and the power of His resurrection, and the fellowship of His sufferings, being made conformable unto His death; if by any means I might attain unto the resurrection of the dead. Not as though I had already attained, either were already perfect: but I follow after, if that I may apprehend that for which also I am apprehended of Christ Jesus. Brethren, I count not myself to have apprehended: but this one thing I do, forgetting those things which are behind, and reaching forth unto those things which are before, I press toward the mark for the prize of the high calling of God in Christ Jesus" (Phil. 3:10—14).

The believer who runs well should make Christ the absorbing object of his heart's devotion, with all energies and activities directed to the interest of Jesus Christ and His glory. When all that we do is done to the glory of God in the name of Jesus, the Lord will delight to give us a full reward in the crowning day.

"*So fight I, not as one that beateth the air.*" Paul

313

is thinking here of boxing, which was included in the Grecian games. A good boxer makes sure that his fists land in the right spot on his opponent to do the most damage. Paul was speaking of a spiritual boxing match against the devil and the emissaries of hell; and as he fought, he did not fight as one who "beat the air." He was determined that each blow against the enemy should land in the right place.

Verse 27: "But I keep under my body, and bring it into subjection: lest that by any means, when I have preached to others, I myself should be a castaway."

The Greek verb used here for "keep under" is *hupo-piazo*, and the literal meaning is "to strike under the eye, or to beat the face black and blue." Paul is not speaking here of *literally* beating himself black and blue; he means that he is determined to keep his body under control, lest passion and lust overcome him. He means that he practiced rigid self-denial in order to keep himself spiritually fit for the Christian race, and for the fights that are sure to come in the life of a believer. Paul realized and preached that the body is the temple of the Holy Ghost. In Romans 12:1 he pleads with believers to present their bodies a living sacrifice, holy and acceptable unto God, which is the reasonable service of every Christian.

". . . *And bring it into subjection*" — that is, he treated his body as a bondslave, refusing to gratify the desires of the flesh and the lust of the world. If the body gets the upper hand of the spirit, then the Christian suffers loss and brings reproach upon the name of Jesus and the cause of Christ. Every believer should have complete mastery over the desires of the flesh, and in order to BE master of the flesh we must rely upon the Holy Spirit. He is able — but we, too, must have deter-

314

mination and be willing to respond to His leadership. The children of God are led by the Spirit of God, and He leads into paths of right living; but we must be willing to follow. If we walk in the Spirit we will not fulfill the lust of the flesh. That is what Paul was teaching the believers in Corinth; *and it is what we need to learn in this day and hour!*

"*. . . Lest that by any means, when I have preached to others, I myself should be a castaway.*" "By any means" points out the idea of "in any way possible." Paul could not allow the flesh, the world, or the devil to get the upper hand in his life and ministry; *he simply must not.* So he buffeted his body daily, and brought it into the position of a slave.

"*When I have preached to others*" signifies the act of giving out the good news. Paul was a herald of the Gospel, giving out the good news that Jesus died, was buried, and rose again to save sinners.

The Greek word *adokimos*, here translated "castaway," does not mean to be cut off from Christ. It means to be *disapproved* as the result of not standing the test of faithfulness in stewardship — rejected from the standpoint of stewardship, not redemption. There are those who refuse to accept this translation, but outstanding Greek authorities declare that this word does not mean "cut off from Christ" in that Paul was afraid he would be lost; but rather that his stewardship and ministry would be rejected. It has to do with loss of reward, not loss of the soul.

The very thought of this should frighten us who name the name of Jesus, if we should entertain any idea of giving Him our second best or proving untrue to Him in testimony or stewardship. We should hear Paul's admonition and we should follow his advice. We should follow in his steps as he followed in the steps of the Christ whom he met on the Damascus road, and who commissioned him as the apostle to the Gentiles.

To point unbelievers to the Lord Jesus Christ and win them for Him should be the foremost desire of our lives — yea, every moment of every hour of every day we should be attempting—through testimony, influence, giving, going, doing whatsoever we can—to point unbelievers to the Lamb of God, who saves to the uttermost all who will come to the Father by Him. We should hear Paul as he cries out, "Whether therefore ye eat, or drink, or whatsoever ye do, do all to the glory of God!" (I Cor. 10:31). "I beseech you therefore, brethren, by the mercies of God, that ye present your bodies a living sacrifice, holy, acceptable unto God, which is your reasonable service" (Rom. 12:1). "Neither yield ye your members as instruments of unrighteousness unto sin: but yield yourselves unto God, as those that are alive from the dead, and your members as instruments of righteousness unto God" (Rom. 6:13).

We should keep our eyes centered on Jesus — and as we look into His face we should also be looking upon the fields that are white unto harvest, and we should go after unbelievers for His name's sake!

CHAPTER TEN

1. Moreover, brethren, I would not that ye should be ignorant, how that all our fathers were under the cloud, and all passed through the sea;

2. And were all baptized unto Moses in the cloud and in the sea;

3. And did all eat the same spiritual meat;

4. And did all drink the same spiritual drink: for they drank of that spiritual Rock that followed them: and that Rock was Christ.

5. But with many of them God was not well pleased: for they were overthrown in the wilderness.

6. Now these things were our examples, to the intent we should not lust after evil things, as they also lusted.

7. Neither be ye idolaters, as were some of them; as it is written, The people sat down to eat and drink, and rose up to play.

8. Neither let us commit fornication, as some of them committed, and fell in one day three and twenty thousand.

9. Neither let us tempt Christ, as some of them also tempted, and were destroyed of serpents.

10. Neither murmur ye, as some of them also murmured, and were destroyed of the destroyer.

11. Now all these things happened unto them for ensamples: and they are written for our admonition, upon whom the ends of the world are come.

12. Wherefore let him that thinketh he standeth take heed lest he fall.

13. There hath no temptation taken you but such as is common to man: but God is faithful, who will not suffer you to be tempted above that ye are able; but will with the temptation also make a way to escape, that ye may be able to bear it.

14. Wherefore, my dearly beloved, flee from idolatry.

15. I speak as to wise men; judge ye what I say.

16. The cup of blessing which we bless, is it not the communion of the blood of Christ? The bread which we break, is

it not the communion of the body of Christ?

17. For we being many are one bread, and one body: for we are all partakers of that one bread.

18. Behold Israel after the flesh: are not they which eat of the sacrifices partakers of the altar?

19. What say I then? that the idol is any thing, or that which is offered in sacrifice to idols is any thing?

20. But I say, that the things which the Gentiles sacrifice, they sacrifice to devils, and not to God: and I would not that ye should have fellowship with devils.

21. Ye cannot drink the cup of the Lord, and the cup of devils: ye cannot be partakers of the Lord's table, and of the table of devils.

22. Do we provoke the Lord to jealousy? are we stronger than he?

23. All things are lawful for me, but all things are not expedient: all things are lawful for me, but all things edify not.

24. Let no man seek his own, but every man another's wealth.

25. Whatsoever is sold in the shambles, that eat, asking no question for conscience sake:

26. For the earth is the Lord's, and the fulness thereof.

27. If any of them that believe not bid you to a feast, and ye be disposed to go; whatsoever is set before you, eat, asking no question for conscience sake.

28. But if any man say unto you, This is offered in sacrifice unto idols, eat not for his sake that shewed it, and for conscience sake: for the earth is the Lord's, and the fulness thereof:

29. Conscience, I say, not thine own, but of the other: for why is my liberty judged of another man's conscience?

30. For if I by grace be a partaker, why am I evil spoken of for that for which I give thanks?

31. Whether therefore ye eat, or drink, or whatsoever ye do, do all to the glory of God.

32. Give none offence, neither to the Jews, nor to the Gentiles, nor to the church of God:

33. Even as I please all men in all things, not seeking mine own profit, but the profit of many, that they may be saved.

This chapter follows in close connection with the last part of chapter 9. The word "moreover" in verse 1, sometimes translated "for," connects the first verse of chapter 10 with the previous chapter. Paul points out that even a true believer may be rejected in regard to his service here on earth. God may place him on the shelf and use him no longer. Not only that, but he may also lose his reward at the judgment seat of Christ if he fails to exercise self-discipline. Paul illustrates this truth by referring to the history of Israel in the wilderness journey, pointing out that many who came out of Egypt were not allowed to enter into the promised land.

This record of the sins of Israel is given by direction of the Holy Spirit and is for our admonition, as clearly shown in verse 11 of this chapter. Believers must not be self-willed nor practice self-complacency, lest we become rejected by the Master, unfit for His use. But we *can* overcome. This assurance is given in verses 12 and 13 of our present chapter.

A defeated Christian has no one to blame but himself, because Jesus will not permit the devil to tempt any believer above that which he is able to bear. God who hath begun a good work in us is able to perform that good work until the day of Jesus Christ — and He will if we let Him.

Israel and Their Experience in the Wilderness a Warning to Believers

Verse 1: "Moreover, brethren, I would not that ye should be ignorant, how that all our fathers were under the cloud, and all passed through the sea."

". . . *I would not that ye should be ignorant* . . . ." Paul is not suggesting here that the believers in Corinth did not know these facts, but there was a possibility that they had failed to see the lesson intended in the account of God's chosen people and their wandering in the wilderness. They no doubt had "head-knowledge" of the Old Testament Scriptures concerning Israel, but head-knowledge without "heart-knowledge" is dangerous.

Paul often uses the term, "I would not that ye should be ignorant." He uses it in I Corinthians 12:1, Romans 1:13; 11:25, II Corinthians 1:8, and I Thessalonians 4:13. In each of these Scriptures except the last, the statement is connected with the truth that precedes it — (in I Thessalonians 4:13 Paul introduces a new subject, the Rapture of the Church) — and in every case Paul speaks of his readers as "brethren." The Greek term is one of love and affection. Paul speaks from a heart overflowing with Christian love.

". . . *How that all our fathers were under the cloud, and all passed through the sea.*" All Israel was under the cloud, and all Israel passed through the sea. This privilege was granted them by Jehovah. Notice that the word "all" is emphasized by being used twice. Paul is emphasizing that ALL Israel was granted this privilege of grace, but he is also laying the foundation for the truth set forth in the next verses—a truth set forth as a warning to believers who may stop short of full dedication to God.

Verse 2: "And were all baptized unto Moses in the cloud and in the sea."

This is typical of the baptism of the believer. The waters of the Red Sea were made to stand divided on either side of the Israelites as they marched through on dry ground: "*He divided the sea, and caused them to pass through; and He made the waters to stand as an heap*" (Psalm 78:13). The cloud above them completed the picture of a watery grave—the waters on either side, the cloud above. They were immersed in the water and the cloud, and then were raised from the watery grave—raised very much alive.

The Holy Spirit is pointing out to us here not only the fact that Moses was the leader of Israel, but also that the baptism of the believer identifies that believer with Christ. One who has received true Christian baptism is buried with Christ in His death and raised in newness of life.

To refer to baptism as "immersion" only is not entirely correct, because *to immerse* is not the full meaning of baptism. We are buried, yes — but we do not *stay buried*. We are *raised* — and if there be no resurrection, then our faith is vain, our preaching is vain, we are still in our sins, and our loved ones who have died are perished. Therefore, baptism sets forth the death, the burial, and the resurrection of the believer.

Verse 3: "And did all eat the same spiritual meat."

The *"spiritual meat"* referred to here is the manna God provided for Israel. The manna was spiritual from two aspects: *First,* in its origin: "Man did eat angels' food: He sent them meat to the full" (Psalm 78:25). *Second,* the manna was spiritual from the aspect of its consequent effects upon those who ate it.

The manna signifies that Christ is the bread of life, and true believers feed upon Him: "Our fathers did eat manna in the desert; as it is written, He gave them bread from heaven to eat. Then Jesus said unto them, Verily, verily, I say unto you, Moses gave you not that bread from heaven; but my Father giveth you the true bread from heaven" (John 6:31,32).

Verse 4: "And did all drink the same spiritual drink: for they drank of that spiritual Rock that followed them: and that Rock was Christ."

"And did all drink the same spiritual drink . . . ." The water Israel drank was natural water — but it was also *supernatural* because of the way it was provided and because it continued to flow. (It is still flowing today.) I visited in the Holy Land for ten weeks and I traveled

through the countries where Moses and the Israelites lived. I drank water from the stream gushing from the rock that furnished water for them in their wilderness journey. There may be many places in the Holy Land that cannot be authentically identified, but all Bible scholars and missionaries to whom I talked declare that *this IS the rock which Moses struck.* The water still gushes forth, and it is the only pure water in that area. Our missionary partner boiled every drop of water we drank until we reached the place where Moses struck the rock; we drank *that* water freely, without boiling it. It is declared to be the purest water in all of Palestine — and certainly we know why.

"*. . . For they drank of that spiritual Rock that followed them.*" In the first part of this verse, the Greek verb translated "to drink" is in the past tense, the same tense used in relation to *eating* in verse 3, indicating that they *had eaten*—an act that was past, with no reference to repetition. However, in the *last part* of verse 4 the tense is imperfect—"they *were drinking*"—pointing out significantly *the constant flow* of the water, and they continued to drink.

What a beautiful picture of the believer's life! Whatever we need daily is as near as a prayer of faith. God is not only *willing*, but anxious and able to supply water, meat, bread. Whatever our needs, physically or spiritually, we find those needs met in Jesus; He is our sufficiency, and we are complete in Him.

"*That Rock was Christ.*" This signifies that the Rock was a type of Christ — but it goes deeper than that. Paul does not say that the Rock *IS* Christ, using the present tense as in Galatians 4:24,25, speaking of Hagar and Mount Sinai: "Which things are an allegory: for these are the two covenants; the one from the mount Sinai, which gendereth to bondage, which *is* Agar. For this Agar *is* mount Sinai in Arabia, and answereth to Jerusalem which now *is*, and *is* in bondage with her children."

Paul says, "That Rock WAS Christ," which certainly implies that the water which gushed forth from the rock was provided by the personal presence of Jesus Christ on the spot; and we know the Angel of His presence was with the chosen people as they journeyed through the wilderness: "In all their affliction He was afflicted, and the angel of His presence saved them: in His love and in His pity He redeemed them; and He bare them, and carried them all the days of old" (Isa. 63:9).

The Rock being described as spiritual and as going along with them is distinctly a divine testimony of the pre-existence of Christ. The smiting of the Rock was a typical foreshadowing of the smiting of Jesus—the judgment stroke that fell upon the Lamb of God, the stroke to which He voluntarily submitted at Calvary when He willingly bore our sins in His own body on the cross; and that stroke fell from the hand of God the Father: "Surely He hath borne our griefs, and carried our sorrows: yet we did esteem Him stricken, *smitten of God*, and afflicted" (Isaiah 53:4).

Verse 5: "But with many of them God was not well pleased: for they were overthrown in the wilderness."

Please note that this does not say "ALL" of them, nor, in the Greek, does it say "many." In Numbers 14: 29-31 we read, "Your carcases shall fall in this wilderness; and all that were numbered of you, according to your whole number, from twenty years old and upward, which have murmured against me, doubtless ye shall not come into the land, concerning which I sware to make you dwell therein, save Caleb the son of Jephunneh, and Joshua the son of Nun. But your little ones, which ye said should be a prey, them will I bring in, and they shall know the land which ye have despised." According to the Old Testament, the rest of the Israelites failed to obtain the desired prize of their hearts and they were rejected.

"For they were overthrown in the wilderness." The literal meaning is "to strew, to overthrow." In other words, because of their disobedience to God the Israelites were literally strewn all over the wilderness, overthrown because they did not please Jehovah.

Verse 6: "Now these things were our examples, to the intent we should not lust after evil things, as they also lusted."

The truth set forth here is simply this: In the things that happened to Israel, God's elect and chosen people, they became types of us and their experiences became *examples* to us, declaring what will happen to us if we do as they did. The Greek word translated "warning" signifies "examples by way of warning." God is warning New Testament believers that if we displease Him we will be cut off—not from the standpoint of redemption, but our earthly testimony and our stewardship will be cut off. We will lose the prize—a full reward, with crowns and trophies to cast at the feet of Jesus when we crown Him King of kings and Lord of lords.

The Greek word used here for "lust" is *epithumeo*, and its primary meaning is "to desire." The Lord Jesus uses the same word in a good sense in Luke 22:15, and it is used in I Peter 1:12 with reference to the holy angels. It is used of good men for good things in Matthew 13:17, I Timothy 3:1, and in Hebrews 6:11. In our present Scripture it is used as having to do with evil desires—the same sense in which it is used in Matthew 5:28, James 4:2, and in the first part of Galatians 5:17.

The word "lust" in the Greek is a noun used with the verb "to be." Thus, *"we should not be lusters."* The record of the lusting of the Israelites is found in Numbers 11:4: "And the mixt multitude that was among them fell a lusting: and the children of Israel also wept again, and said, Who shall give us flesh to eat?"

Their lusting was due primarily to the mixed multitude which came up out of Egypt: "And a mixed multitude went up also with them; and flocks, and herds, even very much cattle" (Ex. 12:38). The example to us is simply this: If Christians do not walk in a separated path, if we are not segregated completely from the world, then as time goes on we will eventually slip and begin to compromise, participating in the habits and practices of the enemies of Jesus Christ.

Then too, if we spend our time and thoughts to satisfy the flesh and gratify only the natural life, the spiritual life is sure to suffer and we will come to disaster and sad disappointment. We will lose our reward.

Verse 7: "Neither be ye idolaters, as were some of them; as it is written, The people sat down to eat and drink, and rose up to play."

It is significant that Paul here points out the things that followed the worshipping of the golden calf, although he does not mention worship of the idol itself. This suggests that he is recalling to the Corinthians the truth he had set forth about sitting at meat in the idol's temple, in chapter 8, verse 10. The believers in Corinth who visited these temples and ate at the feasts did not actually *worship the idol* — but they associated with those who did, and thus their actions were questionable. Spiritually minded believers should *know* better and should *do* better.

Verse 8: "Neither let us commit fornication, as some of them committed, and fell in one day three and twenty thousand."

The subject of fornication has been discussed in chapter six. The evil of fornication existed in the assembly at Corinth, and we are clearly taught in chapter 5 (also in II Corinthians 12:21) concerning this sin. Balaam was an instrument of Satan in seducing Israel into committing fornication. Study Numbers 25; 31:16; Colossians 3:5,6; and Romans 8:13.

In Numbers 25:9 we read that 24,000 were cut off, and Paul mentions 23,000; but the passage in Numbers does not say that 24,000 fell in *one day*, whereas Paul does point out that *23,000* died in one day. Paul is undoubtedly referring to the specific incident of that day, while Numbers 25:9 gives the total number that died *because of the plague*. The believer encounters no difficulty here; only those who attempt to discredit the Scriptures find discrepancies in such passages. There are no contradictions in the Bible when we rightly divide the Word and compare Scripture with Scripture.

Verse 9: "Neither let us tempt Christ, as some of them also tempted, and were destroyed of serpents."

The Greek verb *ekpeirazo* (translated "tempt") used in the first part of this verse is an intensive form of the more frequent verb *peirazo*, and carries with it the meaning of "challenging God." It is used in the same sense in Matthew 4:7, and in Luke 4:12 and 10:25.

However, in the last part of our verse the simpler form of the verb *peirazo* is used. The use of the extremely strong form in the first part of the verse and the lesser in the last part seems to point out that if it was dangerous for *Israel* to tempt God, it is even *more* dangerous for present day believers to do so. We find the same truth in Hebrews 10:28,29: "He that despised Moses' law died without mercy under two or three witnesses: Of how much sorer punishment, suppose ye, shall he be thought worthy, who hath trodden under foot the Son of God, and hath counted the blood of the covenant, wherewith he was sanctified, an unholy thing, and hath done despite unto the Spirit of grace?"

To "tempt God" means for an individual or a people to put God to the test time after time, simply to see the extent of His longsuffering—just how long He will put up with sin and shortcomings. Such a spirit was manifested by the Israelites in their continued rebellion against God. The Greek verb translated "destroyed" (perished) points out that the judgment was continual—day after day—as long as they rebelled against God. The record of the fiery serpents is found in Numbers 21:6.

Verse 10: "Neither murmur ye, as some of them also murmured, and were destroyed of the destroyer."

Here Paul no doubt refers to Numbers 16:14—47. Please read these verses carefully. Murmuring on the part of Christians has its beginning in unbelief. Murmuring denies the goodness, mercy, and longsuffering of God. Believers are exhorted, "In everything give thanks: for this is the will of God in Christ Jesus concerning you" (I Thess. 5:18).

God pity us if we grumble! We may suffer trials, tribulations, and disappointments; but we must remember Romans 8:28. No one thing may *seem* good, but when all things are added up, then "ALL things work together for good."

"*The destroyer*" mentioned in this verse is not Satan, but *God*, through the power of the destroying angel: "For the Lord will pass through to smite the Egyptians; and when He seeth the blood upon the lintel, and on the two side posts, the Lord will pass over the door, and will not suffer the destroyer to come in unto your houses to smite you" (Ex. 12:23). Also see II Samuel 24:16.

Verse 11: "Now all these things happened unto them for ensamples: and they are written for our admonition, upon whom the ends of the world are come."

Here we have a pattern or figure—(and certainly one to be avoided)—warning us of what will happen to us if we practice what Israel did. Strong emphasis is placed upon "THEM"; the Holy Spirit is telling us the things that happened to THEM, in order that we may profit from their sad mistakes. These things were written for our admonition in order that we might profit from the mistakes of Israel. The literal translation of the word *"admonition"* here means *"putting in mind"* and sets forth the picture of training by word—whether it be to encourage, or to warn. It is important for us to remember that the Old Testament Scriptures are not a mere recording of historical facts. They convey a message from God to man . . . they convey the thoughts and law of God concerning men, and hence have a purpose in our lives today. It is important that we read the Old Testament Scriptures with this thought in view.

". . . *Upon whom the ends of the world are come.*" The Greek word here translated "world" should have been *"ages,"* which in Scripture stands for successive periods of time in which God deals with mankind. This age of grace is the closing age of God's dealings with sinful men. From now until the consummation of all things, all who are recipients of God's mercy will receive that mercy only because of God's grace. We have passed through the Age of Innocence, the Age of Conscience, the Age of Human Government, the Age of Law, etc., and are now in the Age of Grace, the final age in which God will deal with peoples upon this earth.

At the end of this age and the consummation of all things, there will be a new heaven — and a new earth

328

"wherein dwelleth righteousness," where the knowledge of the Lord will cover the earth as the waters now cover the sea. All that would hinder will be in hell; nothing that defiles shall enter the City of God. Therefore, after God's dealings, up to the consummation of all things, there will be no more "ages." There will be one long, endless eternity!

The Greek word here translated "are come" means "to arrive at a certain time." Those who study the Scriptures and compare the prophecies of the Bible with current events throughout the world, know that surely the end is near and the coming of Jesus in the Rapture is imminent. Who knows? It may be this day, this very hour, that the Church will be caught up to meet the Lord Jesus in the air!

Verse 12: "Wherefore let him that thinketh he standeth take heed lest he fall."

Here we have the necessary application to each and every believer concerning the truth conveyed in the preceding accounts—that is, the illustrations given concerning God's dealings with Israel. The believer who thinks he *stands* is on good ground for the devil to trip him. Read I Corinthians 8:9–13.

Self-complacency is the danger here – the believer takes his standing for granted and does not look to Jesus for strength to overcome. Self-satisfaction always produces spiritual carelessness, and spiritual carelessness leads to rejection, as pointed out in chapter 9, verse 27. We are more than conquerors, but it is only "THROUGH HIM THAT LOVED US" (Rom. 8:31–39).

Verse 13: "There hath no temptation taken you but such as is common to man: but God is faithful, who will not suffer you to be tempted above that ye are able; but will with the temptation also make a way to escape, that ye may be able to bear it."

From solemn warning, Paul immediately passes to divine encouragement with divine promise. The meaning of *"common to man"* is "such as must—and does—come to all men so long as we live in this body of flesh." It is not a sin to be tempted, and as long as we dwell in the flesh God will permit circumstances to take place out of which will come temptation; but He will always provide a way of escape.

God allows the temptation, God provides *the way of escape*—but the believer must take advantage of that provision . . . that is, we must be alert, not ignorant of the devil's devices. It is God's responsibility to provide a way of escape, but it is OUR responsibility to look to Him and trust Him for the way of escape—and then use it. ". . . God cannot be tempted with evil, neither tempteth He any man: But every man is tempted, when he is drawn away of his own lust, and enticed" (James 1:13,14). God is not the author of sin.

". . . *BUT GOD IS FAITHFUL* . . . ." God cannot be otherwise. At all times, and under all circumstances, He acts consistently with His character. He has made adequate provision for every believer to meet every temptation that may arise. He will supply the strength and the way of escape. The believer who relies upon God's strength, who seeks to be conformed to God's will, and who faithfully looks to God, will always find victory over the world, the flesh, and the devil. Study Hebrews 4:14—16.

". . . *Who will not suffer you to be tempted above that ye are able.*" The Lord God Almighty knows every circumstance surrounding every temptation we face. Not one temptation comes to us without His permissive will — He allows it. But He will not allow the devil to tempt us beyond our breaking point. To Peter Jesus said, ". . . Satan hath desired to have you, that he may sift you as wheat: But I have prayed for thee, that thy faith fail not" (Luke 22:31,32).

We read in John 17:20,21 where Jesus prayed for all who will believe — and I belong to that group. Jesus not only prayed for *Peter* to stand; He prayed for *me*—and for every believer. The restraining power of God is such that the believer can meet and overcome every temptation that faces him when the Holy Spirit is allowed to lead, and the power of the Holy Spirit is allowed to work. If we walk in the Spirit we will not fulfill the lust of the flesh, because He will lead us into paths of right living. He will give us victory over every temptation.

". . . *But will with the temptation also make a way to escape, that ye may be able to bear it.*" The word rendered "way to escape" is *ekbasis* and literally means "a way out." However, it is not merely *a* way of escape, but *THE* way appointed by God and suited to each Christian in each temptation.

There is a glorious fact declared here: *"The temptation and the way out always go together!* A loving God never allows a believer to be the victim of circumstances. We have many marvelous accounts in the Word of God where He provided a way, and His child *did escape* temptation.

Joseph was sorely tempted, but God provided a way of escape, and Joseph took that way (Gen. 39:12).

Daniel was sorely tempted, but God provided a way out of the temptation, Daniel walked therein, and escaped (Dan. 1:8).

No temptation can come to a child of God without the *permissive will* of God, and even then He always provides a way of escape; and for His glory and to His honor we *should* escape. He never allows any temptation to come upon one of His children that they are unable to withstand:

"Blessed is the man that endureth temptation: for when he is tried, he shall receive the crown of life, which the Lord hath promised to them that love Him. Let no man say when he is tempted, I am tempted of God: for God cannot be tempted with evil, neither tempteth He any man: But every man is tempted, when he is drawn away of his own lust, and enticed. Then when lust hath conceived, it bringeth forth sin: and sin, when it is finished, bringeth forth death. Do not err, my beloved brethren" (James 1:12–16).

I advise every believer who does not already know I Corinthians 10:12,13 from memory, to read no further in this book until you memorize those verses. Believe them, hide them in your heart, live by them and walk in them. *You will be a victorious Christian.*

The moment we think we stand, we are on good ground to fall. We must realize in our hearts that no temptation can come upon us apart from the permissive will of God, and in the very temptation *the way of escape is always present.* Because of the faithfulness of God, He will not permit the devil to tempt us or put more upon us than we can bear up under if we rely on HIS strength, not our own.

I repeat: If you are a Christian and you have stumbled, it is not God's fault. If you have succumbed to temptation you have no one to blame but yourself. We are more than conquerors through Christ — not just ordinary conquerors, but MORE than conquerors. He does furnish the strength, the power, and the way to escape temptation.

Verse 14: "Wherefore, my dearly beloved, flee from idolatry."

In this verse Paul returns to the subject of chapter 8—meats, and feasts in the temples where the idols were;

and in addition, he brings to bear what he has declared in the first part of our present chapter concerning Israel. As idol feasts were definitely connected with the subject, he sets forth in the next few verses the contrast of the idol feasts with the significance of the circumstances of the Lord's supper.

Paul gives exhortation here concerning participation in idol feasts, but his instruction goes much, much further than that and can be applied to any and all things which might be set up in the heart of a born again believer which would take the place of full devotion to the Lord Jesus Christ and the stewardship that should be rendered to Him. Christians are to literally *flee* from anything that would cause them to love Jesus less, or render service to Him that is not in full devotion. Believers should have nothing to do with idolatry in any form, and anything that causes Jesus to take second place in one's life certainly becomes an idol to that individual.

Verse 15: "I speak as to wise men; judge ye what I say."

Paul is not speaking here in sarcasm as he did in chapter 4, verse 10. He credits those to whom he is writing with having enough intelligence and spiritual understanding to know what he is saying. The Greek word used here means "prudent"—that is, being able to exercise practical wisdom, that which we refer to as "good common sense." Paul emphasizes "YE." He is saying to the believers, "Judge *ye yourselves* what I declare."

Fellowship at the Lord's Table Demands Full Separation

Verse 16: "The cup of blessing which we bless, is it not the communion of the blood of Christ? The bread which we break, is it not the communion of the body of Christ?"

The *"cup of blessing"* to which Paul refers is the giving of thanks. The love of God abiding in the heart of the believer always causes the heart to praise God. Peter declares, "We rejoice with joy unspeakable and full of glory" (I Pet. 1:8).

". . . *Is it not the communion of the blood of Christ?*" The Greek word translated "communion" is *koinonia*; it signifies "to have in common" and denotes, in its more frequent sense, the share which one has in anything. The meaning here is of great depth, pointing to the fact that the believer shares in the effects of the blood of Jesus shed for the remission of sins. We are *covered* by the blood, redeemed through the blood, and *cleansed* by the blood — and every believer shares in the shed blood, being crucified with Christ, buried with Him in baptism, raised to walk in newness of life. All that we are, all that we have and enjoy, is because of the shed blood of Jesus Christ.

We learn in Leviticus 17:11 that "the life of the flesh is in the blood." The blood was given on the altar for the remission of sin. Jesus shed His blood, He gave His life. He said, "My Father loves me because I lay down my life for the sheep." The basis of all spiritual blessing is the shed blood; it is the blood which makes atonement. *Without* shedding of blood there is *no remission.*

No one should participate in the Lord's Supper unless he has been truly born again, thereby becoming partaker of divine nature (spiritual life) through the death, burial, and resurrection of Jesus. An unsaved person should *never* receive the bread and the fruit of the vine in holy communion. The truth Paul sets forth here is that all believers have fellowship in all that the shed blood of Jesus Christ has made possible; we all share in His shed blood.

"*The bread which we break, is it not the communion of the body of Christ?*"

"*The bread which WE break . . . .*" The fact that

Paul uses the personal pronoun "WE" suggests that each believer broke the bread for himself.

The *communion* with (the fellowship in) the Lord's body is fellowship in what the believer receives from or through the offering of the body of Christ in His death. His body was prepared for Him by the heavenly Father: "Wherefore when He cometh into the world, He saith, Sacrifice and offering thou wouldest not, but a body hast thou prepared me" (Heb. 10:5).

During the Lord's sojourn upon this earth, His flesh was the tabernacle of God. God was in Christ (II Cor. 5:19); Jesus was the God-Man. Throughout the days of His life on earth the flesh was the instrument in which He fulfilled the Father's will in every respect. The cross was the final step. He *willingly* went to the cross, and on the cross proclaimed, *"It is finished!"* Jesus is the living, glorified, Christ—*the bread of life for the souls of believers.*

Verse 17: "For we being many are one bread, and one body: for we are all partakers of that one bread."

This verse points out the oneness of the members of the body of Christ. The Greek word translated "one bread" really means "loaf."

". . . *We are all partakers of that one bread.*" The Greek word translated "partake" denotes "to have a share in that which is being partaken of." In this case the bread is Christ, and so we share in Christ—in His death, in His burial, in His resurrection, and in His life. It is in Him that we live, and move, and have our being.

There is only one true Church, and Jesus is the head and the foundation of that Church. We are members of that body; all believers are baptized into the body of Christ by the Holy Spirit; all believers have been made to drink into one Spirit. We partake of one loaf: *We are one in Christ.*

Verse 18: "Behold Israel after the flesh: Are not they which eat of the sacrifices partakers of the altar?"

"Behold Israel after the flesh." The nation of Israel wandering in the wilderness has a spiritual application, and we should not forget that the things which happened to them happened as examples to us as believers; but Paul is pointing here to the people in their *natural state.*

"Are not they which eat of the sacrifices partakers of the altar?" What Paul is saying here is simply this: "They are in fellowship with Him whose altar it is — and the altar is the Lord's." Even the Israelites after the flesh who ate the sacrifices were partakers with the altar of Jehovah, severed thus in principal and fact from the vanities of the heathen. There are certain offerings in the Old Testament era which, after part of the offering had been burnt on the altar and part had been given to the priest, the remainder of the sacrifice was eaten in the court of the tabernacle. Study Leviticus 7:15–21; Deuteronomy 12:5–7.

To participate in the sacrificial feast meant fellowship with the living God who *appointed* the feast. Here Paul is about to show the spiritual application of these feasts in the matter of partaking of the Lord's Supper.

Verse 19: "What say I then? that the idol is any thing, or that which is offered in sacrifice to idols is any thing?"

The idol is dead and is therefore nothing, thus making the *offering* to the idol nothing. The idol and the offering are lacking in reality; therefore they are nothing. There are no such beings as gods and goddesses such as existed in the minds of those who offered these heathen sacrifices.

Verse 20: "But I say, that the things which the

Gentiles sacrifice, they sacrifice to devils, and not to God: and I would not that ye should have fellowship with devils."

"*. . . They sacrifice to devils, and not to God . . . .*" The idolaters *thought* they were offering a sacrifice to a god, but they were not; they were offering sacrifices to demons. (Where the plural is used the rendering should always be "demons," not *devils*. There is only ONE devil, but there are multiplied millions of demons.) We read of demons in Luke 4:33,34; Acts 19:15; and there are demons who lead unbelievers to practice idolatry. Demons seek to inhabit human bodies, or the bodies of animals (Luke 8:29–32). They are disembodied spirits, and they operate most effectively when they dwell in a body, whether it be human or animal. Someone has defined idolatry in these words: "The ritual of sin—the ceremonial of the rule of evil spirits over men." Those who offer sacrifices to idols are worshipping a god that does not exist, and they are fellowshipping with demons.

"*I would not that ye should have fellowship with demons.*" Paul here points out that believers who visited the feasts in idol temples and ate the meat that had been offered to idols—even though the idol was nothing and the sacrifice was nothing—were nevertheless worshipping in the temple of pagan gods, and thus they were aiding and abetting idolatry. Although they might have been free from evil motives and their consciences might have been clear, they were fellowshipping with demons, nevertheless.

To fellowship with demons is a very dangerous thing for a believer. Born again people today should not attend services that deal in spirits. No believer should attend a spiritual seance where "spiritualists" are supposed to contact the dead.

Verse 21: "Ye cannot drink the cup of the Lord, and the cup of devils: ye cannot be partakers of the Lord's

337

table, and of the table of devils.''

"*Ye cannot drink the cup of the Lord, and the cup of devils (demons) . . . .*" It is a moral impossibility to partake of the cup of the Lord's Supper and then to participate in that which is associated with demons. The Lord's Supper is representative of life received through the shed blood of Christ, and that administered to demons is the cup of death.

". . . *Partakers of the Lord's table . . . .*" The "table" here stands for that which is placed *upon* the table; for example, *the blood of Christ* stands for the giving up of His life in the shedding of His blood in atoning sacrifice. The life is in the blood, so when Jesus gave His blood He gave up His life — and His blood is the atoning sacrifice. Here then the *table* stands for the bread and the cup which are placed upon it. The "bread and the cup" set forth the fellowship believers enjoy with Christ because of His broken body and His shed blood. In the same way, the "table of demons" stands for the things which the table provides for the partakers at the feast and sets forth fellowship with demons and the powers of darkness. Believers in the assembly at Corinth who were attending these feasts in the temple of idols were in danger of partaking of that which was supplied from the altar. It was a very dangerous thing for them to do.

Christians are always at the table of the Lord — we partake of the benefit of His death every moment of every day; but we are not always at the *supper* where His death is proclaimed *in His appointed way*, by the breaking of the bread and the fruit of the vine.

Verse 22: "Do we provoke the Lord to jealousy? Are we stronger than He?"

In connection with this verse please study Deuteronomy 32:21 and Numbers 25:11—13. For a believer to attempt to fellowship with the world, and at the same time, fellowship with the Holy Spirit and with Christ, is to move the Lord to holy indignation and fiery judgment.

Paul asked, *"Are we stronger than He?"* This is a solemn warning given in the form of a question. The believers should have *no fellowship* with the unfruitful works of darkness. We are to come out from the world and be separate. We are to "love not the world, neither the things that are in the world."

We do not hear much negative preaching today, but when we receive the positive (salvation by grace through faith) we should practice the negative—"lust not, be not, touch not." There are many negative commands in the Word of God.

The Law of Love in Relation to Eating and Drinking on the Part of Born Again Believers

Verse 23: "All things are lawful for me, but all things are not expedient: all things are lawful for me, but all things edify not."

"All things" refers to those things concerning which a believer has freedom—the honorable, pure, and right; certainly the reference is not to drunkenness, murder, and such things. Paul repeats the statement in order to lead up to the subject he is about to discuss—meats offered to idols. The principle that should guide each believer in his relationship to others should be that he may be used to edify and build them up spiritually—never to hinder or cause another to stumble. The liberty and freedom that we enjoy at the expense of hindering of others is not *Christian liberty.* Study Romans chapter 14.

No man liveth to himself, no man dieth to himself. We are either encouraging others, or discouraging them. We are building up weaker saints, or tearing them down.

A believer has no right to say, "It is no one's business what I do so long as it does not hurt my own conscience." We must always bear in mind the fact that all Christians are members of the same body, and when one member of the body suffers the entire body suffers. Therefore, if eating meat offends weaker brethren, we should abstain from meats — and that goes for anything that we may eat, drink, or do that might cause a weaker brother to stumble or become discouraged.

In the spiritual sense, we ARE our brother's keeper; and our liberty ends where our practices of life hurt or hinder a weak brother. We are to serve our brothers in Christ as we serve the Lord, and whatever we do is to be done to the glory of God.

Verse 24: "Let no man seek his own, but every man another's wealth."

Self-interest must never be our primary aim in life. For a believer to seek his own advantage is not always sinful — but neither is it always righteous. Only a sanctified life can be used of the Lord to bless and strengthen others, to the everlasting good of others. Day by day, believers should yield soul, spirit, and body entirely to Jesus Christ, and pray for Him to lead them into the path that will glorify Him most and be most beneficial to fellow believers.

Verse 25: "Whatsoever is sold in the shambles, that eat, asking no question for conscience sake."

The Greek word here translated "shambles" means the same as our *market*—in this case, the meat market. The admonition given in this verse has to do with purchasing or eating *in the market*; it has no reference to the feast in the idol temple, as in verse 27. Be careful to note this.

When the Corinthians purchased meat in the market,

in some instances it was impossible for them to know if the meat offered for sale had been offered in the idol temple as a sacrifice. Therefore, the Christian buying or eating meat in the market place was not to be troubled about the meat. Difficulties were not to be created unnecessarily. He was not to ask questions about the meat, because in so doing he could easily start a religious argument which would not bring glory to God nor be of advantage to the individual. And in the case of the market, and the restaurants IN the market, they were to ask no questions; but we will see later that they were not to go to the heathen feasts where they knew the meat had been offered to idols in worship.

Verse 26: "For the earth is the Lord's, and the fulness thereof."

Here Paul quotes from Psalm 24:1. All things were created by Jesus Christ, and through Him. The emphasis here is on *"Lord."* The fulness of the earth belongs to Him. It is true that the devil has corrupted many things, but that does not change God's ownership; and the fact that unbelievers may offer meat to idols does not harm the meat nor make it evil. The born again believer partakes of it for necessary uses *because the earth IS the Lord's,* and the fulness thereof; but we must not eat it if our eating will hinder weak believers, causing them to stumble or become discouraged.

To use this verse of Scripture to argue that the believer may do whatsoever he likes and eat or drink whatsoever he likes is to pervert the Word of God. The purpose in a true believer's heart is to use everything for God's glory and not for self-indulgence. The believer's heart must be dedicated to the mind of God, he must follow the leadership of the Holy Spirit, and he must not do anything that might bring reproach upon the name of Jesus.

For if we fear God as we should, the fear of the Lord is clean and will prevent us from doing that which would bring reproach and shame upon His name.

Verse 27: "If any of them that believe not bid you to a feast, and ye be disposed to go; whatsoever is set before you, eat, asking no question for conscience sake."

This is on the ground of conscience. Remember in verse 25 Paul declared that no questions were to be asked concerning the meat sold in the market or eaten in the restaurant in the market. It was perfectly all right for a believer to buy meat from the market or eat it in the restaurant there; but a believer, on his own and without an invitation, should never go to the heathen temple to one of the feasts. In this verse, however, we have a different picture: Paul is instructing believers concerning an invitation extended to them by an unbeliever, friend, neighbor, or possibly a relative. This does not mean a religious feast, or a feast in the temple, but one in the home.

Paul said, "If an unbeliever invites you to a feast, IF YE BE DISPOSED TO GO, then *go*; and whatever is set before you, EAT. Do not make inquiries as to whether the meat had any connection with idol sacrifices or idol worship."

Verse 28: "But if any man say unto you, This is offered in sacrifice unto idols, eat not for his sake that shewed it, and for conscience sake: for the earth is the Lord's, and the fulness thereof."

In other words, if meat is placed before the believer, and "any man" informs him that the meat has been offered in sacrifice unto idols, *"eat not for his sake that shewed it,* and for conscience sake."

Verse 29: "Conscience, I say, not thine own, but of the other: for why is my liberty judged of another man's conscience?"

One believer may have no conscience against eating meat offered to idols. He may have perfect liberty in his heart concerning such things and can do it with no twinge of conscience. But a weaker brother may have a conscience against it, and if the stronger believer eats in the presence of the weaker, it may lead *him* to do so — and thus his conscience may condemn him and he may become discouraged, which could bring about a tremendous spiritual setback and loss of reward. This principle holds good concerning all matters that would cause weak brethren to stumble.

"For why is my liberty judged of another man's conscience?" Here, Paul clearly puts himself in the place of a strong Christian and shows believers the difficulty he would bring about by bringing upon himself judgment and condemnation of his informant, who with his tender conscience would look upon the stronger brother as having done wrong, and what would Paul have gained by wounding this weaker one and coming under the condemnatory judgment of the weak brother's conscience?

"Let us not therefore judge one another any more: but judge this rather, that no man put a stumblingblock or an occasion to fall in his brother's way. I know, and am persuaded by the Lord Jesus, that there is nothing unclean of itself: but to him that esteemeth any thing to be unclean, to him it is unclean. But if thy brother be grieved with thy meat, now walkest thou not charitably. Destroy not him with thy meat, for whom Christ died" (Rom. 14:13—15).

Verse 30: "For if I by grace be a partaker, why am I evil spoken of for that for which I give thanks?"

Paul believed in giving thanks: but (even though he gave thanks for his food) if all the while in eating it he was wounding a weaker brother and causing him to stumble or become discouraged, was he then, in reality, truly giving thanks to God? To give thanks for what we are doing does not necessarily make that act innocent on our part. We must keep others in mind at all times, regardless of how innocent we may be, for if we are wounding others, it is still wrong.

Verse 31: "Whether therefore ye eat, or drink, or whatsoever ye do, do all to the glory of God."

The glory of God is the manifestation of His character and acts. To do all to the glory of God is to manifest Him in both respects. We as born again Christians represent Christ here on this earth. In a way *true* believers are imitators of God. We have the mind of Christ and we reflect His character and His ways in what we do, the places we go, the things we say, the company we keep. If we are to be true imitators of God, we must walk in love, humility, and self-sacrifice. We must walk in His steps: "Be ye therefore followers of God, as dear children; and walk in love, as Christ also hath loved us, and hath given Himself for us an offering and a sacrifice to God for a sweetsmelling savour" (Eph. 5:1,2).

Jesus said of His disciples, "I am glorified in them" (John 17:10). Therefore, we should have a singular motive first and foremost in our minds in whatsoever we do — and *"whatsoever"* includes not only deeds, but words: "And whatsoever ye do *in word or deed*, do all in the name of the Lord Jesus, giving thanks to God and the Father by Him" (Col. 3:17).

Verse 32: "Give none offence, neither to the Jews, nor to the Gentiles, nor to the church of God."

Paul is here presenting negatively what he presented positively in verse 31. If the believer glorifies God in all that he does, he will not cause another to stumble. Three distinct classes are pointed out here: (1) the Jews, (2) the

Greeks, (3) the Church of God.

Jews and Gentiles are *two classes* of people, but the Church is made up of both Jews AND Gentiles who have been born of the Spirit and washed in the blood—those who have been saved through the Gospel and who form the local assembly.

(No person can rightly divide and understand the Word of God until he understands that God deals with Jews, with Gentiles, and with the Church. It is spiritual robbery to take the promises God made to the Church and give them to the Jews. It is equally wrong to take the promises God made to the Jews and apply those promises to the Church. God has an eternal blueprint, and He will conduct His affairs according to His plans.)

"The church of God" here points to the local assembly in Corinth. It is a term used many times in Paul's writings. In this instance it does not refer to the invisible Church, the body of Christ, made up of all believers the world over.

Verse 33: "Even as I please all men in all things, not seeking mine own profit, but the profit of many, that they may be saved."

The truth set forth in this verse does not mean that Paul was a compromiser, nor that he sought to be popular and get his name in *"Who's Who"* of Corinth—not at all; the last part of the verse makes this very clear. First of all, Paul sought not his own gain or profit. He was not self-willed. He sought, rather, the spiritual profit of all with whom he came in contact, and certainly that would not make him popular. Note Acts 17:32,33.

The second motive uppermost in Paul's mind was the salvation of unbelievers. He lived with the desire in his heart to point unbelievers to the Lord Jesus Christ whom he had met on the road to Damascus. He cried out that he was willing to be accursed from Christ if it would save his brethren (Rom. 9:1–3). And in Romans 10:1 he proclaimed, "Brethren, my heart's desire and prayer to God for Israel is, that they might be saved." His prayer and his desire was for the salvation of sinners.

The Greek word translated "please" means *to be beneficial or useful*; or we could say "profit." Paul wanted to live every moment of every day to the profit of others.

Paul was not satisfied with "a few." His scope was "the many." He wanted to reach the greatest possible number of sinners. He did not believe or preach the doctrine that *some* must be *lost*. Paul believed that "whosoever shall call upon the name of the Lord shall be saved." He believed that no man can call upon God until he hears the Gospel, that no man can hear without a preacher, and that the preacher must be *sent*.

Paul knew that HE was sent by God to preach the Gospel of grace, and on every occasion he had but a singular subject — the cross, the burial, the resurrection, the blood. He longed for MANY to be won for Christ — as many as possible was his desire day by day.

What is MY desire concerning my fellow believers? What is my desire concerning *unbelievers*? Am I content to grow in grace, feed upon the bread, become strong in the Lord—and yet not share my blessings with my fellow Christians? Am I a selfish Christian? Can I rub shoulders with unbelievers and yet allow them to go on in their sins, die without Christ and be tormented in the lake of fire forever? Do I allow them to slip through my opportunities to warn and witness to them? God help me to have, in a measure at least, the spirit, the desire, and the determination of the Apostle Paul.

CHAPTER ELEVEN

1. Be ye followers of me, even as I also am of Christ.

2. Now I praise you, brethren, that ye remember me in all things, and keep the ordinances, as I delivered them to you.

3. But I would have you know, that the head of every man is Christ; and the head of the woman is the man; and the head of Christ is God.

4. Every man praying or prophesying, having his head covered, dishonoureth his head.

5. But every woman that prayeth or prophesieth with her head uncovered dishonoureth her head: for that is even all one as if she were shaven.

6. For if the woman be not covered, let her also be shorn: but if it be a shame for a woman to be shorn or shaven, let her be covered.

7. For a man indeed ought not to cover his head, forasmuch as he is the image and glory of God: but the woman is the glory of the man.

8. For the man is not of the woman; but the woman of the man.

9. Neither was the man created for the woman; but the woman for the man.

10. For this cause ought the woman to have power on her head because of the angels.

11. Nevertheless neither is the man without the woman, neither the woman without the man, in the Lord.

12. For as the woman is of the man, even so is the man also by the woman; but all things of God.

13. Judge in yourselves: is it comely that a woman pray unto God uncovered?

14. Doth not even nature itself teach you, that, if a man have long hair, it is a shame unto him?

15. But if a woman have long hair, it is a glory to her: for her hair is given her for a covering.

16. But if any man seem to be contentious, we have no such custom, neither the churches of God.

17. Now in this that I declare unto you I praise you not, that ye come together not for the better, but for the worse.

18. For first of all, when ye come together in the church, I hear that there be divisions among you; and I partly believe it.

19. For there must be also heresies among you, that they which are approved may be made manifest among you.

20. When ye come together therefore into one place, this is not to eat the Lord's supper.

21. For in eating every one taketh before other his own supper: and one is hungry, and another is drunken.

22. What? have ye not houses to eat and to drink in? or despise ye the church of God, and shame them that have not? What shall I say to you? shall I praise you in this? I praise you not.

23. For I have received of the Lord that which also I delivered unto you, That the Lord Jesus the same night in which he was betrayed took bread:

24. And when he had given thanks, he brake it, and said, Take, eat: this is my body, which is broken for you: this do in remembrance of me.

25. After the same manner also he took the cup, when he had supped, saying, This cup is the new testament in my blood: this do ye, as oft as ye drink it, in remembrance of me.

26. For as often as ye eat this bread, and drink this cup, ye do shew the Lord's death till he come.

27. Wherefore whosoever shall eat this bread, and drink this cup of the Lord, unworthily, shall be guilty of the body and blood of the Lord.

28. But let a man examine himself, and so let him eat of that bread, and drink of that cup.

29. For he that eateth and drinketh unworthily, eateth and drinketh damnation to himself, not discerning the Lord's body.

30. For this cause many are weak and sickly among you, and many sleep.

31. For if we would judge ourselves, we should not be judged.

32. But when we are judged, we are chastened of the Lord, that we should not be condemned with the world.

33. Wherefore, my brethren, when ye come together to eat, tarry one for another.

34. And if any man hunger, let him eat at home; that ye come not together unto condemnation. And the rest will I set in order when I come.

Chapters 11 through 14 speak of the life and testimony of the local church itself, and in *this* chapter Paul deals with the position of men and women IN the assembly and what makes for the recognition of the honor of Christ. He leaves off speaking of things in general and deals with the gathering of the saints to partake of the Lord's Supper. In the following chapters he deals with other details regarding meetings of the church.

Christian Order and the Lord's Supper

Verse 1: "Be ye followers of me, even as I also am of Christ."

Most Bible authorities agree that this should be the closing verse of chapter 10, in which Paul uses himself as an example and exhorts his children in the faith to follow him as he walked—not in the spirit of selfishness or conceit—but in the Spirit of Christ. I doubt that any person ever lived on the face of this earth who walked quite as closely in the footsteps of Jesus as did the Apostle Paul; therefore he could invite his children in the faith to follow him as he followed his Lord.

Verse 2: "Now I praise you, brethren, that ye remember me in all things, and keep the ordinances, as I delivered them to you."

Here, as in the first chapters of the epistle, Paul gives commendation before he rebukes. He is about to reprove the believers because of their actions at the Lord's table, but *before* he rebukes them he again gives honor and praise wherein they deserve it. It is never right to flatter people, but it is good for a minister to give recognition wherein recognition is due.

In speaking of *"the ordinances,"* Paul refers to the apostolic teaching concerning the believer and the assembly. In II Thessalonians 2:15 the same word is used, speaking of Christian doctrine in general. (The same Greek word is sometimes translated *"tradition."*) Paul is speaking of instructions he gave to the churches in general—instructions given upon the authority God had placed upon him as an apostle to the Gentiles.

Verse 3: "But I would have you know, that the head of every man is Christ; and the head of the woman is the man; and the head of Christ is God."

". . . *The head of every man is Christ; and the head of the woman is the man.*" To the Colossians and the Ephesians Paul speaks of Christ as head of the Church. The headship of Christ as having to do with the Church means that He is the head of *the invisible Church*, the body; but here Paul is speaking of the headship of Christ as having to do with *each individual IN the Church.* Christ is the head of each believer, and each believer is under the *authority* of the Lord Jesus Christ. In Him we live and move and have our being. Christ is within us to direct us in the ways of righteousness. He is the head of *all* believers, but He is also the head of each *individual* believer.

Paul is also pointing out the distinction between man and woman by reason of the circumstances of their differing creation. The man is head of the woman, in the same way that Christ is head of the man. The woman as a believer is certainly under the authority of Christ; yet in relative position to the man as having to do with things of earth and the natural life, he is her head, for "the woman is the glory of the man" (verse 7).

This is true in the relationship of husband and wife: "Wives, submit yourselves unto your own husbands, as it is fit in the Lord" (Col. 3:18). "Let the woman learn in silence with all subjection. But I suffer not a woman to teach, nor to usurp authority over the man, but to be in silence" (I Tim. 2:11,12).

In his original state, Adam was under the direct headship of God, his Maker — but he lost that position through sin, and it can be renewed *only through faith,* on the grounds of the shed blood of the Lamb of God—the sacrifice of Jesus on the cross. In this statement Paul is making known the truth concerning the relationship between Christ and every true believer in the assembly. The believing *man* is placed in a position to act in the capacity as "the image and glory of God" (verse 7).

". . . *The head of Christ is God.*" GOD is head of all. Paul does not state this fact here just as a point of doctrine; he presents the pattern of authority and subjection exhibited in his divine relation as having a bearing on the practical realization of the preceding headships — that is, Christ the head of man, man the head of woman, *but GOD as head of all*—the highest order of supremacy. Jesus perfectly manifested His obedience to the Father in the days of His flesh (John 5:30). In John 8:29 He said, "*I do always those things that please HIM.*"

This does not mean that Christ is distinct from God the Father insofar as deity is concerned. Jesus said, "I and my Father are one," and the fact that God is the head of Christ does not make Christ the lesser of the two. God the Father "so loved," He gave the Son—the WORD—and the Son declared God the Father on earth in a way that man could hear the Word, receive the Word, and be saved.

Verse 4: "Every man praying or prophesying, having his head covered, dishonoureth his head."

The Spirit of God uses the natural (physical) head of man as the symbol of both headship and authority. Christ is the "head" of the man; therefore man is under the *authority* of Christ. Man is head of the woman; therefore woman, as the weaker vessel, is to be in subjection to her own husband. Christ is the authority, the final word as having to do with the Church, and a man who prays or prophesies with his head covered "dishonoureth his head." This injunction was neither Jewish nor Greek, for in Paul's day, Jewish men always covered their heads in the synagogue, and the Greeks, both men and women, were uncovered.

Verse 5: "But every woman that prayeth or prophesieth with her head uncovered dishonoureth her head: for that is even all one as if she were shaven."

A clear fact is pointed out here if we are willing to face the Word of God without prejudice, without preconceived ideas: *Paul is not speaking of the assembly here.* In I Corinthians 14:34 he definitely commands the women to be silent in the church. Now would he say that every woman *praying or prophesying* with her head uncovered dishonored her head, and in the very same letter clearly command the women to *keep silent* in the church?

The meaning of I Corinthians 14:34 is unmistakeable: "Let every woman *keep silent.*" Therefore, the statement in our present verse cannot refer to the gatherings of the assembly in the meetinghouse. There are many occasions other than the local assembly when a woman can pray, teach, instruct, exhort—or, if you choose to call it by that name—*preach*. There are many places where a dear woman can give her testimony, pray, teach, or exhort outside of the assembly where the *pastor* is God's undershepherd.

I have no books of Baptist doctrine to go by, no Methodist or Pentecostal books of instruction. I simply have the open Bible, which commands me to compare Scripture with Scripture — and that is what I am doing. In Acts 21:8,9 we read that Philip had four virgin daughters who prophesied. Many use this Scripture in an attempt to prove that there are female prophets in the Church today; but we must face the fact that even though in the Old Testament era there *were* women judges and prophetesses, there is no Scripture to teach that this practice has been brought over into the Church.

Philip's four daughters prophesied in the transition period, and there is no scriptural foundation for teaching dogmatically that they prophesied in the assembly or meetinghouse. Paul's teaching here certainly contradicts such a practice – and not only here, but in other epistles as well. The same is true in the case of Elizabeth as recorded in Luke 1:42–45 and of Anna in Luke 2:38.

If the woman prays or prophesies uncovered, it is *"even all one as if she were shaven."* A woman unveiled would signify that she did not acknowledge a visible human head–the man. Therefore she would shame herself, and she might as well be shorn or shaven. The only way to understand the meaning of this statement is to go to the Old Testament for examples. Study carefully Numbers 5:18, together with the verses that precede and follow.

Among the Greeks, women who were morally clean and upright wore the veil, and *only IMMORAL women,* those of ill repute, *went UNVEILED.* Therefore, every man who saw them knew what they were. The veil served two purposes: (1) It was a sign of inferiority. (2) It was a very great protection. Also, among the Greeks the slave women were shorn–their heads were shaved; and thus any woman seen with her head shaved was known to be a slave. Study Deuteronomy 21:10–17.

Verse 6: "For if the woman be not covered, let her also be shorn: but if it be a shame for a woman to be shorn or shaven, let her be covered."

The Greek word used here literally translated means *"if a woman persist in unveiling herself"*–a continuous act, implying that her not being veiled is her own stubborn, persistent act. The Greek verb translated "to be shorn" points to a single act, while the verb translated "be shaven" denotes a repeated act. So—if a woman insists on uncovering her head *continuously*, then let her have her hair cut short, or shaven — and no woman who possessed the slightest sense of shame would think of doing such a thing! Therefore Paul said, *"If it be a shame for a woman to be shorn or shaven, let her be covered."*

Verse 7: "For a man indeed ought not to cover his head, forasmuch as he is the image and glory of God: but the woman is the glory of the man."

In Genesis 1:26,27 we read that God created man in His own image. The Greek word translated "image" signifies *a visible representation*. God designed man to be His representative. Man was created to display the attributes of God—such attributes as goodness, wisdom, and power. God also created man in His image and likeness for the purpose of manifesting *the glory of God*, His greatness and His majesty. There may be a representation without glory — there may be a shining forth of glory without visible representation. Both are combined in man. Therefore, he whom God created to display His attributes, His glory, greatness, and majesty *is NOT to be covered!*

"But the woman is the glory of the man." Notice Paul does not say that the woman is the *image* of the man — but rather, her honor lies in the fact that she is the manifestation of man's greatness. She was taken out of man, and she adds to his dignity and completeness. Paul is here contrasting the woman and the man, showing that as man is her superior, she is the weaker vessel and cannot suitably represent God the Creator.

God HAS no superior. God is head of the man, and man is head of the woman.

Verse 8: "For the man is not of the woman; but the woman of the man."

The glory of the woman is the reflection of the glory of the man, and here we see a higher relationship of the Church to Christ.

In the twenty-fourth chapter of Genesis there is a beautiful spiritual picture in the account of Rebekah and Isaac. Rebekah asked the servant, "What man is this that walketh in the field to meet us?" And the servant replied, "It is my master." Then Rebekah took a veil and covered herself, and in so doing she not only indicated her prospective position in regard to Isaac, but also set forth the truth that her beauty was for him alone.

Likewise the Church, made up of all born again believers, does not put its glory on display for the gaze of the world. The object of the Church—yea, of *every member* of the Church—is to show forth the glory of God. All that we do should be done to God's glory, and to direct others to *Christ*—not to the beauty of the local assembly, nor to services and rituals. We are to direct others to Christ, the head and the beauty of the New Testament Church.

These verses were given to Paul by the Holy Ghost, penned down to show us the relationship of the Church TO Christ, and every word IN the verses illustrates that high and eternal relationship. When Jehovah God formed Eve from Adam's rib, He said, "I will make him an help meet for him" (Gen. 2:18). Hebrew scholars tell us that the Hebrew word translated *"for"* really means "answer to." Thus we read, "I will make him an help meet *answering to him.*" Woman became man's counterpart, man's compliment; and *in woman* man reaches the full manifestation of himself.

Verse 9: "Neither was the man created for the woman; but the woman for the man."

God created woman for man, not man for woman. (Of course, when God's Word declares that man is head of woman and that woman is to be in subjection and in total obedience to the man, it is understood that the man is to be God-fearing, a Christian and a gentleman.) No person—man OR woman—is to dishonor or disobey God in order to be in subjection to *any* creature. We owe our total devotion, respect, honor and worship to God; but a woman who has a Christian husband is to respect that man as her head. She is to be in subjection to him, answering to him in the Lord.

Verse 10: "For this cause ought the woman to have power on her head because of the angels."

The word here translated *"power"* should be rendered *authority.* The woman should have on her head *the sign of authority*—meaning all that has been declared regarding the relationship of the man to the woman, and of Christ to the Church.

". . . *Because of the angels.*" Angels are observers of the peoples of earth. They are witnesses. Through His Church here on earth the Lord God is making known "unto the principalities and powers in heavenly places . . . THE MANIFOLD WISDOM OF GOD" (Eph. 3:10). *The veiled woman* sets forth the authority of Christ. She has a twofold covering—a *temporary* covering (her veil) and the *permanent* covering mentioned in verse 15 of this chapter.

To those who are not spiritual and who do not understand the deep truths of spiritual things, the woman and her covering may seem small and unimportant. It is true that whether a woman has long hair or short hair has nothing to do with her redemption; but what Paul is setting forth here comprehends truths of the very highest order.

We know that in Paul's day, a woman's veil denoted dignity, and if she discarded the veil she thereby placed herself in a position for open insult by any and all. But Paul's teaching here goes much deeper than the natural. It has to do with the spiritual.

Verse 11: "Nevertheless, neither is the man without the woman, neither the woman without the man, in the Lord."

The Holy Spirit speaks here through the pen of Paul to balance the truth that has preceded, to prevent man's making a wrong application or putting the wrong value on what is attributed to woman in the divine relationship as though woman were inferior to man. Such is not the case, and should not be suggested. Man has no Bible grounds for looking down on woman. This verse makes it very clear that both sexes—male and female—are necessary to each other "IN THE LORD." Where Jesus is in authority, as in the local assembly, both man and woman are dependent upon Him, one just as much as the other, regardless of the sexes: "There is neither Jew nor Greek, there is neither bond nor free, there is neither male nor female: for ye are all one in Christ Jesus" (Gal. 3:28).

Verse 12: "For as the woman is of the man, even so is the man also by the woman; but all things of God."

Paul here confirms what he said in the preceding verse. The first woman was made from man (Gen. 2:21–23), and therefore she is not independent of man; yet in the continuous program of God, man owes his being to woman, and therefore is not independent of her. Man is the *initial* cause of woman's being here — but woman is the *instrumental* cause of *man's* being here.

The first Greek proposition ("of") in verse 12 is *ek*, denoting a single creative act; but the second preposition (by) is *dia*, meaning a constant process. God created man from the dust of the earth, breathed into his nostrils the breath of life, and man became a living soul. Later, God removed a rib from Adam and created woman. She was taken out of man in her original beginning, but now, man originates from woman. And IN THE LORD both man and woman are totally dependent upon HIM.

". . . *But all things of God.*" All things were made by Him; He is the author of all life. All things are by God's counsel, His ordinance, His act. God is sovereign; He knows the end in the beginning and everything that lies *between* the beginning and the end. "All things are of God" is a great, divine truth which fills the entire sixty-six books of our Bible. The statement is repeated by Paul in II Corinthians 5:18.

In the old creation as well as in the new, everything is in *essential harmony* with the nature of God. No man can be happy or have true contentment until he is in the right relationship with God. Regardless of how much wealth, fame, or good fortune man may accumulate, he can never know happiness and true peace until he comes into his proper relationship with his Creator — and the only way for man to BE in the right relationship with God is to believe on God's Son and exercise faith in His shed blood.

Verse 13: "Judge in yourselves: is it comely that a woman pray unto God uncovered?"

Here Paul passes from the subject of divine authority and headship shown by the covering, to the natural instinct and common sense of his readers. In other words, he asks, "Since it is true that the Greek women who are immoral go unveiled—and the fact that they ARE unveiled denotes immorality—and since only slave women are shaven or shorn, would you even consider the thought that a believing woman in the assembly should be uncovered or shorn?"

Verses 14 and 15: "Doth not even nature itself teach

you, that, if a man have long hair, it is a shame unto him? But if a woman have long hair, it is a glory to her: for her hair is given her for a covering.''

Man—created in the image of God, created to display the attributes and glory of God—should not wear long hair. It is a dishonor to him and to God. Even nature teaches him that to have long hair makes him appear feminine and destroys his higher distinction and authority over women. But woman's hair is given to her by nature—a natural covering. A hat or veil is a temporary covering, but her hair is a permanent covering and has the same significance as that of the temporary covering—the veil.

Woman's hair, in the words of Paul, should be kept long. Why? Because *"it is her glory."* It is her glory in that it sets forth the subjection of the Church to Christ. For a woman to shave her head or cut her hair close to her scalp is to rob herself of her natural glory, given to her by nature; and by so doing she denies and sets at nought the dignity of her womanhood, thereby removing the highest possible spiritual significance. Woman's hair is her glory, and *the Church is the glory of Christ on earth.* The Church is in subjection to Christ, and woman's hair denotes *her* subjection to her husband, her head.

All men were without Christ, without hope, and without salvation; dead in sins, walking according to the course of this world, following the lusts of the flesh, fulfilling the desires of the flesh and of the mind. All men were by nature the children of the devil —*"BUT GOD,* who is rich in mercy, for His great love wherewith He loved us, even when we were dead in sins, hath quickened us together with Christ, (by grace ye are saved)'' (Eph. 2:4,5).

Ephesians 4:32 clearly teaches that God saves us for Christ's sake. God saves individuals, and those individuals make up the Church of which Jesus is the head and the foundation. God is calling out the Church— each member saved by His grace, each saved one raised and made to sit in heavenly places in Christ Jesus, FOR THE SINGULAR PURPOSE "that in the ages to come He might shew the exceeding riches of His grace in His kindness toward us through Christ Jesus" (Eph. 2:7).

The Church of Jesus Christ will be displayed in the heavenlies throughout the ceaseless ages of the eternity that lies ahead. All of God's new creation will witness the exceeding riches of His grace; all the new creation will walk in the light of the Pearly White City, the home of the Church (the bride of Christ). *In the woman*, God sets forth the relationship between Christ and the Church. Christ is head of the Church, and we must be in subjection to Him. We are members of His body, bone of His bone and flesh of His flesh. He is the Chief Cornerstone; we are little stones built together into a holy temple.

Woman was taken out of man. God created her to answer to man, and gave her to him to be his helpmate. Nature has given woman a distinction—a natural covering which denotes her subjection to authority, subjection to man—her head, her husband. And IN the woman God sets forth the picture of Christ and the Church, and the relationship between them. It was clearly not the purpose of the Creator that woman should in public adopt the same attitude and boldness of man.

Verse 16: "But if any man seem to be contentious, we have no such custom, neither the churches of God."

The Holy Spirit, through the pen of Paul, makes it crystal clear that what has been set forth in the previous verses, with its tremendous spiritual import, was not a matter to be debated, it was not an issue to cause contention in the church. The "custom" referred to points to the irregularity mentioned in verses 4 and 5. The believers were not to argue about the hair of the man or the woman. There were those in the assembly at Corinth (just as there are people in the assemblies today) who were ready to start an argument or stand up for their liberty, regardless of who it hurt or what dissension it caused. But Paul strictly forbids such behavior in the assembly. The statement is clear: *"WE HAVE NO SUCH CUSTOM, neither the churches of God."*

The devil is shrewd. He is alert and always on the job. His paramount aim and desire is to damn as many souls as possible. Therefore, when an unbeliever trusts the Lord and is saved, thereby becoming a son of God, the devil then begins another program against him. *He immediately seeks to destroy the testimony of that individual,* and if he cannot *destroy* the testimony he attempts to cripple the believer to such degree as to render his testimony ineffective.

If Satan does not succeed in one way, he will try another. Such was the case in the assembly at Corinth— as in many assemblies today. The believers were divided into little groups. They were following men, following teachers who claimed to be wise. They were arguing about baptism, and there was much discussion about the hair and how it should be worn by both men and women.

To sum up the teaching, let me point out what Paul has said and what we have studied up to this point:

The head of every man is Christ; the head of every woman is the man; the head of Christ is God — and therefore, *God is the highest authority.* God is the head of Christ; Christ the head of man; man the head of woman.

Since man is the highest creation of God, he is not to pray or preach with his head covered; but since woman is *in subjection to man,* she is to show submission to him by always keeping her head covered. The Scripture is very clear: When a woman prays or prophesies with her head uncovered she "dishonoureth her head"; and if she is not going to *cover* her head, then let her head be shaven or shorn.

Man ought not to cover his head, because he is the image and glory of God; but the woman is the glory of the man, and therefore she should be covered with her natural covering—her hair—to denote subjection to the man.

Paul points out that man did not originate through woman, but woman through man. God created man, then removed a rib from him and created woman; and because of this she should give due honor to man—and also because the angels are witnesses, observing the peoples of earth at all times. Yet the man is not without the woman, the woman is not without the man *in the Lord*. The woman is of the man, the man also *by* the woman, "BUT ALL THINGS OF GOD."

Since this is true, Paul asks, "Is it according to reason that a woman pray unto God uncovered? Nature itself teaches that if a man have long hair it is a shame to him; but if a *woman* have long hair it is a glory to her, for her hair is given to her for a covering."

There are some who seemingly cannot read this Scripture correctly, putting emphasis where emphasis is due. A woman does not glorify GOD with her long hair — *long hair is a glory to HER*. I do not believe that any woman should cut her hair after the fashion of a man. (To be "shorn" is to have one's hair cut short against the head; to be "shaven" is to use a razor and cut the hair against the scalp.) It is very unbecoming to any woman to cut her hair in fashion as a man cuts his hair, and it is disgusting for a man to wear long hair (although many men in this day do wear their hair much longer than man's custom should be).

Although I have searched, and searched again, I do not find in the Scripture one word, suggestion, or intimation that a woman should not use scissors on her hair in any way. The Word of God simply says that she should not have *short* hair or be shorn. Just what the definition of long hair is, I am frankly at a loss to say. Some ladies have hair that is extremely long, while others wear their hair much shorter. Would it be necessary for a woman to have hair a certain number of inches long in order to be the kind of woman God would have her be? Who would set the rules for the length woman's hair should be worn, since we do not have a verse of Scripture that declares, "O woman, thou shalt have thine hair twelve inches, twenty-four, thirty-four, or forty-four inches long"?

I am not attempting to dodge an issue, nor am I trying to defend anyone. I am simply declaring that the contention, division, animosity, and hard feelings that have come about through discussion of long and short hair in the Church have not brought one iota of glory to God—and never will! Such dissension has brought reproach upon the Church, upon Christ, and upon believers.

It seems to me that if a dear Christian woman lives a clean life, gives a good testimony, walks uprightly and wears clothes that cover the shame of her nakedness, if she has every fruit of righteousness and holiness, then regardless of whether her hair be shoulder length or hang to her waist, spiritually minded believers should understand that God looks upon the heart. It is not the hair — it is the *heart*. It is not the length of the hair — it is *Christ* in YOU. It is not whether the hair hangs over the shoulder, or is balled up on the back of the head, so long as it is not shorn, clipped, or shaven to make her look like a man instead of a woman. "And if any man seem to be contentious, we have no such custom, neither the churches of God.''

Woman's hair is a glory to her. Dear lady, if you know Jesus has saved you and you are a child of God, pray about your dress, the way you fix your face, the way you wear your hair. Seek God's will and follow the leadership of the Holy Spirit. Be as neat and as attractive for Jesus as you possibly can. Walk with Him, live for Him — *and stop your ears to any and all comments by man.* Remember — God looks on the heart, and you will give an account to GOD, not to man.

The Church of the living God is *not* made up of customs, traditions, and man-made rules and regulations:

"Ye shall know the truth, and the truth shall make you free" (John 8:32).

"If the Son therefore shall make you free, ye shall be free indeed" (John 8:36).

Disorderly Conduct at the Lord's Table Rebuked

Thus far in this chapter Paul has dealt with irregularities attributed to ignorance. The Corinthian believers needed more light on the previous subjects discussed. But word had come to Paul that there were divisions among them in connection with the Lord's Supper. Some of them were committing gross sin in their manner of observing this ordinance, and this sin must be dealt with immediately. No longer could Paul say, "I would have you know," or "I would not have you to be ignorant."

Verse 17: "Now in this that I declare unto you I praise you not, that ye come together not for the better, but for the worse.''

(In the original Greek this verse reads, "But in giving you this charge, I praise you not that ye come together not for better, but for worse.'') At the beginning of this chapter Paul was in a position to praise them (note verse 2); but he cannot continue his praise in the matter with which he is now dealing. It is too serious and grave.

". . . *That ye come together not for the better, but for the worse.*" The Greek word translated "better" means "advantageous," and the Greek word translated "worse" means "deterioration." Paul is here pointing out the spiritual effect of their meeting for the Lord's Supper. As previously mentioned, it is the program and purpose of Satan and his host of demons to rob the Lord Jesus of His due praise, honor, glory—and at the same time hinder the believers in spiritual growth and stewardship; and he was having great success in the assembly in Corinth. It is the purpose of the *Holy Spirit* to glorify the Lord Jesus Christ through the believer in each meeting of the assembly; but such was not the case at the time Paul wrote this letter.

Verse 18: "For first of all, when ye come together in the church, I hear that there be divisions among you; and I partly believe it."

"*First of all . . .*" denotes that this is uppermost in the mind of Paul, weighing heavily upon his heart.

"*When ye come together in the church*" does not necessarily mean that they had a building for meeting purposes, but rather refers to the *assembling together* of believers.

"*I hear that there be divisions among you.*" This differs from chapter 1 verse 10 where Paul refers to a party spirit—groups forming and following various leaders such as Paul, Apollos, Cephas, and others. In our present verse the meaning is *dissension*. The believers were divided; they were not right in their hearts toward one another.

". . . *I partly believe it.*" Paul had hopes that, even

though the reports that had come to him were true, there might have been some degree of exaggeration in them. Perhaps the situation was not quite as serious as had been reported and certainly it would carry weight with the spiritually minded believers in Corinth for Paul to assure them that he was giving the church the benefit of the doubt. He had hopes that the reports had been exaggerated, and that when he arrived in Corinth he would find conditions not so ugly and serious as the letter reported.

We should follow Paul's example here. Seemingly, Christians like to believe the worst. They are not willing to allow a little ground for exaggeration. If we hear an evil report about a fellow believer or minister, we are always prone to believe the worst or even worse than reported; but not so with Paul. And in writing to the Corinthian Christians he assured them that he was giving them the benefit of the doubt and hoped in his heart that when he should arrive he would find things better than reported.

Verse 19: "For there must be also heresies among you, that they which are approved may be made manifest among you."

". . . *There must be heresies among you . . . .*" The meaning here is that because of the sin that existed in the lives of some believers in the assembly, there must undoubtedly be *heresies* (divisions or schisms) among them. Divisions in the church always produce factions—little groups cloaking together under the leadership of some individual — and such *should not be* in the Church of the living God. (The word translated "heresies" does not necessarily mean false doctrine, but *sects*, as in Acts 5:17 and 15:5.)

". . . *That they which are approved may be made manifest among you.*" This denotes that God is not the author of confusion. God is not the author of party spirit nor of divisions in the assembly; but rather, He overrules this evil through individual believers who resist such divisions and refuse to take sides. These believers are therefore recognized by God and have His approval. The Christian who is big enough, strong enough, and spiritual enough to stand with Jesus for truth in the midst of divisions, refusing to take sides, is of untold value to God and will be used of Him in the interest of unity in the assembly.

Verse 20: "When ye come together therefore into one place, this is not to eat the Lord's supper."

The meaning here is that when the believers assembled together for the purpose of observing the Lord's Supper, with things as they were in the assembly—with divisions that existed among them, and the spirit of some of the believers—it would be an utter *impossibility* to observe the Lord's Supper in its true meaning. They did assemble, and they did eat a supper — but it was not the LORD'S, for their actions denied the facts relating to the real meaning of the Lord's Supper and prevented the Lord's putting His stamp of approval upon it. As we study the following verses we will see that certainly the Lord could take no part in some of the things that were going on at what was claimed to be "the Lord's table."

Verse 21: "For in eating every one taketh before other his own supper: and one is hungry, and another is drunken."

The statement *"in eating"* points out that actually the occasion was only a simple meal which each of the believers could have eaten *anywhere.* They were probably mixing up the "love-feast" (Agape) with the Lord's Supper. The love-feast was a meal of which the early Christians partook in common. Each participant brought his own share of food, and all contributions were pooled to make a common feast. Thus the poor who could bring but little, shared in the plenty of those who had in abundance. The Corinthians, however, had lost this Christian fellowship and had resorted to class distinction. The poor brought of their scant store and went away hungry, while the wealthy brought abundantly of their rich foods (including wines) and became intoxicated as well as making gluttons of themselves. It seems that they did not put their food together, there was no sharing; but rather, each ate what he brought. So in reality it was not a meal in common — they did not share and share alike. Thus the Christian principle was destroyed at the very meal that should have displayed it in practice. To call such a meal "the Lord's Supper" was unscriptural and did grievous abuse to that observance.

Verse 22: "What? Have ye not houses to eat and to drink in? Or despise ye the church of God, and shame them that have not? What shall I say to you? Shall I praise you in this? I praise you not."

What Paul is saying here is, "If you are assembling together to satisfy your own hunger, then you should eat and drink at home, not in God's house. The Lord's Supper was not instituted to satisfy physical hunger and thirst, but for an altogether different reason with a deep, spiritual significance."

"Despise ye the church of God?" Paul is not referring here to the invisible Church, the body of Christ. He is referring to the local assembly. Whether the believers met in a home or in some type of public building, the phrase "Despise ye the church of God" signifies the *holy character* of the church of God—meaning the local assembly. The house of God (the "meeting-place," as the old-timers called it) is a sacred, sanctified place. We do not worship the building, we do not worship the pews, the pulpit, or other furnishings; but as the house of God where

we meet together in one body to *worship* God, it should not be treated as an ordinary meeting place.

The Lord's Supper was instituted for a twofold purpose:

It shows forth the Lord's death on the cross (I Cor. 11:26).

It points to the return of Jesus for the Church — "Until He come" (I Cor. 11:26b).

Anyone who partakes of the Lord's Supper for any other reason would be far, far better off if he did not partake at all!

"*. . . And shame them that have not*" — or *put to shame utterly.* Paul pressed upon the hearts and minds of his converts the divine truth that *all believers are one in Christ.* In the Church of the living God there are no uppers and lowers, no slaves and slavemasters. We are all ONE, united into one body through the baptism of the Holy Spirit, and therefore it was a disgrace for the assembly in Corinth to observe suppers such as they were observing, with the rich becoming drunken and making gluttons of themselves while the poor left the supper hungry. Such conduct was a shame and disgrace in the sight of God.

"*What shall I say to you? Shall I praise you in this? I praise you not!*" It would have been the joy of Paul's heart to praise them as he did in chapter 1, verses 4 through 7, and again in verse 2 of this chapter. But such actions as he had just ennumerated were not praiseworthy. It was impossible for him to praise them, and he repeated what he had already said in verse 17: "*I praise you not!*"

Is It Wrong to Eat in the Church Sanctuary?

Believers do not agree on the answer to this question. Are church suppers in the house of God *scriptural*? Is it right to sell food to finance the work of the Lord? Any person who will study the Word of God with an open mind, forgetting any preconceived ideas or man-made church doctrine must face the fact that Paul rebuked the believers in Corinth for bringing food into the assembly and eating and drinking in such manner as they were doing in Corinth.

It is not sinful for Christians to have fellowship around the table. Home comings and fellowship suppers are not sinful; *but they should not be held in the sanctuary.* Some may ask, "Is that not straining a point?" I reply in the words of the Apostle Paul: *"Despise ye the church of God*?" Paul must have been referring to the house of God where the assembly met—a sanctified place, dedicated to *the worship of God,* not to the satisfying of the stomach.

It is perfectly scriptural for believers to fellowship around the table, but not in the sanctuary. When a church has a cafeteria or social hall in connection with the sanctuary there is grave danger that the table laden with *food* will be used more than the *table of the Lord* where things of the *Spirit* are served. The devil is shrewd; he does not miss a trick, and if he cannot lead believers away from spiritual living and "first things first" in one way, he will try another. The house of God is a *spiritual* cafeteria, not a place to serve fried chicken, ice cream, and cake! We will learn later in this chapter that some of the believers paid dearly for their misbehavior in the house of God around the Lord's table.

The Meaning of the Lord's Table

Verses 23 and 24: "For I have received of the Lord that which also I delivered unto you, That the Lord Jesus the same night in which He was betrayed took bread: And when He had given thanks, He brake it, and said, Take, eat: This is my body which is broken for you: This do in remembrance of me."

Paul received the Gospel he preached directly from

Christ Himself: *"But I certify you, brethren, that the Gospel which was preached of me is not after man. For I neither received it of man, neither was I taught it, but by the revelation of Jesus Christ"* (Gal. 1:11,12).

What Paul is about to declare concerning the order and meaning of the Lord's table, he received *directly* from the Lord Jesus. All of the other apostles were present when the Lord *instituted* the supper on the night of the Passover; but *they* had not passed the information on to Paul, because he did not confer with flesh and blood when God called and commissioned him as minister to the Church.

Paul received his instructions concerning the Lord's table *directly from the Lord Jesus,* and he sets forth here the divine truth that the risen, glorified Lord confirmed anew the institution of the Lord's Supper, along with confirmation of the fact that we should observe this ordinance during the entire time until He returns for the Church. Paul was not giving the Corinthians new doctrine or new facts; he had *already* given them the details when he was with them in person, but what he had said orally had not been received and obeyed. To tell them by word of mouth should have been sufficient, but evidently it was not; so now Paul repeats his instructions by letter—and thus has the verbally inspired, written Word been bestowed in perpetuity, even unto our present hour!

In the Word we find guidance for believers—"the faith once delivered to the saints" (Jude 3). We need not depend upon human instruction, for we have the "perfect law of liberty." *"That which is perfect"* is come, and all we need to know about God and the devil, Jesus and salvation, heaven and hell—or any other question concerning our spiritual welfare and eternal destiny is contained in the Word of God—and ONLY in the Word of God.

". . . That the Lord Jesus . . . ." The name JESUS

signifies "Saviour," and He is the LORD of all believers. After one is saved he should confess Jesus as Lord, and the Lord's table with the broken bread and the cup points to His broken body and shed blood. (Without shedding of blood is no remission for sin.) Therefore, the name "Jesus" is added to "Lord."

"*. . . The same night in which He was betrayed. . . .*" The Greek reads, "The night He was *BEING betrayed*," signifying that while the previously arranged negotiations between Judas and the chief priests were actually going on, Jesus was at the same time instituting the Lord's Supper. The betrayal negotiations were in progress while He was breaking the bread and offering the cup!

Shortly thereafter, He was betrayed by Judas, who had left the upper room before the Lord instituted the feast. We must remember that the Lord Jesus was omniscient: "Jesus therefore, *knowing all the things that were coming upon Him*, went forth." The detail is pointed out here, not simply as an historical fact, but to declare once again the deity of Christ and to set forth the solemnity of the circumstances in the upper room, in contrast with the loose carelessness of the supper that was being observed in the church at Corinth.

In that night when Jesus was betrayed, "*He took bread . . . .*" (He took a loaf, one of the cakes of bread which had been brought in specifically for the Passover supper.) "*. . . And when He had given thanks . . . .*" In Luke 22:19, the Greek verb *eucharisteo* is used. In the Gospels of Matthew and Mark, the verb *eulogeo* is used, having to do with Christ's giving thanks for the bread, and *eucharisteo* is used in referring to the cup (Matt. 26:27; Mark 14:23). Here is what I want us to see: *Eulogeo* in the Greek translated literally means "to speak well," and in general signifies *to praise*, to acknowledge the goodness of God. This is the meaning in these passages. Please study the references given from Matthew, Mark, and Luke.

The two verbs have much in common and have much the same significance. *Eucharisteo* emphasizes thanksgiving; *eulogeo* emphasizes praise. Therefore the Lord Jesus did not impart a special or divine blessing to the bread and the fruit of the vine. He *gave thanks* for the bread, He gave thanks for the *cup*; but *He did not bless these elements in that they actually became His flesh and blood.* Such doctrine is heresy and is completely foreign to the Word of God.

"*. . . He brake it, and said, Take, eat: this is my body, which is broken for you.*" The pure Greek here reads, "which is *given* for you," just as it reads in Luke 22:19. The word "broken" was probably inserted to go along with the breaking of the bread. It is true that the body of Jesus was marred with spikes and a spear, but in reality He GAVE His body—and Scripture says, "not a bone of Him was broken." IN His body He conquered the world, the flesh, and the devil, and then was nailed to the cross for the remission of sin.

Those who will be reasonable in their thinking cannot accept the teaching of transubstantiation. Christ's human body *was present at the table* and therefore the *bread* offered at the first supper could NOT have been His actual body, nor could the fruit of the vine have been His actual blood. Transubstantiation is a man-made dogma and is definitely unscriptural. When Jesus instituted the Lord's Supper His body had not been given nor had His blood yet been shed.

Jesus was made a little lower than the angels for the suffering of death, in order that He might taste death for every man (Heb. 2:9). The incarnation was in order that

He, through His atoning sacrifice, might yield His body up to death. The bread is a symbol, a token, of His body, given on the cross. Had He NOT surrendered His body to be nailed to the cross and *had He NOT died on the cross*, there could be no spiritual nourishment for us in, by, or through His Person, which the bread at the Lord's Supper symbolizes. (In connection with this, please study John 6:33–51, in which the Lord's Supper is not the subject at all.)

"This do . . ." simply means "Give thanks and break bread, each one for himself." (Note I Corinthians 10:16, *"The bread which we break,"* signifying that each believer broke his own portion.) Any born again believer has a right to go to the Lord's table, give thanks, and break a portion from the loaf. The breaking of the bread, the taking of the cup, are acts for each individual believer to perform: "Let a man examine himself, and so let him eat." (When the Bible refers to *man* in this sense, it is referring to male and female—*mankind.*)

". . . In remembrance of me" —not "in *memory* of me." We are to eat the bread and partake of the cup in remembrance of Jesus. The Greek word used for "remembrance" is *anamnesis*, meaning "bringing to mind." Here it means bringing to mind the Person of the Lord Jesus Christ who came into the world, took a body, and in that body took our place, conquered the world, the flesh and the devil, fulfilled the law every jot and every tittle, and then offered His body on the cross that *through* His shed blood we might enter boldly into the holy of holies by a new and living way—"the veil, that is, *His flesh.*" We should always remember that we are saved, kept, and our needs supplied only because Jesus took our place, paid the sin-debt and purchased eternal life for us!

Verse 25: "After the same manner also He took the

cup, when He had supped, saying, This cup is the new testament in my blood: this do ye, as oft as ye drink it, in remembrance of me."

"After the same manner" simply means that as with the bread, He took the cup which was on the table with the bread, the cup containing the fruit of the vine, and when He had supped, He said, *"This cup is the new testament in my blood."* The cup (i.e. its contents) represents the new covenant, the covenant ratified and sealed by the blood of Jesus, by the giving of His life in atoning sacrifice. The life of the flesh is in the blood, and when the blood of Jesus was shed, *He gave His life.*

The cup *represents* the new covenant, true and sure in virtue of His shed blood; but the cup was not *identical* with the covenant. This is sure testimony to the divine fact that the fruit of the vine in the cup was not *actually* the blood of Jesus, just as the *bread* was not actually His *body.* The bread AND the fruit of the vine are a means of commemoration and communion.

The outstanding and momentous thing about the new covenant is the free bestowment of life eternal upon a hell-deserving sinner through the death of the Son of God's love; and that eternal life is granted by God the Father to the hell-deserving sinner in response to faith in the shed blood of God's only begotten Son. Through the death of Jesus Christ and His shed blood on the cross, God can still be just and yet justify the ungodly—but ONLY on the merit of the shed blood. Please study Romans 3:21—28. I urge each reader to analyze these verses carefully.

"This do ye . . ."—a definite command. Believers should observe the Lord's Supper, but *"as oft as ye drink it"* does not specifically give a time limit between observances. It is not specifically stated anywhere in the New Testament that we should observe the Lord's Supper

every Sunday, every two Sundays, once a month or once a quarter. It simply declares, *"As often* as you drink it, do so in remembrance of me."

In some churches the Lord's Supper is observed every Sunday. Some congregations observe it once a month, some quarterly; but actually there is no ironclad scriptural rule as to how often we should observe the Lord's Supper. We should *do* it, and *as often* as we do it it should be done *in remembrance of Jesus—and for no other reason.*

There is also no scriptural comment as to the *time of day* the Lord's Supper should be observed—whether at the morning worship service or in the evening. I feel that it should be at the most convenient time, when the greatest number of members of the assembly can attend. It seems to me, however, that if we observe the Lord's Supper every Sunday, there is danger of its becoming just another form or ritual, like so many other things in our worship — and yet, this is the most *sacred* of all the Church ordinances for it signifies the shed blood of Jesus, without which there could be no salvation. It also points to His return which, for the Church, is "the blessed hope," the comforting hope, the hope for which we are to look and pray. "Even so, come, Lord Jesus!" Thus John prayed after the last testimony in Revelation 22.

The Lord's Supper, each and every time we observe it, points to the coming of Jesus; but the sad truth is that there are thousands of church members who take the bread and the cup without realizing what they are doing. Some preachers who serve the Lord's Supper do not even *believe* in the second coming of Christ. What a tragedy!

Verse 26: "For as often as ye eat this bread, and drink this cup, ye do shew the Lord's death till He come."

The Greek word translated "shew" means *proclaim.* Thus the very act of receiving the bread and the cup

376

proclaims that Jesus is coming again. The same Greek word (translated "preach") is used in Acts 4:2; 13:5 and 38; 15:36; 17:3 and 13; I Corinthians 9:14 and Colossians 1:28. In all of these Scriptures, the meaning is "to proclaim."

The observance of the Lord's Supper will cease when the Remembered One returns for His own; until then, we should not cease to observe the Supper that sets forth the remembrance of Jesus, who was crucified for us.

Verse 27: "Wherefore whosoever shall eat this bread, and drink this cup of the Lord, unworthily, shall be guilty of the body and blood of the Lord."

"Wherefore" points back to the solemn, divine fact just stated—that partaking of the bread and the cup proclaims the Lord's death—the horrible, atoning death He died for us on the cross. Because of the tremendous importance of the crucifixion of Jesus it is grievous and extremely dangerous to partake unworthily of the bread and the cup which point to His death.

What does it mean to partake of the Lord's Supper unworthily? Of course, no *unbeliever* is worthy to partake of the Lord's Supper; but the warning here is to the spiritual state of the *believer.* To regard the cup and the bread as if they had no spiritual significance (without remembering the Lord's death *as set forth* in the Lord's Supper), is to partake unworthily. It means that a believer who receives the bread and the cup while in a state of cold carnality or while indulging in open sin, receives them unworthily. If one entertains bitterness of spirit against a fellow believer, fails to demonstrate brotherly love, or lives a life that is not spiritual and dedicated, and then observes the Lord's Supper in such a spiritual state, he takes the bread and the cup unworthily. And those who eat the bread and take the cup unworthily *"shall be guilty of the body and blood of the Lord."*

The Greek word here translated "guilty" is *enochos*, and means "liable to the penal effect of a deed." Thus, one who eats and drinks unworthily of the bread and the cup is committing an act which involves him in the guilt of the death of Jesus — and this is dangerous. All believers should be very careful in heart-searching examination when they partake of the bread and the fruit of the vine.

Verse 28: "But let a man examine himself, and so let him eat of that bread, and drink of that cup."

"Let a man examine (prove) himself" does not refer only to the men of the church, but to women as well. The strong word in this verse is *prove*. The believer is to put himself to the test. He is to search his own heart under the direction of the Holy Spirit. He is to be honest with himself and with God; and if there be any unconfessed sin in his life, he is to confess that sin: "If we confess our sins, He is faithful and just to forgive us our sins, and to cleanse us from all unrighteousness" (I John 1:9).

I John 1:4 tells us that the Epistle of John was written that our joy might be full. Full joy and abundant life are the spiritual birthright of every believer; but we cannot enjoy that birthright if there is anything between us and the Saviour. All unconfessed sins should be *confessed and forsaken* by the believer before partaking of the Lord's Supper.

It is significant that eating the bread and drinking the fruit of the vine in this warning are both mentioned three times (verses 27, 28, and 29). The fact that both are mentioned three times denotes the importance of the Lord's Supper for *each believer in the assembly*. It is gross error and man-made doctrine for a minister or priest to eat the bread and drink the cup, instead of allowing each member of the assembly to participate.

Verse 29: "For he that eateth and drinketh unworthily, eateth and drinketh damnation to himself, not discerning
the Lord's body."

In this verse, "*damnation*" does not mean damnation
as we think of the term, but rather, *judgment.* The Greek
word rendered "damnation" in our Bible means discipline,
or chastening, by the Lord. The same word is used in
verse 32 with reference to believers being judged and
chastened. The Holy Spirit is not saying here that if a
born again, blood-washed believer *does* eat the bread and
drink the cup unworthily he will be damned and burn in
hell for so doing. He will be judged, chastened, and dis-
ciplined, but not damned.

". . . *Not discerning the Lord's body.*" Paul is not
here referring to the local assembly in the use of the word
"body," nor is he referring to the Church, the body of
Christ; but to *the Lord's BODY*, the same body spoken of
in verses 24 and 27 in this chapter. For a believer to fail
in recognizing what the bread and the cup really represent
is to fail in the meaning of the Lord's Supper and to eat
unworthily. That is what Paul is warning against, and we
should hear this warning.

Paul knew that those who were making gluttons of
themselves and becoming intoxicated at the Lord's table
certainly could not worship in their hearts, remembering
the crucifixion of Jesus and thinking of the blessed hope
and the glorious appearing of our great God and Saviour,
Jesus Christ. Those who were acting thus were eating
and drinking unworthily and they would be judged, as some
had *already* been judged.

Verse 30: "For this cause many are weak and sickly
among you, and many sleep."

Paul does not mean here that some sleep (are dead)

spiritually, but *physically*. Because they had been misbehaving at the Lord's table, some were weak, some were
sick, and some had died physically and had been buried.
(The Greek word translated "sleep" is *koimaomai*, and is
never used in the New Testament to denote spiritual leth-
argy.)

The Greek word used in our present verse denotes
(in *four* places in the New Testament) *natural* sleep, and
in *fourteen* places it is used in speaking of the *death* of
the body — and always, without exception, it refers to the
death of a believer, never the death of a sinner.

Vine's *Expository Dictionary of New Testament Words*
gives this enlightening comment: "The early Christians
adopted the word *koimeterion* (which was used by the
Greeks as a rest-house for strangers) for the place of in-
terment of the bodies of their departed; thence the English
word *cemetery* ('the sleeping place') is derived."

There is no mistake that Paul is saying here, "Because of the way some of you Corinthian believers have
conducted yourselves around the Lord's table, some are
sick, and many are *dead*!" These who had died had committed the "sin unto death" (I John 5:16).

(It would be well to note here that *the sin unto death*
is committed by believers and has to do with *physical*,
not spiritual, death. The *unpardonable sin* is committed
by unbelievers, never by a born again person.) The "sin
unto death" is *unconfessed sin* in the life of a believer—
known sin that he refuses to confess and forsake. In
I John 5:16 the Scriptures clearly state that it is the sin
of a "brother"—meaning a *believer*. God will cut off the
believer who continues to practice known sin, and who,
knowing he should confess his sin, refuses to do so. Some
of the Corinthians were doing just this.

Verse 31: "For if we would judge ourselves, we

should not be judged."

As believers, we should test ourselves, search our hearts, look to the Lord and allow HIM to search our hearts. We should discriminate between what is right and what is wrong, and *follow righteousness*. We should always give ourselves a thorough examination before we partake of the Lord's Supper. If we would do this, we would not be judged of the Lord.

When believers practice self-judgment they avoid chastening of the Lord; but if we neglect self-judgment, then the Lord has no alternative: He must judge and chasten. But judgment and chastening as having to do with believers never means condemnation or damnation, as we will see in the next verse. Also study II Samuel 7:14,15; 12:13,14; I Corinthians 5:5; I Timothy 1:20; and Hebrews 12:7.

Verse 32: "But when we are judged, we are chastened of the Lord, that we should not be condemned with the world."

This verse is very clear: The purpose of the chastening of the Lord is *that we may not be condemned with the world.*

The Lord chastens in order that we may be "partakers of His holiness" (Heb. 12:10).

The Lord chastens us because He loves us: "Whom the Lord loveth He chasteneth, and scourgeth every son whom He receiveth" (Heb. 12:6).

In Revelation 3:19 we read, "As many as I love, I rebuke and chasten . . . ."

God is love; God is holy. Therefore, God chastens His children, and that chastening is for our profit. We gain in knowledge, in joy, in fellowship — and as we are chastened *we are conformed to Him.* Every blood-washed believer is predestined to be conformed to the image of God's dear Son (Rom. 8:29). Therefore, if we refuse to judge ourselves, search our hearts and clean up our lives as children of God, He has no choice but to chasten us in order that we not be condemned with the world.

Chastening produces "the peaceable fruit of righteousness." Study Hebrews 12—the entire chapter. Not all suffering, disease, heartache and disappointment is due to chastening. Some of God's dearest children, His most consecrated servants, suffer most. They glory in it, and God gets glory out of it. Some of God's saints learn, as did the Apostle Paul, in whatsoever state they find themselves *"therein to be content."*

A believer should not be frightened when God chastens. The Word of God teaches that the Lord chastens every son whom He receives, and anyone who is without chastening is not a child of God: "But if ye be without chastisement, whereof all are partakers, *then are ye bastards, and not sons"* (Heb. 12:8).

No born again, blood-washed believer will be condemned with the world to burn in the lake of fire. All of the chastening we receive as believers will come to us this side of death, for chastening is the sign of sonship.

Lot was a righteous man, so Peter tells us; but he moved into Sodom and began to love the world. He grew cold and indifferent toward the things of God — we would say he "backslid." But he was judged, chastened, and he lost everything he had in the world except two of his daughters (who later disgraced him). He saw Sodom go up in smoke, but God saved him OUT of it because he was God's child.

Verse 33: "Wherefore, my brethren, when ye come together to eat, tarry one for another."

382

Here is exhortation having to do with the importance of love and fellowship among the brethren—but in godly order. The conclusion of the whole subject is simply this: Let everyone—all believers—keep in mind that the Lord's Supper is not an ordinary meal for the purpose of satisfying the hunger of the body. It is a solemn commemoration of the Lord's death until He comes. Those who are hungry are to eat at home, else they invite chastening and judgment from the Lord. They must not be gluttonous and drunken around the Lord's table.

Verse 34: "And if any man hunger, let him eat at home; that ye come not together unto condemnation. And the rest will I set in order when I come."

Hungry folks should eat at home, not in the assembly. Thus Paul definitely and assuredly differentiates between the Lord's Supper and an ordinary meal. The word translated "condemnation" here is the same word translated "judgment" in verse 29. The believers who do not desire to invite judgment or chastening from the Lord should satisfy their hunger at home, not at the house of God at the Lord's table. To do so is to *invite* chastening.

"And the rest will I set in order when I come." This undoubtedly refers to things that were of less importance, details that were insignificant but had connection with questions he had already answered up to this point.

CHAPTER TWELVE

1. Now concerning spiritual gifts, brethren, I would not have you ignorant.

2. Ye know that ye were Gentiles, carried away unto these dumb idols, even as ye were led.

3. Wherefore I give you to understand, that no man speaking by the Spirit of God calleth Jesus accursed: and that no man can say that Jesus is the Lord, but by the Holy Ghost.

4. Now there are diversities of gifts, but the same Spirit.

5. And there are differences of administrations, but the same Lord.

6. And there are diversities of operations, but it is the same God which worketh all in all.

7. But the manifestation of the Spirit is given to every man to profit withal.

8. For to one is given by the Spirit the word of wisdom; to another the word of knowledge by the same Spirit;

9. To another faith by the same Spirit; to another the gifts of healing by the same Spirit;

10. To another the working of miracles; to another prophecy; to another discerning of spirits; to another divers kinds of tongues; to another the interpretation of tongues:

11. But all these worketh that one and the selfsame Spirit, dividing to every man severally as he will.

12. For as the body is one, and hath many members, and all the members of that one body, being many, are one body: so also is Christ.

13. For by one Spirit are we all baptized into one body, whether we be Jews or Gentiles, whether we be bond or free; and have been all made to drink into one Spirit.

14. For the body is not one member, but many.

15. If the foot shall say, Because I am not the hand, I am not of the body; is it therefore not of the body?

16. And if the ear shall say, Because I am not the eye, I am not of the body; is it therefore not of the body?

17. If the whole body were an eye, where were the hearing? If the whole were hearing, where were the smelling?

18. But now hath God set the members every one of them in the body, as it hath pleased him.

19. And if they were all one member, where were the body?

20. But now are they many members, yet but one body.

21. And the eye cannot say unto the hand, I have no need of thee: nor again the head to the feet, I have no need of you.

22. Nay, much more those members of the body, which seem to be more feeble, are necessary:

23. And those members of the body, which we think to be less honourable, upon these we bestow more abundant honour; and our uncomely parts have more abundant comeliness.

24. For our comely parts have no need: but God hath tempered the body together, having given more abundant honour to that part which lacked:

25. That there should be no schism in the body; but that the members should have the same care one for another.

26. And whether one member suffer, all the members suffer with it; or one member be honoured, all the members rejoice with it.

27. Now ye are the body of Christ, and members in particular.

28. And God hath set some in the church, first apostles, secondarily prophets, thirdly teachers, after that miracles, then gifts of healings, helps, governments, diversities of tongues.

29. Are all apostles? are all prophets? are all teachers? are all workers of miracles?

30. Have all the gifts of healing? do all speak with tongues? do all interpret?

31. But covet earnestly the best gifts: and yet shew I unto you a more excellent way.

This chapter continues Paul's answer to the questions he had received from the assembly at Corinth. There were party cliques, divided opinions on many matters, different ideas and beliefs concerning spiritual gifts and their use in the local assembly. Evidently some had unusual power and display of gifts, while others made less show and demonstrated less power. The first group was praised and exalted, while the latter group was ignored and treated as if they were of little value to the church. Such actions would be the tendency in any carnal assembly.

Paul makes it clear that the divine test of the real value of a gift is whether or not the possessor of the gift uses it to glorify the Lord Jesus Christ. It is wrong to place value upon the individual who *possesses* the gift, because the gift is of the Spirit, not of the flesh. Each believer should do all that he does to the glory of God and to the edification of the Church as a whole. Regardless of how powerful the gift may be or how spectacular the results, if the individual is lacking in *love*, the gift is of little value. It is right to desire the best gifts, but love must have pre-eminence in exercising the gifts.

We begin a new section here, which takes in chapters 12, 13, and through verse 40 of chapter 14.

Spiritual Gifts in the Body of Christ— How They Should Be Used in the Local Assembly

Verse 1: "Now concerning spiritual gifts, brethren, I would not have you ignorant."

The subject is *"spiritual gifts"* having to do with matters of or from the Holy Spirit. Again we note the statement used many times by Paul in his epistles: "I WOULD NOT HAVE YOU IGNORANT." There is no excuse for spiritual ignorance, because we have the Word of God, the perfect law of liberty—a lamp to our feet and a light to our pathway. All Scripture is inspired and is profitable. The Holy Ghost is the teacher, and *every believer possesses the Holy Ghost.*

Verse 2: "Ye know that ye were Gentiles, carried away unto these dumb idols, even as ye were led."

Paul is reminding the believers of the time when they were Gentiles (unbelievers). The following rendering brings out the meaning more clearly: "Ye know that ye were

386

constantly being led off to the idols, the speechless things, just as you might from time to time be driven."

It is clearly set forth here that behind these lifeless idols of wood or stone was a mighty, spiritual force, and spiritually minded believers recognize this force as the devil himself, working through the powers of darkness and spiritual rulers of wickedness in high places. These evil spirits operate through human instruments. False teachers (of which there were many in Corinth) were leading astray some who had not been genuinely born again, and even causing some of the believers to become carnal. But *before* they were born again, ALL the believers in Corinth were led away into idol worship through the powers of darkness.

The same is true today in heathendom, and even in our own land there are many idol worshippers — a little statue, a little "gadget," a church building, many things. But wherever there is an idol you may rest assured that the power of darkness is behind it!

Verse 3: "Wherefore I give you to understand, that no man speaking by the Spirit of God calleth Jesus accursed: and that no man can say that Jesus is the Lord, but by the Holy Ghost."

"*I give you to understand* . . . ." (Or, "I make known to you.") Before these people were converted from heathendom, before they left their dumb idols and turned to Jesus, they had no perception concerning spiritual things because "the natural man receiveth not the things of the Spirit of God." But now Paul is making known to them how they can *try the spirits* and know if they be of God. (Compare with I John 4:1–3.)

". . . *That no man speaking by the Spirit of God calleth Jesus accursed.* (In the original, the phrase of blasphemy is 'Anathema Jesus!') *And that no man can say that Jesus is the Lord, but by the Holy Ghost.*" That is, not a single true word can be spoken except by the agency of the Holy Ghost of God. All who truly confess that Jesus is Lord make such a confession under the influence of (or IN) the Holy Ghost.

Paul is here referring to the teachers in Corinth who denied the divinity of Christ. John refers to this group in I John 4:1–3. We still have those who deny the *divinity* of Christ, and those who deny His *humanity*. They deny the incarnation—without which we have no sacrifice, no Saviour, and no grace to save and keep.

Paul makes it clear, therefore, that born again, blood-washed believers speaking in and through the Holy Ghost will not call Jesus accursed—(and to deny His deity or anything the Word of God teaches concerning Him IS to call Him accursed). A born again believer will not do this.

And no man can from the heart truly confess that Jesus is *Lord* except by the Holy Ghost, because He (the Holy Ghost) is in the world to *testify* of Jesus, and the *natural* man cannot from the heart confess Jesus as Lord. Such confession can be made only in and through the Holy Ghost.

In John 16:12–15 Jesus said to His disciples, "I have yet many things to say unto you, but ye cannot bear them now. Howbeit when He, the Spirit of truth, is come, He will guide you into all truth: for He shall not speak of Himself; but whatsoever He shall hear, that shall He speak: and He will shew you things to come. He shall glorify me: for He shall receive of mine, and shall shew it unto you. All things that the Father hath are mine: therefore said I that He shall take of mine, and shall shew it unto you."

The blasphemous phrase "Anathema Jesus!" was frequently used by the Jews. The synagogue prayers included regularly a cursing of all heretics and apostates, and to those Jewish unbelievers Jesus would come under those classifications. The Jewish law laid it down that "cursed is every one that hangeth upon a tree" (Gal. 3:13), and Jesus had been crucified. It is by no means unlikely that the Jews would make those who had been friendly toward the Christians either pronounce this curse or be thrown out of the synagogue as is recorded in John 9:22. Paul said to Agrippa when testifying of his former persecution of Christians, "I often punished them in every synagogue *and forced them to blaspheme*" (Acts 26:11).

Bible history and Bible antiquity tell us that in Paul's day when the saints were gathered for worship and the Gospel was being preached, many times unbelievers or hostile persons would gain admission into the synagogue, and in the midst of the message these men would suddenly spring to their feet and shout out, *"Anathema, JESUS!"* Historians also tell us that the Gnostics demanded that anyone who joined them shout out these words.

The Apostle's statement that no one speaking by the Holy Spirit could use this blasphemous phrase is a preliminary to his second statement that only through the Holy Spirit can one make the declaration that "Jesus is Lord." A believer who is led to the recognition of the Lordship of Christ in his life is led there only through the power of the Holy Spirit, and this work of the Holy Spirit is for one unceasing object—and that is *to glorify Christ.*

Compare this with I John 4:2–4, where John stresses the divine fact of Christ's *humanity.* Here, Paul is driving home the truth of the *deity* of Christ. To deny either His humanity OR His deity is blasphemy.

Born again believers need not fear committing the sin of blasphemy, because "as many as are led by the Spirit of God, they are the sons of God." If you are led by the

Holy Spirit, you may be certain that He will not lead you to blaspheme the name of Jesus, and He will not lead you to blaspheme Himself. (Blasphemy against the Holy Ghost is the unpardonable sin, but a true believer will not, cannot, *commit* that sin.) Christians can commit the sin unto death, but that is death of the *body*, not damnation of the soul.

True Ministry in the Exercise of Spiritual Gifts

Verse 4: "Now there are diversities of gifts, but the same Spirit."

The Greek word translated "diversities" literally means kind, sort, class, or different kinds, and may here have the meaning "distribution or apportionings." The Holy Ghost is the One who apportions (distributes) the different gifts. They are not to be acquired in any other way. And the Holy Ghost has never bestowed a spiritual gift upon anyone except for the singular purpose of glorifying Christ. All glory, praise, worship and honor is due Jesus, and the Holy Spirit is very careful that the praise due Jesus be rendered unto Him. "But of Him are ye in Christ Jesus, who of God is made unto us wisdom, and righteousness, and sanctification, and redemption: that, according as it is written, He that glorieth, let him glory in the Lord" (I Cor. 1:30,31).

Verse 5: "And there are differences of administrations, but the same Lord."

Not "administrations" as in our King James version, but *"ministrations."* The Greek word is *diakonia,* meaning service—a word of general import, and not with the ecclesiastic idea of ministry. Each believer has his particular service to render. God has a ministry for every child of His. He does not expect one believer to carry out a ministry in exact detail as another believer would carry it out.

Each believer has a God-given stewardship, to be carried on for one specific purpose: *to glorify the Lord Jesus Christ.* God saves us for Christ's sake, and all that we do is to be done to His glory. Regardless of whether a ministry be outstanding or humble, each believer in the assembly is to give himself to that ministry or stewardship, performing it with all of his heart, strength, and mind. A believer who discharges the obligation of his stewardship in this manner will receive a full reward.

Paul is especially speaking here of an assembly gathered together to worship and study the Word of God. In an assembly where Christ is recognized as Lord in the life of each believer, there will be no confusion, no temptation for any believer in the assembly to turn to human tradition instead of following the leading of the Holy Spirit of God. The only way to correct any kind of dissension or disorder in the assembly is for *each believer to humble himself* before God, and for the entire assembly to pray fervently unto the Lord for the restoration of the unity that only God can give as each one yields fully to the Holy Spirit. God is not the author of confusion. He is the author of peace and unity, and where the Holy Spirit has His way in the life of each believer there is an assembly that enjoys unity and harmony, not an assembly torn asunder by strife and confusion.

Verse 6: "And there are diversities of operations, but it is the same God which worketh all in all."

In the assembly there are diversities of workings—many ministries to be performed. Some are very humble—not glamorous at all; some are not seen by man, although they are necessary. But whether the ministry be spectacular or humble, it is the same God who accomplishes all of the operations in all of the believers of the entire assembly. There is no schism in the Godhead (and there should be no schism in the Church). Jesus is the head and the foundation of the Church, we are all members of the one body, and therefore we should realize that since there is but one Lord, one God, we are all serving *one cause*—the glorification of Jesus Christ in all that we do, whether humble or great.

If in the assembly we render service to be commended and praised by man, we have our reward; we are not serving God, we are serving man. But if what we do, however great or small, is done in the right spirit and to the glory of God we will receive a full reward. In the sight of God there are no giant Christians and pygmy Christians; we are all sons of God, we all belong to the same body, and we should all be faithful in doing whatever the Lord gives us to do, whether that task be great or small. God knows our ability when He assigns us to service, and "He doeth all things well."

Verse 7: "But the manifestation of the Spirit is given to every man to profit withal."

The singular aim of ALL activities in the assembly is to profit the *entire* assembly. The Godhead—Father, Son, and Holy Ghost—operate in divine unity. They bestow the gifts — and while there are *diversities of endowments*, there is *unity of purpose and effect*.

The manifestation brought about through the gift of the Spirit bestowed upon the individual is not the manifestation of human ability, human wisdom, or human understanding; the manifestation of the indwelling power of the Holy Ghost should be a time of spiritual profit and spiritual growth for each believer IN the assembly at every *gathering* of the assembly. Every believer possesses his own individual gift according to the will of God; but the gifts of all individuals in the assembly are given to them individually for the profit of the entire assembly.

Verse 8: "For to one is given by the Spirit the word of wisdom; to another the word of knowledge by the same Spirit."

There is a difference between "wisdom" and "knowledge." *True wisdom* gauges or measures the true nature and value of a thing or things and their relationship to one another, thereby exercising spiritual insight and understanding. This is the highest kind of wisdom, and comes from God. *Knowledge* consists in the intelligent apprehension of a fact or facts concerning a thing or things, and the principles relating thereto. Knowledge is a much more practical thing. These two are necessary— the wisdom which knows by communion with God the deep things of God, and the knowledge which in the daily life and work can put that wisdom into practice.

All of this applies to divine wisdom and spiritual knowledge, and, in this verse particularly, to that which is ministered by the Holy Spirit concerning the true God, His ways and works, *"in whom are hid all the treasures of wisdom and knowledge"* (Col. 2:3).

The truth of our present verse does not necessarily imply that the gift of knowledge is confined to just one class of believers; such a gift may be given to the ordinary Christian (as we think of people) or to the extraordinary. Neither does it mean that a brother can possess only ONE gift — i.e., that if he has the gift of wisdom, he cannot *also* have the gift of knowledge or the gift of faith. The Spirit may bestow *many* gifts upon one individual.

Verse 9: "To another faith by the same Spirit; to another the gifts of healing by the same Spirit."

"To another faith . . . ." The faith to which Paul refers here is not the faith which is constantly exercised by all true believers. We *live* by faith (Rom. 1:17); but the faith Paul speaks of in this verse is the *special* gift

of faith spoken of in chapter 13, verse 2, which really produces results — a special bestowment of faith that is manifested in the *deeds* of the individual who has that gift.

". . . *To another, the gifts of healing by the same Spirit.*" We must be careful to rightly divide the Word of Truth. We must distinguish between the gifts of the Spirit which were bestowed upon the *apostles*, and the gifts of the Spirit which are permanent and will continue through the Church Age. Some of the gifts were given at a specific time for a specific purpose, and lasted only during the apostolic testimony: *"God also bearing them witness, both with signs and wonders, and with divers miracles, and gifts of the Holy Ghost, according to His own will"* (Heb. 2:4).

During the transition period and in the first century of Christianity, God gave special gifts according to His own will, testifying to the true salvation through the blood of Jesus: ". . . When that which is perfect is come, then that which is in part shall be done away" (I Cor. 13:10). Therefore, when "the faith once delivered unto the saints" was complete and the perfect law of liberty was given in full, there was no longer need for signs and wonders. God has decreed, *"The just shall live by faith,"* and faith does not ask to see, feel, taste, or handle! Faith believes God simply because He IS God; and if God declares it, we can believe it, live by it, stand upon it, and die by it. We need no signs and wonders today to prove what we find in the Word of God. We believe it, we know it is true, simply *because God said it.*

In Paul's day special gifts of healing *were* bestowed upon individuals. Paul not only healed — he also raised a young man from the dead (Acts 20:9–12); yet later in his ministry the gift of healing was not used on behalf of Timothy, Trophimus, Gaius, and many others, although these were God-called, Spirit-filled men. We read in Acts 9:40 that *Peter* also raised the dead.

Now dearly beloved, why can we not be reasonable? Why cannot we who profess to be ministers and teachers of the Word of God *rightly divide* the Word? Why do we proclaim long and loud that *the gift of healing* is upon men today as with the apostles in the early Church — and yet we must admit that no man living today can raise the dead, nor has any man raised the dead in recent centuries? I know God can heal all kinds of diseases, and I know that He DOES heal — He has healed *my* body and He has healed my loved ones. I have seen God work! But for men today to declare that they possess the gift of healing as did Paul and Peter is to handle the Scriptures very carelessly.

In Acts 5:12—16 the sick were placed in the streets, *"that at the least the shadow of Peter passing by* might overshadow some of them . . . and they were healed every one."* I believe in divine healing, and I pray for the sick; but I do not profess to have the gift of healing nor do I claim that I can pray the prayer of faith that will save the sick. I base my prayers for the sick on James 5:14, 15, and when I pray for the sick I close my prayer in the words of the Saviour: "THY will be done."

God DOES heal the sick in answer to prayer — but we must distinguish between the rules laid down in James 5 and the supernatural *gifts* of healing which were temporary, referred to here and in other places in the Scriptures.

In Acts 28:1—9 the Apostle Paul healed an entire island of barbarians—unbelievers — and through the miracle of healing he had the opportunity of telling them about the great Physician of the soul. But this same Paul, near the close of his earthly ministry, left one of his best friends sick and traveled on without him (II Tim. 4:20). I would not presume to be skeptical or sarcastic, but I do ask, WHY?

There are men today who declare that they have the same gift Paul and Peter had; they claim outstanding miracles in their ministries. To the mass of humanity, such an evangelist or teacher is attractive and glamorous; he draws tremendous crowds, and no doubt many are saved through the Gospel that is proclaimed. I judge not, for God will handle these things at the judgment seat of Christ; but I do say in Bible language, *"When that which is perfect is come, then that which is in part shall be done away"* (I Cor. 13:10). And I would warn, in the words of John, "Beloved, believe not every spirit, but try the spirits whether they are of God: because many false prophets are gone out into the world" (I John 4:1).

Paul warns us, ". . . Satan himself is transformed into an angel of light. Therefore it is no great thing if his ministers also be transformed as the ministers of righteousness; whose end shall be according to their works" (II Cor. 11:14,15).

Each morning in the Gospel Hour office the workers meet together for Bible reading and prayer before the day's work is begun, and never a day passes that we do not pray for the sick, the afflicted, the suffering. I thank God for doctors, nurses, hospitals, and medicines; but I also believe in *divine* healing. I believe that only God can heal these bodies of ours.

Verse 10: "To another the working of miracles; to another prophecy; to another discerning of spirits; to another divers kinds of tongues; to another the interpretation of tongues."

"To another the working of miracles . . . ." The Greek word here translated "miracles" is *dunamis*, and denotes unusual power. To some, the gift is given to work

396

works and accomplish things that could be wrought only through a power and strength beyond human possibility. God does give such power to individuals, and they are to use that power to glorify God, not man.

". . . *To another, prophecy . . . .*" To prophesy does not mean simply to foretell the future; it also means to *forthtell* (or tell forth) that which has been foretold. The gift of prophecy includes a divinely imparted ability to tell forth (to preach) "Thus saith the Lord," giving out the good news that God so loved the world that He gave the Son of His love, that we might be saved from sin.

In Paul's day the Church did not have the New Testament; they did not have the Scriptures as we have them today to make known the deep things of God. Therefore, God bestowed upon individuals a divine power to tell forth *the mind* of God. But now we have the complete Scriptures, and we do not have prophets in the same sense that God gave the gift of prophecy in the early days of Christianity and during the transition period. All true ministers today are prophets, however, in that they tell forth the good news that Jesus died to save sinners.

". . . *To another, discerning of spirits . . . .*" To some individuals God gives the power of discernment and discrimination as having to do with true spirits and the spirit of Satan: "Let the prophets speak two or three, and let the other judge" (I Cor. 14:29).

". . . *To another, divers kinds of tongues; to another the interpretation of tongues.*" There were those in the Corinthian church who had the gift of tongues; but the same rule applies to tongues as applies to the gift of healing in Paul's day. The Word of God is very clear on this. Tongues were "for a sign"—a sign to unbelieving Jews. We will study this much more fully in chapter 14.

Notice Isaiah 28:11–13: "For with stammering lips and another tongue will He speak to this people. To whom He said, This is the rest wherewith ye may cause the weary to rest; and this is the refreshing: yet they would not hear. But the word of the Lord was unto them precept upon precept, precept upon precept; line upon line, line upon line; here a little, and there a little; that they might go, and fall backward, and be broken, and snared, and taken."

God gave Israel supernatural testimony; and although it was foretold that this would be *rejected* by Israel, God continued this supernatural testimony to His people and maintained relations with them during the transition period. But such testimonies ceased when God set aside *the kingdom and Israel* for the duration of the Church Age.

These supernatural manifestations such as the unusual gifts of healing, raising the dead, tongues, and prophesying took place during the first twelve years after Pentecost, and such manifestations took place only when and where Jews were present—never in the presence of Gentiles only. You will find the record in Acts. Study Acts 2:22–36; 8:14–17; 10:45; and 19:2–6.

There is no further instance of this kind of supernatural manifestation and demonstration, and no further reference to it recorded in Acts nor anywhere in the Epistles. This was the period of transition—the time when God was making His last call and giving His last testimony to the Jews.

Verse 11: "But all these worketh that one and the selfsame Spirit, dividing to every man severally as He will."

". . . *One and the selfsame Spirit* . . ."—the Holy Spirit. The Bible makes it very clear that no spiritual gift can be developed through human training, nor can a spiritual gift be bestowed upon man by another man.

In verse 6 of this chapter we read that "there are diversities of operations, but it is *the same God* which worketh all in all." God works in all true believers and He must lead in all *acceptable works.* Now we read of the Holy Spirit *"dividing to every man severally as He will."* Thus we see the personality of the Holy Spirit; we see that He is equal with the Father and the Son, because He is declared to do the same thing the Father does. The Godhead works in unity—Father, Son, and Holy Ghost. The Holy Spirit is not merely an influence — *He is a Person.*

We will be rewarded only for the deeds wrought in us by and through the Holy Spirit. Only such stewardship will be approved at the judgment seat of Christ. Both the individual and the assembly should be very careful that the Holy Spirit has right-of-way in every heart. Man-made programs and ideas should never be substituted for the leadership of the Holy Spirit — and if we will yield to Him we can rest assured that He will never lead us astray. He will lead us always in the paths of service where fruit is sure to result. We need not make our own plans and then expect God to bless us; but when the Holy Spirit is allowed to make our plans He will lead us into the right path where God can honor and bless our efforts *in the Holy Spirit.*

All True Believers Are Members of Christ's Body; All True Believers Have a Definite Ministry.

God never saved any individual to be idle; He saves to serve. Regardless of how limited we may be, or how little we may feel, there is a ministry for each and every member of the body of Christ.

Verse 12: "For as the body is one, and hath many members, and all the members of that one body, being

399

many, are one body: so also is Christ."

The Holy Spirit is here using the human body to illustrate the one true Church and its functions. I believe
the local assembly is ordained of God; I believe the local
assembly is included in His program; and I believe every
born again person should unite with a local assembly.
But the Church of the living God is ONE Church, of which
Jesus is the head and the foundation, and all born again,
blood-washed believers are members of that ONE Church.
Our present Scripture points to the invisible Church of
which Jesus is the head, but it also has to do with the
local church to which Paul directs this letter.

Just as the human body is one body, with many members belonging to that one body, *"so also is Christ."*
Some Bible authorities tell us that the Greek reads, "So
also is THE Christ." That is, Christ belongs to the
whole body:

He is the HEAD (Eph. 5:22,23).

He is the FOUNDATION (I Cor. 3:11).

He is the BODY (I Cor. 12:12).

Christ is IN the whole body; He operates throughout
the whole body. He is the Saviour of the body, the Saviour
of the Church (Eph. 5:23).

Verse 13: "For by one Spirit are we all baptized into
one body, whether we be Jews or Gentiles, whether we be
bond or free; and have been all made to drink into one
Spirit."

To me, this verse is crystal-clear and easily understood. Perhaps that is because I am not looking for proof
of a denominational stand. I am not trying to prove anything, I am not defending any denomination. The Word of
God simply states, *"By one Spirit are we all baptized into
one body."* We know this does not refer to water baptism,

because it very clearly declares, "by one *Spirit*." This, then, is a *spiritual baptism*.

Positionally we were baptized into the body of Christ at Pentecost. The Church was foreordained of God, but that has nothing to do with the free will of man. The Church was known of God before the foundation of the world. (God is sovereign; He knows the end in the beginning, and everything *between* the beginning and the end.) Therefore, on the Day of Pentecost, the birthday of the New Testament Church, *the Church as a whole* was baptized into the body of Christ.

To Nicodemus Jesus said, "Except a man be born of the Spirit, he cannot enter into the kingdom of God." To me it is clear that the moment an unbeliever trusts Jesus as Saviour, that individual is born again and *by the Spirit* is baptized into (united with) the body of Christ.

I believe this Scripture has a twofold meaning: It points back to Pentecost when the entire Church was baptized in the Holy Ghost, and it also refers to the moment of conversion when the individual is born of the Spirit, baptized into and united with the body of Christ by the miracle of the Holy Ghost. According to Scripture, there is no such thing as New Testament Christianity apart from the baptism of the Holy Spirit, and that baptism occurs the moment an individual exercises faith in Christ and is born again.

There is no longer the Jew (the chosen one) and the Gentile "dog," as it was before the coming of Christ and during the days of His earthly ministry. NOW it makes no difference whether we be Jew or Gentile, bond or free. All who believe, all who trust in the finished work of Jesus, are baptized by ONE Spirit into ONE body.

"*. . . And have been all made to drink into one Spirit.*"

This statement points back to chapter 10, verse 4. It speaks of the same spiritual drink—Christ, the spiritual Rock from whence comes living water. Special emphasis in this part of the verse is on "ALL" and "ONE"—ALL born again believers drink into ONE Spirit. The spiritual life is sustained through the continual drinking we are made to drink. We drink continually of the one Spirit; therefore we live spiritually. There are different *gifts* of the Spirit, as has been pointed out, but this is *one gift* possessed by all believers. We drink ALL into ONE Spirit.

Verse 14: "For the body is not one member, but many."

The truth of this verse points to the local assembly: *"The body is not one member, but many,"* referring to the many individuals in the church—not all having the gifts of wisdom, knowledge, healing, tongues, etc., but all members of the same body, all drinking into ONE Spirit.

The opening word of verse 14 connects it with verse 13; so actually we read, *"For* by one Spirit are we all baptized into one body . . . *For* the body is not one member, but many." Thus we have the truth concerning the *individual*, and also concerning the local assembly which is made up of *many* individuals; but the deeper meaning points to the Church of the living God, the Church of which Jesus is the head and the foundation, with the believers as members of His body—bone of His bone and flesh of His flesh. He is the Saviour of the body. Read Ephesians 5:23–32.

It is possible to *join* a local church, but the only possible way to become a member of the Church of the living God is to be *baptized into* that Church by the Holy Ghost — and the only way we can live a spiritual life is by drinking into this spiritual Rock, the Lord Jesus, the one Spirit that *sustains* spiritual life.

Verses 15 and 16: "If the foot shall say, Because I am not the hand, I am not of the body; is it therefore not of the body? And if the ear shall say, Because I am not the eye, I am not of the body; is it therefore not of the body?"

There were those in the assembly at Corinth who were grumbling. They were a bit jealous and envious of those who possessed gifts *they* did not possess. Paul has just pointed out that God gives *diversities* of gifts, but there is *only one Spirit*. He then uses the members of the natural body to show these people how childish and foolish they were. Is it not foolish indeed for a person to argue that since the hand is not a foot, it is not part of the body? Or that, since the ear is not the eye, the ear is not a member of the body? Paul points out that it is equally foolish for believers to grumble and complain because some have received gifts more noticeable or spectacular than others.

Happy is that believer who recognizes the sovereignty of God, acknowledging that God knows better than we what service we can best render to Him. If we will be reasonable, we will face this fact. We should actually prefer to perform an *humble* task well, rather than attempt something for which we are not fitted and make a failure of it. If we follow the leadership of the Holy Spirit, He will lay out for us work that we can do, for He knows our capabilities; but if we strive to be "big" and do something spectacular just because someone else has a spectacular gift, we will fail every time — and instead of helping the cause of Christ we will bring reproach upon His name and shame upon ourselves.

Notice that in the contrast Paul makes here, the foot does not speak to the eye nor to the ear; the *foot* speaks to the *hand*. There could be a lesson for us in this. Most of us are not jealous or envious of someone who holds a *much, much higher* position than we; but we are more inclined to become jealous of the person who rises *just a little bit higher* than we are. The devil is shrewd and the flesh is weak. We need to keep our eyes on Jesus, always. When we do this, we will be happy and successful; but when we start looking at others and take our eyes off of Jesus, the devil has a good opportunity to plant the seed of animosity and strife in our hearts, and as a result we will become unhappy and unfruitful.

Verse 17: "If the whole body were an eye, where were the hearing? If the whole were hearing, where were the smelling?"

That is plain enough, is it not? If the whole body were an eye, or an ear, or a nose, *there would BE no body!* It takes the eye, the ear, the nose, the fingers, the toes and other members to *make* the body. So it is with the local church. There are different tasks for different members to perform, and each believer IN the assembly should do his or her job well; for whether it be great or small, it is necessary. No member of the local assembly should covet the work of another. We should each do what the Lord lays out for us to do, and do it heartily *as unto HIM.* And thus we will receive a full reward.

Verse 18: "But now hath God set the members every one of them in the body, as it hath pleased Him."

Paul here states the flawless, perfect plan of Almighty God—omnipotent, omniscient, omnipresent—He who knows the end from the beginning. God knows each individual, He knows our ability, our limitations, and He has set the members of the local assembly, *"every one of them in the body, as it hath pleased Him."* If God be pleased to have us in the position we occupy, then we should be pleased to BE there — because if what we are doing is NOT being done to the glory of God and in the name of Jesus, we would be much better off if we were not doing *anything*. To be hypocritical in our stewardship is worse than having no stewardship at all.

I love to think of the little lad who went to hear Jesus preach. He did not forget to ask his mother to prepare a lunch for him to take—five loaves and two little fishes; but he had no realization of what tremendous blessing his little lunch would be in the hands of the Lord Jesus as He fed the multitudes.

The poor widow gave two mites—*so little*—and yet, *Jesus* said, "She gave more than all the rest." Even a cup of cold water *given in the name of Jesus* is recorded in heaven.

There is a lesson in service in Luke 19:29—32: "And it came to pass, when (Jesus) was come nigh to Bethphage and Bethany, at the mount called the mount of Olives, He sent two of His disciples, saying, Go ye into the village over against you; in the which at your entering ye shall find a colt tied, whereon yet never man sat: Loose him, and bring him hither. . . And they that were sent went their way, and found even as He had said unto them."

Think of it! This occurrence took place as Jesus was about to make His triumphal entry into Jerusalem. These men had followed Him for more than three years. They had walked with Him throughout His earthly ministry, training at His feet. And yet their first assignment was, "Go bring me a donkey." They did as they were told, "and found even as He had said unto them."

I repeat: If we would let the Lord Jesus, through the Holy Spirit, direct us into service, and do whatever He has for us to do, we would be happy; and if we would do the work He gives us to do with all of our hearts, exclusively for the glory of God, we would have a full reward at the end of life's journey.

God help us not to covet the work of a fellow believer nor be jealous of another's success. We are all members of the same body, and instead of being envious and jealous we should rejoice when others do well, because when one member is blessed, the entire body is blessed, just as when one member suffers, all of the body suffers. May God help us to fully realize that we are in Christ and Christ is in us, and let us learn as Paul learned: "I am what I am by the grace of God!"

Verse 19: "And if they were all one member, where were the body?"

Paul repeats here what he has just said in verse 17, pointing out the need for each and every member of the body. Without the existence of ALL members, however insignificant some of them may be, the body could not be complete. When we think of the natural body we think of a variety of members—fingers, toes, feet, hands, arms, eyes, ears, etc. — and we need them all, just as *the local church* needs all members and ministries as the Holy Spirit directs.

If ALL members in the assembly held the *highest positions* in the assembly, the body would cease to exist. There must be offices of distinction, and there must be those of humble service. If God calls us to be a janitor, we should get on our knees and promise God to be *the best janitor* He has! The janitor who keeps the sanctuary spotless to the glory of God will receive a full reward just as truly as any other member of the local assembly.

Verse 20: "But now are they many members, yet but one body."

This same truth was set forth in verse 12. There are many members, but only one body (one assembly); and even though the members differ in their respective ministries, they are dependent one upon the other. God help us to see this in both the local assembly and the invisible Church. The command is, *"Go ye into all the world and preach the Gospel to every creature."* One local assembly could never get the job done; but if all true believers in all assemblies would work diligently and heartily, "as unto the Lord," we *could* get it done. "None of us liveth to himself, and no man dieth to himself" (Rom. 14:7). We are our brother's keeper.

Verse 21: "And the eye cannot say unto the hand, I have no need of thee: nor again the head to the feet, I have no need of you."

In verse 15 we had the illustration of the foot saying to the hand, "Because I am not the hand, I am not of the body." There it was the inferior member grumbling to the higher; but in this verse it is pointed out that the superior member may *despise* the inferior. In the natural life the hand handles the object the eye looks upon — for example, the hand picks up the book, the eye reads the book; therefore the eye needs the hand and the hand needs the eye. The head needs the feet, because the feet walk where the head directs.

So it is in the local assembly. We are not independent one of another. The local assembly is *interdependent*, and if unity is to abound there must be no sense of superiority. We must not look down on any member because of his humble stewardship.

Verse 22: "Nay, much more those members of the body, which seem to be more feeble, are necessary."

Suppose we use the eye as an illustration: The eyeball is one of the most marvelous mechanisms known to man. Our finite minds marvel at color-television — that a person can stand in Los Angeles or New York City and be seen in full color anywhere in the United States where there is a receiver. We marvel at the color-TV tube — and yet, the eyeball was created by God Almighty when He made Adam, and that tiny member of our body contains a color mechanism that enables us to detect colors the moment we open our eyes.

Yes, the human eye is a marvelous creation—but we do not think so much about the *eyelid*—just a little piece of flesh. But when a foreign object aims directly toward the eye, *the lid automatically closes*! We do not stop and think, "I should close my eyelids." When danger threatens the eyeball, the eyelids automatically close to protect it. They are not much to look at, there is not much to them— but *they are very important.*

The same is true in the local assembly. The humble members are sometimes the more needful. What Paul is pointing out here is that the members in the assembly who are prominent and whose ministry makes a big show, should not look down upon the humble servant who keeps the nursery so that others may hear the Word, or those who can only send out postcards to absentees. These people do not receive much recognition, but if they render their service as unto God, they will be rewarded at the end of life's journey.

Verse 23: "And those members of the body, which we think to be less honourable, upon these we bestow more abundant honour; and our uncomely parts have more abundant comeliness."

Paul is still using the human body to illustrate the local assembly and the stewardship and ministry of individual members. "*. . . More abundant honour . . . more abundant comeliness*" points to the extra clothing (or jewels, as the case might be) placed upon these members of the body, while other members remain unclothed. He

408

is pointing out the principle of bestowing honor upon those parts of the body which might be considered as naturally possessing the *least* honor — for instance, if a precious lady has uncomely hands because they were burned and scarred through some tragedy in childhood, she can hide the ugly scars with a pair of beautiful gloves.

So many times, upon that part of the body that seems less honorable, we bestow more abundant honor and spend more time and money than on the more comely members. Instead of despising these uncomely members, we give them special attention and care.

Thus, the members of the local assembly who seem to be less honorable, instead of being ignored should be given more attention and care than we give to the members who are extremely honorable. Only the day of Christ will reveal the true stewardship of those not mentioned in the church bulletin, those who never get their picture in the church paper and never receive publicity from the pulpit. God keeps the record, and in that day we will learn who are the great and the small in the local assembly.

Verse 24: "For our comely parts have no need: but God hath tempered the body together, having given more abundant honour to that part which lacked."

The first part of verse 24 really belongs to the last part of verse 23. Thus it would read, ". . . and our uncomely parts have more abundant comeliness, for our comely parts have no need . . . ."

The human body has three kinds of members: (1) The *less honorable* parts—usually clothed. (2) The *uncomely* parts—always very carefully clothed. (3) The *comely* parts, which have no need of clothing.

"*But God hath tempered the body together, having given more abundant honor to that part which lacked.*"

The Holy Spirit places the emphasis on GOD . . . literally, "*It was God* who tempered (blended) the body together."

God created this natural body of ours, and He knew what was best. He did the right thing in the right way concerning the human body, and the same is true of the local assembly. Those endowed with gifts *received those gifts from GOD.* The bestowal of different spiritual gifts upon different individuals is God's business, and God knows what He is doing. If each believer in the assembly would recognize this, it would bring harmony and unity to the assembly rather than animosity, strife and jealousy.

"Every good gift and every perfect gift is from above, and cometh down from the Father of lights, with whom is no variableness, neither shadow of turning" (James 1:17). The very privilege of being a *child* of God is a gift from God, and we should be thankful for any spiritual gift He bestows upon us, no matter how humble that gift may be or how humble the ministry He gives us. We should praise Him for His goodness and for whatever the gift He bestows upon us, rather than being jealous or envious of those who may seem to have higher positions and greater opportunities than we.

Verse 25: "That there should be no schism in the body; but that the members should have the same care one for another."

Had the Corinthian believers realized that God is the giver of *all* good gifts there would never have been divisions in the assembly, with the party spirit, the jealousy and envy that existed there. All believers in the assembly *need each other.* We should love each other, help each other, and not be critical and envious. We are all children of the same God; we are all members of the same body. We are *blood kin* because we are *covered* by the blood!

Verse 26: "And whether one member suffer, all the

members suffer with it; or one member be honoured, all the members rejoice with it."

Here Paul brings the physical illustration to a close— a very touching, vivid close: When one member of the body suffers, the entire body suffers WITH that member. When even the most insignificant member of the body is wounded or in pain, the whole body suffers *with* that member; and when one member of the body is honored, all members rejoice — *the entire being* rejoices when one member is honored or blessed.

The same should be true in the assembly—(and IS true if the assembly is in the right spiritual relationship with God). If one member of the church suffers, *all* members suffer with that one suffering member; and by like token if one member is honored, the rest of the members will *rejoice* if they are right in their hearts.

Verse 27: "Now ye are the body of Christ, and members in particular."

Paul is now ready to make his application: *"YE are the body of CHRIST!"* Greek authorities tell us that this verse should read, "Ye are BODY of Christ," with stress and emphasis upon "body."

"Body of Christ" denotes the quality or condition of the assembly as a whole. Each individual believer forms a member of the body of Christ. Writing to the believers in Ephesus Paul said, ". . . We are members of His body, of His flesh, and of His bones." When an individual exercises saving faith in the finished work of Jesus Christ, that person is instantaneously united to the body of Christ— and God places him IN the body as it pleases Him. I would again remind you that God knows best what we are capable of doing, and if we would only allow Him to put us where He can use us best, *heaven would gain* and WE would receive a full reward for our stewardship.

Verse 28: "And God hath set some in the Church, first apostles, secondarily prophets, thirdly teachers, after that miracles, then gifts of healings, helps, governments, diversities of tongues."

The Greek verb translated *"hath set"* conveys the thought that God has had a special interest or purpose in placing certain individual believers in the capacity of service where He places them. The literal translation here could read, "And God hath set *for Himself* some in the Church."

". . . *First apostles . . . .*" The local church in Jerusalem was the assembly that primarily contained the apostles. We know there *were* apostles other than the original twelve. For instance, Galatians 1:19 names James, the Lord's brother; in Romans 16:7 we read of Andronicus and Junia; and Acts 14:14 speaks of Paul and Barnabas as apostles.

The apostles were those who had seen the Lord—especially after His bodily resurrection from the grave. In I Corinthians 9:1,2 Paul asks, "Am I not an apostle? Am I not free? Have I not seen Jesus Christ our Lord? Are not ye my work in the Lord? If I be not an apostle unto others, yet doubtless I am to you: for the seal of mine apostleship are ye in the Lord." (See I Corinthians 15:8).

". . . *Secondarily prophets, thirdly teachers . . . .*" The ministry of prophets was by supernatural revelation. God revealed directly to them *His mind* for certain occasions concerning certain matters. The ministry of the prophet was to edify and encourage the believers in the assembly: "But he that prophesieth speaketh unto men to edification, and exhortation, and comfort. . . But if all prophesy, and there come in one that believeth not, or one unlearned, he is convinced of all, he is judged of all: And

412

thus are the secrets of his heart made manifest; and so falling down on his face he will worship God, and report that God is in you of a truth" (I Cor. 14:3, 24, 25).

When the Word of God was completed ("when that which is perfect is come"), prophecy passed away: ". . . Whether there be prophecies, they shall fail . . ." (I Cor. 13:8). The teacher then took the place of the prophet: "But there were false prophets also among the people, even as there shall be *false teachers among you*, who privily shall bring in damnable heresies, even denying the Lord that bought them and bring upon themselves swift destruction" (II Pet. 2:1).

Unlike the ministry of the prophet, the ministry of the teachers in the assembly is gathered from the completed revelation (the perfect law of liberty), and the purpose of that ministry is to make known the revealed thought of God written down in the Scriptures. The pastoral gift and the gift of teaching are Siamese twins: "And He gave some, apostles; and some, prophets; and some, evangelists; and some, *pastors and teachers*" (Eph. 4:11).

You will note that the *evangelist* mentioned in this verse in Ephesians is not mentioned in our present verses in Corinthians, where the Holy Spirit is dealing with the local assembly in Corinth (specifically) and pointing to local assemblies everywhere. The work of an evangelist is chiefly *outside* the local assembly, and in Ephesians the Holy Spirit is referring to the Church of the living God, the *invisible Church*, not the local assembly as Paul deals with it here in Corinthians.

"After that, miracles, then gifts of healings." Notice the change in presentation here. First, "God hath set *some* (referring to individuals) in the church . . . apostles . . . prophets . . . teachers." And then the Holy Spirit *speaks through Paul* in the abstract (the Greek word used

413

is *dunamis*, meaning "power")—that is, *miracles are performed through supernatural power*. The same is true with the gift of healing. These miracles were performed through a special kind of supernatural power.

The power to work miracles and perform healings was designated for the apostolic period and apostolic testimony. As I have said earlier in these messages, signs were given for a specific era. I am not suggesting that the days of miracles are over; we live in an hour of miracles. I am not suggesting that God does not heal today; God DOES heal. But I AM saying that God gave *supernatural* power to men in Paul's day, such as the power Peter possessed when he prayed for a little girl and she was raised from the dead, or such as the power Paul had when he healed the barbarians on the island after his shipwreck.

When we compare Scripture with Scripture and spiritual things with spiritual, we see that this supernatural power was bestowed upon Paul and others at a specific time for a specific reason. This is further evidenced by the fact that Paul did not heal Timothy, Trophimus, and Gaius. I personally believe that if Paul had had the gift of healing at that particular time he would have healed his son in the faith; but instead, he told Timothy, ". . . Use a little wine for thy stomach's sake and thine often infirmities" (I Tim. 5:23). For some reason known only to Paul and to God, he did not pray the prayer of faith on Timothy's behalf, but suggested a remedy.

Oh, yes! *God heals* – and God can raise the dead. But we must rightly divide the Word; we must not take Scripture out of context in order to prove our point. There is a definite and peculiar distinction between the gift of healing as associated with the supernatural power to work miracles, and the formula given for praying for the sick in James 5:14,15. *I believe in praying for the sick accord-ing to this passage from James.*

"Then . . . helps, governments. . . ." The Greek word used here for "helps" is *antilempsis*, meaning "laying hold of, so as to support." Here it means to render assistance to those who are weak and needy: "Now we exhort you, brethren, warn them that are unruly, comfort the feebleminded, support the weak, be patient toward all men" (I Thess. 5:14).

The Greek word for "governments" is *kubernesis*. The meaning denotes "steering." A similar word is used in Acts 27:11 and in Revelation 18:17 with reference to the master of a ship. It means anyone who acts as a spiritual guide or who exercises oversight in the local assembly.

". . . Diversities of tongues"—that is, different kinds of tongues. (Please notice that tongues are mentioned last.) The gift of tongues was temporary, given especially as a sign to the Jews. The use of tongues is recorded in Acts 2:2—11; 10:45,46; and 19:6. Jews were present at each of these gatherings where the people spoke with other tongues.

We read of tongues in the assembly at Corinth, but there is no further mention of the sign of tongues in the epistles. In Matthew 12:38—40 we read, "Then certain of the scribes and of the Pharisees answered, saying, Master, we would see a sign from thee. But He (Jesus) answered and said unto them, An evil and adulterous generation seeketh after a sign; *and there shall no sign be given to it, but the sign of the prophet Jonas: For as Jonas was three days and three nights in the whale's belly; so shall the Son of man be three days and three nights in the heart of the earth."*

Verses 29 and 30: "Are all apostles? are all prophets? are all teachers? are all workers of miracles? Have all the

415

gifts of healing? do all speak with tongues? do all interpret?''

We have here a group of questions which automatically suggest negative answers and which also sum up what has been said in verses 14 through 27. Paul asked these questions with the implied negative answer in order to check the ugly spirit of jealousy, presumption, rivalry, fleshly pride, self-sufficiency and independence displayed by some of the believers at Corinth.

These questions *should be asked today*—over and over again. There are some who suggest (by word of mouth and also through the printed page) that all ministers who are right with God and have the power of God should be able to work miracles, heal the sick, and speak with other tongues. But Paul asks:

"Are all *apostles*?" The answer is ''No.''

"Are all *prophets*?" The answer is ''No.''

"Are all *teachers*?" The answer is ''No.''

"Are all *workers of miracles*?" The answer is ''No.''

"Have all the gift of *healing*?" The answer is ''No.''

"Do all speak with *tongues*?" The answer is ''No.''

"Do all *interpret*?" The answer is ''No.''

It is detrimental to the cause of Christ that some ministers are so narrow and self-righteous that they try to force every other minister into their little circle, suggesting that all who do not work spectacular miracles (or perform great healings such as they themselves claim to perform) could do the same if they were right with God, or if they would allow God to possess them as He should. But according to the Apostle Paul, these ministers are wrong.

God calls men to pastor churches. He calls men to the mission field. He calls evangelists; He calls teachers.

God, who called the Church into being, *"hath tempered the body together"* and set each member in the Church according to His own will and pleasure, *"as it hath pleased Him."* How sad it is that some ministers have the audacity to deliberately demand of their fellow preachers and teachers what God Himself does not expect and what the Word of God does not suggest.

Verse 31: "But covet earnestly the best gifts: and yet shew I unto you a more excellent way."

It is not wrong to covet the best gifts. It is normal to desire such gifts, but not all can possess them. Some are not fitted, some are not physically able, and for various and sundry reasons it is impossible for all to possess the best gifts. Neither can all the members in the assembly be pastors, deacons, or Bible teachers. Where would the *assembly* be if all were preachers and teachers?

If WE cannot ourselves possess the best gifts, we can pray for those who DO possess them. We can pray for God to lead them, give them power, and keep them humble and obedient so that they can be used to glorify Christ. We must remember that whether we possess the best gifts or the most humble, whether our ministry is spectacular or unnoticeable, *we are all members of the same body*, and we should desire to glorify the Lord Jesus Christ, and Him alone.

CHAPTER THIRTEEN

1. Though I speak with the tongues of men and of angels, and have not charity, I am become as sounding brass, or a tinkling cymbal.

2. And though I have the gift of prophecy, and understand all mysteries, and all knowledge; and though I have all faith, so that I could remove mountains, and have not charity, I am nothing.

3. And though I bestow all my goods to feed the poor, and though I give my body to be burned, and have not charity, it profiteth me nothing.

4. Charity suffereth long, and is kind; charity envieth not; charity vaunteth not itself, is not puffed up,

5. Doth not behave itself unseemly, seeketh not her own, is not easily provoked, thinketh no evil;

6. Rejoiceth not in iniquity, but rejoiceth in the truth;

7. Beareth all things, believeth all things, hopeth all things, endureth all things.

8. Charity never faileth: but whether there be prophecies, they shall fail; whether there be tongues, they shall cease; whether there be knowledge, it shall vanish away.

9. For we know in part, and we prophesy in part.

10. But when that which is perfect is come, then that which is in part shall be done away.

11. When I was a child, I spake as a child, I understood as a child, I thought as a child: but when I became a man, I put away childish things.

12. For now we see through a glass, darkly; but then face to face: now I know in part; but then shall I know even as also I am known.

13. And now abideth faith, hope, charity, these three; but the greatest of these is charity.

This chapter is not parenthetical nor is it digressing. It is an essential connection with the subject of various spiritual gifts. Chapter 12 tells of the *existence* of these gifts, chapter 14 tells us how the believer should *exercise* such gifts, and in *this* chapter Paul shows that whatever the believer may do, however great his activity may seem, *apart from love* everything he does is worthless, empty, vain and void. Chapter 13 is an integral part of the tremendous truth set forth in chapters 12 and 14.

Even to the Jew, love was definitely a new sound — and much more so to the Gentiles. The nature and habit of Gentiles in the day of Jesus was to walk in vanity. Their minds were centered on earthly things. Their understanding was darkened by sin. Their hearts were hard, and they were, in the majority, past feeling, having given themselves over to lasciviousness and ungodliness. They were hateful, they hated each other, they were very selfish toward each other, and they lived and thought primarily for self alone.

They were without God, they were shackled by sin, and their godless, sinful nature produced selfishness and other fruits of sin. Love is of God, and he who knows not God cannot love, "for *God IS love.*" Everyone who loves in sincerity is born of God and knows God. One who does not know God cannot love in sincerity. "He that dwelleth in love dwelleth in God, and God in him" (I John 4:16).

Paul taught the believers in Thessalonica that since they possessed God, they must demonstrate love one toward another. All believers should love one another. If we do not love our fellow believer whom we have seen, how can we love God whom we have NOT seen?

To the Colossians Paul declared that love is the bond of perfectness. He admonished Timothy, his son in the ministry, that the end of the charge given him by the Holy Ghost, and the charge given to others through him as God's undershepherd, was love out of a pure heart and a pure conscience, and faith unfeigned.

Let me point out here love's connection with the local assembly and the working of the Holy Spirit IN the assembly through pure love. *Love is always in season.* Love is the breath of the church, and the local assembly could not survive *apart* from pure love. However, where love is not the regulating power of the Spirit-gifts and of the spirit of one believer toward another, then there is danger of envy and strife in the local assembly. But where love governs and leads, where love reigns supremely, all else works smoothly and adds up to the edification of the saints and the glory of the Lord God Almighty.

Paul is reminding the believers in Corinth that the gifts are to be regulated by pure love; and if they had forgotten this, then they must remember that if whatever we do is not done in pure love, to the glory of God and the edifying of other believers, it is definitely out of order and should not be in the local assembly.

Paul definitely sets forth the divine truth that *love* displays divine excellency and surpasses all other gifts—even the gifts that edify. Such gifts may be present where there is no pure love; but where love is, and where love rules in the life and ministry of a believer, then the spiritual gifts will be present and will be used to edify other believers and glorify the Lord Jesus Christ. No other gift surpasses love!

The Necessity for Love in Relation to Gifts Bestowed Upon Individual Believers

Verse 1: "Though I speak with the tongues of men and of angels, and have not charity, I am become as sounding brass, or a tinkling cymbal."

It might be interesting to some of my readers to know that I used this chapter as a text for the first sermon I preached—more than twenty-nine years ago at the time of this writing. I felt strangely impressed of the Lord to use this text, and though I do not know just how much *preaching* I did that morning, the Lord blessed me exceedingly; and I trust that others felt, at least in a measure, what I felt as I walked into the pulpit to deliver the first sermon of my ministry. At the time, I did not realize the magnitude of this chapter, but God blessed His Word and honored the efforts of this unworthy minister.

"Though I speak with the tongues of men and of angels, and have not charity (love) . . . ." In other words, "If I speak with all the powers of earthly and heavenly utterance, if I am not possessed by the love of God, if I do not speak in love, then my words, though they be as the words of an angel, are as sounding brass or a tinkling cymbal."

The "IF" (translated *"though"* in the King James version) in the original Greek suggests a possibility connected with the future. Paul realized that he was not immune from the pitfalls and snares of the devil. He therefore declares that if he should attain the ability to speak with the tongues of men and of angels, and yet was not permeated by the love of God, his message would be as sounding brass or the clanging of a cymbal.

In heathen lands, pagan ceremonies and rituals were accompanied by clanging cymbals and the sounding of brass; and even though a minister might speak with the silver tongue of an accomplished orator, his message is no more powerful than that of the pagan ritual if it is not accompanied by the love of God. It is not the tongue that counts — it is the heart. There are many educated ministers today who can prepare and deliver eloquent sermons; but if the heart is not filled with the love of God, the message will be empty and vain.

Verse 2: "And though I have the gift of prophecy, and understand all mysteries, and all knowledge; and though I

have all faith, so that I could remove mountains, and have
not charity, I am nothing."

"*Though I have the gift of prophecy. . . .*" One might
have the ability to *foretell* what will happen in the future,
and to *forthtell* (proclaim) what has happened in the past—
but if the message is not given in love, it is nothing.

". . . *And understand all mysteries . . . .*" There are
many "mysteries" mentioned in the Word of God. In the
New Testament a mystery is not something *mysterious*, but
rather something not known in the Old Testament era but
made known through the perfect law of liberty—great truths
and the divine purpose of God, made known only to believers, made known only by the Holy Spirit.

". . . *And though I have . . . all knowledge. . . .*" We
learned in chapter 12 that knowledge consists of the intelligent apprehension of facts and principles. Paul is saying, "Though I have the gift of all knowledge, and though
I have the gift of intelligent apprehension of all facts concerning the things of God, *even with this extraordinary
knowledge,* if I am yet devoid of love, *I am nothing!*"

"*And though I have all faith, so that I could remove
mountains . . . .*" (In this particular sense, *mountains* represent stupendous difficulties.) Paul is saying, "If I have
faith to overcome all great difficulties and obstacles and
yet have not love, I am nothing—I am of no value at all
to God!"

Paul is not speaking here of *saving* faith; he is speaking of faith that brings supernatural power through which
miracles are performed and stupendous difficulties are overcome. He is saying that even though an individual possesses such faith and yet does not possess love, that
individual is one great spiritual zero—*nothing!* The most
valuable person in the assembly is one who is capable of
loving the deepest and loving the most. Love is the

essence of Christianity, for GOD IS LOVE; and we love Him because He first loved us.

Verse 3: "And though I bestow all my goods to feed the poor, and though I give my body to be burned, and have not charity, it profiteth me nothing."

Paul is pointing out here that self-sacrifice profits not at all unless the sacrifice is made in the love of God. We may give all that we have to buy food to feed the hungry, and that is the *extent* of sacrifice on the part of what we possess; but Paul goes further:

"*Though I give my body to be burned . . .*" — signifying a most painful death. Many pagan worshippers in those days *did* sacrifice their bodies to be burned in devotion to their god; but if a *believer* should give his body to be burned, and yet not do it because of deep love for God, it would profit nothing. The Lord God Almighty is not seeking men to give their bodies to be burned — He is seeking believers who will present their bodies a *living* sacrifice, holy and acceptable unto God, which is the reasonable service of every Christian (Rom. 12:1).

Here is what Paul has said thus far: Even though a person may be able to speak with the silver tongue of an orator or with the tongue of an angel, if the speaker does not have "charity" (love), he is giving out nothing. Whatever he says is empty and void apart from charity.

In the second place, though one may have the gift of prophecy and the ability to understand all mystery; though he may possess all knowledge and have the faith to remove mountains (transcend all difficulties), if he has not charity, he is nothing.

In the third place, if one spends all of his earthly possessions to buy bread to feed hungry people and, in addition to that, presents his body to be burned on the altar in sacrifice, if he does not have charity in his heart, then all else that he may do adds up to exactly nothing.

Paul said, "Without charity I give out nothing; without charity I gain nothing; without charity I *am* nothing!" Regardless of what we may know, accomplish, give, be, or sacrifice, apart from charity it all adds up to NOTHING!

The Characteristics of Charity

Verse 4: "Charity suffereth long, and is kind; charity envieth not; charity vaunteth not itself, is not puffed up."

"*Charity (love) suffereth long, and is kind . . . .*" So far in this chapter, Paul has declared that love is a divine imperative if we would render stewardship that is acceptable to God — and here begins a striking contrast: Paul begins to point out the character and the value of love.

Christians are Christ-like, and Christ was God manifest in flesh. God is love, therefore Jesus was love—divine love in flesh. Jesus was longsuffering, not willing that any should perish; thus, one of the outstanding characteristics of true love is *"longsuffering."* Love suffers long—and is *kind*. True love does not retaliate in haste, is not anxious to punish. Love is kind, considerate—the exact opposite of anger. God is angry with wickedness and sin, but *He loves the sinner*. We have a Saviour because *"God so loved."* (Notice Exodus 34:6; Romans 2:4; I Peter 3:20.)

One who is longsuffering is willing to forbear and be patient. Kindness is the active quality that renders good deeds and bestows benefits upon those who are less fortunate.

"*Charity envieth not; charity vaunteth not itself, is not puffed up.*" Greek authorities tell us that the verb translated "envieth" means not only to envy, but also to be jealous. The same word is translated both ways in the

New Testament. One who *envies* desires to take from his fellowman what he has. *Jealousy* does not necessarily bring about a desire to *take from* one's fellowman; jealousy deals more with emotion, and craves to have the same thing for one's self. Love does not envy, love is not jealous.

"*Charity vaunteth not itself, is not puffed up.*" To "*vaunt*" one's self means to think one's self superior to anyone else. Paul is speaking here of the local church, and in this case it would be a member of the church who feels that he is superior to all other members—in wisdom, knowledge, spirituality, and in other ways.

One who is "puffed up" is one who shows pride and self-esteem. Such is not the spirit of Christ, nor is it a *fruit of the Spirit.* In connection with this, study I Corinthians 4:6,18,19; 5:2; 8:1; Colossians 2:18. These are the only verses in the entire New Testament where this word is used, and in every instance it refers to those in the assembly who are "puffed up," who feel superior to others.

Verse 5: "Doth not behave itself unseemly, seeketh not her own, is not easily provoked, thinketh no evil."

"*Doth not behave itself unseemly . . . .*" Charity does not have bad manners. To behave unseemly is to behave in bad taste, to be just plain ugly, to act like a spoiled child, or, as in the preceding verse, to be "puffed up." We are to be like children *in faith*, but we are to act like men in our treatment of fellow believers. Charity does not behave itself unseemly.

"*Charity . . . seeketh not her own . . . .*" True love does not think of self, does not pursue selfish interests. Jesus declared that the greatest commandment of all is to love God supremely, love Him to the fullest; and the second commandment is like unto it: "Thou shalt love thy neighbour as thyself. On these two commandments hang all the law and the prophets" (Matt. 22:36—40). Love is the very essence of the Christian religion.

Every believer should pray, "Lord, let me live from day to day/ In such a self-forgetful way,/ That even when I kneel to pray/ My prayer shall be for others!" I believe the most unhappy person on the face of the earth is a self-centered, selfish person; and most assuredly a believer cannot enjoy abundant life if he or she is selfish.

"Charity . . . is not easily provoked. . . ." The meaning here is simply, "Charity does not yield to provocation." True love is not stirred to bitterness nor to a spirit of anger when injured—whether intentionally or unintentionally, whether in fact or in imagination. JESUS was true love, and HE said, "Father, forgive them, for they know not what they do." While being stoned to death by the enemies of Jesus Christ, Stephen prayed, "Father, lay not this sin to their charge." Charity is not easily provoked. Charity does not fly into a rage of anger and bitterness when injured.

"Charity . . . thinketh no evil." The Greek word here is *logizomai* and means "to reckon." What the Holy Spirit is actually saying here is, "Love, when injured, does not make a record of the injury in order to pay back at some later time." Love does not harbor resentment, love holds no malice; love *forgives*, even before an apology is offered.

Verse 6: "Rejoiceth not in iniquity, but rejoiceth in the truth."

Love finds no joy in (*over*) the wrong-doing of others; no satisfaction in sin, regardless of who the sinner may be. Love finds satisfaction in *truth*. JESUS is The Truth; Satan is "The Lie." Since Jesus is truth, love *rejoices* in truth. All wrong-doing and unrighteousness is the result of sin and Satan and is the opposite of truth and righteousness; therefore love finds no grounds for rejoicing in anything that is wrong. True love *expresses* itself in truth, and nothing short of righteous conduct can satisfy love. The same can be said of truth. Pure righteousness and pure truth are closely associated: "For the fruit of the Spirit is in all goodness and righteousness and truth" (Eph. 5:9). Also study II Thessalonians 2:5—12.

Verse 7: "Beareth all things, believeth all things, hopeth all things, endureth all things."

The Greek verb translated "to bear" is *stego* and the meaning is "to support that which is placed upon it, or to cover that which is placed underneath it." In this verse it conveys both ideas — that of supporting what is placed upon it, and covering that which is placed beneath it. That which is covered is protected by that which covers it. Love does just this. Love acts in all ways, love bears all things.

"Charity . . . believeth all things." This does not mean that love accepts as truth all that is stated — true love does not believe a lie. But love is ready to see the best, even if an act is unkind or detrimental. True charity avoids undue suspicion; where there is doubt, charity weighs the matter thoroughly before passing judgment, and gives the other individual the benefit of the doubt until the full truth can be known. Thus, "Charity believeth all things."

"Charity . . . hopeth all things, endureth all things." Pure charity delights to always hope and expect the best. Everyone may seemingly be against us, adverse conditions may be all around us; yet in the midst of it all, *charity hopes for the best.* No *singular* thing may seem to be for the best or for God's glory, but love does not deal in singular things: *True love adds up ALL things—* and the answer is for good to those who love God and

are called according to His purpose (Rom. 8:28).

Charity Cannot Fail — Charity Is Permanent — Charity Is the Capstone of the Pyramid of Grace

Verse 8: "Charity never faileth: but whether there be prophecies, they shall fail; whether there be tongues, they shall cease; whether there be knowledge, it shall vanish away."

"*Charity never faileth.*" Here Paul contrasts the eternal with the temporal. Love abides—not only in time, but throughout all eternity. The Greek verb used here for "fail" denotes "to fall"; and that which falls ceases to be active. If something fails, then it ceases to be active in its normal capacity. LOVE will *never* fail, it will never cease to be active. God is love (I John 4:8); and from everlasting to everlasting, God is God — He has always been, He will never *cease* to be (Psalm 90:1,2).

". . . *Whether there be prophecies, they shall fail.*" In our King James Bible we have the words "shall fail," but the Greek word is *katargeo*, which means "done away." This verb more literally means "to reduce to inactivity" (*kata*, down; *argeo*, idle). Therefore, we have here, in understandable language, the divine fact that the time would come when *prophecies* would be reduced to inactivity and would cease to function.

"When that which is perfect is come, then that which is in part shall be done away" (I Cor. 13:10). God spoke to the fathers through the prophets at various times and in various ways; but *in these last days* God has spoken to us by His Son (Heb. 1:1,2). We now have "the perfect law of liberty." We find in our Bible *everything we need to know* about God and things eternal. There is therefore no need for new prophecies today. We have *the complete written Word of God.*

God has been silent for more than 1900 years. He

speaks today only through His Word. Why? Let me give you this brief outline, and you study it thoroughly. You will be blessed for doing it.

1.   *In Genesis 3:15* the virgin birth of the Lord Jesus Christ ("the seed of the woman") was prophesied. In *Galatians 4:4* we find the fulfillment of this prophecy."When the fulness of the time was come," God did exactly what He promised Adam He would do.

2.   *In Genesis 12:2,3* God revealed to Abraham that he would be the head of the nation with which God would be identified, and through the seed of Abraham the Saviour would be born. In *Acts 3:25* we have the fulfillment of that prophecy.

3.   *In Genesis 49:10* God revealed to Jacob that Jesus would be of the tribe of Judah. In *John 4:22* we read, "Salvation is of the Jews." Thus the prophecy was fulfilled, for *Jesus was of the Jews.*

4.   *In II Samuel 7:12—14* it was foretold that the Saviour would come through the lineage of David. That prophecy was fulfilled in *Luke 1:32*. Gabriel announced to Mary that her Son would sit on the throne of David.

5.   *In Micah 5:2* we have the revelation concerning the birthplace of Jesus. In *Luke 2:4* we find the fulfillment: Jesus was born in Bethlehem as prophesied.

6.   *In Malachi 3:1* it was revealed that Jesus would have a forerunner. In *Matthew 3:1* the fulfillment of that prophecy is recorded: "In those days came John the Baptist," the forerunner of the Lamb of God.

7.   *In Zechariah 11:12* we read the exact price for which Jesus would be sold—thirty pieces of silver, the price of a slave. In *Matthew 26:14,15* Jesus was sold by Judas for exactly thirty pieces of silver.

8.   *In Zechariah 9:9* we read that the Saviour would ride

into Jerusalem on a young donkey. In *Luke 19:29–37* Jesus rode into the city of Jerusalem exactly as prophesied.

9.   To the Psalmist, God revealed the manner of the death of Jesus on the cross (*Psalm 22:16*), and that not one bone of His body would be broken (*Psalm 34:20*). We know that Jesus did die on the cross as prophesied, and *John 19:36* gives the fulfillment of the prophecy that His bones would not be broken. To the Psalmist it was also revealed that Jesus would come back from the dead (*Psalm 16:10*).

What more does God NEED to reveal to man? He has made known every minute detail of His provision, His presentation, and His finished work of redemption in Jesus Christ. We need no new prophecies today; we do not need new revelations. We are saved by God's grace through faith; we overcome the world by faith, we are kept by faith, we live by faith; and "whatsoever is not of faith is sin." Prophecies have therefore ceased — they have become "inactive."

"Whether there be tongues, they shall cease." I feel that any person who will be open-minded and allow the Holy Spirit to speak to his heart can see without comment exactly what these words mean. They are easily understood. We will discuss tongues further in chapter 14.

"Whether there be knowledge, it shall vanish away." It does not appear that knowledge is a "sign-gift" such as tongues, prophecy, and healing. Unlike prophecy, knowledge is not the result of a revelation given by supernatural power, although it is true that God can bestow upon a person *the ability to acquire* knowledge. No one could truly prophesy apart from supernatural power, but knowledge can be acquired.

Knowledge enables one to teach. In our next chapter Paul asks, "Now, brethren, if I come unto you speaking with tongues, what shall I profit you, except I shall speak to you either by revelation, OR BY KNOWLEDGE, or by prophesying, or by doctrine?'' (I Cor. 14:6).

In other words, knowledge could be acquired by individual believers through instruction given by Paul or some other apostle, and therefore *knowledge* did not depend upon the faith once delivered to the saints, nor upon the completion of the Scriptures.

Concerning things spiritual, all true knowledge *since the completion* of the Word of God is derived from the Word of God, whether that knowledge be obtained by the individual believer through personally reading and studying the Bible, or through hearing the preacher or teacher. But one day even knowledge will cease — when we see Him we will have the perfect mind of Christ.

Verses 9 and 10: "For we know in part, and we prophesy in part. But when that which is perfect is come, then that which is in part shall be done away."

In the original Greek, the emphasis is upon *"in part,"* referring to the temporary nature and partial scope of the supernatural gifts named in verse 8. *Charity* will never cease, it will never fail; but these *supernatural* gifts named WILL fail because they are only "in part."

"That which is perfect" refers to the Word of God in its completion. When the faith "once delivered unto the saints" (Jude 3) had come, fully and completely, when the Scriptures were completed (all sixty-six books of the Word of God) then nothing could be added. God's Word is PERFECT.

"So then faith cometh by hearing, and hearing by the Word of God" (Rom. 10:17). If an unbeliever will not trust Jesus through hearing the Word, there is nothing else that can be added or done to *cause* that person to believe. Saving faith can come only by hearing the Word. Regardless of what one may see, feel, or experience, if he does not exercise faith in the finished work of Jesus he cannot be saved.

Woe unto the man who tampers with the Word of God. Nothing can be added to the Word, nothing can be taken away. If any person adds to or takes from the Word, he will suffer eternal destruction for so doing.

We do not need "signs" in this glorious day of grace, in this day when we have *that which is perfect.* "Whosoever will" can be saved by hearing, believing, and receiving the finished work of Jesus as declared in the written Word. We believe what God says in His Word simply because He IS God, and God cannot lie (Heb. 6:18; Titus 1:2). Anyone who hears the Word and *refuses to believe* what God says, thereby calls God a liar: ". . . He that believeth not God hath made Him a liar; because he believeth not the record that God gave of His Son" (I John 5:10).

Verse 11: "When I was a child, I spake as a child, I understood as a child, I thought as a child: but when I became a man, I put away childish things."

(*"I understood as a child"* in the Greek reads, "I *felt* as a child.") Notice three things stated here: "I spake . . . I felt . . . I thought."

"But when I became a man, I put away childish things." Paul illustrates here *the bringing in* of "that which is perfect." The tense of the Greek verb signifies results that are abiding. The Greek verb translated "I have put away" is the same verb used in verses 8 and 10—meaning "reduced to inactivity." That is, the "sign-gifts" which were present during the transition period and the apostolic age have been *reduced to inactivity.*

I want no one to misunderstand what I am saying. *I am not saying* that God does not heal the sick, nor that He does not work miracles — the greatest miracle any person will ever see is the conversion of a sinner. When an unbeliever believes unto salvation and becomes a new creature in Christ Jesus by faith in His shed blood, *THAT is a miracle!* But what I am saying is that such gifts as are spoken of in Hebrews 2:3,4 have been reduced to inactivity:

"... *God also bearing them witness, both with SIGNS AND WONDERS, and with DIVERS MIRACLES, AND GIFTS OF THE HOLY GHOST, according to His own will.*" During the first days of Christianity, God gave signs, wonders, divers miracles, gifts of the Holy Ghost; and through these, God was bearing the apostles witness. I repeat — WE do not NEED signs, we do not need "divers miracles," because *we walk by faith!* We have "that which is perfect." What we need to know, we find recorded in God's Holy Word, and we *believe* it because God cannot lie.

Verse 12: "For now we see through a glass, darkly; but then face to face: now I know in part; but then shall I know even as also I am known."

This verse applies the spiritual principles set forth in verse 10 to the future state of perfection of the Church when it is presented to Christ without spot or wrinkle (Eph. 5:25–30); but the truth declared here also refers to the transition period and the first days of Christianity when gifts of tongues, prophecy, healings, and divers miracles were in force. It points to that time as "partial vision," but now that we have the complete Word of God, we have "*clear* vision."

"... *Now we see through a glass, darkly....*" The King James version says, "in a *glass,*" but the original Greek reads, "in a *mirror.*" The Greek adverb translated "now" is *arti* and means "up to the immediate present," that is, up to the very moment Paul was writing this letter. The Greek preposition here translated "in" is *dia,* meaning "by means of," that is, *by means of a mirror.* Thus,

Paul is saying, "By means of a mirror, up to this present moment we see darkly; but when that which is perfect is come, we will see clearly, as face to face."

To see one in a mirror is not to see a person as he really is. The mirror portrays an imperfect vision as compared with seeing the individual face to face. The Greek word translated "darkly" means "in an *enigma*—a sort of riddle." Paul might have been thinking here of Numbers 12:8: "With him will I speak mouth to mouth, even apparently, and not in dark speeches; and the similitude of the Lord shall he behold: wherefore then were ye not afraid to speak against my servant Moses?"

". . . *But then face to face.*" When we look into the Word of God, we are speaking face to face with God because the Word IS God. The believer possesses the Holy Ghost, and the Word of God was *dictated* by the Holy Ghost, and penned down by holy men of old (II Pet. 1:21). The Holy Ghost then is our Teacher, and we CAN know the deep things of God: ". . . God hath revealed them unto us by His Spirit: for the Spirit searcheth all things, yea, the deep things of God" (I Cor. 2:10).

". . . The anointing which ye have received of Him abideth in you, *and ye need not that any man teach you:* but as the same anointing teacheth you of all things, and is truth, and is no lie, and even as it hath taught you, ye shall abide in Him" (I John 2:27).

The believer need no longer know "in part." The complete Word of God is come, and the believer can see and speak face to face with God in the Word.

"*Now I know in part; but then shall I know even as also I am known.*" The truth set forth here gives us a further and final illustration of the divine principles set forth in verse 10. There is a definite distinction between the two Greek verbs here translated "know." The first is *ginosko*; the second is a compound verb, *epignosko*, which means "to know in full."

Paul is actually saying, "At the present, I am in the process of knowing, but I only know in part. Then, when that which is perfect is come, I shall know fully, even as I am fully known." We can (and we should) fully know God through "that which is perfect"—His holy Word.

I am sure that verse 10 also points to the fulness of our salvation. We are redeemed *now*; we are children of God *now*; and we are just as saved from the penalty of sin as we will *ever* be saved from sin's penalty. We are dead, and our lives are hid with Christ in God. Even NOW we sit together in heavenly places in Christ Jesus, and we are daily being saved from the *power* of sin through Christ our Mediator. In the by-and-by, when the Church is complete and the Rapture takes place, we will be saved from the very *presence* of sin — and *then our salvation will be perfect!*

NOW we have the perfect Word of God, and in the perfect Word we can know God perfectly and become full-grown spiritually. But our *salvation* will not know its completeness or its divine fulness until we see Jesus face to face. NOW we know in part, but THEN we will have the mind of Christ. We will have *perfect knowledge.*

Verse 13: "And now abideth faith, hope, charity, these three; but the greatest of these is charity."

The word "now" is not relating to *time*, but is a logical expression meaning "bringing the entire argument to a conclusion." The same word means "as you see," or "considering everything." Thus we have, "After adding up all things and taking all things into consideration, *the conclusion is*" that faith, hope, and charity abide — they abide in the bosom of every believer.

"*. . . But the greatest of these is CHARITY.*" Faith,

hope, and charity are Bible triplets. All three abide *eternally*; they are not limited to life on earth. Charity (love) is the heart of Christianity. This tremendous chapter opens with the declaration that though we may speak with the tongues of men and of angels, though we possess the gifts of prophecy, the understanding of mysteries, and all knowledge, and faith to move mountains, *if we have not love*, we are nothing!

The chapter closes with the declaration that "now abideth faith, hope, and charity, these three — but the GREATEST of these is charity." Charity is greatest because: "GOD is love," and all true love originates in God and proceeds from God. No person really knows love, nor how to love truly, until he knows God. Yes, "The greatest of these is LOVE."

CHAPTER FOURTEEN

1. Follow after charity, and desire spiritual gifts, but rather that ye may prophesy.

2. For he that speaketh in an unknown tongue speaketh not unto men, but unto God: for no man understandeth him; howbeit in the spirit he speaketh mysteries.

3. But he that prophesieth speaketh unto men to edification, and exhortation, and comfort.

4. He that speaketh in an unknown tongue edifieth himself; but he that prophesieth edifieth the church.

5. I would that ye all spake with tongues, but rather that ye prophesied: for greater is he that prophesieth than he that speaketh with tongues, except he interpret, that the church may receive edifying.

6. Now, brethren, if I come unto you speaking with tongues, what shall I profit you, except I shall speak to you either by revelation, or by knowledge, or by prophesying, or by doctrine?

7. And even things without life giving sound, whether pipe or harp, except they give a distinction in the sounds, how shall it be known what is piped or harped?

8. For if the trumpet give an uncertain sound, who shall prepare himself to the battle?

9. So likewise ye, except ye utter by the tongue words easy to be understood, how shall it be known what is spoken? for ye shall speak into the air.

10. There are, it may be, so many kinds of voices in the world, and none of them is without signification.

11. Therefore if I know not the meaning of the voice, I shall be unto him that speaketh a barbarian, and he that speaketh shall be a barbarian unto me.

12. Even so ye, forasmuch as ye are zealous of spiritual gifts, seek that ye may excel to the edifying of the church.

13. Wherefore let him that speaketh in an unknown tongue pray that he may interpret.

14. For if I pray in an unknown tongue, my spirit prayeth, but my understanding is unfruitful.

15. What is it then? I will pray with the spirit, and I will pray with the understanding also: I will sing with the spirit, and I will sing with the understanding also.

16. Else when thou shalt bless with the spirit, how shall he that occupieth the room of the unlearned say Amen at thy giving of thanks, seeing he understandeth not what thou sayest?

17. For thou verily givest thanks well, but the other is not edified.

18. I thank my God, I speak with tongues more than ye all:

19. Yet in the church I had rather speak five words with my understanding, that by my voice I might teach others also, than ten thousand words in an unknown tongue.

20. Brethren, be not children in understanding: howbeit in malice be ye children, but in understanding be men.

21. In the law it is written, With men of other tongues and other lips will I speak unto this people; and yet for all that will they not hear me, saith the Lord.

22. Wherefore tongues are for a sign, not to them that believe, but to them that believe not: but prophesying serveth not for them that believe not, but for them which believe.

23. If therefore the whole church be come together into one place, and all speak with tongues, and there come in those that are unlearned, or unbelievers, will they not say that ye are mad?

24. But if all prophesy, and there come in one that believeth not, or one unlearned, he is convinced of all, he is judged of all:

25. And thus are the secrets of his heart made manifest; and so falling down on his face he will worship God, and report that God is in you of a truth.

26. How is it then, brethren? when ye come together, every one of you hath a psalm, hath a doctrine, hath a tongue, hath a revelation, hath an interpretation. Let all things be done unto edifying.

27. If any man speak in an unknown tongue, let it be by two, or at the most by three, and that by course; and let one interpret.

28. But if there be no interpreter, let him keep silence in the church; and let him speak to himself, and to God.

29. Let the prophets speak two or three, and let the other judge.

30. If any thing be revealed to another that sitteth by, let the first hold his peace.

31. For ye may all prophesy one by one, that all may learn, and all may be comforted.

32. And the spirits of the prophets are subject to the prophets.

33. For God is not the author of confusion, but of peace, as in all churches of the saints.

34. Let your women keep silence in the churches: for it is not permitted unto them to speak; but they are commanded to be under obedience, as also saith the law.

35. And if they will learn any thing, let them ask their husbands at home: for it is a shame for women to speak in the church.

36. What? came the word of God out from you? or came it unto you only?

37. If any man think himself to be a prophet, or spiritual, let him acknowledge that the things that I write unto you are the commandments of the Lord.

38. But if any man be ignorant, let him be ignorant.

39. Wherefore, brethren, covet to prophesy, and forbid not to speak with tongues.

40. Let all things be done decently and in order.

In this chapter, Paul brings to a climax the subject of spiritual gifts. When love is made the main object and pursuit of the believer's life, love will regulate the use and exercise of any and all special gifts bestowed upon that individual. In chapter 13, Paul shows that love gives character and conduct to the individual. In *this* chapter, he sets forth the truth that the *influence* of love places true value and correct *use* upon all spiritual gifts. Thus, love is the center and heart of all that has to do with spirituality and spiritual gifts.

Prophecy — Greatest of the Gifts

Verse 1: "Follow after charity, and desire spiritual gifts, but rather that ye may prophesy."

We are commanded in the outset of this chapter to *"follow after charity."* The second command is that we *"desire spiritual gifts,"* with which prophesying and speaking in tongues are compared. The reason we are commanded to follow after charity is *"that ye may PROPHESY"*—which, according to the Word of God, is superior to the gift of tongues. In Paul's day, the prophet was not just a minister. He was inspired of the Holy Ghost, and through him God gave revelation relating to the believer and the local assembly. This continued until the New Testament was completed.

During the infant days of the Church, God gave His prophets revelations having to do with the new dispensation—the Dispensation of Grace; but now, *since that which is perfect is come*, there is no reason for new revelations. All that we need to know about God, eternity, and things having to do with God and ourselves, is recorded in our Bible.

Today the prophet is one who forthtells what has been foretold. God is not anointing men today to give new revelations, because that which is perfect *has been revealed* and there ARE no new revelations. But God does call and anoint men to forthtell—to give out the good news of the grace of God and salvation by grace, to tell of the *keeping* power of Jesus, and of the blessed hope of the Church and the individual believer.

Verse 2: "For he that speaketh in an unknown tongue speaketh not unto men, but unto God: for no man understandeth him; howbeit in the spirit he speaketh mysteries."

The original Greek does not say "an *unknown* tongue." It says simply, "He that speaketh in a *tongue*." The genuine gift of tongues was the supernatural gift of speaking in another language without its having been learned. This verse makes it clear that he who speaks in a tongue, unless the tongue is interpreted, would be speaking "not unto men, but unto God." The same is true in verse 14 where Paul refers to *praying* in a tongue. He would edify *himself alone* unless he interpreted, in which case his interpretation would have the same value as the superior gift of prophesying.

The gift of tongues, though a dangerous gift, was highly coveted in the Corinthian church, and the person who possessed this gift was very likely to develop a certain spiritual pride in such possession. Also, the very desire TO possess the gift of tongues could produce a kind of self-hypnotism, a deliberately-induced hysteria which issued forth in a synthetic, completely false and deluded speaking with tongues.

The Greek word translated "understandeth" in the original means "heareth with understanding." Therefore, if a believer speaks in a tongue he is addressing God, and other believers do not hear nor understand him. For that reason, he is not to speak in a tongue unless there is someone present to interpret what is being said. We will study this a little later in the chapter.

". . . *Howbeit in the spirit he speaketh mysteries.*" The believer who speaks in a tongue without interpreting "speaketh mysteries," and the language being unknown, "no one heareth"; no one understands.

It is not God's will in this dispensation for mysteries to *remain* mysteries; they are to be revealed. To the Apostle Paul, God revealed the mystery of the *grace of God* — how Jew and Gentile, bond and free, *are all in one body* by grace. The Divine intention in mysteries in this day is that they be revealed. Therefore, if there is no one present to interpret, the believer who speaks in a tongue speaks a mystery, and this should not be.

Verse 3: "But he that prophesieth speaketh unto men to edification, and exhortation, and comfort."

In other words, *he who prophesies* speaks words that are addressed to fellow believers. He who prophesies speaks words that bring results, for through his speaking, believers are edified, comforted, and consoled. The command of Jesus to Peter was, "Feed my lambs; feed my sheep." Paul's exhortation to young Timothy was, *"Preach the Word!* Be instant in season, out of season; reprove, rebuke, exhort with all longsuffering and doctrine" (II Tim. 4:2). The good minister preaches the Word of God, as Paul instructs, "in words easy to be understood" (verse 9).

The minister who is ordained of God and who preaches in the Spirit, will deliver messages that edify—(edification develops Christian character). God's minister also delivers messages that encourage believers—(encouragement stimulates the will). God's minister preaches sermons that are *consoling*—(consolation strengthens the spirit of the individual believer) — and God the Father knows believers need to be edified, encouraged, and consoled, especially in these perilous times.

"Prophesying," as it was in the days of Paul, has given way to *teaching* in this day and hour. We find Bible proof of this in I Peter 2:1,2: "Wherefore laying aside all malice, and all guile, and hypocrisies, and envies, and all evil speakings, as newborn babes, desire the sincere milk of the Word, that ye may grow thereby."

The Word is MILK to the babes in Christ, MEAT to those who are growing into spiritual maturity, and BREAD to those who are spiritually hungry. Therefore, we need no new spiritual rations. The perfect diet ("that which is perfect") has come, and we need no new revelations or prophecies. God's minister has a perfect diet with which to feed his parishioners.

Verse 4: "He that speaketh in an unknown tongue edifieth himself; but he that prophesieth edifieth the Church."

If a man speaks in a tongue that he understands not, he may be enriching his own spiritual experience, but he is not enriching the souls of others. Therefore, Paul here attempts to show the Corinthian believers that whatever is done in the assembly must be done to benefit *the entire assembly*, not just one individual. Whatever we do must be done, first of all, to glorify God; but in glorifying God *we also edify and bless our fellow Christians*. Since all born again people belong to the body of Christ, all that we do should be done to edify the entire Church. We should not do anything for selfish reasons — and he who speaks in a tongue in the church IS selfish because while he may be edifying himself, unless he uses an interpreter no one else is edified by what he says because no one else *understands* what is said.

"*. . . But he that prophesieth edifieth the Church.*" The teacher, the preacher, or the evangelist, *speaking from the Word of God*, edifies all believers, because when he gives out the Word of God he is literally giving out milk, meat, and bread. The Word of God will not return void; it will accomplish that whereunto God sends it. The true prophet (preacher) always preaches *the Word*.

Verse 5: "I would that ye all spake with tongues, but rather that ye prophesied: for greater is he that prophesieth than he that speaketh with tongues, except he interpret, that the Church may receive edifying."

The first desire here expressed by the Apostle does not indicate by any means that speaking with tongues was a gift to remain permanently in the Church. The circumstances at Corinth were within the period limited to the use of sign-gifts (or the transition period), while the Scriptures were not yet completed and God was still dealing with His earthly people in that manner.

Paul makes it plain that prophecy is to be desired and preferred over and above the gift of tongues, because prophecy is more useful in the assembly; *prophecy* edifies ALL the Church. The truth here clearly implies that a man may speak in a tongue or another language without even *himself* knowing what he is saying (verse 14). Paul wanted all of the believers in Corinth to be spiritually minded and dedicated — remember, some were carnal and the assembly was divided. He said, "I feed you with *milk* when you should be eating *meat*." He wanted them all to be strong in the Lord, spiritually capable of speaking with tongues but also capable of interpreting, thus edifying the Church through prophecy—not *foretelling*, but simply *giving out* the Word of God. If they spoke with tongues and also had the gift of interpreting, they would edify the entire church; but if they did not have someone present to interpret, then they should speak words easy to understand so that the whole assembly would be edified.

Jesus said to His disciples, "The harvest truly is plenteous, but the labourers are few; Pray ye therefore the Lord of the harvest, that He will send forth labourers into His harvest" (Matt. 9:37,38).

In John 4:35 Jesus said, "Say not ye, There are yet four months, and then cometh harvest? Behold, I say unto you, Lift up your eyes, and look on the fields; for they are white already to harvest!"

Please note that Jesus did not instruct His disciples to *seek* the gift of tongues (nor *any other gift*, for that matter). *He instructed them to make known the Gospel story of salvation in the finished work of the Lamb of God.* "The fields are white, the labourers are few, the need is very great. So preach the Word to every creature, teaching them to observe all things whatsoever I have commanded you." Therefore, *He who prophesies (preaches, teaches, or evangelizes) is GREATER than he who speaks with tongues!*

Verse 6: "Now, brethren, if I come unto you speaking with tongues, what shall I profit you, except I shall speak

444

to you either by revelation, or by knowledge, or by prophesying, or by doctrine?"

The Greek word translated "now" is not relative to time, but is used as a logical conclusion, and might be better expressed by our word "really." Thus the opening phrase of this verse would read, *"Really,* brethren, if I come unto you. . . ." Paul here gives reasons why speaking with tongues in the assembly is unprofitable. In Paul's day, before "that which is perfect" had come, God was bearing witness with signs, wonders, divers miracles, and gifts of the Holy Ghost "according to His own will" (Heb. 2:4). Revelation and spiritual knowledge were received in those days as supernatural gifts by the minister whom God ordained to give out His revelations and make known spiritual truths (which were not then recorded, because the New Testament was not yet complete).

Teaching and preaching were external manifestations of the internal knowledge and revelation God had given to the minister. Revelation from God *always precedes* prophesying. True spiritual knowledge—definitely a gift from God through the Spirit—precedes true Bible teaching. No person can teach the Word of God simply from the standpoint of human knowledge, wisdom, or understanding. Real Bible teaching is definitely a gift from God, and the knowledge to teach is ours through the Holy Ghost.

Paul is saying here, "Really, brethren, if I come to you speaking with tongues, what will YOU be profited? Will you be *edified*? Will you be *exhorted* or *comforted*? Unless I shall speak by revelation, by knowledge, by prophesying, or by doctrine, will you be profited?" (*Doctrine* here is the faith once delivered unto the saints, as in Jude 3.)

Any person who delivers to an assembly a message that does not edify or profit the assembly, is definitely out of order. Anything done in the assembly which does not contribute to the spiritual growth of the believers IN the assembly is contrary to New Testament procedure. A pastor should be very cautious in securing speakers for a missionary conference, a revival, a Bible conference, or for any special occasions where someone else fills his pulpit. He should never allow any man in his pulpit until he knows the exact doctrine of that man, because the true pastor is God's undershepherd and must at all cost keep the wolves out of the flock. He will have to give an account to God for who he allows in his pulpit.

Verse 7: "And even things without life giving sound, whether pipe or harp, except they give a distinction in the sounds, how shall it be known what is piped or harped?"

Paul uses an understandable illustration here to confirm his reason given against the use of tongues in the assembly. He speaks of musical instruments. Whether brass or strings, each instrument must give a distinct tone of melody if the music is to be understood. If the instruments give out sound with no distinction, just a conglomeration of notes, then how shall the listeners appreciate what is being played on the instruments? Such music is of no value, it edifies no one, it blesses no one. It is simply an unharmonious mixture of notes that make *noise*, not music.

Verse 8: "For if the trumpet give an uncertain sound, who shall prepare himself to the battle?"

Here, Paul uses an even stronger illustration, pointing out the trumpet or bugle. The Greek word translated "uncertain" means "lacking in clearness, indistinct." If the soldier is to understand the message from the trumpet, then the trumpet must give a distinct signal that differs from all other sounds—a sound that calls men to battle. If the trumpet does not give the correct signal, it misses the intended effect upon the soldier.

When we deliver the Word of God, we must not give an uncertain sound; we must not deliver a message that lacks in clearness. All who speak in the assembly should speak words that make clear the meaning of what the speaker is saying. There must be no uncertainty in the message. *The Word of God* is clear and to the point, and the minister who tells forth the Word must speak clearly, in words easily understood.

Verse 9: "So likewise ye, except ye utter by the tongue words easy to be understood, how shall it be known what is spoken? For ye shall speak into the air."

"*The tongue*" here does not mean the *gift* of tongues, but the physical organ. When a believer stands in the assembly to give testimony or deliver a message, that message should not be delivered merely to impress the listeners, but rather to edify, encourage, and strengthen them. The speaker should never use big, highsounding words, because in so doing he speaks "*into the air*," and the hearers are neither blessed nor edified.

I say this in love: I have never been able to understand why some preachers take great pains to prepare sermons, using highsounding words and flowery phrases, when JESUS, the greatest Preacher, the greatest Teacher, who ever lived illustrated His sermons in simple words like "water. . .bread. . .light. . .sparrows. . .lilies. . .the sower. . .the seed"—words that everyone uses and that even a child can understand. One need not use a dictionary to look up the meaning of any word Jesus ever used, in preaching or in prayer.

The minister who is led by the Spirit has no desire to use highsounding words. He uses simple, down-to-earth words that make his message plain and clear, a message that can be understood and received by those who hear it.

447

When God's preacher speaks "into the air," no eternal good is accomplished. God is not glorified, the Church is not blessed, and that preacher's ministry is empty and vain. The same can be said of the Sunday school teacher, and of all who deliver messages or testimonies in the assembly.

Verse 10: "There are, it may be, so many kinds of voices in the world, and none of them is without signification."

"Voices" here means languages. There are many languages and dialects. *"It may be"* (or "perhaps") points out that the exact number of languages is immaterial. There are many, many languages, not one of which is unintelligible, for every language on earth is understood by those who speak it. But to a *Greek*, an address in a foreign language is of no value, and is no more than gibberish to him. This holds true in the Church. Unless there be an interpreter, he who speaks in an "unknown" tongue does not know what he is saying, nor do those who listen; and the voice of language is useless.

Verse 11: "Therefore if I know not the meaning of the voice, I shall be unto him that speaketh a barbarian, and he that speaketh shall be a barbarian unto me."

The "barbarian" was one in Corinth who could not speak Greek. Naturally, those who could not speak Greek, and the Greeks who could not speak other languages, could not carry on an intelligent or profitable conversation with each other. Ignorance of another's language is an almost insurmountable barrier to fellowship. How then could fellowship be maintained in an assembly where tongues were exercised for display and without an interpreter? No one would be edified or blessed, and Jesus would not be glorified. Nothing should be allowed in the assembly that would hinder fellowship among believers.

I know the hindrance of a language barrier, because I have personally preached many times through interpreters on the mission field. In the jungles of Ecuador, South America, I spoke through *two* interpreters. I spoke in English, the missionary repeated my message in the language of the people to whom he ministered, and then a native translated the message into Indian dialect. It is difficult to preach through an interpreter, and it is nothing short of a miracle when people are converted through the Gospel message delivered by way of TWO interpreters. I am deeply grateful for God's promise that His Word will not return unto Him void.

Verse 12: "Even so ye, forasmuch as ye are zealous of spiritual gifts, seek that ye may excel to the edifying of the Church."

It is not wrong to desire spiritual gifts nor to be zealous for the Lord and covet *the best gifts*, as Paul has already pointed out; but the desire for these spiritual gifts must be with the motive to encourage believers, and to edify the Church, and to glorify God.

We must not covet spiritual gifts for self-esteem or self-gratification, nor from the standpoint of being superior to others. Whatever is done in the assembly must be for the benefit and welfare of everyone IN the assembly. All ministry, preaching, teaching, or exhorting must be to the spiritual edification of all believers present.

Verse 13: "Wherefore let him that speaketh in an unknown tongue pray that he may interpret."

If any individual did speak in tongues in the assembly, he should pray that he might be able to interpret what he said, therefore making known to all the assembly what he had uttered in a tongue. Paul is speaking here of private devotions – the individual who speaks with a tongue should pray earnestly *at home*, that when he does exercise the gift of tongues he may be able to interpret what he has said in order that all may benefit. This has nothing to do with *praying* in tongues, referred to in our next verse.

Verse 14: "For if I pray in an unknown tongue, my spirit prayeth, but my understanding is unfruitful."

Paul makes it clear that if he prays in the assembly in a tongue, his spirit prays, but his understanding is unfruitful. He may have had private delight in the exercise of the gift, but there was no spiritual benefit for anyone. The assembly does not profit from such a prayer, and it is not right to pray in public if no one is blessed, edified, or encouraged through that prayer.

Keep in mind that Paul is here giving instruction concerning tongues in the public worship service of the local assembly. If one is in his private prayer closet, and such burden possesses the heart that the individual prays in a tongue, certainly there would be nothing against such praying, because "the Spirit itself maketh intercession for us with groanings which cannot be uttered" (Rom. 8:26). If we pray in a genuine tongue and not in self-induced hysteria, it is the Spirit praying; but even the individual does not understand. The Spirit knows the burden, the Spirit knows HOW to pray when we do not know how, and when we do not know what we should pray for.

Verse 15: "What is it then? I will pray with the spirit, and I will pray with the understanding also: I will sing with the spirit, and I will sing with the understanding also."

What Paul is saying here is this: "The spirit (which is the highest element of the individual) and the understanding (which is the reasoning faculty of the individual) are to cooperate—in singing, praying, teaching, or preaching, which we see have their rightful place in the assembly. Whether a man is praying, singing, or speaking in the assembly, he must do it not only with his spirit, but with his mind. *He* must know what is going on, and others must be able to understand it.

Verse 16: "Else when thou shalt bless with the spirit, how shall he that occupieth the room of the unlearned say Amen at thy giving of thanks, seeing he understandeth not what thou sayest?"

Paul goes a step further in his attempt to show the believers in Corinth exactly what they were to do in the assembly in regard to speaking, praying, or singing in a tongue that could not be understood by the group in the assembly. The meaning of the Greek word translated "bless" is simply to offer praise to God, and if the individual believer offered praise to God with the spirit but not with the understanding, how could others in the assembly say "Amen!" when they did not understand the meaning of the tongue used when thanksgiving was made to God?

"The unlearned" refers to those without understanding—that is, unless someone interpreted the tongue, they could not know what was going on. Evidently the assembly at Corinth believed in saying "Amen!" Paul here follows the practice of God's chosen people Israel in this matter:

"And Benaiah the son of Jehoiada answered the king, and said, *Amen:* The Lord God of my lord the king say so too" (I Kings 1:36).

"Blessed be the Lord God of Israel for ever and ever. And all the people said, *Amen,* and praised the Lord" (I Chron. 16:36).

"Blessed be the Lord God of Israel from everlasting to everlasting: and let all the people say, *Amen.* Praise ye the Lord" (Psalm 106:48).

When someone in the assembly at Corinth gave thanks

and blessed God, Paul wanted all believers to be edified, strengthened, and at the end of the thanksgiving, be able to say *"Amen!"* But if the one giving thanks did so in a tongue, then the assembly would not know whether to say "Amen."

"And the four beasts said, *Amen*! And the four and twenty elders fell down and worshipped Him that liveth for ever and ever" (Rev. 5:14).

"And the four and twenty elders and the four beasts fell down and worshipped God that sat on the throne, saying, *Amen*! *Alleluia*!" (Rev. 19:4).

Christians who do not believe in a little emotion in the assembly on earth have my heartfelt sympathy when they reach heaven! I do not advocate fanaticism or foolishness in God's house; but words of praise are always in order if the Spirit is present and the congregation is blessed.

One reason so many people have dropped out of church in our day is because of dead, formalistic, cut-and-dried services. Where there is life, there is activity. There is very little activity in a cemetery, and I am afraid some of our churches today are spiritual graveyards. May God help us to realize what we possess when we know Jesus! It is definitely in order to praise God. Let all believers "praise ye the Lord" in words easily understood.

Verse 17: "For thou verily givest thanks well, but the other is not edified."

Paul is very careful to assure the believers in Corinth that he is not against speaking in a tongue—*if the speaker is possessed of the Holy Ghost* and is not acting in the energy of the flesh, for his own satisfaction and self-gratification. If one speaks in a tongue to the glory of God, if all the church is blessed and edified, then Paul says, "Amen!" But if only the one giving thanks is

452

blessed and edified, that is selfish; because one person is only a very small part of the assembly—one of many members. The gift is wonderful — but if those who listen cannot know what is being said, if they cannot say "Amen," then the purpose of the thanksgiving is missed altogether.

Verse 18: "I thank my God, I speak with tongues more than ye all."

So Paul did not deny that the gift of tongues existed. No one could say to him that it was a case of "sour grapes," for he possessed the gift more than anyone else. I think the one thing we need to learn from this statement is that those in the local assembly who possess the greatest gifts, those who are most spiritual, dedicated, and gifted, are the ones who advertise it the least. To parade one's gifts and abilities completely spoils the usefulness of such gifts and frustrates the results that could be attained. There is no place in the Christian religion for pride. Jesus Christ was the most humble personality who ever walked on this earth, and we are to follow in His steps. We are to demonstrate His spirit in our daily living.

Verse 19: "Yet in the church I had rather speak five words with my understanding, that by my voice I might teach others also, than ten thousand words in an unknown tongue."

Some outstanding Bible scholars believe that Paul is not only thinking here of the *supernatural gift* of tongues. This man Paul spoke *many languages.* It is not recorded just how many languages Paul *did* speak, but he was one of the best educated men of his day and he was undoubtedly an accomplished linguist.

I believe that Paul spoke tongues not only in the assembly, but elsewhere. Seemingly he used the gift of tongues outside the assembly much more than IN the assembly, because he said that *in the church*, before his fellow believers, he had rather speak *five* words that would be understood than to speak *ten thousand* words that would NOT be understood.

When we divide five into ten thousand, we see the percentage here. Therefore I cannot see why some precious preachers spend more time talking about tongues than they spend in expounding the grace of God! They spend more time inviting people to seek the gift of tongues than they spend in altar calls inviting people to be saved by God's grace, through faith.

It seems to me that when some precious ministers read verses 18 and 19 of this chapter, they would re-work some of their sermons. Paul, in his own words, excelled "more than ye all," but he desired to edify each believer— both when he spoke in the assembly, and when he prayed publicly.

Verse 20: "Brethren, be not children in understanding: howbeit in malice be ye children, but in understanding be men."

It is not difficult to understand what Paul is saying here: "*Brethren* (born again believers), *do not be children in mind. Do not THINK as a child.*" A child likes to be noticed, likes to be in the limelight. It is natural for children to desire praise; but it is *unnatural* for a full-grown adult to act in such a way. Paul here rebukes the pride of intelligence. A person whose heart is right will not be puffed up with pride, even though he may be far above average in intelligence. He will not demonstrate self-satisfaction and selfishness toward his fellowman.

The Greek word translated "*be not*" literally means "cease to be." Some of the believers in the church at Corinth were acting like children. They were boasting, bragging, advertising their gifts. They were exercising a "holier-than-thou" attitude, and it is not right for a believer

454

to behave in such a way.

"Be not children"—(literally, "*become* not children")—
is to "cease to be in the attitude of malice one toward
another." It rebukes pride of intelligence. Self-satisfaction
often produces evil thinking and acting toward others.
Paul is pointing out to the believers that their estimate
of "tongues" was an estimate such as a child would make
if he were showing off his gifts and demonstrating ugly
pride. They were not really showing intelligence in their
thinking and in their practice in the local assembly.

". . . *Howbeit in malice be ye children, but in understanding be men.*" The Greek word translated "malice"
is *kakia*, and it has the meaning, "badness in quality, or
vicious character."

In ill-will we are to be as babes; but in the use of
intelligence, especially concerning spiritual matters, we
are to be men. We are to grow spiritually as we grow
physically; and in the very beginning of his letter Paul
declared that some of the believers in Corinth were still
spiritual babies, needing to be fed with milk, although
they had been converted long enough to be eating meat. But
they could not be fed with spiritual meat because of their
childish attitude.

Verse 21: "In the law it is written, With men of other
tongues and other lips will I speak unto this people; and
yet for all that will they not hear me, saith the Lord."

The Holy Spirit through the pen of Paul here quotes
Isaiah 28:11,12: "For with stammering lips and another
tongue will He speak to this people. To whom He said,
This is the rest wherewith ye may cause the weary to
rest; and this is the refreshing: yet they would not hear."
(When the New Testament refers to the law, unless it
specifies the Law of Moses it is speaking of the entire
Old Testament. An example of this is found in John 10:34;

12:34; 15:25; and Romans 3:19.)

Paul now brings the subject to bear upon the presence of *unbelievers* who were attending services in the Corinthian assembly. Thus, if the believers spoke in a tongue, the unbelievers could not understand and the message would have no meaning for them.

Paul is saying here that in the Old Testament era, God spoke to His people through Isaiah and other prophets, and their messages met with hardened hearts and unbelieving criticism. God gave warning that His retribution would be through foreign invaders who spoke a language utterly strange to His rebellious people:

"And if ye will not be reformed by me by these things, but will walk contrary unto me; then will I also walk contrary unto you, and will punish you yet seven times for your sins. And I will bring a sword upon you, that shall avenge the quarrel of my covenant: and when ye are gathered together within your cities, I will send the pestilence among you; and ye shall be delivered into the hand of the enemy" (Lev. 26:23–25).

An example of this was the invasion of the Assyrians who conquered the Israelites and occupied their cities, speaking a tongue utterly unintelligible to God's rebellious people. Such a tongue was a sign of humiliation and of God's judgment. Just as God's warning message fell upon deaf ears in those days, in like manner the use of tongues would fail to effect any purpose for unbelievers in Paul's day, save that of providing a sign.

Verse 22: "Wherefore tongues are for a sign, not to them that believe, but to them that believe not: but prophesying serveth not for them that believe not, but for them which believe."

In keeping with the passage from Isaiah, tongues in the church at Corinth were *"for a sign"* indicative of judgment upon the unbelieving, NOT a sign to lead them to *faith*, as was true on the Day of Pentecost.

"*. . . Tongues are for a sign, not to them that believe, but to them that believe not.*" If tongues are a sign, *of what* are they a sign? The only way to know the answer is to compare spiritual things with spiritual and let the Word of God speak while we keep silent.

The people on the Day of Pentecost marvelled when they heard a few men speak every language on earth at that time. Present on that day were men from all over the known world, and each man heard the Gospel in his own tongue. Tongues on the Day of Pentecost were a sign that the Holy Ghost had been poured out. The Gospel message was made known, and *each man*, in his own tongue (language), heard the Gospel story of the death, burial, and resurrection of Jesus.

It is clearly stated in our present verse that tongues are *for a sign*—a sign of judgment (as God spoke to His people Israel in the Old Testament)—not a sign that one has been baptized in the Holy Ghost. There is no such suggestion anywhere in the New Testament. Tongues are for a sign to the unbelievers, testifying to them that God is speaking in a supernatural way, attempting to get them to realize that He IS supernatural, that God loves and Jesus saves. Keep in mind that when an interpretation was given it was no more an unknown tongue, but served as prophesying. But since "that which is perfect" is come, tongues are no longer necessary.

I shall never cease to praise God that in the beginning of my Christian life, in the early days of my ministry, He literally took me out of denominationalism and man-made religious ideas. I am a member of a Baptist church, but it is an independent church, not connected with any denominational organization—just united to Jesus Christ, the head of the true Church. Since I am not attempting to prove any religious points or defend any denomination, I am willing to compare Scripture with Scripture, spiritual things with spiritual, and rightly divide the Word of Truth.

In Mark 16, Jesus upbraided His disciples because of their unbelief. He said to them, "Go ye into all the world, and preach the Gospel to every creature. He that believeth and is baptized shall be saved; but he that believeth not shall be damned. *And these SIGNS shall follow them that believe*: In my name shall they cast out devils; they shall speak with new tongues; they shall take up serpents; and if they drink any deadly thing, it shall not hurt them; they shall lay hands on the sick, and they shall recover" (Mark 16:15–18).

Now why do precious ministers claim all of these gifts *except the drinking of deadly poison without being hurt*? There are well-meaning, honest men, born again, who announce that they can and do cast out demons. They speak with other tongues – and some have even taken up serpents without harm. Many lay hands on the sick, and announce that all manner of sickness is healed under their ministry. But I have yet to hear the announcement, "Come and see me drink a vial of deadly poison—poison *declared deadly* by a licensed physician!"

I have yet to see anyone (who claims to have exactly what Paul, Peter, James and John had) drink a vial of poison without hurt! I believe in accepting and preaching ALL of the Word of God; but the only gift I can claim is the gift of salvation by grace through faith. Having been put into the ministry by the will of God, I preach the Word with the ability God gives me. I claim no gifts except the grace of God. In the words of Paul, "I am what I am *by the GRACE of God*, and the life I now live in the flesh I live by the faith of the Son of God, who loved me and gave Himself for me." I have nothing of which to brag or boast. I am only a sinner saved by grace, called of God to preach the Word — and I want to preach the Word in language "easy to be understood."

"But prophesying serveth not for them that believe not, but for them which believe." In Paul's day there were prophets to whom God gave new revelation—truths not yet given, because the Word of God was not complete. But when "that which is perfect" had come, that which was "in part" ceased. Today we have the perfect law of liberty. The Word of God is complete. We need no new revelation, no new prophecies. All God needs to say *has been said.*

Preaching the Gospel is not displaying knowledge or ability to speak. Preaching the Gospel is giving out the good news of salvation, demonstrating the power of the Spirit of God, to the edifying of all believers in the assembly.

The Divine Order Concerning the Ministry of the Gift of Tongues in the Local Assembly

Verse 23: "If therefore the whole church be come together into one place, and all speak with tongues, and there come in those that are unlearned, or unbelievers, will they not say that ye are mad?"

"If . . . the whole church be come together. . . ." In Paul's day it was uncommon for the whole church NOT to assemble with every member present. I wonder what some pastors would do today if all of their members assembled at one time? There are not many church auditoriums that would seat the membership, because most of the time only half—or less than half—of the members show up for services.

We are not to suppose that every member in the assembly was speaking at the same time with tongues, but it does seem that there were times when *several* of the members had spoken in tongues all at one time, and Paul makes it clear that such conduct in the assembly is not in accord with the leadership of the Spirit. Regardless of what we do in the church, it should always be done to the glory of God and the edifying of other believers. Any other conduct on the part of a Christian is not in harmony with the leading of the Spirit.

Paul is here giving an illustration of what would happen if the entire membership of the local church were gathered together, and all began to speak in tongues simultaneously. Should all of the members begin to speak in tongues, and unbelievers or unlearned people should come into the assembly and hear many people speaking at the same time in many languages, Paul asks, *"Will they not say that ye are MAD?"*

Greek authorities tell us that the Greek word translated "mad" could have been rendered "lunatic." Thus, if the entire assembly be gathered for a service and all the members begin to speak in a tongue, if sinners (or people who know nothing at all about the Spirit and His gifts) should walk into the assembly, they would exclaim, "These people are *lunatics!*"

Dearly beloved, there is no room for misunderstanding here. What Paul is saying is that God's purpose in the assembly of the Church is that believers be edified and unbelievers be reached with a message that is simple and understandable, appealing to the conscience and heart of the unbeliever, causing him to turn from Satan to Jesus.

God speaks through individuals in this day and hour, and He wants us to use words that will bring conviction and salvation to the *unbeliever*, and at the same time bring comfort, edification, and instruction to the believer. This would not be possible if all began to speak in tongues; for even though *they themselves* might be edified and blessed, the purpose of the meeting is missed entirely insofar as God is concerned.

Whatever testimony is given in the assembly—whether by minister or layman—should appeal to the heart and touch the conscience of all present—*especially the conscience of the unbeliever.* Any service that does not produce such effect is not a service where God has His way, because if God has HIS way the saints will be edified and sinners will be brought under conviction.

Verse 24: "But if all prophesy, and there come in one that believeth not, or one unlearned, he is convinced of all, he is judged of all."

"*If all prophesy*" does not mean that all WILL prophesy, but it is *possible* for all to exercise the gift of prophecy. It is true that God appoints some evangelists, some pastors, some teachers, some missionaries — but God is *able* to give to *any* believer whatever gifts. *other* believers are able to receive. There is no distinction in the body of Christ.

The Greek verb here translated "convinced," in the original reads "reproved," meaning to be *convicted* of sin—though not necessarily *convinced.* There are those who are convicted of sin who are not convinced of the need of a Saviour, and they go on in their sins. There is a definite distinction between being *convicted of sin,* and being convinced that one *needs Christ.*

The meaning here is that the testimony or prophecy given by the individual strikes home to the heart and conscience of the unbeliever, and "*he is judged*"—that is, his heart is searched and he is convicted inwardly because the Word of God points out sin. The Word, preached in its fulness and purity, will cause the unbeliever to examine and judge himself; and when *successive speakers* give out the message of the Word of God, conviction is deepened and the work of redemption is performed in the heart. Jesus said, "Verily, verily, I say unto you, He that heareth my word, and believeth on Him that sent me, hath everlasting life, and shall not come into condemnation; but is passed from death unto life" (John 5:24).

Verse 25: "And thus are the secrets of his heart made manifest; and so falling down on his face he will worship God, and report that God is in you of a truth."

Hearing the Word of God brings to the unbeliever a realization of his lost condition — *and no person will ever realize his lost condition until he does hear the Word of God.*

Hearing the Word brings conviction, self-condemnation, and self-judgment. Thus through hearing the Word of God, *"the secrets of his heart are made manifest."* The unbeliever recognizes and evaluates his thoughts, his motives, and his desires; and through the Word he knows that he is lost; his own heart condemns him: "For if our heart condemn us, God is greater than our heart, and knoweth all things. Beloved, if our heart condemn us not, then have we confidence toward God" (I John 3:20,21). If the heart is right with God, then the heart gives assurance, not condemnation.

Thus an unbeliever, having heard the Word, being convicted, convinced, the secrets of his heart made manifest, he is ready for salvation. He sees his sad spiritual state and realizes his need of a Saviour.

". . . And so falling down on his face he will worship God, and report that God is in you of a truth." In the assembly where both believers and unbelievers are gathered, all preaching and teaching should be done from the Word of God; and the singular purpose of all ministry is to lead unbelievers into the knowledge of salvation and bring believers closer to God. If believers are NOT edified, if unbelievers are NOT born again, then there is no purpose whatsoever for the assembly. The joy of God is to save the lost and bless believers.

Verse 26: "How is it then, brethren? when ye come together, every one of you hath a psalm, hath a doctrine, hath a tongue, hath a revelation, hath an interpretation. Let all things be done unto edifying."

(The Greek suggests, "Taking into consideration what I have pointed out, how is it with you Corinthians?") And I might ask, "How is it with YOU who read these lines? What is the uppermost desire in your life when you testify, teach, preach, exhort, or witness? What is the motivating purpose in your heart as you enter the assembly?" I might ask, "How is it with ME? Am I preaching for the right purpose? Is the motive of my ministry according to the Bible; or am I preaching for some other reason?" As believers, we need to answer the question Paul put to the Corinthians: *How is it with US?*

This verse is not a commendation; Paul is not praising the believers when he declares, *"When ye come to-gether, everyone of you hath a psalm, hath a doctrine, etc."* The Holy Spirit will lead in the assembly if He is *permitted to lead*; but in the assembly at Corinth, individual believers were preparing their psalms, their teaching, their revelation, tongues, and interpretation before they came to the meeting place, with the intention of "doing their little bit" whether the Spirit led or not.

We should always be prepared, spiritually and physically, to do what the Holy Spirit leads us to do; but if we think we are so gifted and so good that we just *must* give our little testimony or quote our little psalm, then we are definitely out of order. Such practice abuses the cause of Christ and hinders the testimony of the Church!

There are those who, though born again, blood-washed

believers, are offended if they are not asked to sing or take some outstanding part in every service in the church. Many times on Sunday morning, by the time all of the singers have sung and all of the "talents" have been displayed, the pastor has but a few minutes left in which to deliver God's message. Many times in revival services, when all of the singing and special numbers are finished it is time to go home, because the congregation is so tired they are neither mentally nor physically fit to listen while God's man preaches.

The Christian who is easily provoked or angered if not called upon to perform in some capacity at every service, is not right with God. In services conducted *in the Spirit* the Holy Ghost will lead as to who and how many should sing, who should pray, who should perform in *any* capacity. God pity born again children of God who act like babies in the church!

"Let all things be done unto edifying." Paul is not suggesting here that anyone quench the Spirit. He is pointing out that each one who takes part in the service should be sure that his aim (in song, prayer, testimony, teaching, or preaching) is the true aim of the ministry of the Gospel—*first and foremost to glorify God*, and then to edify all believers in the assembly and bring sinners under conviction.

Verse 27: "If any man speak in an unknown tongue, let it be by two, or at the most by three, and that by course; and let one interpret."

The truth declared here is easily understood if we will read the Word of God with an open heart and an open mind, forgetting preconceived ideas, religious dogma, and man-made doctrine.

"If any man speak in an unknown tongue . . . ." If a believer is moved by the Holy Ghost to speak in a tongue,

then, *". . . let it be by two, or at the most by three, and that by course."*

I see no reason for anyone to misunderstand the instruction here. The Holy Ghost declares that two (never more than three) should speak in "a tongue" in the assembly, and that they should speak *"by course"*—that is, only one at a time. It is unscriptural, out of order, unchristian and unkind for any person to stand up and begin speaking in a public meeting in the church while someone else is speaking. This is clearly taught in our verse. Only one should speak at a time, and never more than three in any one service.

". . . And let one interpret." It does not say let one interpret for each speaker, but *let one interpret* (for all three). If three believers deliver a message in a tongue in the assembly, and one believer is able to interpret for all three and tell the congregation exactly what has been said, it could be known that the Holy Ghost was in the messages and in the interpretation.

According to the teaching of the New Testament, whatever takes place in the assembly is to be free from confusion, for God is not the author of confusion. Whether praying, testifying, or singing, all is to be done to the *edifying* of the whole assembly, not to the *confusion* of all. Therefore only one person is to speak at one time, and then whatever is said is to be interpreted.

Verse 28: "But if there be no interpreter, let him keep silence in the church; and let him speak to himself, and to God."

From this verse it is clear that there is to be no speaking with another tongue in the assembly if there is no interpreter present.

". . . And let him speak to himself, and to God." The emphasis in the Greek language is on *"to himself"*—

that is, the believer is to exercise his spiritual gift of tongues in privacy—perhaps in his own home—not in the assembly when an interpreter is not present.

Another clear conclusion that can be drawn from this verse is that he who has the gift of another tongue must first be assured that there is someone present in the assembly who has the gift of *interpreting* tongues; otherwise how would he know whether or not to keep silent in the assembly?

There are many things in the local church today that are definitely out of order, and there will be a reckoning day with tremendous loss of reward for those who behave unscripturally in the house of God. *Man* is receiving most of the praise that should go to Jesus Christ. God have mercy on any person who performs in the church and does it in the flesh or to show off talent or ability!

Verse 29: "Let the prophets speak two or three, and let the other judge."

During the transition period, the Word of God was not complete. The gift of prophecy was given to men, and these men had the supernatural ability to tell forth the mind of God—things that had not then been written down. We have these truths today in the Word of God.

In Paul's day God gave men the gift of prophecy—for edification, comfort, and exhortation. He also gave the gift of teaching, together with special anointings of knowledge. But there were also *false teachers* who claimed to be endowed of God, and the early Christians were warned to be on guard against them. We need to be careful today about such teachers. (Notice II Peter 2:1 and I Peter 5:8.)

Again the rules and regulations are clearly set forth: Prophets should speak by two or three, *"and let the other judge.''* This statement simply means that a person who is born of the Spirit will recognize the Spirit of God in a speaker. I say without hesitation and without fear, that when you listen to a minister, if you cannot discern whether he is a fundamental preacher, or a modernist, or a liberal, then I am sorely afraid that you do not possess the Holy Spirit — in fact, I fear that you have not been born again!

In I Peter 2:6 we read, ''Wherefore also it is contained in the Scripture, Behold, I lay in Sion a chief corner stone, elect, precious: and he that believeth on Him shall not be confounded (confused).'' Born again people cannot be confused, and if the Holy Ghost is speaking through me when I stand in the pulpit or as I write these lines, *if you are saved* you will judge (discern or understand) that the message I give to you is of the Lord. If you do not recognize a man of God when you hear him, if you do not know whether what you read is truth or error, then I would advise you to fall upon your knees and cry out to God for Holy Spirit salvation; it is entirely possible that the devil has slipped you a counterfeit.

Paul's instruction here is simply this: ''Let the prophets prophesy—never more than three in one assembly— and let others judge (discern) if those prophets are of God.'' False prophets and false teachers should not be permitted to speak in the church. It is absolutely unscriptural to allow such a person to stand in the pulpit and preach spiritual poison.

Verse 30: ''If any thing be revealed to another that sitteth by, let the first hold his peace.''

The meaning here is simply that no speaker in the Corinthian church was to prolong his message to undue length, or take up the entire time of the worship service. Each was to recognize that others possessed the gift the same as he. Although the assembly should have a reasonable length of time together, the meetings should not be too long lest there be grave danger of failing to reach those who need the message. A service should not be prolonged until those in attendance are mentally and physically tired, and unfit to receive the things of the Spirit of God.

Each individual must realize that he is not the only one to whom God has given a gift. Selfishness is not a fruit of the Spirit, and we should never feel that we have priority on either God's gifts or His message. We should be willing to let someone else witness, testify, or teach occasionally.

". . . *Let the first hold his peace*" might signify to "bring his message to a close." That is, if the Spirit prompts the individual who is speaking to close his message, he should close it. He should not continue just for the sake of pride, even though he may have been speaking but a short time. If the Spirit bids, he should bring his message to a close and allow someone else to whom the Holy Spirit has spoken, to witness or testify.

Verse 31: "For ye may all prophesy one by one, that all may learn, and all may be comforted."

Paul is not saying here that every member of the church may speak in one assembly, nor does he imply that all will take part in one service. What Paul is suggesting here is the ability (and the possibility) of each individual giving a testimony or a message. Verse 27 declared that two (never more than three) should take part in one service—and the length of the service should depend upon the leadership of the Holy Spirit. We should never lay down an ironclad rule that a service cannot last more than forty-five minutes or an hour. The Spirit might lead otherwise.

Gifts of the Spirit should be exercised in such manner that all present may receive exhortation, comfort, instruction—and, if need be, *reproof and rebuke.* In the local church to which Paul was writing, it was customary for more than one person to speak; but if the Spirit was in the service, each successive speaker would carry on the message begun by the Holy Spirit in the first speaker. If two or three gave messages, each would amplify what the other had said, for the Holy Spirit is the author of peace and unity.

Verse 32: "And the spirits of the prophets are subject to the prophets."

(The original reads, "And spirits of prophets are subject to prophets." The definite articles are not used.) The meaning here is that the *true* prophet did not act like a *false* prophet; he was not controlled by a false spirit, nor did he speak to glorify or satisfy the flesh or to expound false doctrine. The true prophet exercised self-control. Although speaking by the directing power of the Holy Spirit, he was not carried away by the supernatural influence. A Christian who does not employ self-control does not glorify God. He is detrimental to the cause of Christ, rather than an asset.

The Holy Spirit of God speaks to and uses the understanding of a minister who is called of God and who is led of God in his speaking. Such a minister will speak intelligently, he will speak with self-control, and he will not prolong his speaking just to monopolize the time.

Verse 33: "For God is not the author of confusion, but of peace, as in all churches of the saints."

A service controlled by the Spirit of God (and a preacher who is under the *guiding power* of the Spirit of God) will be marked by self-control, discretion, humility, longsuffering, and love. The message will bring peace and order, rather than disorder and tumult in the assembly. The Holy Spirit has nothing to do with the message that causes rivalry, dissension, or division among believers. Such a message is of the flesh and is instigated by Satan, not by the Holy Spirit. God is a God of harmony, a God of unity and love.

If the Holy Spirit has His way, He will maintain a service that is in order and that will glorify God from the first moment until the last. Jesus will have pre-eminence, because the Holy Spirit is in the world to glorify the Lord Jesus Christ—not to glorify Himself. In Jesus we have our fulness, completeness, and our sufficiency. There is no room left for the glory of man: "But of Him are ye in Christ Jesus, who of God is made unto us wisdom, and righteousness, and sanctification, and redemption: that, according as it is written, He that glorieth, let him glory in the Lord" (I Cor. 1:30,31).

Verse 34: "Let your women keep silence in the churches: for it is not permitted unto them to speak; but they are commanded to be under obedience, as also saith the law."

This verse is considered by many to be controversial. There are many varied ideas about it. Some have attempted to use the original Greek words to make it mean what they want it to mean in order to keep their beliefs concerning the ladies in the church.

No one on the face of this earth appreciates born again mothers, wives, and young ladies more than I do. Were it not for the Christian women—godly mothers and consecrated wives—I am sure my ministry could never have reached the vast coverage it has today by means of radio.

I appreciate the men, and I realize that many of the dear ladies who send gifts to keep our radio ministry on the air receive the money from their working husbands who, in all probability, seldom if ever get to hear the broadcast. Many men DO support us liberally, but a large percentage of our letters come from godly women. It is therefore understandable that I have a very warm spot in my heart for born again ladies, and I would not intentionally hurt any one of them; but I cannot skip over this verse or butcher it to make it say what it *does NOT* say.

There are those who say that this means the ladies should take no part in the business affairs of the church. Others teach that the women in the Corinthian church were speaking in tongues and breaking up the service. They suggest that the verb here means "to chatter, or to speak unintelligibly."

The Greek verb used here is *laleo*. The same word is used 18 times in this chapter. It is used in verses 3 through 29 relative to speaking with tongues; in verse 19 it refers to "speaking with the understanding," and in verse 21 it is used in "the utterance of God through human agency." Now why should this word be translated 18 times in this chapter as having to do with speaking in tongues, speaking with understanding, speaking to God— and then in this one place make the same word mean "to chatter or speak unintelligibly"?

We dare not take any word out of its setting, nor force it to mean what we want it to mean in order to prove our viewpoint. The Word of God was not given to prove points. The instruction to *"let your women keep silent in the churches"* is preceded by only a few verses with the statement that if there be no interpreter present, *"let HIM keep silent in the church."* At certain times, under certain conditions, the *man* is to be silent, and the same word is used pertaining to women keeping silent. Therefore the meaning is plain:

It is simply unscriptural for a woman to speak in the position of a minister over the assembly in the church. Women are to refrain from preaching or addressing the assembly gathered for worship. It is clear that women are not to take part in the oral ministry of the church.

Of those who would differ with me in this interpretation, I ask this simple question: If it is divinely ordered of God for ladies to pastor churches and direct the affairs of local assemblies, why did Jesus Christ call *twelve MEN* to be His apostles; and by like token, why is there not one single book in the New Testament authored by a woman?

Great Christian women are *named* in the New Testament, but not one received the dictation of an epistle from Almighty God. I shall never cease to be grateful to God for the born again ladies. They have a very definite and essential place in God's Church and in His program, but they are not to usurp authority over the men.

"But they are commanded to be under obedience, as also saith the law." In Genesis 3:16 we read, "Unto the woman He said, I will greatly multiply thy sorrow and thy conception; in sorrow thou shalt bring forth children; and thy desire shall be to thy husband, and he shall rule over thee."

"Wives, submit yourselves unto your own husbands, as unto the Lord. For the husband is the head of the wife, even as Christ is the head of the Church: and He is the Saviour of the body. Therefore as the Church is subject unto Christ, so let the wives be to their own husbands in every thing" (Eph. 5:22–24).

It is perfectly scriptural for women to teach in Sunday school or in the young people's organization; but it is not scriptural for them to teach the men's Bible class or exercise the duties of a pastor over men in the assembly. This may seem to be a hard saying, but it is God's Word.

Verse 35: "And if they will learn any thing, let them

ask their husbands at home: for it is a shame for women to speak in the church.''

"*. . . Let them ask their husbands at home . . . .*" This is a general statement. Unmarried girls could ask their mothers or fathers if they desired to ask questions about the assembly and the meeting.

"*For it is a shame for women to speak in the church.*" This part of the verse is self-explanatory. I see no need to add anything to it.

Verse 36: "What? Came the Word of God out from you? Or came it unto you only?"

"*The Word of God*" points to the Gospel message of the death, burial, and resurrection of Jesus—the Gospel which is "the power of God unto salvation to all who believe." Paul is asking questions that imply negative answers. I believe that he is using just a little irony or sarcasm. He asks, "*What?* Do you mean to tell me that the Gospel had its starting point in the city of Corinth? Was it to YOU that God first revealed the Gospel message? Were YOU the only recipients of the message of God's saving grace? Did the inspired Word come out FROM you — or did I bring the Word of God TO you when you were in heathenism, worshipping idols?"

From the way the Corinthian believers were living, teaching, and preaching, they indicated that they considered themselves the custodians of the Word of God and that they therefore had a right to add to, take from, or rearrange the Word as having to do with doctrine and faith. Some things were very wrong in the Corinthian church. They were condoning fornication in the membership, going to law against each other, intermarrying with unbelievers, arguing about the eating of meats — and by their attitude suggested that God had given them the authority to draw up the New Testament doctrines for the Church.

Verse 37: "If any man think himself to be a prophet, or spiritual, let him acknowledge that the things that I write unto you are the commandments of the Lord."

"If any man think himself to be a prophet . . . ." Paul refers here to the supposedly wise teachers in Corinth, the self-appointed prophets. In other words, Paul says, "If these individuals think they are prophets and teachers, then let them carefully study the things which I write"—and this statement refers to the entire sixteen chapters of this letter plus the second epistle which is to follow. These are verbally inspired words which God gave to Paul to pen down.

". . . The things that I write unto you are the commandments of the Lord." The Greek word is singular—*"commandment."* Whatever Paul had taught or penned down had come to him through divine authority. Paul was God's mouthpiece. He was ordained of God and sent by God to give the Corinthians the truth in *"the things which I write,"* and the instruction given by God through Paul to the church at Corinth stands for the churches today, insofar as order of service and conduct of believers is concerned. Notice I Corinthians 4:17; 7:17; 11:16; 14:33.

The cure for all division, all misunderstanding, and all ills that exist in local assemblies can be summed up in one simple statement: Let God's Holy Spirit completely control every thought, motive and action of a God-called, Spirit-filled pastor, and let that pastor teach from the Word of God after he has studied diligently and rightly divided the Word of Truth. No minister has any right to wrongly divide the Word of God in order to prove his denominational points or religious ideas. There is one God, one Church, one Holy Spirit, one Mediator, one WORD OF GOD. If God's true ministers would allow the Holy Ghost to lead them, then the differences and confusion would vanish and we would have a glorious church right here upon this earth!

God is the author of peace, peace comes through Jesus Christ, and knowledge of Jesus Christ comes through the simple Gospel message of salvation by grace through faith in the finished work of God's only begotten Son. "This then is the message which we have heard of Him, and declare unto you, that God is light, and in Him is no darkness at all. . . And this is the record, that God hath given to us eternal life, and this life is in His Son. He that hath the Son hath life; and he that hath not the Son of God hath not life" (I John 1:5; 5:11,12).

Verse 38: "But if any man be ignorant, let him be ignorant."

If anyone refused to acknowledge the divine authority of Paul's teachings through professed lack of knowledge of the facts, the deplorable condition of that person must continue. Unwillingness to submit prevents the possibility of being instructed. There are some dear people whom even the Lord God cannot help because their minds are made up, they are not willing to listen to reason, they will not allow their hearts and minds to be opened by the Word of God through the Holy Spirit. Peter speaks of such people as being "willingly ignorant" (II Pet. 3:5).

". . . The Word of God is quick, and powerful, and sharper than any twoedged sword, piercing even to the dividing asunder of soul and spirit, and of the joints and marrow, and is a discerner of the thoughts and intents of the heart" (Heb. 4:12). The Holy Spirit is in the world to convict, convince, and bring unto Jesus all who will allow Him to work in their hearts through the inspired Word of God. Paul was God's anointed apostle; through him God spoke to the believers in Corinth, and through his writings God speaks to you and to me—and to all who will hear the Word.

Verse 39: "Wherefore, brethren, covet to prophesy, and forbid not to speak with tongues."

The closing admonition of this tremendous and vital chapter of instruction is simply this: *"Wherefore"* (because of the divine instruction set forth in the preceding verses) *". . . covet to prophesy."* Paul again contrasts between the gifts of tongues and prophecy. The gift of prophecy is to be coveted, and the instruction concerning tongues is *"Do not forbid."*

In verses 5, 12, 22, 24 and 25 of this chapter we are clearly taught that prophesying is more honorable, more profitable in the assembly, and more to be desired than tongues. In chapter 12, verse 31, Paul said, "But covet earnestly the best gifts: and yet shew I unto you a more excellent way." In chapter 14 verse 1 we read, "Follow after charity, and desire spiritual gifts, BUT RATHER that ye may PROPHESY . . . for GREATER IS HE THAT PROPHESIETH than he that speaketh with tongues, except he interpret, that the church may receive edifying" (verse 5).

We are nowhere instructed to covet the gift of tongues; but we read clearly, "COVET to prophesy, and *forbid not* to speak with tongues."

During the transition period, God gave signs and wonders. In the second chapter of Hebrews we read of the great salvation that began to be spoken by the Lord and was confirmed to us by them that heard Him *"through signs and wonders."* One of the "signs and wonders" was the gift of tongues, but when the perfect law of liberty (the full Word of God) came, we no longer *need* signs or wonders. ("The *just* shall live by FAITH.") In chapter 13 of our present study Paul tells us, "When that which is perfect is come, that which is *in part* will be done away."

There is no reason why anyone should seek the gift

of tongues today. We have the completed Word of God, we *believe* God's Word, and we trust in the *promise* of His Word — and His promise cannot be broken (Rom. 3:4; Titus 1:2; Heb. 6:18).

Verse 40: "Let all things be done decently and in order."

Everything in the church should be done according to the leadership of the Holy Spirit, according to divine arrangement. All activities of the church should be carried on in humility, in an orderly manner, and to the ultimate glory of God. Be earnestly desirous to prophesy, to tell the good news of the grace of God.

I have never forbidden anyone to speak with another tongue, even though I believe the gift of tongues was for a definite period only; nor have I ever invited anyone to *seek* the gift of tongues. In our meetings I urge all of the converts to surrender soul, spirit, and body to the Lord Jesus, to study the Word of God diligently, and to unite with a Bible-believing, Bible-preaching local church where God's ordained minister preaches the grace of God— *pure Gospel*—uncompromisingly.

I believe the paramount mission of every Christian is to earnestly strive to point unbelievers to the Lamb of God—by all that they say, by all that they do, and by living a consistent Christian life day by day. I believe the nearest and dearest thing to the great heart of God is the salvation of the sinner who is only one step from eternal damnation. There is no way in which any individual can bring more glory to God than by winning souls. Therefore, my fellow believers, *"COVET to prophesy!"*

CHAPTER FIFTEEN

1. Moreover, brethren, I declare unto you the gospel which I preached unto you, which also ye have received, and wherein ye stand;

2. By which also ye are saved, if ye keep in memory what I preached unto you, unless ye have believed in vain.

3. For I delivered unto you first of all that which I also received, how that Christ died for our sins according to the scriptures;

4. And that he was buried, and that he rose again the third day according to the scriptures:

5. And that he was seen of Cephas, then of the twelve:

6. After that, he was seen of above five hundred brethren at once; of whom the greater part remain unto this present, but some are fallen asleep.

7. After that, he was seen of James; then of all the apostles.

8. And last of all he was seen of me also, as of one born out of due time.

9. For I am the least of the apostles, that am not meet to be called an apostle, because I persecuted the church of God.

10. But by the grace of God I am what I am: and his grace which was bestowed upon me was not in vain; but I laboured more abundantly than they all: yet not I, but the grace of God which was with me.

11. Therefore whether it were I or they, so we preach, and so ye believed.

12. Now if Christ be preached that he rose from the dead, how say some among you that there is no resurrection of the dead?

13. But if there be no resurrection of the dead, then is Christ not risen:

14. And if Christ be not risen, then is our preaching vain, and your faith is also vain.

15. Yea, and we are found false witnesses of God; because we have testified of God that he raised up Christ: whom he raised not up, if so be that the dead rise not.

16. For if the dead rise not, then is not Christ raised:

17. And if Christ be not raised, your faith is vain; ye are yet in your sins.

18. Then they also which are fallen asleep in Christ are perished.

19. If in this life only we have hope in Christ, we are of all men most miserable.

20. But now is Christ risen from the dead, and become the firstfruits of them that slept.

21. For since by man came death, by man came also the resurrection of the dead.

22. For as in Adam all die, even so in Christ shall all be made alive.

23. But every man in his own order: Christ the firstfruits; afterward they that are Christ's at his coming.

24. Then cometh the end, when he shall have delivered up the kingdom to God, even the Father; when he shall have put down all rule and all authority and power.

25. For he must reign, till he hath put all enemies under his feet.

26. The last enemy that shall be destroyed is death.

27. For he hath put all things under his feet. But when he saith all things are put under him, it is manifest that he is excepted, which did put all things under him.

28. And when all things shall be subdued unto him, then shall the Son also himself be subject unto him that put all things under him, that God may be all in all.

29. Else what shall they do which are baptized for the dead, if the dead rise not at all? why are they then baptized for the dead?

30. And why stand we in jeopardy every hour?

31. I protest by your rejoicing which I have in Christ Jesus our Lord, I die daily.

32. If after the manner of men I have fought with beasts at Ephesus, what advantageth it me, if the dead rise not? let us eat and drink; for to morrow we die.

33. Be not deceived: evil communications corrupt good manners.

34. Awake to righteousness, and sin not; for some have not the knowledge of God: I speak this to your shame.

35. But some man will say, How are the dead raised up? and with what body do they come?

36. Thou fool, that which thou sowest is not quickened, except it die:

37. And that which thou sowest, thou sowest not that body that shall be, but bare grain, it may chance of wheat, or of some other grain:

38. But God giveth it a body as it hath pleased him, and to every seed his own body.

39. All flesh is not the same flesh: but there is one kind of flesh of men, another flesh of beasts, another of fishes, and another of birds.

40. There are also celestial bodies, and bodies terrestrial: but the glory of the celestial is one, and the glory of the terrestrial is another.

41. There is one glory of the sun, and another glory of the moon, and another glory of the stars: for one star differeth from another star in glory.

42. So also is the resurrection of the dead. It is sown in corruption; it is raised in incorruption:

43. It is sown in dishonour; it is raised in glory: it is sown in weakness; it is raised in power:

44. It is sown a natural body; it is raised a spiritual body. There is a natural body, and there is a spiritual body.

45. And so it is written, The first man Adam was made a living soul; the last Adam was made a quickening spirit.

46. Howbeit that was not first which is spiritual, but that which is natural; and afterward that which is spiritual.

47. The first man is of the earth, earthy: the second man is the Lord from heaven.

48. As is the earthy, such are they also that are earthy: and as is the heavenly, such are they also that are heavenly.

49. And as we have borne the image of the earthy, we shall also bear the image of the heavenly.

50. Now this I say, brethren, that flesh and blood cannot inherit the kingdom of God; neither doth corruption inherit incorruption.

51. Behold, I shew you a mystery; We shall not all sleep, but we shall all be changed,

52. In a moment, in the twinkling of an eye, at the last trump: for the trumpet shall sound, and the dead shall be raised incorruptible, and we shall be changed.

53. For this corruptible must put on incorruption, and this mortal must put on immortality.

54. So when this corruptible shall have put on incorruption, and this mortal shall have put on immortality, then shall be brought to pass the saying that is written, Death is swallowed up in victory.

55. O death, where is thy sting? O grave, where is thy victory?

56. The sting of death is sin; and the strength of sin is the law.

57. But thanks be to God, which giveth us the victory through our Lord Jesus Christ.

58. Therefore, my beloved brethren, be ye stedfast, unmoveable, always abounding in the work of the Lord, forasmuch as ye know that your labour is not in vain in the Lord.

The Rapture of the Church — The First Resurrection

Whether or not the Corinthian assembly had questioned Paul on the subject of the resurrection, we do not know. Apparently a report had reached him that there were false teachers in Corinth who were teaching error *concerning* the resurrection. Possibly some of the converts in the assembly were Sadducees, and the Sadducees did not believe in the bodily resurrection of the dead. It is more likely that some of the Greek members had brought *their* belief on the subject over into the church. Study Acts 17:18–34.

The important fact is that the resurrection of the dead was doubted and denied by some in Corinth. In some way, Paul had learned of this doctrinal error in the church, and whether they asked for it or not he gave them a clear, understandable outline concerning true doctrine as relating to the resurrection of the dead.

The greatest bombshell ever to explode in the face of an unbelieving world was the bodily resurrection of Jesus Christ. To their own satisfaction His enemies explained away Calvary, they explained away His miracles— but they could not explain away the empty tomb—nor have the enemies of the Gospel explained away the bodily

481

resurrection of Jesus Christ until this present hour.

Christianity is the only religion that has a risen Saviour—testified as having been seen by many, even by five hundred at one time. History records the names of many great men, some of whom founded great religions and inspired multitudes of followers; but only Christ, the head of Christianity, lived, died, *rose again—AND SHOWED HIMSELF after His resurrection.* He proved that He was flesh and bone by eating in the presence of His disciples and inviting them to touch Him and determine that He was not a spirit. (Study the entire twenty-fourth chapter of Luke.)

The Gospel

This chapter has to do primarily with the second coming of Jesus Christ for His Church. The dead in Christ will be raised incorruptible, the living saints will be changed, and together we will be caught up to meet the Lord Jesus in the clouds in the air. But the *first part* of the chapter gives the best definition of the Gospel to be found anywhere in the Bible.

Verse 1: "Moreover, brethren, I declare unto you the Gospel which I preached unto you, which also ye have received, and wherein ye stand."

Paul is repeating the foundation of "the truth" which he had delivered to the Corinthians when they were converted from heathenism to Christianity. He points out three proofs that the message he delivered was true:

1. Even though they had been pagans, they had heard, *received*, and accepted his message when he came to them and delivered the Gospel.

2. They were even that very moment *saved*, and *standing* in the truth that had set them free.

3. They were at that very moment *looking for the blessed*

hope and the glorious appearing of the great God and Saviour, Jesus Christ, who would save them from even the very *presence* of sin and give them the fulness of their salvation—a new body just like the glorious body of Jesus.

The Corinthians had been pagans when Paul came to them. Now they were believers. They were saved, and their salvation had come through the message he delivered—the message of the death, burial, and resurrection of Jesus Christ.

Verse 2: "By which also ye are saved, if ye keep in memory what I preached unto you, unless ye have believed in vain."

This does not imply that salvation depends upon the individual's holding fast to the Gospel. If that were true, then we would not be saved by the free gift of God, the unmerited favor of His grace. Salvation is OF the Lord, BY the Lord, THROUGH the Lord, IN the Lord. Salvation is altogether THE LORD.

What the Holy Spirit is saying through Paul is simply this: If the Corinthians denied the truth of the bodily resurrection of Jesus Christ, that would be proof that they were NOT holding fast what Paul had taught them.

". . . *Unless ye have believed in vain.*" The Greek word here translated "in vain" is *eike* and means "without cause, or to no purpose." That would be true if Christ had not been raised.

The whole thing in a nutshell is this: If Christ did not rise from the dead then the message Paul preached had no grounds for truth — it was not valid, it was a lie; and they therefore had no reason to believe his message . . . *IF Christ had not been raised bodily from the grave.* The question here is not whether they would "hold on" or "hold to" — but if they did not believe in the bodily resurrection, then they had never believed from the heart:

"That if thou shalt confess with thy mouth the Lord Jesus, and shalt believe in thine heart that God hath raised Him from the dead, thou shalt be saved. For with the heart man believeth unto righteousness; and with the mouth confession is made unto salvation" (Rom. 10:9,10).

Verse 3: "For I delivered unto you first of all that which I also received, how that Christ died for our sins according to the Scriptures."

"First of all" does not refer to a point of time – i.e., the *first message* Paul delivered, but *the first in DIVINE IMPORTANCE*. The Gospel is first in pointing men to Jesus Christ—the simple, down-to-earth Gospel, not the wisdom of men nor the tongues of angels. Paul is showing the believers that the Gospel is the foundation of their salvation; they had accepted the message because it WAS the Gospel. He delivered unto them the message he had received on the road to Damascus—the message of Jesus Christ, crucified, buried, risen.

As to how Paul *received* the Gospel, we read, ". . . *I have received of the LORD that which also I delivered unto you . . .*" (I Cor. 11:23). "But I certify you, brethren, that the Gospel which was preached of me is not after man. For I neither received it of man, neither was I taught it, but by the revelation of Jesus Christ" (Gal. 1:11,12). Also study carefully the entire ninth chapter of Acts.

The message Paul received of God and delivered to the Corinthians was *"how that Christ died for our sins according to the Scriptures."* The meaning here is "as a sacrifice," or "to make atonement for" our sins. Study Hebrews 5:1–3; 7:27; and 10:12. Paul states the *fact* of the crucifixion of Jesus–("Christ died"); the *purpose* of the crucifixion–("for our sins"); and the basic *testimony*– ("according to the Scriptures").

The FACT of the death of Jesus on the cross is in

484

perfect accord with the Old Testament *prophecies* concerning His death and the manner of His death. There is perfect harmony in every detail between the Old and New Testaments as related to the death of Jesus for the sins of the whole world.

The appeal and invitation of the minister to unbelievers must always be in accord with "what saith the Word of God?" In this day of grace it is not the sin-question, but the SON-question: "What think ye of CHRIST? Whose Son is He?"

Verse 4: "And that He was buried, and that He rose again the third day according to the Scriptures."

The first point in the Gospel message is that Christ *died* for our sins —"according to the Scriptures" (Isaiah 53:5,6).

The second point is that He was *buried* —"according to the Scriptures" (Isaiah 53:9). The fact that Jesus was buried is essential to the doctrine of His *bodily resurrection* "according to the Scriptures." Isaiah prophesied, "He made His grave with the wicked, and with the rich in His death." Therefore it was imperative that the body of Jesus be put in the grave, even though afterward the tomb was found empty.

". . . *And that He rose again the third day according to the Scriptures.*" The mention of "the third day" fulfills the statement of Jesus to the Pharisees (Matt. 12: 38–42) that no sign would be given them except the sign of Jonah: "As Jonas was three days and three nights in the whale's belly, so shall the Son of man be three days and three nights in the heart of the earth." Jesus was buried, and according to the Scriptures He rose on the third day as prophesied.

In the Greek language the tense of the verb *changes* here from the past tense to the perfect — "*He hath been raised."* In the first two cases, the verb points to *the FACT of* His death and burial; and here, the verb declares that Jesus Christ the risen One *remains* alive — that is, *"He ever lives, He is alive to die no more."* The fact of His death and the fact of His burial point to a *condition— dead; buried.* The truth of His bodily resurrection points to His present *position* — He sits at the right hand of God to make intercession, to mediate for us (Heb. 1:1–3; I Tim. 2:5).

Verse 5: "And that He was seen of Cephas, then of the twelve."

Notice the wording here: *"He was SEEN."* It is not as some versions render, "He *appeared.*" To say that Jesus *appeared* could mean that He appeared in a vision, or in spiritual form; but that is not the case. He was seen *bodily.* John makes this clear in I John 1:1–3:

"That which was from the beginning, which we have heard, which we have *seen* with our eyes, which we have *looked upon,* and *our hands have handled,* of the Word of life; (For the life was manifested, and we have *seen* it, and bear witness, and shew unto you that eternal life, which was with the Father, and was manifested unto us;) *That which we have SEEN and HEARD* declare we unto you, that ye also may have fellowship with us: and truly our fellowship is with the Father, and with His Son Jesus Christ."

Jesus did not "appear" in a vision. He was *SEEN literally,* in a body of flesh and bone.

". . . Then of the twelve." *"The twelve"* had become a technical or official phrase for the complete apostolic company—although Judas was not present (nor was *Thomas*) on the first occasion. Hence the number is used as a *name* for the group, or in a conventional way, not actually numbering twelve men present. There is therefore no

discrepancy here. The important point is the double confirmation of the resurrection.

Verse 6: "After that, He was seen of above five hundred brethren at once; of whom the greater part remain unto this present, but some are fallen asleep."

The occasion of this event is not known, nor is it important. What IS important is the fact that the resurrected Lord was seen by more than 500 believers at one time—and 500 believers could not be wrong! Certainly if that many people saw Jesus at one time, it was Jesus *in a body*. This fact provides indisputable proof of the bodily resurrection of Jesus Christ.

". . . *Of whom the greater part remain unto this present, but some are fallen asleep.*" The Greek word used here for "asleep" is used in reference to the death of the body, and is used relative to the death of those who belong to Christ, never of Christ Himself. It denotes rest, and when we think of sleeping we think of rest. When a believer dies, we think of his going to rest.

The believer dies — *but he does NOT cease to exist.* In spite of the fact that he is absent from the body, he continues to exist and to KNOW. Those of us who remain cannot speak with our loved ones who have departed, but they are conscious. They are resting with Jesus.

However, sleep has its waking. Those who sleep will awake; those who are dead in Christ will be raised incorruptible. The body, not the spirit, is under discussion here. The Greek word used in this instance means "to lie down," and certainly we do not think of spirits as lying down. We think of *the body* as lying down — we lie down to sleep, we lie down to rest whether we sleep or not. Thus, the body of the believer lies down to rest in Jesus until the resurrection. The body goes back to dust;

the spirit returns to God who gave it.

In Daniel 12:2 we read of "them that sleep in the dust of the earth," and the Hebrew word used in this statement points to the body, not the spirit. So it is *bodies* that sleep in the dust, and it is bodies that will be raised when Jesus comes!

Verse 7: "After that, He was seen of James; then of all the apostles."

"... *He was seen of James* ...." This is probably James, the brother of our Lord (that is, as having to do with the *flesh*). Some contend that there were no other children after the birth of Jesus, but the Bible teaches that while Jesus was Mary's firstborn, other children were later born to her.

"... *Then of all the apostles*"—or, *the apostles as a complete body*. This suggests that the James mentioned was not the Apostle James. This part of the verse also adds confirmation to the previous statement that Jesus was seen of "the twelve."

Verse 8: "And last of all He was seen of me also, as of one born out of due time."

Jesus was seen by the Apostle Paul *"as of one born out of due time."* The phrase "one born out of due time" translates the one noun *ektroma*, meaning "born *before* the due time." The Greek word denotes an abortion, an untimely birth. Paul thinks of himself here as one of the Israelites born into the family of God before the time for all Israel to be saved nationally: "For I say unto you, Ye shall not see me henceforth, till ye shall say, Blessed is he that cometh in the name of the Lord" (Matt. 23:39). "Who hath heard such a thing? Who hath seen such things? Shall the earth be made to bring forth in one day? Or shall a nation be born at once? For as soon as Zion travailed, she brought forth her children" (Isa. 66:8).

The conversion of Paul, recorded in Acts 9:3−6, is an illustration of the rebirth of Israel as a nation. In Ezekiel 20:35−38, Hosea 2:14−17, Zechariah 12:10; 13:6, and Romans 11:25−27 we are clearly taught that *Israel WILL be saved as a nation*; however, that does not mean that each and every Israelite will be saved and will enter the joys of the kingdom.

There will be a remnant who will see Him, "and one shall say unto Him, What are these wounds in thine hands?" He will reply, "Those with which I was wounded in the house of my friends" (Zech. 13:6). When they see and recognize their Messiah, they will be converted just as *Paul* was converted when he saw the Lord on the road to Damascus.

Verse 9: "For I am the least of the apostles, that am not meet to be called an apostle, because I persecuted the Church of God."

We see humility in this verse. In I Timothy 1:15 Paul confessed that he was "chief of sinners." In Ephesians 3:8 he refers to himself as "less than the least of all saints." As he writes these lines he no doubt remembers his sinful state before he met the Lord Jesus on the road to Damascus. Perhaps the stoning of Stephen flashed through his mind, along with many other days of bloody persecution; but now, though humbly considering himself chief of all sinners and least of all saints, he had become a recipient of God's marvelous saving grace. He had persecuted the Church of God with all zeal, but in spite of his exceeding sinfulness he had received the saving grace of God, the unmerited favor of Jesus Christ.

Verse 10: "But by the grace of God I am what I am: and His grace which was bestowed upon me was not in vain; but I laboured more abundantly than they all: yet not I, but the grace of God which was with me."

Paul gives credit where credit is due: *"I am what I*

am by the grace of God.'' The same might be truthfully said of US — we are what we are by the grace of God, and *apart from* the grace of God we would all be miserable sinners, headed for hell. All that we are, all that we ever hope to be; all that we have or ever hope to have; all that we have accomplished or ever hope to accomplish is because of God's marvelous grace.

"And His grace which was bestowed upon me was not in vain." This entire verse testifies to the truth of James 2:26: ". . . Faith without works is *dead.''* We are not *saved* by works, but true salvation *produces* works. Any person who professes to be a child of God and yet does not produce spiritual works is deceived; he is not genuinely saved. He may have "religion," but he does not have CHRIST; he is not a Christian.

"For we are His workmanship, created in Christ Jesus unto good works, which God hath before ordained that we should walk in them" (Eph. 2:10).

In Titus 2:11–14 we read, ". . . The grace of God that bringeth salvation hath appeared to all men, teaching us that, denying ungodliness and worldly lusts, we should live soberly, righteously, and godly, in this present world; looking for that blessed hope, and the glorious appearing of the great God and our Saviour Jesus Christ; Who gave Himself for us, that He might redeem us from all iniquity, and purify unto Himself *a peculiar people, ZEALOUS OF GOOD WORKS.''*

It is absolutely foreign to the Word of God that one can be a Christian and not produce good works, for grace *automatically* produces works. We may bring forth a hundredfold, sixty, thirty, or tenfold—*but never zero.* I sincerely believe that God wants all of us to produce a hundredfold—but whether we produce a hundredfold or not, *we PRODUCE if we are saved!*

Greek authorities tell us that two Greek words in our English Bible are translated "vain." The first (used in our present verse) is *kenos*, and means "empty, lacking in anything which should be possessed"—in this particular case, a person who does not produce good works. The same word is used in verse 14: ". . . Then is our preaching vain"—that is, empty and lacking power.

The second Greek word translated "vain" is *mataios*, meaning "lack of results." For example, in James 2:20 we read of the "vain man." The word used there is *kenos*, meaning that the vain man is empty of divinely imparted wisdom and knowledge; but in James 1:26 we read of *vain religion*, and the word used is *mataios*, meaning *a religion that is empty and produces nothing profitable*. *Kenos* emphasizes lack of QUALITY; *mataios* emphasizes lack of EFFECT.

". . . *But I laboured more abundantly than they all.*" Paul is not saying here that he is doing more than all the rest of the Church combined, but that he is doing more than any other *one person* in the assembly—and certainly he is not boasting. He makes the statement as proof of the resurrection of Jesus Christ — for apart from the resurrection of Jesus, the work he had accomplished could not have been possible.

It is only in *the living Christ* that the Church lives and grows. Therefore, Paul declares that he is laboring "more abundantly" (doing more) than any other one individual in the Church, because he believes and trusts continually in the resurrected, living Lord; and thus, *because Christ lives*, the work that he is doing continues to live and grow.

". . . *Yet not I, but the grace of God which was with me.*" Paul makes it clear that he is only the instrument, the mouthpiece, through which God works. The grace of

God is the *power*, the wherewithal, that brings about the accomplishment. Paul was a dedicated man. He was willing, he was zealous, he was alert, he was active; but he was only a tool in the hands of God. He completely ruled *himself* out of the picture — *and each of us should do the same.* It is the grace of God that *produces* in our lives.

To the Ephesians Paul said, "You are saved by grace, through faith—NOT OF YOURSELVES." To Titus he said, "Not by works of righteousness which WE have done . . . ." And now he says, "YET NOT I." So Paul rules man out — and the hardest thing on earth for any minister to do is to get across to his congregation the fact that man is definitely out of the picture. It is GOD—God's love, God's grace, God's Christ—who is our sufficiency, our all in all. *In Him* we find completeness; *out of Him* (without Him) we are nothing.

Read Matthew 7:21–23 and you will clearly see that *it IS possible* to work and produce results apart from the grace of God, but those results are only temporary; they have no lasting, eternal value. Paul said, "I am what I am by the grace of God, and whatever I accomplish is through the grace of God. It is not I — *it is grace!*"

Verse 11: "Therefore whether it were I or they, so we preach, and so ye believed."

Here Paul sums up what he has said thus far in this chapter on the resurrection. Whether Paul or others of the apostles gave the message, *"So WE preach."* That is, "We ALL preach the same message because we are all the apostles of Jesus Christ, and Christ is not divided. There is only one Gospel; there is only one message."

". . . *And so ye believed.*" In other words, "Because you heard, received, and believed the Word, *you are saved*, you are standing in the Word, and you are laboring *because of the grace of God.*"

Christ's Resurrection a Divine Imperative

Verse 12: "Now if Christ be preached that He rose from the dead, how say some among you that there is no resurrection of the dead?"

No other event in history has ever so shaken mankind as did the empty tomb of Jesus. Here Paul introduces the second part of this great chapter. As we study the following verses, we will learn the consequences of the denial of the bodily resurrection of the Lord Jesus Christ (verses 12–19), consequences of *accepting* His bodily resurrection "according to the Scriptures" (verses 20–28), and arguments from experience (verses 29–34). And the experiences of Paul because of his message were not peculiar to him alone; believers down through the ages have had (and will have) such experiences (II Tim. 3:12) until Jesus comes to receive His Church unto Himself.

Paul approaches the subject of the resurrection from this point of view: *"Now if Christ be preached that He rose from the dead . . . ."* This WAS being preached—not only by Paul, but by Timothy and many others. Therefore, since the preaching of this message was transforming lives and working miracles in individuals, how could some of the members of the church declare that there IS no resurrection? The evidence was with them and all around them — *overwhelming* evidence of Christ's resurrection. And since Jesus HAD been raised from the dead, the teaching that there was no resurrection was without foundation. Such heresy should be ignored and ruled out by all believers.

Verse 13: "But if there be no resurrection of the dead, then is Christ not risen."

If Christ DID rise from the dead, then it must be admitted that the dead IN Christ will be raised. Jesus said, *"I am the resurrection, and the life:* he that believeth in me, though he were dead, yet shall he live" (John 11:25).

493

To deny that believers who have died will rise from the dead is to deny that JESUS arose from the dead; and if Jesus be not risen, then how shall we explain away the more than five hundred who saw Him literally after His resurrection? Paul makes it plain that the bodily resurrection of Jesus Christ is an undeniable fact. It cannot BE explained away!

Verse 14: "And if Christ be not risen, then is our preaching vain, and your faith is also vain."

Most religious groups believe in some sort of spiritual existence after death; *but that is not enough.* Those who deny the *bodily* resurrection of Christ deny that His death, burial, and resurrection were sufficient to afford the sinner salvation from the condemnation of sin. To deny His bodily resurrection is to deny His sacrificial death—yes, *and every doctrine contained in the fundamentals of the faith!* If there be no resurrection, if Jesus Christ did not rise *bodily* from the dead, then all preaching is an empty, worthless lie because the fundamentals of the faith hinge completely upon the bodily resurrection of Christ.

Verse 15: "Yea, and we are found false witnesses of God; because we have testified of God that He raised up Christ: whom He raised not up, IF so be that the dead rise not."

Paul is saying here, "If you fellows can prove that Jesus did not rise from the dead, then *we are discovered to be liars and false witnesses,* and we have been giving a lying testimony concerning God Almighty and Jesus Christ."

Paul and his co-laborers preached the bodily resurrection; and if Jesus did not rise, then they had been actually giving testimony against God — they had been preaching that God did what God actually *did not do.* The contention here is as clear as can be: *If there BE no resurrection of the dead,* then God could not have raised up JESUS from the dead. Thus the whole matter is either a lie—entirely false, or it is pure truth—ALL truth.

Verse 16: "For if the dead rise not, then is not Christ raised."

Paul here amplifies the argument for the bodily resurrection of Jesus Christ. If the dead rise not, then *Christ* is not risen. And if Christ is not risen, then we are of all men most miserable, and extremely foolish.

Verse 17: "And if Christ be not raised, your faith is vain; ye are yet in your sins."

If Jesus did not return from the grave, then our faith is empty and to no avail; it has produced no eternal results. Here, the Greek word used is *mataios*, which we discussed in verse 2. As used in this verse it means that if Christ is not raised from the dead, then *FAITH in Christ* will not and cannot produce salvation.

The bodily resurrection of the Lord Jesus Christ is founded upon His atoning sacrifice, and apart from the resurrection there can BE no atoning sacrifice. The *death* of Jesus "according to the Scriptures" was a divine imperative. His *burial* "according to the Scriptures" was a divine imperative. And His *bodily resurrection* "according to the Scriptures" is a divine imperative. To deny one is to deny all.

The Corinthian assembly held *living proof* of the bodily resurrection of Jesus Christ, because many individuals *in* that assembly had exercised faith in His death, burial, and resurrection, and *as a result of that faith* they were NEW CREATIONS in Christ. They proved this by their daily living and by the hope in their hearts.

Verse 18: "Then they also which are fallen asleep in Christ are perished."

Positionally, believers are in Christ NOW: "For ye are dead, and your life is hid with Christ in God" (Col. 3:3).

495

". . . And hath raised us up together, and made us sit together in heavenly places in Christ Jesus" (Eph. 2:6).

"In Christ" expresses the spiritual union between a born again believer and the Lord in His atoning death and resurrection, and the death of the body is pointed to as *"falling asleep."* If there be no resurrection of Jesus Christ, then those who had fallen asleep (supposedly IN Christ) were perished, because apart from the resurrection there could BE no life beyond the grave.

To teach that those who are IN CHRIST should perish denies the fundamentals of the faith, denies the foundation of truth and saving faith. ". . . He which hath begun a good work in you will perform it until the day of Jesus Christ" (Phil. 1:6).

The Greek verb translated "perish" is *apollumi.* It does not mean annihilation or extinction; it means *loss—* not loss of being, but loss of *well-being*; not loss of the spirit, but the ruin of a person insofar as the purpose for existence is concerned. God did not create man to burn in hell; it is not His will that any perish. "God sent not His Son into the world to condemn the world, but that the world through Him might be saved." Those who perish do not perish because it is God's will, but because of their *own stubborn* will. I repeat – the Greek verb used here *does not mean extinction*; it means spiritual and eternal loss—disaster! Paul declares the impossibility of departed believers having lost their eternal life and happiness – but there is no alternative view: *if Christ has NOT been raised*, then ALL have perished! Apart from His bodily resurrection there is no hope.

Verse 19: "If in this life only we have hope in Christ, we are of all men most miserable."

The original does not read "we HAVE hoped," nor "we have HOPE." Literally translated, it is "we *are having* hope," thus stressing the character of the persons who have exercised saving faith in the death, burial, and resurrection of Jesus, not the act of hoping. We do not hope to "*finally* make it" into the Pearly White City. We KNOW whom we have believed; we know that He is able to keep that which we have committed unto Him against that day. We are sure that we will see Him and that we shall be like Him.

If we are men who have hope in Christ in only this short span of life, if we do not have hope *beyond* this life, then we are indeed most pitiable — and we who profess to be followers of Jesus Christ, having announced faith in His death, burial, and resurrection, are even MORE pitiable than all others; we are truly miserable.

The Order of the Resurrections

Verse 20: "But now is Christ risen from the dead, and become the firstfruits of them that slept."

The Greek word here translated "firstfruits" comes from two Hebrew words, one of which means "the chief or principal part" (Num. 18:12; Prov. 3:9), and the other means "the earliest ripe of the crop, or the earliest ripe fruit on the tree" (Ex. 23:16; Neh. 10:35). The two words together mean "the first of the firstfruits" (Ex. 23:19).

". . . *Now is Christ . . . become the firstfruits.*" In Ephesians 4:8—10 Paul reveals that "He who *ascended*" first *descended* into the lower parts of this earth and led captivity captive. Jesus arose from the dead, brought the saints out of the Paradise side of Hades, and ascended far above all heavens. NOW there ARE no saints in the Paradise that was in the heart of the earth before the resurrection of Jesus; they are now in the Paradise above— the Paradise seen by Paul and of which he tells us in II Corinthians 12:1—5. *JESUS FIRST*. He is the resurrection and the life. He is risen, so that death has no more dominion over Him; He is risen — the pledge that those who have fallen asleep in Him shall also rise. Those who sleep in Jesus will be raised first; then those who are alive will be changed — "in a moment, in the twinkling of an eye."

Verse 21: "For since by man came death, by man came also the resurrection of the dead."

In Romans 5:12 we have a clear explanation of the statement, ". . . *since by man came death*":

"Wherefore, as by one man sin entered into the world, and death by sin; and so death passed upon all men, for that all have sinned." Through Adam, death moved upon all men. God told Adam, "The day you eat thereof, you shall surely die." The wages of sin is death.

By man (Adam) came death. By Man (the last Adam, Jesus Christ) came also the *resurrection* of the dead. Christ (possessed in the Godhead from eternity) voluntarily took a body; and in that body He tasted death for every man. He was God, yet He was man; in Him was complete combination of deity and manhood — *and in the flesh JESUS satisfied God.*

Jesus was *man* (who offended God), and yet He was *God* (whom man offended). God was in Christ, reconciling lost man unto Himself:

"But we see Jesus, who was made a little lower than the angels for the suffering of death, crowned with glory and honour; that He by the grace of God should taste death for every man. . . Forasmuch then as the children are partakers of flesh and blood, He also Himself likewise took part of the same; that through death He might destroy him that had the power of death, that is, the devil; and deliver them who through fear of death were all their lifetime subject to bondage" (Heb. 2:9, 14, 15).

"Who His own self bare our sins in His own body on

the tree, that we, being dead to sins, should live unto righteousness: by whose stripes ye were healed" (I Pet. 2:24).

Verse 22: "For as in Adam all die, even so in Christ shall all be made alive."

Adam is the head of the human family, and because of our natural relationship to him, death is common to all men.   But *Christ* is the head of the *spiritual* life, and if any man be in Christ, *he is a new creation.*   All who believe on Him and trust in His finished work shall be made alive.

There is no such thing as "the Fatherhood of God and the brotherhood of man," in the spiritual sense.   We are all brothers from the standpoint of Adam and the fact that in Adam all are sinners; but those who are *in Christ* are alive eternally.   In death, the body will return to dust, *but the spirit will never die!*

We enter the *human* family by birth, born of earthly parents.   We enter the *heavenly family* by birth, born of the Holy Spirit.   Jesus said to Nicodemus, "Except a man be born again, he cannot see the kingdom of God. . . Except a man be born of water and of the Spirit, he cannot enter into the kingdom of God. . . Marvel not that I said unto thee, Ye must be born again" (John 3:3, 5, 7).

To be born of the Spirit, thus becoming a son of God, partaker of divine nature, we are baptized into the body of Christ and hid with Christ in God.   The miracle of the new birth alone guarantees resurrection unto life eternal; but all who are out of Christ will perish forever: "He that hath the Son hath life; and he that hath not the Son of God hath not life" (I John 5:12).

Those who have fallen asleep in Christ will be raised at the first resurrection, which will take place a thousand years before the resurrection of the wicked: "And I saw thrones, and they sat upon them, and judgment was given unto them . . . and they lived and reigned with Christ a thousand years. *But the rest of the dead lived not again until the thousand years were finished. This is the first resurrection.* Blessed and holy is he that hath part in the first resurrection: on such the second death hath no power, but they shall be priests of God and of Christ, and shall reign with Him a thousand years'' (Rev. 20:4–6).

Unbelievers *will be raised:* ''But this I confess unto thee, that after the way which they call heresy, so worship I the God of my fathers, believing all things which are written in the law and in the prophets: And have hope toward God, which they themselves also allow, *that there shall be a resurrection of the dead, BOTH OF THE JUST AND THE UNJUST''* (Acts 24:14,15).

Unbelievers will appear before the Great White Throne judgment: ''And I saw a great white throne, and Him that sat on it, from whose face the earth and the heaven fled away; and there was found no place for them. And I saw the dead, small and great, stand before God; and the books were opened: and another book was opened, which is the book of life: and the dead were judged out of those things which were written in the books, according to their works. And the sea gave up the dead which were in it; and death and hell delivered up the dead which were in them; *and they were judged every man according to their works.* And death and hell were cast into the lake of fire. This is the second death. *And whosoever was not found written in the book of life was cast into the lake of fire''* (Rev. 20:11–15).

Verse 23: ''But every man in his own order: Christ the firstfruits; afterward they that are Christ's at His coming.''

The Greek word here translated ''order'' is generally used as a military term referring to troops in order of rank.

In this verse, two orders are given: *"Christ the firstfruits"* and *"they that are Christ's."*

Christ holds the place of pre-eminence in the resurrection, the first to rise from the dead. Then, those who are His, and who *"at His coming"* are to be raised by virtue of His bodily resurrection. The Greek word translated "coming" has a twofold meaning: It not only means an "arrival," but also means "presence with." Thus, the coming of Jesus in the Rapture not only means that He is coming FOR His saints "in the twinkling of an eye," but also that the saints will be with Him FOREVER (I Thess. 4:17b). The Church will not only be caught up to meet Jesus in the clouds in the air, but we will be with Him through the Millennial reign here on earth, and will continue with Him throughout the eternity of eternities.

"Be patient therefore, brethren, unto the coming of the Lord. Behold, the husbandman waiteth for the precious fruit of the earth, and hath long patience for it, until he receive the early and latter rain. *Be ye also patient; stablish your hearts: for the coming of the Lord draweth nigh"* (James 5:7,8).

Verse 24: "Then cometh the end, when He shall have delivered up the kingdom to God, even the Father; when He shall have put down all rule and all authority and power."

The Greek word here translated "then" does not mean "immediately," but indicates a sequence in time. That is, *"after an interval"* Jesus will come for His saints, we will be caught up to meet Him in the air, we will be rewarded for our stewardship, and then we will return with Him to reign for one thousand glorious years here upon earth. We will be with Him in the final consummation of time and of God's dealings with man upon this earth, and then we will move into the Pearly White City.

"The end" refers to the consummation of all things

on earth, just before the new heaven, the new earth, and the Pearly White City described in Revelation 21. The Greek word translated "end" is *telos*, and points to the last event in a *series* of events.

"... *When He shall have delivered up the kingdom to God, even the Father ...*." The Scriptures clearly teach that God the Father has given to the Son all authority in heaven and on earth (Matt. 28:18; John 5:22–27; 17:2; I Pet. 3:22). When Jesus shall have delivered up the kingdom to God the Father, this momentous act will complete that which the Father committed unto the Son to accomplish. He (the Son) must reign until He has put all enemies under His feet, until all enemies have become His footstool.

"*When He shall have put down all rule and all authority and power.*" The Greek word here is *katargeo*, which means "to reduce to inactivity." Christ will have all authority in heaven and earth until He has reduced to inactivity all that is against God the Father and righteousness.

Verse 25: "For He must reign, till He hath put all enemies under His feet."

"*He MUST reign ...*." God has declared it, and it cannot be changed. "The Lord said unto my Lord, Sit thou at my right hand, until I make thine enemies thy footstool... *For ever, O Lord, thy word is settled in heaven*" (Psalm 110:1; 119:89). Not until Jesus has conquered and subdued all enemies, regardless of how great or how small, will He deliver up the kingdom to God the Father.

Just before Jesus went to Calvary, He said to the Father, "I have glorified thee on the earth: I have finished the work which thou gavest me to do" (John 17:4). This refers to the work on earth insofar as salvation is concerned. Jesus came the first time to redeem the soul;

He is coming the second time to redeem the body—and all creation:

"For we know that the whole creation groaneth and travaileth in pain together until now. And not only they, but ourselves also, which have the firstfruits of the Spirit, even we ourselves groan within ourselves, waiting for the adoption, to wit, the redemption of our body" (Rom. 8:22,23).

"Beloved, now are we the sons of God, and it doth not yet appear what we shall be: but we know that, when He shall appear, we shall be like Him; for we shall see Him as He is" (I John 3:2).

Verse 26: "The last enemy that shall be destroyed is death."

Since Adam, death has been an enemy to the human family—an *active* enemy, taking no vacation; "it is appointed unto men to die." Through the disobedience of Adam, sin and death moved upon all men; but there is coming a day when there will be no more victims for death to claim; it will be rendered inactive.

The final annihilation of physical death will take place when "death and hell" are cast into the lake of fire at the Great White Throne Judgment (Rev. 20:14). As long as Satan has access to earth and its inhabitants there will be sin, and as long as there is sin there will be death. In Revelation 20:10 we are told that Satan will be put into the lake of fire where the beast and the false prophet will already be, and he will be tormented day and night forever and forever.

The subject of this chapter is the fact of the resurrection of the believer, Christ being the firstfruit. What is here stated about death being abolished, affords no grounds for the idea that the wicked dead will in the end be delivered from death. The state of the unsaved dead is not here in view, nor is it being dealt with. Those who die without Christ will spend eternity separated from God, tormented forever in the lake of fire that burns with brimstone—death unending; but for the believer, death will be destroyed.

Verse 27: "For He hath put all things under His feet. But when He saith all things are put under Him, it is manifest that He is excepted, which did put all things under Him."

There is special emphasis on *"all things."* Paul is emphasizing here what he has already declared in verse 24. Through disobedience, Adam lost the position of authority delegated to him by God in the beginning—authority over all creation. Everything on earth was subject to Adam (Gen. 1:26,28), but he lost that position through sin.

The last Adam *bought back* all that the first Adam lost through disobedience to the command of God; therefore *the act is already accomplished* . . . it cannot fail. We have assurance that final victory and deliverance are sure, because *Jesus, the last Adam*, cannot fail.

"He hath put ALL things under His feet"—with one exception: The Father Himself was not put in subjection to the Son. The Father has done and is doing all to the glory of the Son. We are saved for the sake of the Son of His love (Eph. 4:32), and we will be on display in the Pearly White City through all eternity to show forth the exceeding riches of God's grace in His kindness toward us through Christ Jesus (Eph. 2:6,7).

Verse 28: "And when all things shall be subdued unto Him, then shall the Son also Himself be subject unto Him that put all things under Him, that God may be all in all."

". . . *When all things shall be subdued* . . . ." No one knows the exact day or moment, but *whensoever* all things have been subjected unto Him, then (immediately) shall *the Son also* be subjected to God the Father who subjected all things unto the Son. The truth set forth here is clear:

When the Son of God (who became the Son of man) has completed the work of subjecting all things unto Himself (and God the Father gave Him authority to do just that), then with great delight He will voluntarily subject *Himself* to God the Father, from the standpoint of eternal governmental reign and rule. And yet, the Son will be no less in the Godhead than He was in the beginning. He is equal with the Father in omnipotence, omniscience, and omnipresence.

And WHY does the Son willingly and joyfully subject Himself to God the Father? ". . . *THAT GOD MAY BE ALL IN ALL!*" When that glorious moment comes, all—yes, ALL—in heaven, in the new earth, in the vast regions of space, in the Pearly White City, will be merged in the absolute, divine, infinite supremacy of God the Father.

God the Father will then be everything IN everything. He will never again be forced to turn His head while His only begotten Son dies on a cruel cross. He will never again be forced to see His children stoned, jailed, beaten, martyred. There will be no special work for God the Son or God the Holy Spirit to carry out, because all things will have been accomplished, all things that are opposed to God and His righteousness will have been put down and reduced to inactivity. God the Father, God the Son, and God the Holy Ghost will then be united and will be as ONE in all things everywhere — in the third heaven, in the new heaven, in the new earth. I pray with John the Beloved, "Even so, COME, Lord Jesus!"

Verse 29: "Else what shall they do which are baptized for the dead, if the dead rise not at all? Why are they then baptized for the dead?"

This is one of those verses so difficult for believers to understand, and I would not profess to know all about it. The only way we can deal with a verse like this is to compare Scripture with Scripture and never try to make the verse say what we might *like* for it to say.

Some say that this verse refers to certain ceremonies which took place when a believer was buried; but there is not one line of Scripture to substantiate such an argument, nor does history record any evidence of such ceremonies. Therefore, we do not accept such teaching.

Greek authorities tell us that when Paul penned these words under inspiration, the original was without punctuation marks. Let us put the first question mark after the word "baptized," and it would read thus: "Else what shall they do which are baptized? It is for (in the interest of) the dead. If the dead are not raised at all, why then are they baptized for them?"

The question is, *"If there be no resurrection of the dead, than what is the value of being baptized?* Baptism denotes death, burial, and resurrection. We are buried with Christ in baptism, and raised to walk in newness of life. But if there IS no resurrection, *then what is the purpose of baptism in the first place?"*

When we are baptized we testify through water baptism that we have died to the world, we are buried with Christ, and we are raised as a new creation in Him, to walk in newness of life; but if there is no resurrection, then why baptize? If there be no resurrection of the dead, the ordinance of baptism—instead of setting forth the identification of the believer with the risen Christ—has no meaning at all, either for HIM or for them, for all perish at death. Both His command and their obedience in the ordinance are null and void. They testify to doctrines that have no significance. Their baptism then is in the interest of death—not life.

Never entertain the idea that Paul would suggest that a *living* person could be baptized for one who had departed this life. Baptism was for those who had exercised faith in the finished work of Jesus, thereby becoming believers— dead IN sin before they believed, dead TO sin AFTER they believed unto salvation. The whole truth set forth here is that if there be no resurrection from the dead, it is void and foolish to baptize those who have professed faith in the finished work of Jesus Christ, who through the rite of baptism are taking the places in the church left vacant by those who have died—because the Gospel IS the death, burial, and resurrection of Jesus, "according to the Scriptures."

Verse 30: "And why stand we in jeopardy every hour?"

If all perish with death, then why should Paul and his fellow laborers suffer as they were suffering? Paul had been in jail, he had been stoned, he had been beaten, he had been shipwrecked—all for the sake of the Gospel; and if there *is no resurrection* then it is absurd for one to sacrifice as Paul and his co-workers were doing.

Verse 31: "I protest by your rejoicing which I have in Christ Jesus our Lord, I die daily."

Paul's joy in the believers in Corinth was not just human boasting. He gloried in them because of his relationship to Christ—and theirs. They were members of the same body, they had the same eternal life that Paul had *"in Christ Jesus our Lord."* Christ was not only their Saviour, but Lord of their lives as well; so Paul speaks here of the oneness of himself with the believers in Corinth and with Christ Jesus.

". . . *I die daily.*" This statement points to Paul's unusual physical sufferings, and it also points to the extreme perils of which he speaks — as in II Corinthians 4:11: "For we which live are alway delivered unto death for Jesus' sake, that the life also of Jesus might be made manifest in our mortal flesh!" It was Paul who said, "We are accounted as sheep for the slaughter . . ." (Rom. 8:35,36). He also said, "Yea, and all that will live godly in Christ Jesus shall suffer persecution" (II Tim. 3:12). We have the promise, "If we suffer (with Him), we shall also reign with Him" (II Tim. 2:12). Paul suffered physically, mentally, and was constantly aware that his life was in danger — but he counted it a privilege and joy to suffer for Jesus, who suffered that we might have life.

Verse 32: "If after the manner of men I have fought with beasts at Ephesus, what advantageth it me, if the dead rise not? Let us eat and drink; for to morrow we die."

"If after the manner of men . . . ." This statement simply means, "If I did it with human motives, with the idea of personal gain, pride, and prestige." (And if Jesus did not rise from the dead, then Paul could have had no purpose *other* than human gain.)

". . . I have fought with beasts at Ephesus . . . ." Paul was a free-born Roman Jew; he did not buy his citizenship nor earn it. He was *born* free, and therefore he could not be compelled to fight with the beasts in the arena in Rome. He was a citizen of Rome, and he could not be thrown to the beasts because of his citizenship. So undoubtedly the beasts to which he refers here were the maniacal mobs who attacked him and so brutally beat him. Most outstanding Bible scholars believe that on one occasion they actually killed Paul and dragged him outside the city, leaving him for dead; but the saints gathered round and prayed, and Paul was literally raised from the dead. Study the entire nineteenth chapter of Acts, and Acts 14:19,20.

". . . *What advantageth it me, if the dead rise not?*"
Paul is asking, "If there be no resurrection and no rewarding day, why should I go on suffering for the Gospel?"
Thus he makes it crystal-clear that there IS a rewarding
day coming for all suffering saints. At the judgment seat
of Christ, when believers have been raised from the dead,
they will be rewarded for their stewardship (I Cor. 3:11–15;
II Cor. 5:10).

If the dead rise not, "*Let us eat and drink*; *for to
morrow we die.*" To reject the Bible doctrine of the bodily resurrection of Jesus Christ and the consequent resurrection of the dead—saved and unsaved—opens the door to
unbridled sensuality. Those who believe that man is no
more than any other animal, as a rule will follow the
practice of eating, drinking, and making merry—many times
in the most debased way imaginable! But to accept the
Bible fact that death does *not* end it all and that there will
be a resurrection and a judgment day, provides a moral
safeguard against sensuality.

Verse 33: "Be not deceived: evil communications
corrupt good manners."

Satan is a deceiver; his first desire is to damn your
soul. But if you are saved and you cling to the Rock of
Ages, then the devil sets about to destroy your testimony
and rob you of your joy and your spiritual birthright.

"*Be not deceived . . . .*" The Greek language here
is in the present tense, meaning for the believers in Corinth to *cease BEING deceived.* Seemingly, they were
continually succumbing to deception. There were those
in the assembly who were practicing immorality, suffering
moral decline, making gluttons and drunkards of themselves at the Lord's table.

". . . *Evil communications (or companions) corrupt
good manners.*" Paul here warns believers not to fellow-

ship with those who are living contrary to the leadership of the Holy Spirit. In II Corinthians 6:14—17 he warns, "Be ye not unequally yoked together with unbelievers . . . what part hath he that believeth with an infidel? And what agreement hath the temple of God with idols? For ye are the temple of the living God. . . Wherefore, come out from among them, and be ye separate, saith the Lord, and touch not the unclean thing . . . ." How can an infidel and a believer walk together? *"Can two walk together, except they be agreed?"* (Amos 3:3).

Therefore, be not deceived; evil company DOES corrupt good manners. ("Good manners" means literally, *"good things"* — not only behavior, but all that is good and profitable.) We must abstain from all appearance of evil, we must have no fellowship with the unfruitful works of darkness.

Verse 34: "Awake to righteousness, and sin not; for some have not the knowledge of God: I speak this to your shame."

"Awake to righteousness . . . ." The tense of the Greek verb here signifies that they are to awaken *immediately, at once,* and permit righteousness to occupy its rightful place in their hearts and in their daily practices of life.

". . . *And sin not."* Here, the tense of the Greek verb denotes present, continuous action — that is, the believer is to have no mapped-out, daily-pursued course of unrighteousness or sin. He is not to play with error, for to do so is to invite grave risk of being *led into* sin, and a continuation of such would lead eventually to the dulling of spiritual feelings or senses, thereby causing the believer to grow cold and carnal.

"For some have not the knowledge of God." There were some in the assembly who were proud of their ability,

wisdom, intelligence, and holiness — and yet they allowed error to exist in their midst—error concerning the resurrection. They were willingly ignorant, unable to recognize the character and power of God: and these few who had not the knowledge of God were affecting the entire assembly. Thus, Paul speaks to the entire group when he says, *"I speak this to your shame."* That is, to the shame of the entire church. Something must be done about the situation, immediately. Those who believed error must either repent and believe the Gospel, or else the believers were to have no fellowship with them. In other words, Paul says, "Either set the church right—or stop advertising your intelligence and wisdom; because actually, *you are ignorant.*"

The Method of Resurrection

Verse 35: "But some man will say, How are the dead raised up? and with what body do they come?"

In the following verses, Paul answers two questions concerning the resurrection:

1. The question having to do with *the possibility* of resurrection.
2. *The kind of body* that is to be raised.

He speaks first from the standpoint of nature, and then settles the questions *according to the Word of God.*

In the very outset of the epistle Paul had declared that "the natural man receiveth not the things of the Spirit of God: for they are foolishness unto him: neither can he know them, because they are spiritually discerned." It is impossible for the human mind to comprehend the resurrection of the body from the dust to which it returns at death. Paul knew that from the human standpoint some would ask just how the resurrection is to take place, and what kind of body believers will have in their eternal state.

Verse 36: "Thou fool, that which thou (thyself) sowest is not quickened, except it die."

Paul suggests that only a foolish one would ask such a question. The Greek emphasizes the second "thou," actually meaning *"thou thyself."* Thus, by his own experience one should know the answer to this question; for as the seed perishes and produces a new and more abundant life, so it is with the body of the believer: It is sown in corruption, it will be raised in incorruption; it is sown in mortality, it will be raised in immortality.

Jesus referred to the sower and the seed on several occasions while He was here on earth. We can learn much from the earth and from nature if we will but realize that God is the Creator of all things, and that all things were made BY Him and FOR Him.

Verses 37 and 38: "And that which thou sowest, thou sowest not that body that shall be, but bare grain, it may chance of wheat, or of some other grain: but God giveth it a body as it hath pleased Him, and to every seed his own body."

Paul continues his illustration: The grain that we sow is not the grain that will come forth from the ground. Paul is here contrasting the little grain—dry and certainly not beautiful—with that which it produces, the beautiful plant that springs from the grain that is sown. The seed receives its new body from God, for God is the author of ALL life: and in the same way, He will provide a resurrection body for every believer—a body like unto His own glorified body.

God the Father will fashion the resurrection body *"as it hath pleased Him."* Here we have the declaration of the omnipotence and the absolute foreknowledge of God. Redemption was completed from start to finish before ever the foundation of this world was laid. God is sovereign: He knows the end in the beginning, and everything *between* the beginning and the ending. Each believer's resurrection body is already foreordained "as it hath pleased Him"—that is, as God willed, according to His predetermined counsel.

Verse 39: "All flesh is not the same flesh: but there is one kind of flesh of men, another flesh of beasts, another of fishes, and another of birds."

Paul lays down the fact that even in this world as we know it, there is more than one kind of body. That argument proves that God gives to each living creature (and created thing) a body suitable for and adjusted to its part in creation. If that be so, it is only reasonable to expect that He will give *us* a new body, *fitted for the resurrection.*

Verses 40 and 41: "There are also celestial (heavenly) bodies, and bodies terrestrial (earthly): but the glory of the celestial is one, and the glory of the terrestrial is another. There is one glory of the sun, and another glory of the moon, and another glory of the stars: for one star differeth from another star in glory."

The Greek word translated "glory" is *doxa.* The basic idea set forth by this word is that of manifestation. God's acts, His Being, and His character are manifested through His glory. Paul mentions inanimate things here—the sun, the moon, the stars. The manifestation of the *nature* of these heavenly bodies is their differing degrees of beauty and splendor.

"The heavens declare the glory of God; and the firmament sheweth His handywork. Day unto day uttereth speech, and night unto night sheweth knowledge. There is no speech nor language, where their voice is not heard" (Psalm 19:1–3).

The stars testify to God's infinite wisdom and the omnipotence of His inexhaustible power as Creator of all things. The Holy Spirit here points out the different degrees of splendor and beauty of the stars—their difference in brilliance, lustre, and glory. However, we are not to think that this teaches that there will be different degrees of glory in the bodies of the saints in resurrection; we will all be like Jesus. Paul is simply pointing out here the inexhaustible power of God the Creator.

Through this illustration we are assured that the God who had the power to create the sun, the moon, the stars in all of their glory and splendor, certainly has power to bring about the state of glory that will be manifested in the glorified bodies of His saints in the resurrection.

Verses 42 and 43: "So also is the resurrection of the dead. It is sown in corruption; it is raised in incorruption: It is sown in dishonour; it is raised in glory: it is sown in weakness; it is raised in power."

Here is confirmed the truth that there will be no difference in degrees of glory in the bodies of the resurrected saints. "*The dead*" mentioned here are believers only— "they that are heavenly." In that glorious resurrection morning, *all believers*—those whose bodies sleep in the dust and those who are alive at His coming—will be given bodies that possess incorruptibility, bodies of glory and power, yea, like unto the Lord's glorious resurrection body!

Here we are shown that just as there is a definite and intimate connection between the seed sown and the plant which the seed produces, so will there be a definite likeness between the natural body and the resurrection body. It is clearly stated and four times emphasized in our present Scripture that this body is *sown* (in corruption, in dishonor, in weakness, a natural body), and that *this body is RAISED* (incorruptible, in honor, in power, a spiritual body). There are some who contend that this body will not be raised; but according to the Word of God the body of the individual believer is to be *redeemed* (Rom. 8:23).

This old body of corruption will be made incorruptible by the same God who was made *flesh* in order that WE might be made sons of God through the miracle of the new birth. Jesus was God in flesh, and in that body of flesh He conquered the world, the flesh, the devil, death, hell, and the grave; and He who provided the Saviour in flesh *will redeem these bodies of flesh!* A bit later in our study we will see that our incorruptible bodies will resemble this natural body and that we will "know as we are known."

Verse 44: "It is sown a natural body; it is raised a spiritual body. There is a natural body, and there is a spiritual body."

The body of the believer is sown in dishonor — a body of corruption and weakness that will return to dust; but that body which is sown in dishonor, corruption, and weakness will be raised in *incorruption, glory, and power.* The resurrection body will not be just a body of flesh; it will be a spiritual body, not limited by earthly conditions as our present bodies are. It will be a body of flesh and bone as was the body of Jesus when He invited His disciples to handle Him and see that He was not a spirit. Our resurrection bodies will be able to take food, although we will not NEED food. Jesus ate broiled fish and honeycomb to prove to His frightened disciples that He was not a spirit.

"*There is a NATURAL body, and there is a SPIRITUAL body.*" This is a clear, concise statement. Just as surely as the believer has a physical body suited and fitted for this earthly life, he will just that surely have a *spiritual* body fitted for the Pearly White City and life eternal with Jesus.

GOD fashioned these bodies of flesh, and when we

consider the human body we must admit that it is truly a miracle — but we must remember that we were *created by the GOD of miracles*; and the God who constituted our earthly bodies for earth, with its responsibilities and trials, will fashion our spiritual bodies to meet the conditions of the glory in which we will live.

The Christian who lives by faith and walks by faith spends no time worrying about what kind of body he will have on the resurrection morning. It will be a spiritual body — but it will not be simply a *spirit*. As Christ's body was in His resurrection, so shall our bodies be. Please study Luke 24:36–44.

Verse 45: "And so it is written, The first man Adam was made a living soul; the last Adam was made a quickening spirit."

God formed Adam out of the dust of the ground, breathed into his nostrils the breath of life — *and he became a living soul*; but this first Adam failed in his responsibility toward God, and *lost* man's perfect estate.

The last Adam was a life-giving spirit, the Lord Jesus Christ — obedient, suffering, victorious over all. He took a body of flesh, and in that body He conquered the world, the flesh, and the devil. He laid His life down as the purchase price to buy back all that the first Adam lost.

The Scriptures clearly show us that the Lord Jesus Christ became "a quickening spirit" when He rose from the dead. It was *AFTER His resurrection* that He breathed on His disciples, saying, "Receive ye the Holy Ghost" (John 20:22). Just now we are not looking primarily at either the incarnation or the ascension, however important they are. The subject of this chapter is not necessarily the *death* of Jesus, though His death was a divine imperative since He was the only One who could pay the sin-debt. But the heart of chapter 15 is *the glorious resurrection of the Lamb of God*. And because HE was raised, WE shall also be raised at His coming.

Verse 46: "Howbeit that was not first which is spiritual, but that which is natural; and afterward that which is spiritual."

Paul here states a divine principle relating to the development of human life, which begins with the natural, and subsequently receives the spiritual through the miracle of Almighty God. There is no such thing as the natural man *growing into* a spiritual man. Jesus paid the sin-debt, satisfied the law of God and God's righteousness, and when we receive HIM we receive and possess all that He purchased through His sacrificial death, His burial, and His glorious resurrection.

". . . *That was not first which is spiritual* . . . ." You will notice that all through the Word of God, the natural precedes the spiritual—i.e., *first Cain*, then Abel; *Ishmael*, then Isaac; Esau, *then* Jacob. The term "spiritual" here signifies more than the spiritual body. Indeed we *now* have a *natural* body, and in the hereafter we shall have a *spiritual* body—and that is the primary teaching of the passage. But it also holds good in that in our unregenerate state we had natural tendencies which caused us to do evil because of our descent from Adam; but after we accepted Christ as Saviour, *spiritual* life was imparted to us — and since that time the natural is to be under the control of the spiritual.

The last Adam (the Lord Jesus) did what the first Adam could not do because of the weakness of the flesh. In clear, understandable terms, God laid down what Adam could do, and what he was *forbidden to do*. Adam openly and deliberately disobeyed God's command. Flesh *cannot* please God; but those of us who are born again are not in the flesh: "But ye are not in the flesh, but in the Spirit, if so be that the Spirit of God dwell in you. Now if any man have not the Spirit of Christ, he is none of His" (Rom. 8:9).

Verses 47—49: "The first man is of the earth, earthy: the second man is the Lord from heaven. As is the earthy, such are they also that are earthy: and as is the heavenly, such are they also that are heavenly. And as we have borne the image of the earthy, we shall also bear the image of the heavenly."

As was the first man, so are the children of Adam. We inherited Adam's nature, and in Adam all die.

As was the Heavenly One, so are the believers. As we bore the image of the first man, so shall we who are saved bear the image of the second Man (Christ). Believers are now IN CHRIST, and we shall bear *the image of Christ* in the glorious resurrection body which He will give us when He comes for His saints. Every believer is predestined to be conformed to the image of God's dear Son.

It is true that we grow in grace, and we should become more and more like the Master every day; but there is a day coming when we will receive *full and final conformity* which cannot be ours until Christ calls the Church to meet Him in the air. When the Church is complete, when the soul that completes the body of Christ is saved and the first resurrection takes place, then He will transform these bodies of humiliation into conformity with His glorious body according to the working of His ability even to subdue all things unto Himself. We have the promise made by Him who cannot lie, and we are sure that one day *we shall be LIKE Him.*

Because of Adam's sin, *in Adam all die.* Because of the obedience and victory of the second Man, *in Christ shall all be made alive.* By the grace of God, Jesus tasted death for EVERY man (Heb. 2:9). The first Adam became a sinner and *because of his sin* was sentenced to death before he became the head of the human family. The last Adam, the Lord Jesus Christ, bore our sins in His own body and died FOR sin before HE became the head of the Church and of those who believe (Eph. 5:25—32).

Jesus told the Pharisees that unless a grain of wheat should fall into the ground and die, it would abide alone; but in dying it would bring forth much fruit. Until Jesus died, *He abode alone*; but after He died He bore much fruit, and is still bringing many sons into the Church.

There is life in none other. Jesus is the Way, the Truth, the Life, the Door to heaven, and the Good Shepherd of the sheep. He is the author of eternal life, the author and finisher of our faith. Believers are dead, and their lives are hid with Christ in God. Even NOW we sit together in heavenly places in Christ Jesus.

There was never hope for man in any other. The blood sacrifices of the Old Testament could not take away sin. Jesus is our only hope today. No man cometh unto the Father but by Him.

Jesus told His own people, ". . . Ye WILL NOT come to me, that ye might have life. . . I am come in my Father's name, and ye receive me not: If another shall come in his own name, him ye will receive" (John 5:40,43). Jesus refers here to Antichrist, and those who follow him will perish everlastingly in the lake of fire. But the believer has life eternal in Christ, and is predestined to be conformed to His image and be glorified with Him.

Verse 50: "Now this I say, brethren, that flesh and blood cannot inherit the kingdom of God; neither doth corruption inherit incorruption."

The truth set forth in this verse confirms what has preceded it, but it also prepares the way for the answer to the question concerning what will happen to believers who are alive when Jesus comes in the Rapture. Flesh and blood constitute a nature that is perishable, and we know that nothing perishable shall enter the kingdom of God. Flesh and blood will eventually produce corruption, and *incorruption* characterizes all that has to do with the kingdom of God.

The resurrection body will be a body of flesh and bone. There will be no blood in the resurrection body, because "the life of the flesh is in the blood" and Jesus gave His life (His blood) for the remission of sin. (Personally, I believe He presented His blood to the heavenly Father when He returned to the Father immediately after His resurrection — John 20:17.)

"... *Flesh and blood*"—that is, man as he is here upon earth—positively CANNOT inherit the kingdom of God. Man at his very best is altogether vanity. Apart from the resurrection, man cannot enter into the kingdom of God. True, the resurrection was brought about by another Man — but the Man Christ Jesus was not only man — He was also God. Apart from the death, burial, and resurrection of Jesus, man could never inherit the kingdom of God, he could never have lived where God reigns. What a glorious truth, that born again believers will be raised incorruptible and will reign with Christ.

Verses 51 and 52: "Behold, I shew you a mystery: We shall not all sleep, but we shall all be changed, in a moment, in the twinkling of an eye, at the last trump: For the trumpet shall sound, and the dead shall be raised incorruptible, and we shall be changed."

"... *I shew you a mystery* ...." The "mystery" here mentioned refers to the fact that in the Rapture (the first stage of the second coming of Christ), living believers will inherit the kingdom of God despite their being flesh and blood — but we are also to learn of the miracle which will make this possible.

"We shall not all sleep, but we shall all be changed . . . ." Not all believers will die physically before the Lord's return. The use of the pronoun "we" does not necessarily suggest that Paul expected to be alive when the Rapture occurred. He used similar expressions on several occasions. Greek authorities tell us that this passage should be translated "We, *the living*," meaning born again believers. Both I Thessalonians 4:15 and our present verse tell us that when Jesus comes in the Rapture, believers will be divided into two classes—the living and the dead.

The Word of God teaches that believers should be prepared to meet death, with courage and without fear (Phil. 1:21–23; 3:20,21); but it also teaches that we should consistently be looking for the glorious appearing of the great God and our Saviour, Jesus Christ. We are not to be "star-gazers," but we are to occupy until He comes.

All believers will be taken in the Rapture. The saints who have died will be raised incorruptible and the living saints will be translated—*"in a moment, in the twinkling of an eye."* Here is pointed out the *suddenness* of the Rapture—and even though there may not be "signs" of His coming, the absence of signs is no proof that He is not near.

Actually, the signs of the times point to the *Revelation*—the time when "every eye shall see Him." No man knows the day nor the hour of His coming, but there are many, many signs that point to the Revelation of Jesus—and since that be true, surely the Rapture must be upon us! It could take place at any moment.

". . . For the trumpet shall sound . . . ." The trumpet here is literal. It is not to be confused with the trumpet in Revelation 11:15, also literal. The seals, the vials,

521

and the trumpets in Revelation all occur *after* the Rapture of the Church, and certainly Paul would not have been writing to the Corinthians and the Thessalonians concerning prophecies that had not even been made at that time! The trumpet mentioned in our present verse, and in I Thessalonians 4:16 is a literal trumpet, not symbolic.

"*. . . The dead shall be raised incorruptible, and we shall be changed.*" In I Thessalonians 4:16 we read, "The dead in Christ shall rise *first*." The fact that some believers are dead will not be of any disadvantage to them in the resurrection. I personally believe that the bodies of the saints who have died will be raised up to the level of the living saints, and then TOGETHER we will ALL be caught up in one body in the clouds, to meet the Lord in the air. There will be no interval between the raising of the dead in Christ and the changing of the living saints. It will all be over in the twinkling of an eye.

Only the saved will have part in this resurrection. The resurrection of unbelievers is not referred to here. It will take place a thousand years later (Rev. 20:5). Anyone who refers to a "general resurrection" or a "general judgment" is advertising scriptural ignorance.

The statement here having to do with the raising of the dead in Christ confirms the truth of verses 42–44. The living believers will receive the same incorruptible body as will those who are resurrected at His coming.

Verse 53: "For this corruptible must put on incorruption, and this mortal must put on immortality."

"*. . . This corruptible MUST put on incorruption. . . .*" It is a divine necessity that this body be changed to prepare it for the kingdom of God. The Greek verb rendered "put on" signifies putting on a garment. It points out the nature of the change that will occur at the resurrection, as well as confirming the truth taught in previous verses. It also confirms the definite and positive connection between the body we now possess and the body that is raised or changed.

This mortal body, sown in corruption, *must "put on"* immortality. This definitely points out the connection between the former body and the raised (or changed) body. Study Philippians 3:21 and II Corinthians 5:4.

Verse 54: "So when this corruptible shall have put on incorruption, and this mortal shall have put on immortality, then shall be brought to pass the saying that is written, Death is swallowed up in victory."

Tremendous words! *"Death is swallowed up in victory!"* The fact that death is *swallowed up* expresses the final, complete, eternal removal of every trace of the physical effects of sin that moved upon the whole human race through Adam. For those who are saved, every trace of the curse of Satan's power will be removed. When death is swallowed up in victory, every minute trace and scar will be eternally removed:

"He will swallow up death in victory; and the Lord God will wipe away tears from off all faces; and the rebuke of His people shall He take away from off all the earth: for the Lord hath spoken it" (Isa. 25:8). This prophecy, which had special and significant reference to Israel, is now true concerning each and every believer. Jesus conquered death, hell, and the grave. He was dead, He is alive for evermore, and He holds the keys of hell and of death (Rev. 1:18).

Verse 55: "O death, where is thy sting? O grave, where is thy victory?"

We are told that the best Greek manuscripts read, "O *death*, where is thy victory? O *death*, where is thy sting?"

The truth here is stated in Hosea 13:14: "I will ransom

them from the power of the grave; I will redeem them from death: O death, I will be thy plagues; O grave, I will be thy destruction: repentance shall be hid from mine eyes."

The Hebrew word translated "grave" is *Sheol*, which is NOT the grave, but a region which we believe to be in the center of the earth where all spirits went at death in the Old Testament. It was divided into two compartments. The rich man died, and "in hell he lifted up his eyes, being in torments." The beggar Lazarus died, "and was carried by the angels into Abraham's bosom" (Luke 16:19–31). It is said of Jesus, "Thou wilt not leave my soul in hell" (Psalm 16:10; Acts 2:25–27).

But since the death, burial, resurrection and ascension of Christ, there IS no Sheol for the believer. Jesus died, descended into the lower parts of this earth, announced to the spirits in prison that the sin-debt had been paid. He then led captivity captive and ascended far above all heavens, taking with Him the spirits of the righteous (Eph. 4:8–10).

It is *death*, not the grave, which gains victory over the body of flesh. In this body we die, and the grave is just a place where the body is deposited after death. It is *death* that is to be swallowed up in victory. It is *death* that is to be robbed of its sting and its poison. Jesus has already conquered death; therefore, WE are conquerors because HE conquered. For the believer, death has no sting. It is simply a valley of shadow where Jesus walks with us—not INTO, but THROUGH it (Psalm 23:4).

Verse 56: "The sting of death is sin; and the strength of sin is the law."

In connection with this, please study Romans 5:21; 6:12, 14, 17; 7:11, 14, 20, 23, 25; 8:2; Hebrews 3:13; 11:25; 12:4; and James 1:15.

The wages of sin is death. When sin is finished it brings forth death. Paul said, *"I had not known sin had not the law said, Thou shalt not covet."* By the deeds of the law there shall no flesh be justified; by the law is the knowledge of sin (Rom. 3:20). God's law is holy, just, and good; but what the law could not do (not because the *law* was weak, but because of the weakness of the flesh), God sent His own Son to accomplish. Jesus, in the likeness of sinful flesh, *condemned sin IN the flesh*, that we in Him might be made the righteousness of the law.

Jesus removed the sting of death. (The *hornet* is as harmless as a *housefly* if he has no stinger.) Death cannot harm the Christian. True, it separates us from our loved ones and from earthly ties; but it is only the doorway through which we step from earth to Paradise in a fleeting moment of time — absent from the body, *present with the Lord*!

"The sting of death is sin, and the strength of sin is the law." (But Jesus *fulfilled* every jot and tittle of the law.) Therefore, sin has been conquered, defeated, and put away. Sin gives death its power, and the law gives *sin* its power; but the Lord Jesus Christ is "the end of the law for righteousness to everyone that believeth" (Rom. 10:4). Through the death, burial, and resurrection of Jesus Christ, sin and death have already been overcome and conquered.

It is true that to the believer death retains its outward form. Saints die (fall asleep in Jesus); but death has lost its power to harm the born again believer. If you are afraid to die, if it frightens you to think about death, you had better make a double-check on your conversion experience! It is very likely that the devil slipped you a counterfeit.

Verse 57: "But thanks be to God, which giveth us

the victory through our Lord Jesus Christ."

"... *God ... GIVETH us the victory ...*" (present tense) — pointing to a constant process through which the believer, because of the death and resurrection of Jesus, constantly gains the victory over sin. We are victorious over sin because greater is He that is in us than he that is in the world (I John 4:4).

"... *Through our Lord Jesus Christ.*" We overcome because of the strength imparted to us through Christ and His finished work. We believe on Him, embrace His finished work, and become partaker of divine nature. The Holy Spirit then dwells in our bosom, we are led by Him into paths of right living, and therefore we do not fulfill the lust of the flesh.

Yes, thanks be unto God, we are MORE than conquerors through the Lord Jesus Christ — but *without Him* we can do nothing! In Jesus we are victorious over the world, the flesh, and the devil, death, hell, and the grave. Without Jesus we are helpless, hopeless, and hell-bound!

Verse 58: "Therefore, my beloved brethren, be ye stedfast, unmoveable, always abounding in the work of the Lord, forasmuch as ye know that your labour is not in vain in the Lord."

"*Therefore*" points back to the tremendous truths set forth previously, and glorious promises and victories that have been declared.

"... *Be ye stedfast, unmoveable ....*" According to the first part of this epistle, many of the Corinthian brethren were neither *steadfast NOR unmoveable.* They were led about by teachers of error. They were babes in Christ when they should have been spiritually full grown. But Paul loved them, and his affection remained unchanged in spite of their faults and failures.

The Greek here reads, *"become ye"*—that is, *"Prove yourselves"* by being steadfast, firmly rooted and grounded in the pure doctrine of the grace of God. Do not allow any of the forces of the enemies of Christ to draw you away from Him in the least degree."

". . . Always abounding in the work of the Lord. . . ." Work in the work of the Lord with all of your might, do whatever He gives you to do, and do it with diligence. *"For we are His workmanship, created in Christ Jesus unto good works, which God hath before ordained that we should walk in them"* (Eph. 2:10).

"For as the body without the spirit is dead, *so faith without works is dead also"* (James 2:26).

We should be good stewards, doing whatsoever we do to the glory of God, remembering that there is coming a day when we will be *rewarded* for our stewardship. At that time, we will either receive a reward for our service, or we will see our works burned. Therefore, Paul pleads with the brethren to be—not just ordinary workmen, but ABOUNDING in the work of the Lord.

". . . Forasmuch as ye know that your labour is not in vain in the Lord." The verb "to know" signifies assured knowledge; hence we may read it thus: "Ye are fully ASSURED that your labor is not in vain."

The Greek word translated "labour" is *kopos*, meaning "toil resulting in weariness." Compare John 4:6: "Now Jacob's well was there. Jesus therefore, *being wearied with His journey*, sat thus on the well . . . ."

"Work" pertains to what is done; it can be easy and pleasant. But "labor" has to do with the performing of the work, the pains taken, and the strength spent. However, where love is the motive, a labor of love is not wearisome and hard. Read I Thessalonians 1:3.

The true quality and fruitfulness of service rendered by the believer is determined by whether or not it is rendered *"in the Lord."* He is the one foundation, and if we build on that foundation gold, silver, and precious stones, we shall receive a full reward, no matter how small and insignificant our service may be in the eyes of man. It is not the *amount* of service that counts, but the "sort" (I Cor. 3:11-15).

The resurrection of Christ is divine proof that He is the Saviour of sinners. He laid His life down, He took it up again as He promised (John 10:18).

The resurrection of Christ is the witness of salvation. We confess with our mouth that Jesus is Lord, we believe in our heart that God raised Him from the dead, and we are saved (Rom. 10:9,10).

The resurrection of Christ is the guarantee of victory over the world, the flesh, the devil, death, hell, and the grave. Because HE lives, WE live. We are more than conquerors through Him that loved us (Rom. 8:28-39).

The resurrection of Christ guarantees reward for faithful stewardship. Even a cup of cold water given in His name is not overlooked. There is a Man in heaven—the Man Christ Jesus—seated at the right hand of God the Father, beholding every son of God as he lives and labors upon this earth, looking for the blessed hope and the glorious appearing of the great God and our Saviour, Jesus Christ (I Tim. 2:5; Heb. 1:1-3).

CHAPTER SIXTEEN

1. Now concerning the collection for the saints, as I have given order to the churches of Galatia, even so do ye.

2. Upon the first day of the week let every one of you lay by him in store, as God hath prospered him, that there be no gatherings when I come.

3. And when I come, whomsoever ye shall approve by your letters, them will I send to bring your liberality unto Jerusalem.

4. And if it be meet that I go also, they shall go with me.

5. Now I will come unto you, when I shall pass through Macedonia: for I do pass through Macedonia.

6. And it may be that I will abide, yea, and winter with you, that ye may bring me on my journey whithersoever I go.

7. For I will not see you now by the way; but I trust to tarry a while with you, if the Lord permit.

8. But I will tarry at Ephesus until Pentecost.

9. For a great door and effectual is opened unto me, and there are many adversaries.

10. Now if Timotheus come, see that he may be with you without fear: for he worketh the work of the Lord, as I also do.

11. Let no man therefore despise him: but conduct him forth in peace, that he may come unto me: for I look for him with the brethren.

12. As touching our brother Apollos, I greatly desired him to come unto you with the brethren: but his will was not at all to come at this time; but he will come when he shall have convenient time.

13. Watch ye, stand fast in the faith, quit you like men, be strong.

14. Let all your things be done with charity.

15. I beseech you, brethren, (ye know the house of Stephanas, that it is the firstfruits of Achaia, and that they have addicted themselves to the ministry of the saints,)

16. That ye submit yourselves unto such, and to every one that helpeth with us, and laboureth.

17. I am glad of the coming of Stephanas and Fortunatus and Achaicus: for that which was lacking on your part they have supplied.

18. For they have refreshed my spirit and your's: therefore acknowledge ye them that are such.

19. The churches of Asia salute you. Aquila and Priscilla salute you much in the Lord, with the church that is in their house.

20. All the brethren greet you. Greet ye one another with an holy kiss.

21. The salutation of me Paul with mine own hand.

22. If any man love not the Lord Jesus Christ, let him be Anathema Maran-atha.

23. The grace of our Lord Jesus Christ be with you.

24. My love be with you all in Christ Jesus. Amen.

Instructions Concerning Collections for the Saints

Verse 1: "Now concerning the collection for the saints, as I have given order to the churches of Galatia, even so do ye."

Paul is speaking here of a special collection to supply the need of the poor among the saints at Jerusalem: "For it hath pleased them of Macedonia and Achaia to make a certain contribution for the poor saints which are at Jerusalem" (Rom. 15:26).

This matter was known in the local church at Corinth. The instructions Paul had given concerning this special collection contained Christian principles which apply to the offerings of believers in general even to this present day and hour. In connection with this, also study II Corinthians, chapters 8 and 9.

Verse 2: "Upon the first day of the week let every one of you lay by him in store, as God hath prospered him, that there be no gatherings when I come."

". . . *The first day of the week*" is not a term used in this passage alone. We also find it in Mark 16:2,9; Luke 24:1; John 20:1,19; and Acts 20:7. Nowhere in the New

Testament is the first day of the week called "the Sabbath." The fact that *the first day of the week* is pointed out on several occasions signifies its importance. Saturday is the Sabbath; the first day of the week is Sunday.

". . . *Let every one of you lay by him in store* . . . ." Please notice that the collection was to be presented by each and every one of the members. Regardless of how poor the believer may be, there is always a penny or two (even the widow's mite) that can be given.

". . . *As God hath prospered him* . . . ." As the individual has prospered through the goodness and mercy of God, so he is to give. No actual proportionment is given. Any reasonable person who is not bound by denominational dogma must admit that the tithe would be entirely *too little* for some to give, and by like token it would be a great deal more for others.

For example, if a widow received an old-age pension of fifty dollars a month, her tithe would be five dollars, leaving her only forty-five dollars to live on for the entire month. On the other hand, a business man may have a net profit of three thousand dollars a month (and many business men make more than that). *His* tithe would be *three hundred dollars* a month — but he would still have more than two thousand dollars left to live on for thirty days. Do you think such a percentage of giving would be right in the sight of God?

There is no ironclad rule laid down in the New Testament for giving to the Lord's work. In many cases it is honorable and right to tithe, but each individual believer is to give according as God has prospered that individual. In accordance with the amount God gives us, we should lay aside an amount that would glorify Him. "God loveth a cheerful giver," and if we sow sparingly, we shall reap sparingly.

There is absolutely no place in the New Testament that teaches what some ministers preach as "storehouse tithing." Many Christians are lean and poor *spiritually* because they are "tightwads" toward God, *financially.* Many believers live in a very small world; they store their tithe in one little assembly, and most of the money never *leaves* that immediate assembly. But he who looks on the fields "white unto harvest" acquires far-reaching vision, and does not store his giving in one little corner of God's great vineyard. He will sow seed to the uttermost parts of the earth by *giving*—not only to the local assembly, but to others who are winning souls around the world by pointing men and women to the Lamb of God!

Jesus died for the sins of the whole wide world—and yet, the vision of many is limited to their own little group. There is entirely too much selfishness among God's people. They do not see with the eyes of Jesus (John 1:29; I John 2:2).

Verses 3 and 4: "And when I come, whomsoever ye shall approve by your letters, them will I send to bring your liberality unto Jerusalem. And if it be meet that I go also, they shall go with me."

The Corinthian believers were instructed to lay by each week as the Lord had prospered them, and have the collection ready when Paul arrived. He planned to visit the assembly in Corinth, and *"whomsoever"* the assembly approved by letter, Paul would send to Jerusalem with the money.

It seems that the church was to prepare letters which would be sent (along with the individuals appointed BY the church) to the assembly in Jerusalem to present the money to the church there.

". . . *If it be meet that I go also, they shall go with me.*" Here is a point that needs to be emphasized. Money matters and financial affairs of the church should never be in the hands of only one person. Several men should be responsible for the money and the handling of funds in the church. Every precaution and care should be exercised to avoid error or suspicion in handling money given by believers in the assembly.

Money matters in the church have been used of the devil to divide many local assemblies. It is unfair—both to the church and to the individual—to let any one person handle the Lord's money. All possible precaution should be taken by the pastor and officials concerning offerings given in the local assembly, in order that its financial affairs be above reproach in every way.

Verse 5: "Now I will come unto you, when I shall pass through Macedonia: for I do pass through Macedonia."

We know from II Corinthians 1:15 and 16 that Paul had previously planned to go directly to the church in Corinth, and from there on to Macedonia and back to Corinth; but he changed his plans—perhaps for the reason mentioned in II Corinthians 1:23: "Moreover I call God for a record upon my soul, that *to spare you* I came not as yet unto Corinth."

Verse 6: "And it may be that I will abide, yea, and winter with you, that ye may bring me on my journey whithersoever I go."

". . . *Abide . . . and winter with you* . . . ." Greek authorities tell us that *"with"* expresses more than just being present with them bodily. It implies a deep spiritual interest, a very intimate feeling and fellowship. He would be present physically, but he would also be with them in spirit, to fellowship in the Lord and feed upon His Word as they fellowshipped together, even throughout the winter. The possibility (*"It may be . . ."*) of his spending the winter with them might be due to the fact that it was extremely hazardous for ships to sail at that time of year, making it almost imperative for Paul to spend the winter in Corinth.

"*. . . That ye may bring me on my journey whithersoever I go.*" This simply means that Paul would travel in the ministry wherever God led him, through the gifts that the Corinthian church would give him. We find a similar reference in Romans 15:24: "Whensoever I take my journey into Spain, I will come to you: for I trust to see you in my journey, *and to be brought on my way thitherward by you,* if first I be somewhat filled with your company." And in II Corinthians 1:16 we read, "And to pass by you into Macedonia, and to come again out of Macedonia unto you, *and of you to be brought on my way* toward Judaea."

Visiting ministers and other servants of God should be sent on their way in a worthy manner, bountifully supplied with practical help and the necessities of this life. This is a God-given responsibility of the local church. It is a noble privilege for an assembly to take care of the servants of God in a worthy way. God pity the church that has funds through which they *could* help their pastor and visiting ministers and missionaries but because of selfishness fail to do so! They bring reproach upon the name of Jesus, and such an assembly will suffer severely for exercising a selfish spirit in caring for God's servants.

Verse 7: "For I will not see you now by the way; but I trust to tarry a while with you, if the Lord permit."

"*. . . I trust to tarry a while with you . . . .*" In verses 6 and 7, the emphasis is on "YOU," denoting Paul's love for and interest in the believers at Corinth. He yearned to see them and fellowship with them. Then too, in view of the fact that there were many things that needed to be corrected and much instruction that needed to be given, a *brief* visit was out of the question. It was necessary that Paul spend some time with the assembly in Corinth.

". . . *If the Lord permit.*" All believers should be totally dependent upon the Lord's leading and dealing with us. We should never run ahead of Him. We should allow the Spirit to direct us in all details of life. We are not our own, we are bought with a price, and we should glorify God in all that we do. This was true in the life and ministry of the Apostle Paul.

Verse 8: "But I will tarry at Ephesus until Pentecost."

It is indicated here that this epistle was written at Ephesus, and the time of the writing was no doubt around Easter time.

Verse 9: "For a great door and effectual is opened unto me, and there are many adversaries."

Paul did not want to remain at Ephesus simply to keep the feast at Pentecost. A door of opportunity had opened to him there — an immediate and very special opportunity for him to minister to the converts and give them instructions that they needed as babes in Christ.

II Corinthians 2:12, Colossians 4:3, and Revelation 3:8 also mention an open door — a door opened for preaching and teaching the Gospel of the grace of God; and this was the nearest and dearest thing to the heart of Paul. It *should be* the nearest to the heart of *any* minister of the Gospel, or any representative of the saving grace of God.

Paul says, "*a great door and effectual* . . ." — GREAT because of the opportunities it afforded, extended opportunities to deliver the glorious message of the grace of God; EFFECTUAL because of its power. The Greek word used here is *energes*, meaning "powerful in action." Paul was assured that the Gospel he preached was "the power of God unto salvation to everyone that believeth."

And since the Holy Spirit had opened so great and effectual a door for *preaching* the Gospel, God's minister must buy up the opportunities to give out the good news of the grace of God.

"*. . . And there are many adversaries.*" Paul had *many* adversaries (note again I Corinthians 15:32). Ephesus was a center of superstition and there were many enemies of the pure Gospel—a mob bitterly antagonistic to Christianity. Study Acts 19 and you will see that the Gospel entered and prevailed in Ephesus only through much suffering and persecution. But Paul was a good soldier; he did not run from the battle. The enemies of the Gospel presented even greater challenge for him to remain and preach the Gospel of the saving grace of God, in the midst of superstition and error.

Verses 10 and 11: "Now if Timotheus come, see that he may be with you without fear: for he worketh the work of the Lord, as I also do. Let no man therefore despise him: but conduct him forth in peace, that he may come unto me: for I look for him with the brethren."

"*. . . IF Timotheus come . . . .*" Timothy was Paul's own son in the ministry. Paul uses "IF," pointing out that it was uncertain as to whether or not Timothy would reach Corinth by or before the time the letter reached the believers there, as he was to go by way of Macedonia (Acts 19:22). If the bearers of the letter traveled by sea, directly from Ephesus to Corinth, they would reach the city before Timothy did.

From II Corinthians 10:10 we know that there were some in Corinth who were critical, and at times very impolite. Seemingly this minority had no conscience toward the feelings of Paul, and they would possibly treat Timothy in the same way. There is no Scripture to suggest that Timothy was timid, or that he labored under an inferiority

complex; but Paul wanted him to be treated with respect.
He was much younger than the Apostle, but the Corinthian
believers were to receive him with the same confidence
and assurance with which they would receive Paul—*"without
fear."* Believers should not despise any servant of
God because of youth, weakness, physical handicaps, or
for any other reason if that servant of God is carrying out
the duties of the ministry.

Paul wanted young Timothy's visit to the Corinthian
church to be such that when they sent him away he would
leave the church with a good feeling in his heart and
would bring with him a good report. The love the believers in Corinth had for Paul should compel them to treat
Timothy with the same love and respect as they would
treat the older apostle.

Verse 12: "As touching our brother Apollos, I greatly
desired him to come unto you with the brethren: but his
will was not at all to come at this time; but he will come
when he shall have convenient time."

From this verse it would seem that the believers in
Corinth had also invited Apollos to visit them, and Paul
makes it clear that he, too, had earnestly hoped that
Apollos would visit the Corinthian assembly. But it was
not possible for Apollos to come to them at that particular
time. Paul makes it quite clear that there was no feeling
of rivalry or jealousy between himself and Apollos. It
was Apollos himself who made the decision not to visit
Corinth at that time. Paul wanted it clearly understood
that there was no ill will between himself and his fellow
minister. (Read also I Corinthians 1:12; 3:4–6; 4:6; and
Titus 3:13.)

". . . *But he will come when he shall have convenient time."* The Greek verb used here suggests more than
just *having opportunity* to come — it points to "a more

favorable time." It seems that Apollos thought that his visit to the church in Corinth at that particular time might in one way or another rekindle the party spirit or cause divisions as mentioned in the first part of the epistle. He therefore felt that it was not a favorable time for him to visit the church. But when such favorable time arrived he would visit the believers in Corinth.

Two true servants of God, working in the same assembly or in the same part of God's great vineyard, should take every precaution to see that a spirit of unity prevails; and that is exactly what Apollos was doing.

Verse 13: "Watch ye, stand fast in the faith, quit you like men, be strong."

More than once Paul exhorts believers to be good soldiers. The four exhortations given here have a definite military tone:

"Watch ye." Christians must be on guard. They must maintain a position that will bring glory to God, rather than bringing reproach upon His name. They must be on the alert against moral decay, alert to spiritual dangers.

"Stand fast in the faith." No false doctrine, no teaching of error, no influence—either from within or without the assembly—should cause the Christian to deviate from the fundamentals of the faith once delivered to the saints.

"Quit you like men." There is no place for a spiritual coward in the army of the Lord. The God who saves us will furnish the grace and courage needed, even though we "wrestle not against flesh and blood, but against principalities, against powers, against the rulers of the darkness of this world, against spiritual wickedness in high places" (Eph. 6:12).

"Be strong!" Paul said, "I can do all things THROUGH

CHRIST WHO STRENGTHENETH ME" (Phil. 4:13). God will furnish the strength, the might, and the *power* for each and every battle His soldiers must fight. We who name the name of Jesus today should heed these admonitions.

Verse 14: "Let all your things be done with charity."

The Greek here reads "IN charity (love)." We are to do all things in the very element and atmosphere of love and for no other reason. FAITH is a divine imperative; HOPE is a divine fruit of saving grace; but CHARITY (love) is the greatest gift of all (I Cor. 13:13). Jesus said, "By this shall all men know that ye are my disciples, if ye have love one to another" (John 13:35).

If party spirit and division continued to exist in the church at Corinth, the believers could not serve the Lord "in love." John asks, ". . . He that loveth not his brother whom he hath seen, how can he love God whom he hath not seen?" (I John 4:20). In I John 3:14 we read, "We know that we have passed from death unto life, because we love the brethren. He that loveth not his brother abideth in death."

Verses 15 and 16: "I beseech you, brethren, (ye know the house of Stephanas, that it is the firstfruits of Achaia, and that they have addicted themselves to the ministry of the saints,) that ye submit yourselves unto such, and to every one that helpeth with us, and laboureth."

". . . *The house of Stephanas . . . firstfruits of Achaia* . . . ." "Firstfruits" is used here in the same way that it is used in Romans 16:5 with reference to the earliest converts, the first believers, in a district, in relation to those who are saved later. That these early believers were ministering to their fellow believers clearly proves that the Spirit of God had called them to render voluntary spiritual service, and the Holy Spirit had *equipped* them for such service.

The house of Stephanas was not appointed in this capacity by the apostles, but by the Holy Spirit Himself — and how wonderful it is that the Spirit *names* the house of Stephanas, even though incidentally, because that household stands for all who name the name of Jesus in every place and at any time during the Church Age.

Please notice that the house of Stephanas had not been appointed in a spectacular way, not by laying on of hands or by outward signs and wonders. But quietly, in the heart of each member of that household, the call to service had been heard and answered: "Lord, here am I. Send me." The members of that household may not have had their names in the church bulletin, they might not have had much recognition from the pulpit — *but they were recognized by the Holy Spirit*, and that is what will count in that day when Christians are rewarded for their stewardship!

Dear believer, you may not be a minister, a missionary, or an evangelist. You may not even be a teacher in the Sunday school nor one who is called upon to do outstanding service in the eyes of others; but no matter how humble or how ill-equipped you may feel, *you can always belong to "the house of Stephanas."* And if you will allow the Holy Spirit to lead you, He will give you a ministry that will be profitable to others, and that will bring *reward for YOU* at the end of the way!

". . . *That ye submit yourselves unto such . . . .*" Believers in the assembly were to have regard to the responsibilities of "those of the house of Stephanas," even though they were neither apostles nor apostolic appointees. The HOLY SPIRIT had appointed them, and therefore the believers were to recognize them. Such a spirit of subjection and recognition would create a spirit of harmony in the assembly, thus preventing animosity, strife, and rivalry among believers.

Verse 17: "I am glad of the coming of Stephanas and Fortunatus and Achaicus: For that which was lacking on your part they have supplied."

The Greek here reads, "*I am rejoicing in the presence . . . .*" These brethren were already *with Paul* as he was writing this message.

"*. . . For that which was lacking on your part they have supplied.*" Evidently these brethren brought Paul gifts or supplies that the church had failed to supply, and their gifts had greatly refreshed him.

Verse 18: "For they have refreshed my spirit and your's: therefore acknowledge ye them that are such."

The visit by Stephanas, Fortunatus, and Achaicus had relieved Paul's anxiety in that they brought him news from the church in Corinth; and their visit had relieved the Corinthian assembly from fear of being misrepresented to Paul. For even though the assembly was divided and party spirit was there, as a whole the saints in Corinth loved the old apostle and down deep in their hearts they were united in loyalty to Him.

"*. . . Therefore acknowledge ye them that are such.*" Paul makes it clear that the Corinthians are to give due and generous recognition to those who render such service to the church and to the Lord's anointed.

Verse 19: "The churches of Asia salute you. Aquila and Priscilla salute you much in the Lord, with the church that is in their house."

"*The churches of Asia salute you.*" This has reference to the province of Asia, of which Ephesus was the capital city. Study Acts 19:10—26.

"*Aquila and Priscilla salute you . . . .*" This couple came from Corinth to Ephesus with Paul (Acts 18:2,18).

541

There was an assembly in the house of Aquila and Priscilla (notice Romans 16:5 and II Timothy 4:19). It seems evident that they had opened their house to the assembly and the believers met in their home regularly.

". . . *In the Lord*" has to do with matters pertaining to the life of the believer here in this world, whereas "*in Christ*" refers to the spiritual life and *heavenly position* of the believer. We are dead, and our lives are hid with Christ in God. Positionally we sit together in heavenly places "*in Christ Jesus.*" Therefore Paul said, "Aquila and Priscilla salute you . . . IN THE LORD," thus relating to the stewardship of believers in the local assembly that met in the home of these two.

Verse 20: "All the brethren greet you. Greet ye one another with an holy kiss."

The Greek word here translated "holy" is *hagios* and means "free from anything inconsistent with the calling and practice of believers as saints." In the early Christian church, the kiss was a common form of salutation between persons of the same sex (never between those of opposite sexes). Men were to greet men with a kiss, and women were to greet women in like manner.

The enemies of the saints often referred to Christians as "evildoers," and it was therefore extremely important that believers conduct themselves in such manner as would not bring reproach upon the name of Jesus. Their conduct must be pure in the sight of the Lord and honorable before men. Study I Peter 3:16; Romans 14:16; II Corinthians 8:21. The kiss of greeting was not to be mere formality—and certainly not a kiss of hypocrisy. The Greek language in I Peter 5:14 speaks of it as "*a kiss of love.*"

The greeting by a holy kiss must be one of character and meaning, and there was to be no discrimination in this greeting. They were to greet the poor as well as the rich, the least in the assembly as well as the most outstanding.

Verse 21: "The salutation of me Paul with mine own hand."

This removes all doubt as to who wrote this letter to the believers in Corinth.

Verse 22: "If any man love not the Lord Jesus Christ, let him be Anathema Maran-atha."

This first epistle to the Corinthians ends with a denunciation similar to that found in the first chapter of the epistle to the Galatians. Paul admonished the Galatian church that if anyone—*man*, or angel from heaven—should come to them preaching any gospel except the Gospel they had received, *"let him be accursed!"* In other words, "Let him drop into hell!" In Galatians 5:12 Paul said, "I would they were even *cut off* which trouble you." These are strong words; but what Paul is actually saying is that the Church (and the world) would be better off if these legalizers and those who would mix law and grace (thus robbing Jesus of His finished work) were cut off—DEAD.

In closing this letter to the Corinthians, he makes *the same declaration* in other terms. Paul counted all things loss for the sake of the Gospel. He was jealous for Jesus. His cry was, "God forbid that I should glory save in the cross! I am what I am by the grace of God; and therefore, whether I eat or drink, or whatsoever I do, I will do it all to the glory of God!"

Verse 23: "The grace of our Lord Jesus Christ be with you."

Always, in Paul's epistles, grace is part of the *greeting* and grace occurs in the *benediction*. Whether Paul declared the Lord Jesus to be the source of grace, either alone (as here), or in association with God the Father (as in II Thessalonians 1:12), he was declaring the deity of Christ.

543

Verse 24: "My love be with you all in Christ Jesus. Amen."

How tender, personal, and loving is this last note in the letter! In spite of all their faults and failures, in spite of the fact that some of them had spoken disparagingly of Paul as having to do with his physical handicaps, in spite of their lack of maturity in the things he had taught them, he closes his letter with the assurance of his deep, unchanging love for them!

Such assurance should cause them to take to heart the admonitions and solemn warnings he had given them concerning the evils in the assembly and lead them to do something about it. The love Paul had for his children in the faith was because of the love of God, love "in Christ Jesus." This was not just human love, a changeable love. It was love like unto the love displayed by Jesus on the cross.